Janet

Child and Youth Psychiatry: European Perspectives
Volume I
ANOREXIA NERVOSA

CHILD AND YOUTH PSYCHIATRY: EUROPEAN PERSPECTIVES

Series Editors: H. Remschmidt (Marburg) and M. H. Schmidt (Mannheim)

Advisory Board
F. ALMQVIST, Helsinki, Finland
H. van ENGELAND, Utrecht, Holland
C. GILLBERG, Göteborg, Sweden
H.-C. STEINHAUSEN, Zurich, Switzerland
K. MINDE, Kingston, Canada
P. J. GRAHAM, London, England
Y. TSIANTIS, Athens, Greece
K.-J. NEUMÄRKER, Berlin, Germany
K. OGURA, Tokyo, Japan

Volume I: ANOREXIA NERVOSA
Editors: H. Remschmidt (Marburg) and M. H. Schmidt (Mannheim)

Volume II: DEVELOPMENTAL PSYCHOPATHOLOGY
Editors: H. Remschmidt (Marburg) and M. H. Schmidt (Mannheim)

ANOREXIA NERVOSA

Edited by

Helmut Remschmidt, Marburg

and

Martin H. Schmidt, Mannheim

Hogrefe & Huber Publishers
Toronto • Lewiston, NY • Bern • Göttingen • Stuttgart

Library of Congress Cataloging-in-Publication Data

Anorexia nervosa / edited by Helmut Remschmidt and Martin H. Schmidt.
  p. cm. — (Child and youth psychiatry, European perspectives ; v. 1)
  Includes bibliographical references.
  Includes index.

  1. Anorexia nervosa. I. Remschmidt, Helmut. II. Schmidt, Martin H. III. Series.
  [DNLM: 1. Anorexia nervosa. WM 175 A61512]
  RC552.A5A572 1990   616.85'262—dc20   90-4848 CIP

Canadian Cataloguing in Publication Data

Main entry under title:
Anorexia nervosa

(Child and youth psychiatry, European perspectives ; v. 1)
Includes bibliographical references.

1. Anorexia nervosa. I. Remschmidt, Helmut. II. Schmidt, Martin H. III. Series.
RC552.A5A5   1990   616.85'262   C90-094417-X

No part of this book may be reproduced, stored in a retrieval system, or transmitted, in any form or by any means, electronic, mechanical, photocopying, microfilming, recording or otherwise, without written permission from the publisher.

© Copyright 1990 by Hogrefe & Huber Publishers

P. O. Box 51
Lewiston, NY 14092

12–14 Bruce Park Ave.
Toronto, Ontario M4P 2S3

ISBN 3-456-81957-9
ISBN 0-88937-041-9
Hogrefe & Huber Publishers • Toronto • Lewiston, NY • Bern • Göttingen • Stuttgart

Printed in Germany on acid-free paper

Editors' Preface

This volume is the first in the new series entitled "Child and Youth Psychiatry: European Perspectives." It is the intention of the editors and the publishers to publish a theme-centered volume approximately once a year, containing high-quality original research, reviews, and theoretical considerations concerning the main fields of child and adolescent psychiatry.

This first volume is devoted to anorexia nervosa, a condition that has become increasingly important during the last decade. There are studies from several European countries and from the United States describing a remarkable increase in this condition as well as in bulimia nervosa. But despite intensive research all over the world, the etiology is still poorly understood. Genetic factors, individual predisposition, family structure, endocrinological and other somatic factors as well as sociocultural influences have been considered as important factors influencing the manifestation of this disorder.

Some of these issues as well as epidemiological and follow-up studies are included in this volume, which reflects recent tendencies in Europe. Of course, these tendencies can only be a selection from the rich body of empirical studies in the field.

The editors wish to thank all contributors for their excellent work and their discipline with respect to the time-table. We would also like to thank Dr. Beate Herpertz-Dahlmann and Mrs. Elisabeth Le Guillarme for their assistance in the editorial work, and—last not least—the publishers Dr. C. J. Hogrefe Sr. and Dr. G.-J. Hogrefe Jr., who accepted our proposal for this new series with enthusiasm and engagement. Finally, our special thanks go to Mr. Joseph A. Smith, who was most helpful and supportive during all phases of the editorial work.

The editors hope sincerely that this volume will contribute to enhance the knowledge in the field of anorexia nervosa and related disorders, and will stimulate empirical research in the field in order to facilitate the better understanding of the condition and to develop better ways of providing therapy and help.

Helmut Remschmidt
Martin H. Schmidt
April 1990

Table of Contents

Editors' Preface _____ v

Epidemiology

Eating and Weight-Control Problems in a Community Population of Adolescent Girls Aged 15–20 Years
   Elizabeth Monck, Philip Graham, Naomi Richman, Rebecca Dobbs _____ 1

Psychobiology

Psychobiology of Human Starvation
   Manfred M. Fichter and Karl-Martin Pirke _____ 13

The Noradrenergic System in Anorexia and Bulimia Nervosa
   K. M. Pirke _____ 30

Central Versus Peripheral Disturbances in the Norepinephrine Metabolism of Adolescents with Anorexia Nervosa
   A. Rothenberger, H.-U. Müller and W. E. Müller _____ 45

Anorexia Nervosa and Urinary Excretion of Peptides and Protein-Associated Peptide Complexes
   M. Råstam, C. Gillberg, O. Trygstad, I. Foss _____ 54

Etiology

Genetic Vulnerability to Eating Disorders: Evidence from Twin and Family Studies
   Janet Treasure and Anthony Holland _____ 59

Anorexia Nervosa and Depression: A Continuing Debate
   Beate Herpertz-Dahlmann and Helmut Remschmidt _____ 69

Diagnostic and Psychopathological Issues

Self-Perception of Anorectic and Normal-Weight Adolescents
   G. Lehmkuhl, H. Flechtner, I. Woerner, W. Woerner, J. Masberg _____ 85

The Assessment of Body-Image Distortion Using a Semantic Differential: A Methodological Study
   Hans-Christoph Steinhausen _____ 95

Construction of a Questionnaire on the Body Experience of Anorexia Nervosa
   H. Van Coppenolle, M. Probst, W. Vandereycken, M. Goris, R. Meermann _____ 103

Behavioral and Self-Report Methods in the Study of Family Interaction Concepts
   W. Vandereycken, H. Vertommen, E. Kog, R. Meermann _____ 114

Follow-Up and Prediction

The Long-Term Course of Anorexia Nervosa
   Helmut Remschmidt, Franz Wienand, Christoph Wewetzer _____ 127

Anorectic Psychopathology in Young Women
   Fredrik Almqvist _____ 137

Prediction of Long-Term Outcome in Anorectic Patients from Longitudinal Weight Measurements during Inpatient Treatment: A Cross-Validation Study
   Helmut Remschmidt, Martin H. Schmidt, Cornelius Gutenbrunner _____ 150

Name and Subject Indexes _____ 169

Eating and Weight-Control Problems in a Community Population of Adolescent Girls Aged 15–20 Years

Elizabeth Monck, Philip Graham, Naomi Richman, Rebecca Dobbs

A community population of 15–20-year-old adolescent girls living in London were screened for eating control problems using the 26-item Eating Attitudes Test (EAT-26). A second intensive interview was held with girls with high EAT-26 scores and a control group with low scores, in the course of which data were obtained on clinically significant eating problems. The rate of anorexia was found to be 1%, but a further 13% showed heterogeneous but serious problems. High EAT-26 socres were related to self-reported and clinically significant affective disorder, and to the girls being over- rather than underweight. Neither high EAT-26 socres nor clinical eating disorders were related to the girls' social class, age, or educational achievement.

The experience of feeling fat and subsequent dieting is common among female adolescents (Nylander, 1971; Crisp, 1977, Huenemann, Shapiro, Hampton & Mitchell, 1966; Mann, Wakeling, Wood, Monck, Dobbs & Szmukler, 1983). Several authors have commented on contemporary cultural pressures on girls and women in Western developed nations to achieve low weight-to-height ratios (Garfinkel & Garner, 1982). Among adolescent girls, it seems that the fear of obesity and the adoption of inappropriate eating habits are pervasive, regardless of body weight or nutrition knowledge (Moses, Banilivy & Lifschitz, 1989). In contrast, the concern of males, especially in adolescence, is to gain rather than to lose weight (Huenemann et al., 1966). Anorexia nervosa is, like general concern with weight, a syndrome predominantly found among girls and young women; onset is commonly between the ages of 13 and 18 years, though not uncommon up to the late 20s. There is recent evidence that prepubertal onset is more common than formerly supposed (Fosson, Knibbs, Bryant-Waugh & Lask, 1987). Nevertheless, the links between the concerns of adolescent girls with weight control and the more extreme behaviours associated with anorexia or bulimia nervosa are unclear.

Anorexia nervosa can be distinguished by an overwhelming drive to lose weight by controlling and limiting the intake of food, and by taking excessive exercise. By contrast, the diagnostic criteria for bulimia nervosa, first described by Russell (1979), include an intractable urge to overeat and a morbid fear of becoming fat, which leads to avoidance of the fattening effects of food by purging, vomiting, or excessive exercise (Fairburn & Cooper, 1984). Despite an obsession with weight and shape control, weight loss is much less marked than with anorexia; this frequently enables the sufferer to go undetected by family, friends, or professionals.

Patients with anorexia nervosa frequently display a range of psychiatric symptoms, of which the most common is depression (Stonehill & Crisp, 1977; Herzog, 1984), and some authors have suggested that both anorexia and bulimia nervosa may be related to affective disorder (Cooper & Fairburn, 1986). It has, however, also been argued that affective disorders follow rather than pre-date the

---

Department of Child Psychiatry, Institute of Child Health, Guilford Street, London WC1N 3JH, UK.
The study on which this paper is based was undertaken with a grant from the Wellcome Trust. Our thanks are due to Dr Marjorie Smith for her helpful comments in the preparation of this paper.

onset of eating problems (Laessle, Kittl, Fichter, Wittchen & Pirke, 1987). Distortion of body image is common among patients with anorexia and bulimia nervosa (Slade & Russell, 1973), but this has also been noted among normal females (Moses, Banilivy & Lifschitz, 1989). Obsessionality has been noted as a distinctive feature of young anorectic patients (Higgs, Goodyer & Birch, 1989).

Studies of clinic populations have led to assertions that the families of anorectic patients are characterized by intense, overinvolved relationships between mother and anorectic daughter, by poor conflict resolution, and by strong rule-boundedness of the child/adolescent by the parent(s) (Bruch, 1977; Minuchin, Rosman & Baker, 1978). These conclusions were drawn from observations of families in treatment and have not included systematic observations of comparison groups. The majority of studies of the aetiology of anorexia nervosa have concerned clinic populations or groups selected on the basis of relatively high educational attainment (Button & Whitehouse, 1981; Thompson & Schwartz, 1982; Clarke & Palmer, 1983) or occupational preference (e.g., studies of dance students; Garner & Garfinkel, 1980).

Early studies of patients described anorexia nervosa as occurring more frequently in higher social classes, predominantly among girls and young women with high academic achievements, but recent community population studies have thrown some doubt on these findings (Cullberg & Engstrom-Lindberg, 1988; Johnson-Sabine, Wood, Patton, Mann & Wakeling, 1988). Estimates of the prevalence of anorexia or bulimia nervosa in the general population are difficult to establish, though recent studies suggest that neither syndrome is as rare as was once supposed (Meadows, Palmer, Newball & Kenrick, 1986; Szmukler, 1985; Johnson-Sabine et al., 1988). Among adolescent girls, Szmukler (1985) reported a prevalence for anorexia of about 1%. Mann et al. (1983) found no cases of anorexia in a 15-year-old schoolgirl population, and King (1989) reported no cases of anorexia in a survey of male and female attenders at general practitioners' surgeries in south London. The prevalence of bulimia nervosa is similarly low: Fairburn and Cooper (1983) reported 1%–2% in a study of women attending a family planning clinic, and King (1989) found 6 females (1.1%) in a general practice population.

Nonclinic studies, even in high-risk groups such as dancers or beauticians, suggest that both conditions are more common in females than males, and that there is a continuum of disturbed behaviour and attitudes, which only in the extreme forms can be defined as clinical anorexia or bulimia (Button & Whitehouse, 1981; King, 1989). The term partial syndrome is now used to describe those who show some but not all features of the clinical conditions. The prevalence of partial syndrome eating disorders has been variably estimated at between 3% and 5% (Button & Whitehouse, 1981; Mann et al., 1983; King, 1989).

As with other relatively rare conditions, it has become common to seek information about anorexia nervosa and bulimia in the general population through the use of self-report screening questionnaires. The most commonly used screening questionnaires are the 40-item and the 26-item *Eating Attitudes Tests* (EAT-40 and EAT-26) (Garner & Garfinkel, 1979; Garner, Olmsted, Bohr & Garfinkel, 1982). Both questionnaires were developed using patient groups, but the authors have made clear that they expected the EATs to be useful as screening devices in general populations.

It is important to distinguish between the prevalence of cases of eating disorders and the prevalence of high scores on self-report screening questionnaires. The latter will identify a range of disturbed and distorted behaviour and attitudes, by no means necessarily linked to classical disorders of eating control: the questions are general enough in content for a high proportion of normal respondents to answer positively (King, 1989).

In the UK, the use of the two versions of the *Eating Attitudes Tests* in community population screening have shown some similar results. Using the EAT-40, Button and Whitehouse (1981) found that 6.3% (all females) of a college population had high scores, while Clarke and Palmer (1983) found 11% (all females) in a similar population. Using the EAT-26, Mann et al. (1983) reported 6.9% with high scores in a 15-year-old female population, and Johnson-Sabine et al. (1988) found

8.2% with high scores in a 14–16-year-old population.

This paper reports a study of girls between the ages of 15 and 20 years, living in inner and outer London, in which a screening questionnaire was used to identify those at risk of eating disorders. Prevalence rates of clinically significant disorders were estimated, and the association between eating problems and personal and family variables was assessed. It was hypothesised that girls from higher socioeconomic groups and those with high educational achievements or expectations would be more likely both to record high scores on the screening questionnaire and to show clinically significant eating control problems. It was also further predicted that the existence of a large number of parental rules, conflict between the girl and her parent(s), and evidence of emotional overinvolvement between mother and daughter would carry a higher risk of clinical eating disorders.

Method

The sample was drawn from the age/sex registers of eight General Practices in north and east London. The names of the girls in the chosen age group were submitted to the General Practitioners, who excluded those members of cultural minorities who could not speak English well enough to hold an extended interview, as well as those with marked learning problems.

In a two-stage design, an initial, screening interview was held in the girl's home, with the girl and her key relative. Data were collected on the composition of the household, and the girl's school, employment, and health history. The girl and her key relative were asked to fill in the 26-item *Eating Attitudes Test* (EAT-26) (Garner et al., 1982). Items on the EAT-26 relate to preoccupation with food, weight, bodily appearance, dieting, overeating, and vomiting. The girls were also asked to fill in a self-report questionnaire (*The Great Ormond Street Mood Questionnaire—GOSQ*) designed to elicit affective disorder. Both questionnaires had been validated for use with an adolescent female population (Mann et al., 1983). The girls and their key relatives also filled in third-person versions of the questionnaires on each other. All the girls were weighed and measured.

A second, intensive interview was held at home with a subsample drawn from among those girls who lived with their mothers (92% of the total population), and included the girls who had scored over the cut-off point on the EAT-26 as well as a comparison group of girls with low EAT-26 scores.

The second interviews were held with mothers and daughters separately but at the same time, by interviewers blind to the girl's scores on either self-report questionnaire. The girl's interview included standardised psychiatric questions designed to elicit evidence of current psychiatric disorder (Goldberg, Cooper, Eastwood, Kedward & Shepherd, 1970). Both mothers and daughters were asked questions on the girl's attitudes toward eating, weight control, exercise, and associated behaviour; these questions were derived from the eating disorders interview designed by Szmukler (1983). Other sections of the two interviews covered the girl's friendship network and confiding relationships; relationships within the family, with particular attention paid to family discord; and the system of parental control in selected areas of adolescent life.

Measures

Eating Disorders

- Self-reported symptoms identified with the use of the 26-item version of the *Eating Attitudes Test*; three factors form subscales found to be meaningfully related to anorexia, bulimia, weight and body-image variables; the subscales were termed *Dieting, Bulimia and Food Preoccupation,* and *Oral Control* (Garner et al., 1982).

- Clinical rating of symptoms reported from the clinical sections of the second interview. Using these data, girls were placed in one of five diagnostic categories by the two psychiatrists (PG and NR) (Mann et al., 1983). Agreement was reached independently in 80% of cases, and when disagreement occurred, the final rating was reached by consensus.
  —Normal: no concern over weight or fatness; no dieting.
  —Normal dieters: dieting to control weight, but not a major preoccupation; no marked weight changes or food abstinence.
  —Partial syndrome (all or most of the following are present): major preoccupation with weight control and food intake; persistent drive to lose weight; severe guilt about eating; marked concern with shape and size; excessive exercise or laxative abuse to control weight. However, weight remains within normal limits, and menstruation continues.
  —Anorexia nervosa: attitudes similar to partial syndrome, but with severe weight loss and amenorrhoea; positive identification with an emaciated body, and morbid fear of weight gain. *Bulimia nervosa:* attitudes similar to partial syndrome, but with marked binge eating and frequent self-induced vomiting or laxative abuse.
  —Mixed disorders: This included girls who held distorted views on appropriate food intake and were depressed and anxious about weight; for these persons a diagnosis of food avoidance emotional disorder would be appropriate (Higgs et al., 1989).

Affective Disorders

- Self-reported symptoms: *Great Ormond Street Mood Questionnaire:* 28 items with a cut-off point of 24/25 gives specificity of 79.6 and sensitivity of 56.2.
- The two psychiatrists made a diagnosis using DSM-III criteria and assessed severity using data from the standardised clinical interview.

Confiding Relationships

Both mother and daughter were asked in detail about whether the girl confided fully, in part, or not at all with parents, siblings, friends, and others.

Family Relationships

On the basis of reports by the mother and the daughter, supported by observation of their behaviour together, ratings were made of the warmth and criticism of mother to daughter and vice versa; and of the degree of emotional overinvolvement of each in the other. Warmth between father and daughter was rated on reports only. The girls were asked directly how well they got on with each parent, and ratings were also made of the quality of the parents' partnership from the reports of the mother and her daughter.

Arguments and Rows

Information was collected in detail on the frequency, duration, and severity of rows between the girl and both her parents individually in the previous 6 months. Information was collected about the last row in each of the following categories:

- *Minor:* irritable outbursts or interaction; very short duration; no significant after effects.
- *Moderate:* more heated exchanges, lasting several minutes and leading to sulkiness or

withdrawal; an outsider would judge that the participants were quarrelling.
- *Serious:* one or both participants lose control; shouting, screaming, or tears.
- *Serious with violence:* clear evidence of the intention to hurt or frighten.

Parental Rules

Both girls and mothers were asked to describe whether there were parental controls on the behaviour of the girl in 25 areas of family/adolescent life. The issues were chosen to reflect the normal concerns of parents with adolescent children (e.g., time of coming home at night, drinking alcohol, smoking, premarital sex, having friends in the home). Answers were rated as indicating the following:

- *A parental rule:* clear evidence that parent(s) had laid down a rule, and that the girl knew it existed. Compliance was not necessary to confirm the rating.
- *Parental advice:* the issue had been discussed by parent(s) and their daughter; parent(s) have not avoided the topic, but have not handed over complete control.
- *Adolescent autonomy:* it is clear that decisions on the issue can be made by the girl herself.
- *Internalised rules:* parental rules have existed, and explicit reference is made to them, but decisions now lie with the adolescent.
- *Issues not discussed*, and parental position unclear.

Educational Achievement

Information was collected on the full range of national examinations or aptitude tests (e.g., athletic or music competitions) the girl had succeeded in passing. The younger girls were asked what exams they intended taking, and a crude assumption made of a two-thirds pass rate. The girl was also asked about her intention to continue her education after the end of compulsory school attendance (age 16+).

Height/Weight Ratio

This figure (weight adjusted for height) was derived for mothers and daughters from the measurements taken in the screening interview and was calculated according to the formula Wt/ht^2 (Tanner, Whitehouse & Takaishi, 1966).

Results

From the General Practitioners' lists, 645 girls were identified as eligible for inclusion in the study; 116 girls or families (17.9%) refused, and 529 screening interviews were completed. At the second stage, 176 mother and daughter pairs were approached; 23 (13%) refused, and 153 intensive interviews were completed. The results are reported in two parts: first, the total screened group of 529 girls; second, a subsample (N = 115) of the intensively interviewed group. The subsample was composed of all girls living with their mother who had a score above the cut-off point on the *Eating Attitudes Test*, and a control group of girls with low EAT scores. This latter group was reconstituted to include a proportion of girls with low scores on both the EAT-26 and the *Great Ormond Street Mood Questionnaire* (low EAT and low GOSQ), and a proportion with low EAT scores but high GOSQ scores, which ensured that the controls were representative of the screened population.

The Screened Sample (N = 529)

Self-Reported Eating Disorders

Of the 529 girls who completed the self-report *Eating Attitudes Test* (EAT-26), 43 (8.1%) scored over the cut-off point (20/21) which identified them as being at risk of significant eating disorders. The distribution of EAT-26 scores is shown in Figure 1.

EAT-26 Subscores

The EAT-26 produces three subscores on *Oral Control*, *Dieting*, and *Food Preoccupation* with bulimia (Garner et al., 1982). Nearly 75% of the present sample had nil scores on the questions tapping preoccupation with food, and another 10% scored only 1. The dieting questions were more likely to be answered positives: only 9% scored nil, and another 22% scored only 1. For the oral control questions, 50% scored nil, and a further 14% scored 1. Further analysis revealed a factor structure with strong similarities to that reported by Garner et al. (1982). The *Dieting* factor loaded on 12 of the 13 questions Garner and colleagues had identified; the *Food Preoccupation* factor loaded on the same six questions; only the *Oral Control* factor lacked the robustness found by Garner et al. (1982).

None of the subscores showed any relationship with weight/height ratios, though *Dieting* subscores did show a significant linear trend with higher scores predominating among the heavy-for-height girls.

Self-Reported Affective Disturbance

Table 1 shows the highly significant association between self-reported eating problems and self-reported affective problems ($\chi^2 = 14.04$, 1 df, $p<0.0002$); 44% of the girls with EAT-26 scores over the cut-off point also reported affective symptoms that took their GOSQ score over the cut-off point. There was a significant relationship between a high EAT-26 score and the girl's own unemployment ($p<0.03$), but this was explained by the strong association between the girl's self-reported GOSQ (depression/anxiety) score and her own unemployment.

Weight and Weight/Height Ratios

Six girls refused to be weighed. For the remaining 523 no association was found between the height and age of the girls: this accords with data on the Tanner-Whitehouse

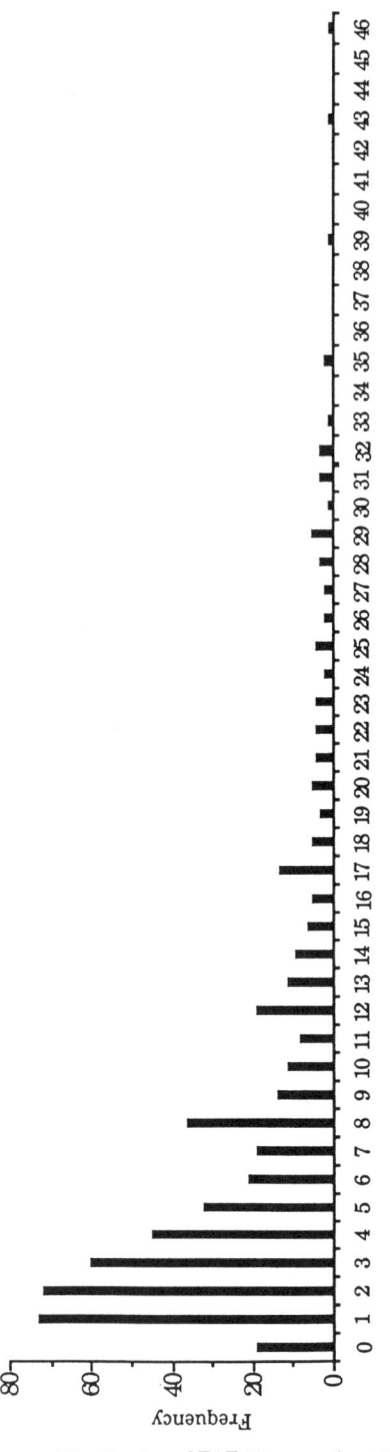

Figure 1. Distribution of EAT-26 scores (n = 529).

Table 1. Girls' self-reported affective symptoms and self-reported eating problems.

Eating Attitudes Test score	Great Ormond Street Mood Questionnaire score					
	0–24		25+		Totals	
	N	%	N	%	N	%
0–20	395	81	91	19	486	100
21+	24	56	19	44	43	100
Totals	419	79	110	21	529	100

$\chi^2 = 14.04$, 1 df, p<0.0002

growth charts for the UK, which indicate that the difference between age 15 and 17 years (when maximum growth is achieved) is only about 2 kg (Tanner, Whitehouse & Takaishi, 1966). Similarly, there was no linear association between age and weight/height ratio. These results provide the necessary assurance that, in terms of weight and weight/ height ratios, this population is a homogeneous one despite spanning the age group 15 to 20 years.

Table 2 shows the significant tendency for the mean EAT-26 scores to increase as weight increased. While a small group of girls (n = 9) weighing less than 40 kg had notably higher scores than the other low-weight girls, there was otherwise a consistent tendency for mean EAT-26 scores to rise with rising weight.

There was a significant linear association between weight/height ratio and the girls' EAT-26 scores (F = 24.91, 1 df, p<0.0001), with girls who were overweight for their height reporting the higher scores.

Social Class and Educational Achievement

Against prediction, there was no relationship between the girl's EAT-26 score and either the socioeconomic status of the chief wage-earner or school examination achievement (four or more passes in the General Certificate of Education examination (O-level) or the equivalent (Grade 1) in the Certificate of Secondary Education). Other methods of assessing personal achievement also showed no association with the girl's EAT-26 scores.

Mothers' Eating Problems

Mother's self-reported EAT-26 score was related to her daughter's EAT-26 score (Pearson's r 0.20, p<0.0001). If the mother scored over the cut-off point on the EAT-26, her daughter was more than twice as likely to do so as well, but the number of such mother/daughter pairs are small (n = 10), and by far most mother/daughter pairs scored together below the cut-off point on the EAT-26.

Mother's Perception of Daughter's Eating Control Problems

The mothers' (third-person) EAT-26 scores on their daughters were highly correlated with the daughters' own reports (Pearson's r 0.49, p<0.0001).

Table 2. The distribution of mean EAT-26 scores by weight.

Girl's weight	N	Mean EAT-26 score	Standard deviation
0–39.9 kg	9	9.33	7.74
40–44.9 kg	50	5.36	4.81
45–49.9 kg	103	4.66	4.84
50–54.9 kg	116	6.87	8.61
55–59.9 kg	97	7.76	7.23
60–64.9 kg	77	8.92	7.92
65–69.9 kg	33	11.03	9.49
70–74.9 kg	12	11.50	10.44
75–79.9 kg	15	10.60	11.58
80–84.9 kg	7	12.14	8.45
85+ kg	6	12.66	13.36

F 4.07, 10 df, p<0.00001

Table 3. Distribution of eating disorders by *Eating Attitudes Test* scores (subsample n = 115).

Eating Attitudes Test score	Normal N (%)	Normal dieting N (%)	Partial syndrome N (%)	Anorexia nervosa N (%)	Mixed disorders N (%)	Totals N
<21	49 (92)	29 (66)	2 (40)	0 (0)	10 (100)	90
21+	4 (8)	15 (34)	3 (60)	3 (100)	0 (0)	25
Totals	53 (100)	44 (100)	5 (100)	3 (100)	10 (100)	115

$\chi^2 = 28.10$, 4 df, p<0.0001

Table 4. Eating diagnosis and mean EAT-26 scores.

Diagnosis of eating disorder	N	Mean EAT-26 scores	SD
Normal	53	6.09	6.98
Normal dieter	44	15.20	11.97
Partial syndrome	5	25.20	7.56
Anorexia nervosa	3	22.66	1.52
Mixed disorders	10	9.30	4.62

F = 10.53, 4 df, p<0.0001

Table 5. Clinically confirmed "cases" of eating disorder and scores on the *Eating Attitudes Test*.

Eating Attitudes Test score	Clinical confirmation Noncase N (%)	Case N (%)	Totals N (%)
0–20	78 (87)	12 (13)	90 (100)
21+	19 (76)	6 (24)	25 (100)
Totals	97 (84)	18 (16)	115 (100)

$\chi^2 = 0.97$, 1 df, NS

The Intensively Interviewed Sample (N = 115)

Of the 43 girls with high EAT-26 scores, 5 were not eligible for the second interview because they did not live with their mothers. Among the remaining 38 girls, 8 were "lost" during an unforeseen break in the fieldwork, and 30 girls who lived with their mothers became eligible for the second, intensive interview; among these, 5 girls refused, so that 25 interviews were completed. The reconstituted subsample consisted of these 25 high EAT-26 girls and 90 representative controls.

Self-Reported Eating Problems and Clinical Diagnosis of Eating Disorders

Table 3 identifies the significant association between a high EAT-26 score and the diagnoses of eating disorders. There is a notable absence of high EAT-26 scores in the "mixed" category, which included at least two "recovered" anorectics. Table 4 shows the significant differences in the mean EAT-26 scores between the diagnostic categories, with an increase in the means from the normal to the anorectic groups (F = 10.53, 4 df, p<0.0001). The mean for the "mixed" group falls between the normal and the normal dieting group.

Despite the strong association with individual diagnostic categories such as classical anorexia nervosa, a high EAT-26 score was not significantly associated with the compound definition of "case/noncase" (Table 5).

Prevalence of Eating Disorders

Table 5 shows that 6 "cases" of clinically significant eating disorders were identified among the 25 girls with high EAT-26 scores, and 12 "cases" among the remaining 90 girls with low EAT-26 scores. Extrapolating these figures back to the full sample of girls living with their mothers who were not given a second interview, a prevalence rate of clinically significant eating disorders of 14.4% was established. This figure does not apply to the 41 girls who did not live with their mothers (or mother surrogates). The small numbers involved do not allow a meaningful estimate of the rate of classical anorexia or bulimia nervosa. For this selected subsample, the specificity of the EAT-26 was only 33.0%, the sensitivity being 80.4%.

EAT-26 Subscores and Diagnostic Categories

Mean subscores for *Dieting* and *Oral Control* were significantly related to the diagnostic categories with high scores associated with partial syndrome and anorexia nervosa (*Dieting* F = 7.45, 4 df, p<0.0001; *Oral Control* F = 3.50, 4 df, p<0.01). The mean subscores for *Food Preoccupation* showed only a nonsignificant tendency, with the girls in the normal dieting and partial syndrome categories showing the highest scores.

Affective Disorders

Table 6 shows that there was a significant relationship between eating disorder "caseness" and self-reported affective disturbance (a high score on the GOSQ) (p<0.01). There was a stronger relationship with the psychiatrists' definition of clinically significant affective disorder (p<0.005).

Menarche

The age at menarche of the girls with scores above the cut-off point on the EAT-26 was significantly earlier than in the general population (p<0.01). There was also a significant tendency for girls identified as "cases" of eating disorder not to have regular periods; 4 girls (4/18 = 22%) had irregular periods, and 2 (11%) were not menstruating (p<0.003).

Height/Weight Ratios

Both self-reported and clinically identified problems of eating control were related to the extent to which the girl's weight-for-height ratio deviated from the norm for her age, but not in the predicted direction. There was a significant tendency for girls with high EAT-26 scores and for those with a clinical classification of eating problems to be overweight. It is noteworthy that 32% of the girls with high EAT scores were more than two standard deviations above the weight-for-height norm for their age, compared with only 15% of the low-scoring group.

Social Class and Educational Achievement

As with the self-reported EAT-26 scores, there was no association between a clinical diagnosis of eating disorders and either the socioeconomic status of the family or the educational achievement of the girl.

Emotional Overinvolvement of Mother and Daughter

A high level of emotional overinvolvement between mother and daughter was not related to a high EAT-26 score or to a diagnosis of eating disorder. However, there was a significant relationship between the presence of an eating disorder and the girl saying that she confided in her mother only (and in no one else), which might be some indication of overinvolvement that was not otherwise observed by the second-stage interviewers. The number of such girls was very small (7).

Family Conflict and Rule-Boundedness

There was a significant relationship between the relative absence of moderate and serious arguments between the daughter and both her father and her mother, and a diagnosis of eating disorder. The girls with a diagnosis of normal or normal dieter were significantly more likely to have rows and to have had recent rows with their parents.

Table 6. Clinical cases of eating disorders and self-reported affective symptoms.

Scores on Great Ormond Street Mood Questionnaire	Eating disorders Noncase N (%)	Case N (%)	Totals N (%)
0–24	76 (91)	8 (9)	84 (100)
25+	21 (68)	10 (32)	31 (100)
Totals	97 (84)	18 (16)	115 (100)

χ^2 = 7.22, 1 df, p<0.01

An extensive analysis of the girl's and of the mother's reports of the existence of parental rules in the family showed no significant relationship with a diagnosis of "caseness." Again, this may be a product of the choice of family rules as a way of assessing rule-boundedness.

Mothers' Perception of their Daughters' Eating Disorders

Like the girls' self-report (EAT-26) scores, the girls' clinical diagnoses were unrelated to the mothers' third-person versions of the EAT-26.

Discussion

The prevalence of self-reported severe eating-control problems (identified by a score of 21+ on the 26-item *Eating Attitudes Test*) was similar to that found in other studies of community samples. In the current study, 8.1% of the girls gave scores on the EAT-26 above the cut-off point. This compares with 6.9% reported from an earlier study of 15-year-old schoolgirls (Mann et al., 1983), 8.2% in a population of 14–16-year-old schoolgirls (Johnson-Sabine et al., 1988), 11.5% among female university students (Clarke & Palmer, 1983), and 6.3% in the female student population studied by Button and Whitehouse (1981). Neither of the latter two groups would have included any 15-year-olds and very few 16-year-olds. Reports from studies of adults suggest similar findings: King (1989) found a rate of 13.3% high EAT-26 scorers among adult women in four London general practices, although Cooper, Waterman and Fairburn (1984) reported a rate of 20.6% high scorers among women attending a family planning clinic.

The usefulness of the EAT-26 as an accurate screening instrument for finding the "cases" of eating-control problems in this population of girls in their late adolescence was limited. In a subsample of 115 girls who were intensively interviewed and who could therefore be assigned to diagnostic groups, 18 were described as "cases" of eating disorders by the two psychiatrists; of these only 6 (33%) had EAT-26 scores above the cut-off point. Of the 25 girls with high EAT-26 scores, 19 were not defined as "cases" by the psychiatrists.

Several authors have confirmed that the two EATs are of only limited use in identifying cases of anorexia nervosa or bulimia, and suggest that high self-report scores should be treated as a measure of concern about weight and eating control. Williams, Tarnopolsky and Hand (1982) have pointed to the limitations of screening questionnaires in the identification of conditions with a prevalence below 20%. This study thus confirms that it would be unwise to use only a screening test to identify cases of eating disorders in the community, and an interview is essential to confirm "caseness."

The strong relationship between affective disorders and eating-control problems found in the responses to the self-report questionnaires in this study repeats the findings of several previous studies (e.g., Cantwell, Sturzenberger, Burroughs, Salkin & Green, 1977).

The absence of association between a high EAT-26 score and parental socioeconomic status was similar to that found in recent studies of schoolgirls (Eisler & Szmukler, 1985) and of adults in four London general practices (King, 1989). However, it should be noted that the proportion of older girls attending the University or Polytechnic was lower than the national average, indicating that the current population may not be sufficiently representative of high educational achievement to test the relationship with self-reported eating problems noted in other studies.

Significant differences were found between the mean EAT-26 scores of the diagnostic subgroups, which mirrors the findings in other studies. King (1989), however, found much higher mean scores in groups of normal dieters and partial syndrome adults identified in the community. This may suggest that if the habits associated with bulimic or anorectic behaviour persist from adolescence through into adult life, they are likely to be more severe and appear as higher scores. The adults may also be more honest in their responses to the EATs.

Clearly, the important questions about which of the adolescent girls diagnosed as having clinically significant eating disorders will continue to show disturbed behaviour or attitudes in adult life cannot be answered in the present study. It is important to record that only two girls—one with a diagnosis of "recovered" anorexia, the other with a diagnosis of food preoccupation and emotional disorder—had received any treatment from the medical profession. In neither case was the anorectic behaviour the reason for the referral: in one case, it was the associated amenorrhoea, and in the other a severe kidney infection.

These findings suggest that there is a worryingly high rate of adolescent girls in the general population whose preoccupation with weight and appearance dominates their lives. It might well be appropriate for health education in schools to put more emphasis on the wide range of normality in appearance in order to counter some of the emphasis on the desirability of extreme thinness still permeating much media and advertising material.

Summary

A survey of eating control problems in a community population of 15–20-year-old girls was carried out in eight General Practices in inner and outer London. In a two-stage design, 529 girls were initially screened using the 26-item *Eating Attitudes Test* (EAT-26). A second interview was held with high-scoring girls and low-scoring controls who lived with their mothers. This clinical interview established that 14.4% of the girls who lived with their mothers could be expected to be "cases" and have significant eating control problems; the rate of anorexia nervosa was 1%, and the remaining 13% showed heterogeneous but serious eating problems. A high EAT-26 score was highly related to self-reported depression/anxiety as well as to a clinical diagnosis of affective disorder, and was significantly related to girls being over- rather than underweight. Neither high self-report (EAT-26) scores nor clinical eating disorders were related to age or social class. There was a significant tendency for serious arguments with both parents to occur less frequently among girls defined as "cases." Only one "case" had ever received any treatment for eating disorder.

References

Bruch, H. (1977). Psychological antecedents of anorexia nervosa. In R. A. Vigersky (Ed.), *Anorexia nervosa* (pp. 1–10). New York: Raven Press.

Button, E. J., & Whitehouse, A. (1981). Subclinical anorexia nervosa. *Psychological Medicine, 11,* 509–516.

Cantwell, D. P., Sturzenberger, S., Burroughs, J., Salkin, B., & Green, J. K. (1977). Anorexia nervosa—An affective disorder? *Archives of General Psychiatry, 34,* 1087–1093.

Clarke, M. G., & Palmer, R. L. (1983). Eating attitudes and neurotic symptoms in university students. *British Journal of Psychiatry, 142,* 299–304.

Cooper, P. J., & Fairburn, C. G. (1986). The depressive symptoms of bulimia nervosa. *British Journal of Psychiatry, 148,* 268–274.

Cooper, P. J., Waterman, G. C., & Fairburn, C. G. (1984). Women with eating problems: A community survey. *British Journal of Clinical Psychology, 23,* 45–52.

Crisp, A. H. (1977). Diagnosis and outcome of anorexia nervosa. *Proceedings of the Royal Society of Medicine, 70,* 464–470.

Cullberg, J., & Engstrom-Lindberg, M. (1988). Prevalence and incidence of eating disorders in a suburban area. *Acta Psychiatrica Scandinavica, 78,* 314–319.

Eisler, I., & Szmukler, G. I. (1985). Social class as a confounding variable in the Eating Attitudes Test. *Journal of Psychiatric Research, 19,* 171–176.

Fairburn, C. G., & Cooper, P. J. (1983). Binge-eating and self-induced vomiting in the community: A preliminary study. *British Journal of Psychiatry, 142,* 139–144.

Fairburn, C. G., & Cooper, P. J. (1984). The clinical features of bulimia nervosa. *British Journal of Psychiatry, 144,* 238–246.

Fosson A., Knibbs, J., Bryant-Waugh, R., & Lask, B. (1987). Early onset in anorexia nervosa. *Archives of Diseases in Childhood, 62,* 114–118.

Garfinkel, P. E., & Garner, D. M. (1982). *Anorexia nervosa, a multidimensional perspective.* New York: Brunner/Mazel.

Garner, D. M., & Garfinkel, P. E. (1979). The Eating Attitudes Test: An index of the symptoms of anorexia nervosa. *Psychological Medicine, 9,* 273–279.

Garner, D. M., & Garfinkel, P. E. (1980). Socio-cultural factors in the development of anorexia nervosa. *Psychological Medicine, 10,* 647–656.

Garner, D. M., Olmsted, M. P., Bohr, Y., & Garfinkel, P. E. (1982). The Eating Attitudes Test: Psychometric features and clinical correlates. *Psychological Medicine, 12,* 871–878.

Goldberg, D. P., Cooper, B., Eastwood, M. R., Kedward, H. B., & Shepherd, M. (1970). A standardised psychiatric interview for use in community surveys. *British Journal of Preventive and Social Medicine, 24,* 18–23.

Herzog, D. B. (1984). Are anorexic and bulimic patients depressed? *American Journal of Psychiatry, 141,* 1594–1597.

Higgs, J. F., Goodyer, I. M., & Birch, J. (1989). Anorexia nervosa and food avoidance emotional disorder. *Archives of Diseases in Childhood, 64,* 346–351.

Huenemann, R. L., Shapiro, L. R., Hampton, M. C., & Mitchell, B. W. (1966). A longitudinal study of gross body composition and body conformation and their association with food and activity in a teenage population. *American Journal of Clinical Nutrition, 18,* 324–338.

Johnson-Sabine, E., Wood, K., Patton, G., Mann, A. H., & Wakeling, A. (1988). Abnormal eating attitudes in London school-girls—A prospective epidemiological study: Factors associated with abnormal response to a screening questionnaire. *Psychological Medicine, 18,* 615–622.

King, M. B. (1989). Eating disorders in a general practice population. Prevalence, characteristics and follow-up at 12 to 18 months. *Psychological Medicine* (Monograph Suppl.), 14.

Laessle, R. G., Kittl, S., Fichter, M. M., Wittchen, H.-U., & Pirke, K. M. (1987). Major affective disorder in anorexia nervosa and bulimia: A descriptive diagnostic study. *British Journal of Psychiatry, 151,* 785–789.

Mann, A. H., Wakeling, A., Wood, K., Monck, E., Dobbs, R., & Szmukler, G. (1983). Screening for abnormal eating attitudes and psychiatric morbidity in an unselected population of 15-year-old schoolgirls. *Psychological Medicine, 13,* 573–580.

Meadows, G. N., Palmer, R. L., Newball, E. U. M., & Kenrick, J. M. T. (1986). Eating attitudes and disorder in young women: A general practice based survey. *Psychological Medicine, 16,* 351–357.

Minuchin, S., Rosman, B. L., & Baker, L. (1978). *Psychosomatic families: Anorexia nervosa in context.* Cambridge, MA: Harvard University Press.

Moses, N., Banilivy, M. M., & Lifschitz, F. (1989). Fear of obesity among adolescent girls. *Pediatrics, 83,* 393–398.

Nylander, I. (1971). The feeling of being fat and dieting in a school population. *Acta Sociomedica Scandinavica, 3,* 17–26.

Russell, G. E. (1979). Bulimia nervosa: An ominous variant of anorexia nervosa. *Psychological Medicine, 9,* 429–448.

Slade, P. D., & Russell, G. M. (1973). Awareness of body dimensions in anorexia nervosa: Cross-sectional and longitudinal studies. *Psychological Medicine, 3,* 188–199.

Stonehill, E., & Crisp, A. H., (1977). Psychoneurotic characteristics of patients with anorexia nervosa before and after treatment and at follow-up four years later. *Journal of Psychosomatic Research, 21,* 187–195.

Szmukler, G. I. (1983). Weight and food preoccupation in a population of English schoolgirls. In J. G. Bergman (Ed.), *Understanding anorexia nervosa and bulimia: Fourth Ross Conference on Medical Research* (pp. 21–28). Columbus, OH: Ross Laboratories.

Szmukler, G. I. (1985). The epidemiology of anorexia nervosa and bulimia. *Journal of Psychiatric Research, 19,* 143–153.

Tanner, J. M., Whitehouse, R. H., Takaishi, M. (1966). Height velocity and weight velocity in British children, 1966. *Archives of Disease in Childhood, 41,* 454–471 and 613–635.

Thompson, M. G., & Schwartz, D. M. (1982). Life adjustment of women with anorexia nervosa and anorexic-like behaviour. *International Journal of Eating Disorders, 1,* 47–60.

Williams, P., Tarnopolsky, A., & Hand, D. (1982). The problem of screening for uncommon disorders—A comment on the Eating Attitudes Test. *Psychological Medicine, 12,* 431–434.

Psychobiology of Human Starvation

Manfred M. Fichter* and Karl-Martin Pirke**

In a series of experiments, 5 female subjects aged 21 to 25 years were investigated longitudinally on the basis of psychological and laboratory tests. The phases included a baseline with normal body weight, fasting, weight restoration, and a final baseline maintaining body weight. This group was compared with 16 patients suffering from anorexia nervosa and 27 suffering from bulimia nervosa. The hypothesis that reduced caloric intake in healthy subjects leads to multiple neuroendocrinological changes was confirmed. Under starving conditions, healthy subjects showed a hyperactivity of the hypothalamic-pituitary-adrenal axis and insufficient cortisol suppression following DST, regression in the 24-hour pattern of gonadotrophic hormones, a diminished TSH response to stimulation with TRH, increased basal growth hormone secretion, and—after subsequent weight gain—a blunted growth hormone response to stimulation with clonidine. The same neuroendocrine disturbances have been described for emaciated patients with anorexia nervosa, normalizing after weight gain. Patients with bulimia nervosa show similar neuroendocrine disturbances, though to a lesser degree than healthy starving subjects and patients with anorexia nervosa.

During the evolution of mankind, the biological adaptation to time of famine was of great importance. Keys, Brozek, Henschel, Mickolson and Taylor (1950) have documented the major times of famine in history in their important three-volume work on the *Biology of Human Starvation*. They present evidence for the time of famine in ancient Egypt; in the "stele of famine" about 2,000 years before the biblical drought in Abraham's time, the Pharaoh wrote: ". . . their souls are afflicted, their legs do not carry them anymore and they drag themselves along on the floor and their hands rest on their chest. Helplessness governs the great advisors on court." In the Old Testament, there are also numerous references to times of famine as a result of severe droughts, floods, earthquakes, and the devastation of wars. In the past centuries of our time (7 million died during the Irish famine in the mid-1800s) and decades (Leningrad during World War II) and up to the present-day droughts and wars (shortage of food in Third-World countries) there have also been numerous episodes of famine recorded.

Fasting—the deliberate reduction of food intake in times without food shortage—is a rite that many cultures prescribe to their members. Buddhism, Hinduism, Islam, Christianity, and other religions make use of fasting. The Old Testament contains many references to fasting (Leviticus 16:29, 23:27; 1st Samuel 1:7, 20:34; 2nd Samuel 1:12, 12:16; Isaiah 58:2, Jeremiah 14:12, 36:9) as does the New Testament (Matthew 6:16, 9:14, 17:21; Luke 18:12). In both the Old and the New Testament, fasting is supposed to purify one from sins and guilt. This association is also of importance for the psychodynamics of anorexia nervosa. Many famous physicians during the Greek and Roman empires as well as during the Middle Ages made the assumption that stringent fasting purified the body and used this method in attempts to treat various diseases. For example, Hippocrates, Celsius, and Sydenham reported that prescribed fasting resulted in cures for illnesses.

Besides its presumed cathartic effect, fasting can also have another meaning: Fasting can be used to put pressure on another person

---

*Klinik Roseneck (Prien), affiliated with the Medical Faculty of the Ludwig-Maximilians-University, Munich, and Research Division "Psychiatric Epidemiology and Evaluation" of the Department of Psychiatry, University of Munich, West Germany.
**Max Planck Institute of Psychiatry, Munich, West Germany.
Dedicated to Prof. Hanns Hippius on the occasion of his 65th birthday.

or as a form of revenge. Aggressive impulses against another person can be transformed into fasting in order to humiliate and to shame another person (Wellhöfer, 1981). Fasting has been used as a political weapon by the British suffragettes in their fight for the right to vote, by Mahatma Ghandi during his fight for India's independence, in the Irish war of independence, and by present-day imprisoned terrorists, for example, by the RAF (Red Army Fraction) in West Germany. If fasting can lead to the independence of an entire country, why should it not be used by an adolescent in his or her striving for personal independence from parents. In the case of anorexia nervosa, fasting is a powerful weapon in a family struggle, though it also has its price. Long-term follow-up studies over 20 or more years have shown a high mortality of 15% (Russell, 1987) and 18% (Theander, 1985).

The scientific exploration of the effects of hunger or fasting on the human body began only fairly recently, at the end of the 19th century, when the physician Tanner, using himself as subject, conducted the first fasting experiment. Benedict (1915, 1919) conducted the "Carnegie Nutrition Laboratory Experiment" on the effects of semistarvation in a group of male volunteers. The study focused on the metabolism of macronutrients. The classical, most thoroughly conducted study on the effects of semistarvation was the "Minnesota Experiment" conducted by Keys et al. (1950): A group of male volunteers participated in this semistarvation experiment over a period of 168 days. Keys et al. were the first to note mental changes during semistarvation in detail. More recently, fasting experiments have been conducted by Kollar, Slater, Palmer, Doctor and Mandell (1964), Consolazio, Matousk, Johnson, Nelson and Krzywicki (1967), and Palmblad, Levi, Burger, Melander, Westgren, v. Schenck and Skude (1977). In addition, there are several studies on the effects of protein-calorie malnutrition in involuntarily starved patients in Third-World countries (Cooke, James, Landon & Wynn, 1964; Smith, Bledsoe & Chhetri, 1975; Chopra & Smith, 1975).

The results of these studies indicated that starvation and semistarvation has marked effects on the metabolism in general, and on neuroendocrine regulation in particular. Amenorrhea is considered a cardinal symptom for the diagnosis of anorexia nervosa according to the DSM-III-R criteria (APA, 1987) and according to the ICD-10 (WHO, 1987). After Simmonds (1916), anorexia nervosa was seen as a disease caused by the primary pituitary insufficiency. Although this had been proved wrong, it has stimulated the search for other primary biological causes and "biological markers" for anorectic and bulimic eating disorders ever since. Anorectic and bulimic eating disorders show many neuroendocrine and neurotransmitter dysfunctions and other medical complications. In eating disorders, it is very important to separate the effects of reduced caloric intake and body weight from possible primary dysfunctions in the brain. According to our "nutritional hypotheses," neuroendocrine and neurotransmitter disturbances in anorectic and bulimic eating disorders are the result of temporarily reduced food intake. Since the effects of starvation and possible primary causes for the eating disorder may be confounded when patients with anorexia or bulimia nervosa are studied, we designed a fasting experiment with healthy normal subjects of the same age as our eating-disturbed patients.

Method

Samples

Starvation Study with Healthy Subjects: The Munich University Starvation Experiment (MUSE)

Five healthy female subjects aged 21–25 years (23.2 ± 2.2) were thoroughly screened on the basis of psychological and laboratory tests. The designs of the study were such that the subjects were studied longitudinally in four experimental phases:

- During the initial baseline phase (A), the subjects kept their body weight stable at 58 ± 4.9 kg (mean ± SD).
- During the fasting phase (B), the subjects remained in our research unit in order to ensure close medical supervision; during this phase, which lasted on the average 21 days, the healthy subjects lost an average of 8 kg (from 10.29% ± 2.7% of ideal body weight (IBW) to 87.8% ± 1.7% of IBW).
- During the weight restoration phase (C), the subjects gained weight until they reached their original body weight (101.8% ± 2.3% of IBW).
- In a final baseline phase (D), the subjects kept their body weight stable for 6 weeks until the end of the study.

Blood samples for endocrine assessments were drawn over 24 hours in 30-minute intervals before fasting (I), after fasting (II), and after weight gain (III).

Patients with Anorexia Nervosa (acc. to DSM-III; APA, 1980)

Sixteen patients with anorexia nervosa aged 13 to 29 were studied longitudinally during in patient treatment (Pirke, Fichter, Lund & Doerr, 1979; Doerr, Fichter, Pirke & Lund, 1980). Blood samples were drawn 1 week after admission at an average weight of 63% of IBW, after initial weight gain of 10% of IBW, and before discharge (average weight 88% of IBW). Fifteen of the anorectic patients were women, one was a boy.

Patients with Bulimia Nervosa (acc. to DSM-III; APA, 1980)

Twenty-seven bulimic patients of an average age of 26.7 years and an average duration of illness of 4.9 years were assessed. Body weight was on the average 98% of matched population mean weight (cf. Kemsley, 1953, cit in Crisp, 1980). Patients were trained to keep a detailed record of food intake over 21 days and were closely monitored by a nutritional counselor. These records were analyzed with the computer program KALI, version 2.14, which calculates caloric intake separately for carbohydrates, fat, and protein, and estimates the consumption of alcohol, vitamins, and minerals. Three patients with marked alcohol abuse were excluded from further analyses. After 10 days of recording food intake, nocturnal basal blood samples were obtained in 30-minute intervals from 6 p.m. to 6.30 a.m. At 7 a.m., blood samples for determining beta-hydroxy-butyric (BHBA) and T_3 were taken.

There were four control groups of healthy normal-weight females of about the same age as the bulimic patients (25 ± 4 years):

1) A control group of 15 females was used for comparison of the results of the dexamethasone suppression test;
2) other 15 healthy female controls served as controls for the nocturnal cortisol secretion;
3) 11 healthy females served as controls for nocturnal gonadotropins, prolactin, and growth hormone;
4) 12 healthy females served as controls for the TRH test.

Tests of Endocrine Functioning and Laboratory Assessment

The subjects in all studies (healthy females in the fasting experiment, patients with anorexia nervosa, patients with bulimia nervosa, and healthy controls) were kept off any medication (except for tests for endocrine function) throughout the complete course of the study, including contraceptives. However, vitamins and minerals were supplemented in the Munich Starvation Experiment. Healthy subjects in the Munich Fasting Experiment (in each phase of the study), patients with anorexia nervosa, and patients with bulimia nervosa and their healthy controls participated in the following assessments.

24-Hour Nocturnal Basal Hormone Secretion

Blood samples were drawn through an indwelling catheter, which was placed in the forearm vein. Blood samples were drawn in 30-minute intervals through a catheter, which was extended into an adjoining room to avoid sleep disturbances. About 600 ml NaCl solution (0.9%) were perfused at night. The lights were turned off at 10 p.m., and sleep EEG was recorded. Nocturnal blood samples were used to measure plasma cortisol, gonadotropins (LH, FSH), growth hormone, and prolactin.

Dexamethasone Suppression Test (DST)

On day 2 of the neuroendocrine assessments, the subjects took 1.5 mg fortecortin orally at 11 p.m. On the following day 3, blood samples were obtained for determination of plasma cortisol and plasma dexamethasone levels at 9 a.m., 4 p.m., and 9 p.m.

TRH Test

This test was performed on day 5 of the neuroendocrine assessments in the subjects participating in the fasting experiment (in each phase of the study) and in patients with bulimia nervosa and their controls, but not in patients with anorexia nervosa. Starting at 9 a.m., a TRH test was performed with injection of 1.0 ml TRH (= 0.2 mg relefact-TRH) intravenously, and 7 blood samples were taken at −60, −30, 0, +15, +30, +45, and +60 minutes.

Laboratory Assessments

Cortisol was determined by radioimmunoassay (Biosigma Co.); the interassay variability was 4.5% at an average concentration of 12.1 µg/dl at a limit of detection of 0.17 µg/dl. For the dexamethasone suppression test (DST), a level plasma cortisol above 5 µg/dl on the day following injection of fortecortin was defined as insufficient suppression. At 9 a.m. following oral administration of fortecortin, dexamethasone plasma levels were measured using a radioimmunoassay (Haak, Vecsei, Lichtwald, Klee & Gless, 1980). The interassay variability was 8.5% at an average concentration of 220 ng/dl and a limit of detection of 10 ng/dl. Plasma TSH was measured using radioimmunoassay (Serono Co., Freiburg) as described by Schlesser, Rush, Fairchild, Crowley and Orsulak (1983). The TSH interassay variability was 8.6% at an average concentration of 4.2 mU/ml. Plasma LH and plasma FSH were determined using radioimmunoassay as described by Pirke et al. (1987) (Serono Co., Freiburg); the interassay variability was 7.2% for LH (average concentration = 10.6 mU/ml) and 8.1% for FSH (average concentration = 12.1 mU/ml). Radioimmunoassay was also used for measuring plasma prolactin (Serono Co., Freiburg) as described by Neill (1980); the plasma prolactin interassay variability was 7.4% at an average concentration of 5.6 n/ml. Plasma T_3 levels and plasma beta-hydroxy-butyric acid (BHBA) levels were used as indicators for reduced caloric intake in the preceding weeks or days. BHBA was determined using the method described by Williamson and Mellonby (1974); the interassay variability was 4.1% at an average concentration of 0.53 µmol/ml. Plasma T_3 was determined by radioimmunoassay (Serono Co., Freiburg); the interassay variability was 6.1% at an average concentration of 1.1 n/ml.

Statistical Analyses

When the data were normally distributed, parametric statistical testing was performed. Nonparametric tests (U-test, Wilcoxon-test) were performed when the data were not normally distributed. For analyzing the effects of nutrition, the data of the total bulimic group was split at the median of variables, which indicated high or low caloric intake. Both bulimic groups were compared with each other and with healthy controls.

Results

Hypothalamic Pituitary Adrenal (HPA) Axis

In Munich University Starvation Experiment (MUSE)

The average level of the basal 24-hour plasma cortisol showed a significant rise during the 3-week fasting period with a 15% weight loss from 7.3 ± 4 to 12.4 ± 3 µg/dl (df = 4; p<0.05). The hypercorticolism observed after fasting in the healthy subjects normalized again after the subjects had regained their original (normal) body weight; cortisol levels were then 6.7 pmg/dl (df = 4; p<0.05). A significant increase was also observed in the plasma cortisol half-life, which was 79 minutes before fasting and 125 minutes after the fasting phase (df = 4; p<0.05). The restoration of body weight also resulted in a normalization of the plasma cortisol half-life (72 minutes). Fasting also resulted in an increase in the total amount of time spent in secretory activity: 258 minutes in 24 hours during the initial baseline and 420 minutes in 24 hours after the fasting phase (df = 4; p). The number of secretory episodes in 24 hours showed an increase that was, however, statistically not significant. In summary, fasting resulted in increased cortisol secretion and decreased cortisol caboli-

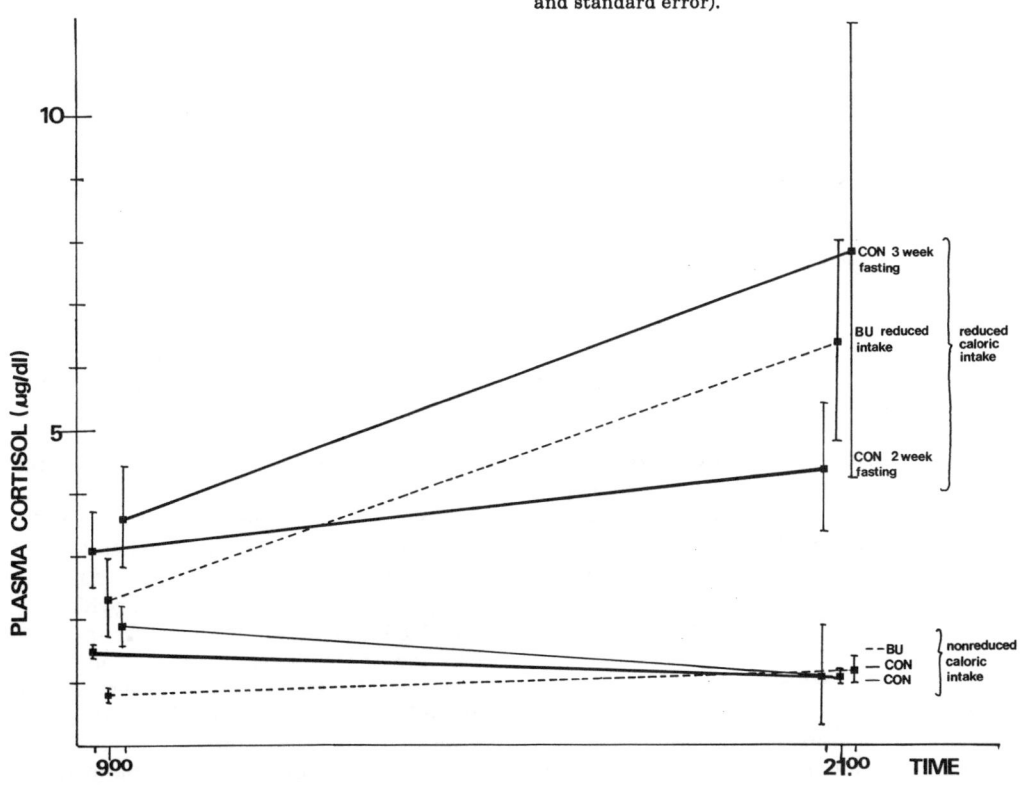

Figure 1. Plasma cortisol levels following ingestion of dexamethasone in healthy controls (CON) before and after experimental starvation, and in bulimic patients (BU) with higher or lower caloric intake (mean and standard error).

zation, which in turn resulted in marked increases in plasma cortisol levels.

The dexamethasone suppression test (DST) was sufficiently suppressed in all 11 DSTs performed in the 5 subjects during initial baseline. In the fasting phase, 7 of 14 DSTs (50%) showed insufficient suppression of cortisol levels above 5 µg/dl. All 11 DSTs performed were normally suppressed during the weight gain phase (C). In the final baseline phase (D), 17 of 18 (94.4%) cortisol probes at 4 p.m. and 9 p.m. were normally suppressed. Figure 1 shows the cortisol levels at 9 a.m. and 9 p.m. following ingestion of fortecortin for healthy subjects before, during, and after fasting as well as for bulimic patients as compared to healthy controls.

Insufficient cortisol suppression in starving healthy patients was most pronounced after 3 weeks of fasting (as compared to 1 or 2 weeks of fasting). Post-DST plasma cortisol levels at 9 p.m. were 1.1 ± 1 during baseline (A1), 4.4 ± 1 during the second week of starvation (A2), and 7.8 ± 4 µg/dl during the third week of starvation (A3). The differences were statistically significant (t-test: df = 4; p<0.05). When the subjects began to eat again after the fasting phase, post-DST cortisol levels normalized quickly—there were indications that this normalization occurred at least within days. The last DST in the fasting phase B (with insufficient cortisol suppression) was followed by the first DST in the weight gain phase C by an average of 7.6 days, and cortisol was then normally suppressed.

A remarkable finding was also that the dexamethasone plasma levels obtained in 4 of the 5 healthy female subjects were substantially reduced during fasting; the levels were 413 and 478 ng/dl in the 2 initial baseline weeks (A1 and A2), 278 and 357 ng/dl in the first and second fasting week (B1 and B2). Levels increased again during the weight-gain phase (C1 and C2) to 595 and 544 ng/dl. Apparently, the cortisol response to dexamethasone was affected by the absorption, distribution, or metabolization of dexamethasone itself.

In Anorexia Nervosa

The 24-hour plasma cortisol level was elevated in anorexia nervosa patients on admission: It was 18.1 µg/dl on admission, 10.1 µg/dl after initial 10% weight gain, and 8.9 µg/dl before discharge at 88% of ideal body weight. On admission, body weight was on the average 63% of ideal body weight. In the emaciated state 1 week after admission, anorectic patients showed a statistically significant increase in the number of secretory episodes in 24 hours, a significant increase in the total time spent in secretory activity and a significant increase in the average cortisol half-life in the plasma.

Following admission, all but one of the anorectic patients showed insufficient cortisol suppression following application of dexamethasone (DST). Small increases in body weight led to a normalization of this finding: After an increase of only 10% in ideal body weight, all except 3 patients showed normal cortisol suppression. Dexamethasone plasma levels were not measured in anorectic patients.

In Bulimia Nervosa

Patients with bulimia nervosa usually have fairly normal weight. In our study, the body weight of bulimic patients was on the average 98% of matched population mean weight. Characteristically, bulimic patients have marked weight fluctuations with weight loss as a result of dieting, restricted food intake and purging behavior, and weight gain as a result of uncontrolled eating. Since a minor reduction in body weight in healthy starving subjects resulted in hypercorticolism and insufficient cortisol suppression in the DST, and since minor increments in body weight led to a normalization of the HPA-axis in anorectic patients, it is reasonable to assume that disturbances in the HPA-axis in bulimia may exist. Our results show that bulimic patients (as compared to healthy female controls) did not show increased nocturnal plasma cortisol levels in the time from 1 a.m. to 6.30 a.m. The average cortisol plasma level during this time was 6.1 ± 1 (standard error of the mean, SEM) µg/dl for the bulimic patients, and 7.0 ± 1 µg/dl for the 15 controls. At 9 p.m. on the day following ingestion of dexamethasone, plasma cortisol levels were elevated and thus insufficiently suppressed in bulimic patients as compared to controls; this difference, however, did not quite reach statistical significance using two-sided testing (t = 2.0; df = 36; p = 0.058). The cortisol levels at 9 p.m. on the day following ingestion of dexamethasone (DST) were 3.4 ± 1.1 for the total bulimic group and 1.1 ± 0.1 for the control group. The difference in the 9 p.m. post-DST plasma cortisol levels were seen between the calorie-restricting bulimics (6.4 ± 1.6 µg/dl) and the nonrestricting bulimics (1.2 ± 0.2 µg(dl) (t = 2.0, df = 8, p = 0.08). Since the split-half calculations reduced the cell number, statistical significance was harder to achieve. A trend for statistical significance was also observed for the comparison between the two bulimic groups at 4 p.m. and the comparison between the calorie-restricting bulimics and the control group at 4 p.m. and 9 p.m. on the day following ingestion of dexamethasone. Beta-hydroxy-butyric acid (BHBA) is an indicator for reduced food intake in the previous days. Bulimics with high BHBA plasma levels had somewhat higher 9 p.m. post-DST plasma cortisol levels than controls (t = −.70, df = 13, p = 0.10). A high degree of depression in the bulimic patients was not associated with higher basal or post-DST cortisol levels. In fact, the 9 p.m. post-DST cortisol levels were higher in bulimics with low scores in their self-rating of depression than in controls. There were no differences in post-DST plasma levels at 4 p.m. or 9 p.m. between bulimics with high and bulimics with low depression scores in the self- or in an expert rating.

Hypothalamic Pituitary Gonadal Axis

In Healthy Females During Fasting

All 5 healthy subjects had normal (adult) secretory patterns of the luteinizing hormone (LH) as defined by Pirke et al. (1979). A remarkable finding was that 3 of the 5 healthy female subjects showed a regression to an infantile (!) plasma LH secretory pattern after fasting. The two other subjects continued to have an adult plasma LH secretory pattern. Concerning LH regression, the phase of the menstrual cycle in which fasting began may have been of importance. Those subjects who showed regression in the LH secretory pattern began fasting at a later point of time in their menstrual cycle. It is important to note that the infantile secretory pattern in 3 of 5 subjects was observed following a minor weight loss (8 kg on average) when compared to amenorrheic patients with anorexia nervosa. In addition, the regression in LH secretory pattern occurred within a relatively short period of time (14–23 days). The body weight of the 3 healthy female subjects responding with a LH regression was markedly higher than the weight of patients with anorexia nervosa, who were assessed at low body weight on admission and after 10% weight increase. A similar reduction in plasma LH and FSH levels was recently reported for monkeys during dietary restriction (Cameron, 1989). In our Munich University Starvation Experiment (MUSE), one subject had a menstrual period at the beginning of the fasting phase (days 5–8); all other subjects were amenorrheic during fasting, weight gain, and final baseline phase.

In Anorexia Nervosa

Fourteen of 16 patients with anorexia nervosa had an infantile plasma LH secretion pattern on admission. LH and FSH secretion increased with increasing body weight. All 16 patients with anorexia nervosa developed a pubertal or adult pattern after 10% weight increase or at the time of discharge (Pirke et al., 1979). Two patients, one of which had an adult and the other a pubertal pattern after weight gain at discharge, had a relapse 3 and 13 weeks after discharge, respectively. Immediately after the second hospital admission, both patients again showed a regression to an infantile LH secretion pattern, which matured again with subsequent weight gain to a pubertal pattern in one case and an adult pattern in the other case at second discharge. The increase in average 24-hour LH plasma values per week was significantly higher in younger than in older anorectic patients. In addition, a longer duration of illness was associated with a slower maturation of the LH pattern.

In Bulimia Nervosa

Russell (1979), Fairburn and Cooper (1984), and Leon, White-Phelan, Kelly and Patten (1986) have reported amenorrhea in more than a third of patients with bulimia nervosa. In 15 patients and in 9 healthy controls, we obtained nocturnal blood samples in 30-minute intervals in the beginning of the second week of the menstrual cycle (or the observation week, respectively). The average LH plasma concentrations over 6 hours at night and the average LH peak amplitude was significantly lower in bulimics with anovulatory cycles (estradiol maximum below 444 pmol/l) than in bulimics with ovulatory cycles and in healthy controls. The number of LH peaks over the 6 hours at night was also lower in bulimics with anovulatory cycles than in bulimics with ovulatory cycles and in healthy controls, though this difference did not reach statistical significance. Bulimic patients with ovulatory cycles and luteal phase defects (LPD) only did not show a decrease in the nocturnal LH average plasma concentration, the number of LH peaks over the 6 hours at night, or the average LH peak amplitude.

In another sample of 24 patients with bulimia according to DSM-III criteria, we also measured nocturnal LH and FSH secretion, but did not control for the time of the menstrual cycle. These bulimic patients had a significantly lower LH and FSH average plasma level over 12 hours at night than healthy female controls. In this study we also controlled for caloric intake. The gonadotropin plasma levels were significantly lower in bulimics with a reduced caloric intake, bulimics with lower body weight, and bulimics with a higher number of fasting days (caloric intake below 1000 cal) than in the control groups and in bulimic patient with no indication of reduced food intake. Bulimics with a high percentage of protein intake (which corresponds to a low percentage of carbohydrate intake) had significantly lowered plasma gonadotropin levels compared to healthy controls and compared to bulimics with a lower percentage of protein intake (and a higher percentage of carbohydrate intake).

In the 15 bulimic patients in the first bulimia study on gonadotropin secretion mentioned above and 15 additional bulimic patients, we also studied the secretion of estradiol, progesterone, and LH over the total period of the menstrual cycle. The age of these 30 bulimic patients was on average 23.7 ± 3.6 years, which was equivalent to the age of 19 female controls (22.9 ± 2.9 years). Blood was sampled over a 6-week period each Monday, Wednesday, and Friday between 7 a.m. and 10 a.m. starting with a new cycle except for cases with amenorrhea. This design allowed a detailed analysis of gonadotropin and gonadal hormones over the whole period of the menstrual cycle. According to the results of the endocrine analyses, patients were classified into the following categories:

1) *normal gonadal functioning*, with a mid-cycle LH peak and a first estradiol peak at the time of ovulation and a second estradiol peak and a progesterone peak during the luteal phase;

2) *luteal phase defect (LPD)*, with a mid-cycle LH and an estradiol peak and a lack of the estradiol and progesterone peak during luteal phase;

3) *anovulatory cycle*, with flat LH estradiol and progesterone secretion throughout the menstrual cycle.

Only 3 out of 30 bulimic patients (10%) showed the normal pattern of secretion over the menstrual cycle (category 1). Twelve of the 30 bulimic patients (40%) showed a luteal phase defect (LPD) with estradiol peaks of more than 200 pg/nl during the follicular phase. Fifteen of the 30 bulimic patients (50%) showed continuously low estradiol and progesterone plasma levels, indicating that there is no growth of a dominant follicle. Clinically, this pattern presents as amenorrhea or oligomenorrhea. The fact that half of the bulimic patients showed anovulatory cycles with flat LH secretion over the total menstrual cycle is not only of importance for reproductive functions and fertility, but it also is most likely a "ticking time bomb" for the development of osteoporosis at a later point of time. This risk appears to be highest for emaciated patients with anorexia nervosa and for bulimics who have oligo- or amenorrhea for a longer period of time during adolescence and young adulthood. During this time, normal estrogen secretion is necessary for the take-up of calcium into the bone structures. With the recent increase of eating disorders, it is most likely that osteoporosis and other medical complications of eating disorders will be seen at a higher frequency in future years.

Growth Hormone (HGH) and HGH Response to Clonidine

In Healthy Subjects under the Conditions of Starvation (Munich University Starvation Experiment—MUSE)

In our 5 female healthy subjects, the basal growth hormone (HGH) levels over 24 hours were elevated at the end of the fasting phase; it was 3.7 ± 1 ng/ml at baseline and rose to 4.8 ± 2 ng/ml at the end of the fasting phase (df = 4; ns). At the end of the study (final baseline), the basal growth hormone levels were low (2.2 ± 1 ng/ml). Basal plasma HGH levels at the end of fasting were significantly higher than HGH levels after weight restoration (df = 4; p<0.05). The increased basal growth hormone levels after fasting must be taken into account when interpreting the results of the growth hormone response to clonidine.

The clonidine test was performed after two days without neuroendocrine testing at 8 a.m. with perfusion of 150 µg clonidine in 10 ml NaCl solution (0.9%) in 10 minutes. The HGH response to injection of clonidine was measured in 3 of the 5 females subjects. Clonidine is an alpha$_2$-adrenergic receptor agonist, and its injection normally leads to a temporary increased growth hormone secretion. Blunted growth hormone responses to injection of clonidine have been observed in depression (Checkley, Slade & Shur, 1981; Charney, Henninger, Sternberg, Hafstad, Giunings, & Landis, 1982; Ansseau, Frenckell, Certontaine, Papart, Franck, Timsit-Berthier et al., 1988). In our normal healthy subjects, injection of clonidine resulted in a normal growth hormone response at the end of the initial baseline phase, elevated basal growth hormone levels, and a normal growth hormone response to clonidine after 3 weeks of fasting and a blunted growth hormone response after the weight gain phase (t-test for paired observations, df = 2, p<0.05). In this study, however, the time of the menstrual cycle at which the clonidine injection occurred was not taken into account. According to our results, adrenoceptors appear to respond to fasting with a time delay.

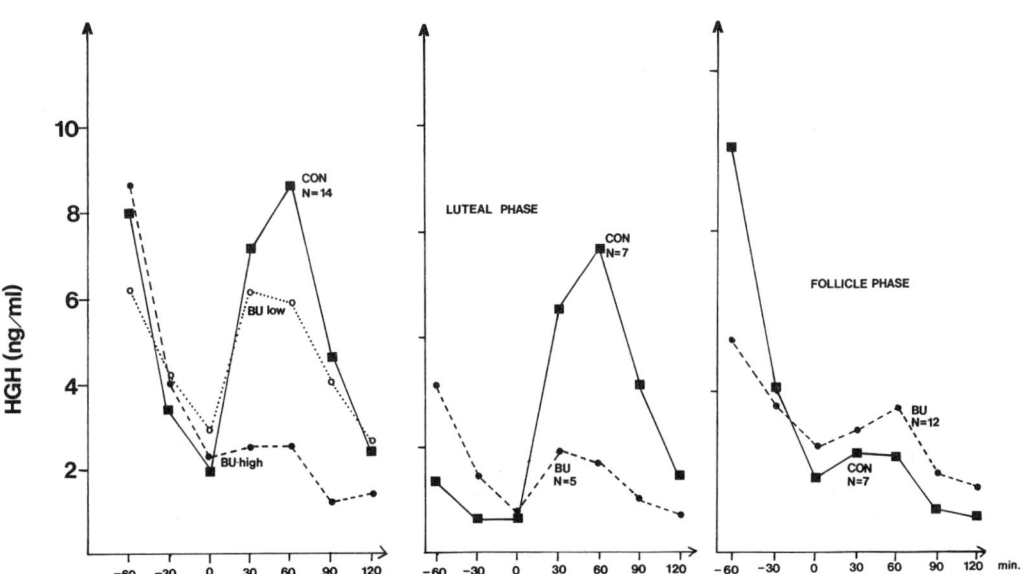

Figure 2. Growth hormone (HGH) response to clonidine. BU = bulimia nervosa, CON = healthy control, low = low caloric intake, high = higher caloric intake.

In Anorexia and Bulimia Nervosa

A clonidine challenge test has not been performed in patients with anorexia nervosa. Since clonidine lowers the blood pressure, the use of this test in hypotonic patients did not appear appropriate. In our study with 24 patients with bulimia, there was a trend for toward increased basal nocturnal growth hormone levels (9 p.m.–6 a.m.) with 4.0 ± 0.7 ng/ml for bulimic subjects compared to 3.5 ± 7 ng/ml for controls (one-tailed, $t = 0.6$, $df = 26$, $p = 0.28$). Therefore, 5 bulimic patients with basal growth hormone levels above 5 ng/ml were excluded from further analyses. Injection of 2 µg/kg clonidine showed a significantly lower growth hormone response in the remaining bulimic patients compared to controls ($p<0.05$). Because the clonidine test is sensitive to the menstrual cycle (Ansseau et al., 1988), patients and controls were subdivided with respect to the phase of the menstrual cycle. During the luteal phase, the differences between bulimics and controls were most pronounced, while both groups did not differ in their HGH response to clonidine in the follicle phase. However, the slightly higher HGH basal levels in bulimics have to be taken into account in interpreting the results. A blunted growth hormone response to clonidine presumably reflects a reduction in postsynaptic alpha$_2$- adrenergic receptor sensitivity. A blunted growth hormone response to clonidine has been shown in depression, in healthy subjects after fasting and regain of body weight, and in (food-restricting) bulimics during the luteal phase in our study. In another study with anorectic and bulimic patients, Heufelder, Warnhoff and Pirke (1985) assessed platelet alpha$_2$-adrenoceptors and adenylate cyclase and concluded that the activity of the sympathetic nervous system was reduced in both patient groups.

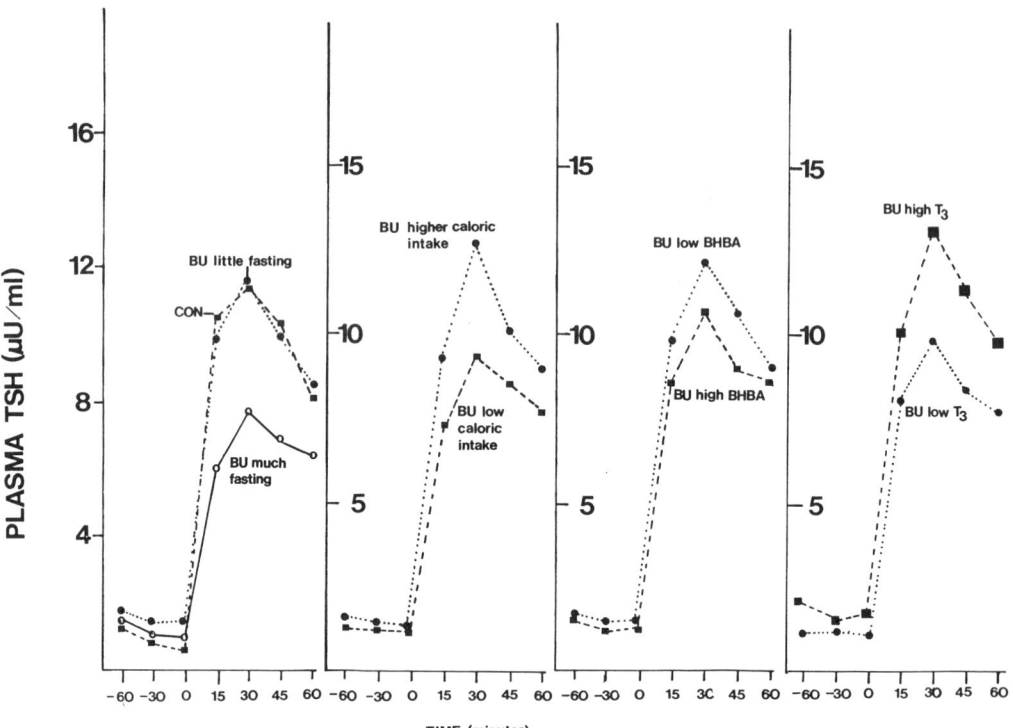

Figure 3. Response of plasma TSH to injection of TRH in patients with bulimia nervosa and in healthy controls. BU = bulimia nervosa, CON = healthy controls, BHBA = beta-hydroxy-butyric acid, o- - -o = bulimic patients with signs of reduced food intake.

Hypothalamic Pituitary Thyroid Function

In Healthy Subjects under Conditions of Starvation (Munich University Starvation Experiment—MUSE)

As expected, plasma T₃ levels were significantly reduced in healthy female subjects during starvation. The TRH- test showed a significantly reduced TSH response to TRH during the fasting phase as compared to the preceding baseline phase (paired t-test, df = 3, one-tailed, p<0.05). The TSH response to TRH normalized when body weight was restored. For depression, a blunted TSH response to TRH injection has been extensively documented (Extein, Pottash & Gold, 1981; Fleming, Extein, Sternbach, Pottash & Gold, 1983; Gold, Pottash, Sweeney, Martin & Davies, 1980; Gold, Pottash, Extein, Martin, Howard, Müller & Weeney, 1981; Kirkegaard, Bjorum, Cohn, Farber, Lauridsen & Nerup, 1977; Kirstein, Gold, Extein, Martin & Pottash, 1982; Loosen & Prange, 1980; McGrath, Quitkin, Stewart, Asnis, Novacenko & Puig-Antich, 1984; Schlesser et al., 1983; Winocur, Amsterdam, Oler, Mendels, Snyder, Caroff & Brunswick, 1983). A possible explanation for the blunted TSH response to TRH in depression could be the reduced appetite and consequent weight loss, which are frequent symptoms in depression.

In Bulimia Nervosa

For anorexia nervosa we did not assess the TSH response to TRH. This has, however, been studied by others: Casper and Frohmann (1982), Norris, O'Malley and Palmer (1985), and Kiyohara, Tamai, Karibe, Kobayashi, Fujii Fukino, Nakagawa et al. (1987) reported a blunted and delayed TSH response following injection of TRH. Our bulimic patients showed a lower 30-minute TSH response to TRH than 12 healthy controls (df = 33, one-tailed, p = 0.035). In order to analyze the effects of reduced caloric intake, we split the bulimic group at the median with respect to the variables indicating reduced caloric intake (low caloric intake, high beta-hydroxybutyric acid plasma levels and low T₃ plasma level). A trend for a reduced TSH response to TRH (which did not reach statistical significance) was seen for bulimics with reduced caloric intake, for bulimics with high beta-hydroxy-butyric acid plasma levels, and for bulimics with low T₃ plasma levels. A significantly decreased 30-minute TSH response was seen in those bulimics with a low percentage of carbohydrate intake compared to healthy controls (t = −2.8, df = 23, p = 0.004) and compared to bulimics with a high carbohydrate intake (t = −1.9, df = 19, one-tailed p = 0.035). Older compared to younger bulimics also had a significantly reduced TSH response to TRH (t = 2.4, df = 22, p 0.03, two-tailed testing). Age and duration of illness was positively correlated. A high degree of depression in bulimic patients was not associated with a decreased TSH response to TRH. Norris, O'Malley and Palmer (1985) also described a low TSH response to TRH in bulimics compared to healthy controls; however, their case number was low and their results were statistically not significant. Kiyohara et al. (1987) reported a rate of 58% of normal-weight bulimics as showing an abnormal TSH response to TRH.

We also observed a slightly reduced prolactin response to TRH, which did not reach statistical significance. For depression, a blunted prolactin response to TRH has been reported by Winocur et al. (1983) and Witchy, Schlesser, Fulton, Orsulak, Giles, Fairchild et al. (1984). For anorexia nervosa, conflicting results have been reported: Brambilla, Cocchi, Nobile and Müller (1981) and Giusti, Mazzochi, Mortara, Mignone and Giordano (1981) did find a blunted prolactin response to TRH, while Caspar and Frohmann (1982) did not confirm this finding.

Mood and Food

In the Minnesota Fasting Experiment, Keys et al. (1950) found depression-like symptoms in their subjects during semistarvation. The rank order of the expression of these symptoms was tiredness, sensitivity to noise, irritability, apathy, lack of concentration, loss of libido, disturbances in vigilance, moodyness, depression, and reduced motoric activity. In the Munich University Starvation Experiment (MUSE) with healthy females under conditions of total food abstinence, we did find an average increase in the *Hamilton Depression Scale* (Hamilton, 1967) and in the *Depression Self-Rating Scale* by von Zerssen (1976) (Fichter, 1985). This finding was the result of one subject reacting with substantial depressive symptoms to the 3 weeks of total food abstinence. There have been several reports on depressive symptoms as a result of harsh dieting (Robinson & Winnek, 1973). The issue of dieting and depression has been critically reviewed by Wadden, Stunkard and Smoller (1986) and by Smoller, Wadden and Stunkard (1987). Apparently, dieting and food composition do have an effect on mood. Schweiger, Laessle, Kittl, Dickhaut, Schweiger and Pirke (1986) reported a high negative correlation between carbohydrate intake and global mood ($r = -0.74$, $p<0.01$) and between the ratio of plasma tryptophan to other large neutral amino acids and global mood ($r = -0.52$, $p<0.05$). Tryptophan is a precursor of the neurotransmitter serotonin, and according to Wurtman (1981) the ratio of tryptophan to other large nutrial amino acids is a predictor of tryptophan flow into the brain. Schweiger et al. (1986) made their dieting study on the basis of the results of the Munich University Starvation Experiment (MUSE) and assessed the effects of different ways of dieting on the plasma level of large nutrial amino acids and mood. Kendler, Mohs and Davis (1983) studied the effects of different diets on the plasma levels of the dopamine metabolite homovanillic acid (HVA) in healthy young males. Compared to polycose meal, the high monoamine meal significantly increased pHVA.

Discussion

In a series of experiments, we studied the hypothalamic pituitary function in

1) healthy females under conditions of total food abstinence (starvation),

2) anorexia nervosa patients longitudinally during treatment and regain of body weight,

3) patients with bulimia (nervosa).

Our hypothesis was that reduced caloric intake (total food abstinence) in healthy subjects leads to multiple neuroendocrine changes. This hypothesis was confirmed. In starving healthy subjects, we found a hyperactivity of the hypothalamic pituitary adrenal (HPA) axis and insufficient cortisol suppression following DST, regression in the 24-hour pattern of gonadotrophic hormones (LH), a diminished TSH response to stimulation with TRH, increased basal growth hormone secretion, and—after subsequent weight gain—a blunted growth hormone response to stimulation with the alpha$_2$-adrenergic receptor against clonidine. The same neuroendocrine disturbances have been described for emaciated patients with anorexia nervosa; these endocrine dysfunctions in anorexia nervosa normalized with weight gain.

Patients with bulimia (nervosa) are more or less at normal weight. Nevertheless, they do show similar neuroendocrine disturbances, though to a lesser degree than healthy starving subjects and patients with anorexia nervosa. The most likely reason for this is that not the absolute body weight, but *temporarily reduced food intake* affects the hypothalamic pituitary function. Bulimic patients characteristically show high fluctuations in body weight as a result of fasting and dieting alternating with phases of increased food intake and binges. In bulimic patients, we found, in accordance with the literature, a trend for insufficient cortisol suppression following injection of dexamethasone; this trend was most pronounced in bulimics with signs of restricted caloric intake (higher number of fasting days in 3 weeks, lower number of consumed calories per day). Increased basal plasma cortisol levels were not detected in our bulimic patients, but have been reported by Kennedy, Garfinkel, Parienti, Costa and Brown (1989). In our studies, the dexamethasone plasma level following injection of dexamethasone was significantly reduced in bulimics compared to healthy subjects during total food abstinence. The insufficient cortisol suppression in the DST may be explained on this basis, although it is unknown whether the low dexamethasone plasma levels in the DST are a consequence of insufficient absorption or distribution or of increased metabolization.

In addition, we found

1) significantly lower plasma FSH levels in bulimics with signs of restricted caloric intake (higher number of fasting days, lower number of calories consumed),

2) significantly lower plasma LH levels in bulimics with signs of reduced caloric intake (low T_3 levels, high beta-hydroxy-butyric acid levels, reduced caloric intake or higher number of fasting days),

3) reduced nocturnal prolactin levels in bulimics with signs of restricted caloric intake in the previous days (increased beta-hydroxy-butyric acid plasma levels),

41) a significantly reduced prolactin response to TRH in bulimics with a history of anorexia nervosa,

5) a trend toward a blunted TSH response to stimulation with TRH.

There was also a trend toward a reduced TSH response to TRH in bulimics with a low percentage of carbohydrate intake; older bulimic patients (with a long history of an eating disorder) had a significantly lower TSH response to TRH. Blunted TSH responses to TRH in bulimia (nervosa) have also been reported by Gwirtsman, Roy-Byrne, Yager and Gerner (1983), Mitchell and Bantel (1983), and Norris, O'Malley and Palmer (1985), while this was not found by Kaplan, Garfinkel and Brown (1989).

The Munich University Starvation Experiment (MUSE) was the first well-controlled study on neuroendocrine functioning in healthy subjects under conditions of complete food abstinence using modern radioimmunoassay techniques for determining plasma hormone levels. Our findings concerning the DST in healthy starving subjects have recently been confirmed by a group in New Zealand (Mullen, Linsell & Parker, 1987). In addition, these authors reported a reduced rapid-eye-movement (REM) latency in 14 healthy male subjects following semistarvation. Reduced REM latencies have also been said to be a "biological marker" for depression (Kupfer, 1984). The same has been claimed for the dexamethasone suppression test (Carroll, 1982), for a reduced TSH response to TRH (Loosen, Wilson & Prange, 1980), and for blunted HGH response to stimulation with clonidine (Checkley, Slade & Shur, 1981). Our results and those of Mullen, Linsell and Parker (1987) confirm the nutritional hypothesis and shed doubt on the notion that the above-mentioned dysfunctions constitute a biological marker for (endogenous) depression, anorexia nervosa, or bulimia. There are several studies in depressed patients showing no association between body weight and disturbances in the HPA axis, but the methodology of these studies must be questioned (Keitner, Brown, Qualls, Haier & Barnes, 1985; Yerevanian, Baciewicz, Iker & Prirtera, 1984; Kline & Beeber, 1983; Targun, 1983, Coppen, Harwood & Wood, 1984; Zimmerman, Pfohl & Coryell, 1984). According to our results, not body weight but a reduction of food intake in the preceding days or weeks is of major importance for these neuroendocrine changes, and there are no studies in depression actually measuring the food intake in the weeks prior to endocrine testing. "Poor appetite or significant weight loss when not dieting" are frequent symptoms in depression and constitute a criterion for major depression in the DSM-III-R (APA, 1987). The study of neuroendocrine responses in healthy subjects before, during, and after starvation appears to be a purer model for studying these effects.

It has been shown in several studies that physical exercise increases the hypothalamic pituitary adrenal activity (Luger, Deuster, Kyle, Gallucci, Montgomery, Gold et al., 1987). Kendler, Mohs and Davis (1983) also reported an increase in pHVA following physical activity consisting of 30 minutes of exercise on a bicycle ergometer. Physical hyperactivity is a common symptom in anorexia nervosa and is also observed in some bulimic patients. Physical hyperactivity may also account for some of the neuroendocrine dysfunctions seen in these disorders.

According to a Gallup Poll in November 1985, 31% of American women aged 19–39 dieted at least once a month and 16% considered themselves as perpetual dieters (cit. in Brownell, Greenwood, Stellar & Shrager, 1986). The present ideals of body slimness have a high impact on dieting behavior especially for young females. The term "yoyo dieting" was coined for a form of dieting behavior with repeated cycles of losing and regaining body weight. In an animal model, Brownell et al. (1986) found significant increases in food efficiency (weight gain/kcal food intake) in the second food restriction and refeeding periods compared to the first in rats). Thus, weight loss occurred at half the rate and weight regain at three times the rate in the second cycle of weight loss and subsequent regain. At the end of the experiment, weight-cycled animals had a four-fold increase in food efficiency compared to controls. Other studies have shown similar effects in obese and lean animals during a single bout of food restriction and refeeding (Bjorntorp & Yang, 1982; Boyle, Storlien, Harper & Keesey, 1981; Boyle, Storlien & Keesey, 1978; Levitsky, Faust & Glassman, 1976; Robinson, Hodgson, Bradford, Robb & Peterson, 1975; Rolls & Rowe, 1979, 1980; Walks, Lavau, Presta, Yang & Bjorntorp, 1983). The study of Brownell et al. (1986) has shown that the energy efficiency not only endures but increases further with subsequent cycles of food restriction and refeeding. As mechanisms for increased energy efficiency, the following possibilities have been suggested: increased activity of lipoprotein lipase, lowered heat increment in response to food, decreased metabolic weight, flux of energy from plasma to peripheral tissue, adipose tissue pathology, and changes in intestine enzymes. While the effect of food restriction and refeeding resulting in increased energy efficiency has been well studied and documented in animals, this important area of investigation has been almost completely neglected in humans. Bennett, Williamson and Powers (1989) reported a lower resting metabolic rate in severe bulimics than in less severe bulimics and normals. Bulimic and obese patients often report weight increases in spite of low caloric intake. The dieting behavior of obese and bulimic patients and of many other food-restricting humans most likely has the effect of increasing energy efficiency. As in times of famine, the body adapts to low caloric intake by increasing energy efficiency. This means that a woman after "yoyo dieting" will gain weight when she consumes the same amount of calories that formerly resulted in stable body weight. At present this is a hypothesis that needs scientific investigation in humans.

References

American Psychiatric Association (1980). *Diagnostic and statistical manual of mental disorders (DSM-III)*. Washington, DC: APA.

American Psychiatric Association (1987). *Diagnostic and statistical manual of mental disorders—Revision (DSM-III-R)*. Washington, DC: APA.

Ansseau, M., Frenckell, R. v., Cerfontaine, J. L., Papart, P., Franck, G., Timsit-Berthier, M., Geenen, V., & Legros, J. J. (1988). Blunted response of growth hormone to clonidine and apomorphine in endogenous depression. *British Journal of Psychiatry, 153*, 65–71.

Benedict, F. G. (1915). *A study of prolonged fasting*. Washington, DC: Carnegie Institute, Vol. 203.

Benedict, F. G., Miles, W. R., Roth, P., & Smith, H. M. (1919). *Human vitality and efficiency under prolonged restricted diet*. Washington, DC: Carnegie Institute, Vol. 280.

Bennett, S. M., Williamson, D. A., & Powers, S. K. (1989). Bulimia nervosa and resting metabolic rate. *International Journal of Eating Disorder, 8,* 417–424.

Bjorntorp, P., & Yang, M. U. (1982). Refeeding after fasting in the rat: Effects on body composition and food efficiency. *American Journal of Clinical Nutrition, 36,* 444–449.

Boyle, P. C., Storlien, L. H., Harper, A. E., & Keesey, R. E. (1981). Oxygen consumption and locomotor activity during restricted feeding and realimentation. *American Journal of Physiology, 241,* 382–387.

Boyle, P. C., Storlien, L. H., & Keesey, R. E. (1978). Increased efficiency of food utilization following weight loss. *Physiological Behav., 21,* 261–264.

Brambilla, F., Cocchi, D., Nobile, P., & Müller, E. E. (1981). Anterior pituitary responsiveness to hypothalamic hormones in anorexia nervosa. *Neuropsychiatry, 7,* 225–237.

Brownell, K. D., Greenwood, M. R. C., Stellar, E., & Shrager, E. E. (1986). The effects of repeated cycles of weight loss and regain in rats. *Physiology & Behavior, 38,* 459–464.

Cameron, J. L. (1989). Influence of nutrition on the hypothalamic-pituitary-gonadal axis in primates. In K. M. Pirke, W. Wuttke & U. Schweiger (Eds.), *The menstrual cycle and its disorders* (pp. 66–78). Heidelberg, New York: Springer-Verlag.

Carroll, B. J. (1982). The dexamethasone suppression test for melancholia. *British Journal of Psychiatry, 140,* 292–304.

Casper, R. C., & Frohman (1982). Delayed TSH release in anorexia nervosa following injection of thyrotropin-releasing hormone (TRH). *Psychoneuroendocrinology, 7,* 59–68.

Charney, D. S., Henninger, G. R., Sternberg, D. E., Hafstad, K. M., Giunings, S., & Landis, D. H. (1982). Adrenergic receptor sensitivity in depression: Effects of clonidine in depressed patients and healthy subjects. *Archives of General Psychiatry, 39,* 290–294.

Checkley, S. A., Slade, A. P., & Shur, E. (1981). Growth hormone and other responses to clonidine in patients with endogenous depression. *British Journal of Psychiatry, 138,* 51–55.

Chopra, I. J., & Smith, S. R. (1975). Circulating thyroid hormones and thyrotropin in adult patients with protein-calorie malnutrition. *Journal of Clinical Endocrinol. Metabolism, 40,* 221–227.

Consolazio, C. F., Matousk, L. O., Johnson, H. L., Nelson, R. A., & Krzywicki, H. J. (1967). Metabolic aspects of acute starvation in normal humans. *American Journal Clinical Nutrition, 20,* 672–683.

Cooke, J. N. C., James, V. H. T., Landon, J., & Wynn, V. (1964). Adrenocortical function in chronic malnutrition. *British Medical Journal, 1,* 662–666.

Coppen, A., Harwood, J., & Wood, K. (1984). Depression, weight loss and the dexamethasone test. *British Journal of Psychiatry, 145,* 88–90.

Crisp, A. H. (1980). *Anorexia nervosa: Let me be.* London: Academic Press.

Doerr, P., Fichter, M. M., Pirke, K. M., & Lund, R. (1980). Relationship between weight gain and hypothalamic pituitary adrenal function in patients with anorexia nervosa. *Journal Steroid Biochemistry, 13,* 529–573.

Extein, I., Pottash, A. L. C., & Gold, M. S. (1981). Relationship of thyrotropin-releasing hormone test and dexamethasone test abnormalities in unipolar depression. *Psychiatry Research, 4,* 49–53.

Fairburn, C. P., & Cooper, P. J. (1984). The clinical features of bulimia nervosa. *British Journal of Psychiatry, 144,* 238–243.

Fichter, M. M. (1985). *Magersucht und Bulimia. Empirische Untersuchungen zur Epidemiologie, Symptomatologie, Nosologie und zum Verlauf.* Berlin, Heidelberg, New York, Tokyo: Springer-Verlag.

Fleming, J. E., Extein, I., Sternbach, H. A., Pottash, A. L. C., & Gold, M. S. (1983). The thyrotropin-releasing hormone and dexamethasone suppression tests in the familial classification of depression. *Psychiatry, 9,* 53–58.

Giusti, M., Mazzochi, G., Mortara, R., Mignone, D., & Giordano, G. (1981). Prolactin secretion in anorexia nervosa. *Horm. Metabolism Research, 13,* 585–585.

Gold, M. S., Pottash, A. L. C., Sweeney, D. R., Martin, D. M., & Davies, R. K. (1980). TRH-induced TSH response in unipolar, bipolar and secondary depressions. Possible utility in clinical assessments and differential diagnosis. *American Journal of Psychiatry, 137,* 101–102.

Gold, M. S., Pottash, A. L. C., Extein, I., Martin, D. M., Howard, E., Müller, E. A., & Weeney, D. R. (1981). The TRH-test in the diagnosis of major and minor depression. *Psychoneuroendocrinology, 6,* 159.

Gwirtsmann, H. E., Roy-Byrne, P., Yager, J., & Gerner, R. H. (1983). Neuroendocrine abnormalities in bulimia. *American Journal of Psychiatry, 140,* 559–563.

Haak, D., Vecsei, P., Lichtwald, K., Klee, H. R., & Gless, K. H. (1980). Some experiences on radioimmunoassays of synthetic glucocorticoids. *Allergology, 3,* 259–263.

Hamilton, M. (1967). Development of a scale for primary depressive illness. *British Journal Social & Clinical Psychology, 6,* 278–296.

Heufelder, A., Warnhoff, M., & Pirke, K. M. (1985). Platelet alpha-2-adrenoceptor and adenylate cyclase in patients with anorexia nervosa and bulimia. *Journal Clinical Endocrinol. Metabolism, 61,* 1053–1060.

Kaplan, A. S., Garfinkel, P. E., & Brown, G. M. (1989). The DST and TRH-test in bulimia nervosa. *British Journal of Psychiatry, 154,* 86–92.

Keitner, G. I., Brown, W. A., Qualls, C. B., Haier, R. J., & Barnes, K. T. (1985). Results of the dexamethasone suppression test in psychiatric patients with and without weight loss. *American Journal of Psychiatry, 142,* 246–248.

Kendler, K. S., Mohs, R. C., & Davis, K. L. (1983).

The effects of diet and physical activity on plasma homovanillic acid in normal human subjects. *Psychiatry Research, 8,* 215–223.

Kennedy, S. H., Garfinkel, P. E., Parienti, V., Costa, D., & Brown, G. M. (1989). Changes in melatonin levels but not cortisol levels are associated with depression in patients with eating disorders. *Archives of General Psychiatry, 46,* 73–78.

Keys, A., Brozek, J., Henschel, A., Mickolson, O., & Taylor, H. L. (1950). *Biology of human starvation.* Minneapolis: University of Minneapolis Press.

Kirkegaard, C., Bjorum, N., Cohn, D., Farber, J., Lauridsen, U. B., & Nerup, J. (1977). Studies on the influence of biogenic amines and psychoactive drugs on the prognostic value of the TRH-stimulation test on endogenous depression. *Psychoneuroendocrinology, 2,* 131.

Kirstein, L., Gold, M. S., Extein, I., Martin, D., & Pottash, A. L. C. (1982). Clinical correlates of the TRH infusion test in primary depression. *Journal of Clinical Psychiatry, 43,* 181–194.

Kiyohara, K., Tamai, H., Karibe, C. Kobayashi, N., Fujii Fukino, O., Nakagawa, T., Kumagai, L. F., & Nagataki, S. (1987). Serum thyrotropin (TSH) responses to thyrotropin-releasing hormone (TRH) in patients with anorexia nervosa and bulimia: Influence of changes in body weight and eating disorders. *Psychoneuroendocrinology, 12,* 21–28.

Kline, M. D., & Beeber, A. R. (1983). Weight loss and the dexamethasone suppression test. *Archives of General Psychiatry, 40,* 1034–1035.

Kollar, E. J., Slater, G. R., Palmer, J. O., Docter, R. F., & Mandell, A. J. (1964). Measurement of stress in fasting. Man. *Archives General Psychiatry, 11,* 113–125.

Kupfer, D. J. (1984). Neurophysiological "markers"—EEG sleep measures. *Psychiatry Research, 18,* 467–475.

Leon, G. R., White-Phelan, P., Kelly, J. T., & Patten, S. R. (1986). Symptoms of bulimia and the menstrual cycle. *Psychosomatic Medicine, 48,* 415–421.

Levitsky, D. A., Faust, J., & Glassman, M. (1976). The ingestion of food and the recovery of body weight following fasting in the native rat. *Physiological Behav., 17,* 575–578.

Loosen, P. T., Wilson, I. C., & Prange, A. J. Jr. (1980). Endocrine and behavioral changes in depression after TRH: Alteration by pretreatment with thyroid hormone. *Journal of Affective Disorders, 2,* 267–278.

Luger, A., Deuster, P. A., Kyle, S. B., Gallucci, W. T., Montgomery, L. C., Gold, P. W., Loriaux, D. L., & Chrousos, G. P. (1987). Acute hypothalamic-pituitary-adrenal responses to the stress of treadmill exercise. Physiologic adaptions to physical training. *New England Journal of Medicine, 318,* 1309–1315.

McGrath, P. J., Quitkin, F. M., Stewart, J. W., Asnis, G., Novacenko, H., Puig Antich, J. (1984). A comparative study of the pituitary TSH-response to thyrotropin in outpatient depressives. *Psychiatry Research, 12,* 185–193.

Mitchell, J. E., & Bantle, J. P. (1983). Metabolic and endocrine investigations in women at normal weight with the bulimic syndrome. *Biological Psychiatry, 18,* 355–365.

Mullen, P. E., Linsell, C. R., & Parker, D. (1987). Der Einfluß von Schlafentzug und Kalorienrestruktion auf biologische Merkmale der Depression. *Lancet (German edition), 1* (2), 114–118.

Neill, J. (1980). Neuroendocrine regulation of prolactin secretion. *Frontiers in Neuroendocrinology, 6,* 129–155.

Norris, P. D., O'Malley, B. P., & Palmer, R. L. (1985). The TRH-test in bulimia and anorexia nervosa: A controlled study. *Journal of Psychiatry Research, 19,* 215–219.

Palmblad, J., Levi, L., Burger, A., Melander, A., Westgren, U., v. Schenck, H., & Skude, G. (1977). Effects of total energy withdrawal (fasting) on the levels of growth hormone, thyrotropin, cortisol, adrenaline, noradrenaline, T4, T3, and rT3 in healthy males. *Acta Medica Scandinavica, 201,* 15–22.

Pirke, K. M., Fichter, M. M., Lund, R., & Doerr, P. (1979). Twenty-four-hour sleep-wake pattern of plasma LH in patients with anorexia nervosa. *Acta Endocrinol. (Kbh), 92,* 193–204.

Pirke, K. M., Fichter, M. M., Chlond, C., Schweiger, U., Laessle, R. G., Schwingenschlögel, M., & Hoehl, C. (1987). Disturbances of menstrual cycle in bulimia nervosa. *Clinical Endocrinology, 27,* 245–251.

Robinson, D. W., Hodgson, D., Bradford, G. E., Robb, J., & Peterson, D. W. (1975). Effects of dietary restrictions and fasting on the body composition of normal and genetically obese mice. *Journal of Animal Science, 40,* 1058–1062.

Robinson, S., & Winnek, H. Z. (1973). Severe psychotic disturbances following crash diet weight loss. *Archives of General Psychiatry, 29,* 559–562.

Rolls, B. J., & Rowe, E. A. (1979). Exercise and the development and persistence of dietary obesity in male and female rats. *Physiological Behavior, 23,* 241–247.

Rolls, B. J., Rowe, E. A., & Turner, R. C. (1980). Persistent obesity in rats following a period of consumption of a mixed, high-energy diet. *Journal of Physiology, 298,* 415–427.

Russell, G. F. M. (1987). Cit in Hsu, L. K. G. (1988). The outcome of anorexia nervosa: A Reappraisal. *Psychological Medicine, 18,* 807–812.

Russell, G. F. (1979). Bulimia nervosa: An ominous variant of anorexia nervosa. *Psychological Medicine, 9,* 429–448.

Schlesser, M., Rush, A., Fairchild, C., Crowley, G., & Orsulak, P. (1983). The thyrotropin-releasing hormone stimulation test: A methodological study. *Psychiatry Research, 9,* 59–68.

Schweiger, U., Laessle, R., Kittl, S., Dickhaut, B., Schweiger, M., & Pirke, K. M. (1986). Macronutrient intake, plasma large neutral amino acids and mood during weight-reducing diets. *Journal Neural Trans., 67,* 77–86.

Simmonds, M. (1916). Über Hypophysenschwund mit tödlichem Ausgang. *Deutsche Medizinische Wochenschrift, 42,* 190.

Smith, S. R., Bledsoe, T., & Chhetri, M. K. (1975). Cortisol metabolism and the pituitary-adrenal axis in adults with protein-calorie malnutrition. *Journal Clinical Endocr. Metabolism, 40,* 43–52.

Smoller, J. W., Wadden, T. A., & Stunkard, A. J. (1987). Dieting and depression: A critical review. *Journal of Psychosomatic Research, 31,* 429–440.

Targum, S. D. (1983). Reported weight loss and the dexamethasone suppression test. *Psychiatr. Res., 9,* 173–174.

Theander, S. (1985). Outcome and prognosis in anorexia nervosa and bulimia: Some results of previous investigations, compared with those of a Swedish long-term study. *Journal of Psychiatry Research, 19,* 493–508.

Wadden, T. A., Stunkard, A. J., & Smoller, J. W. (1986). Dieting and depression: A methodological study. *Journal of Consulting and Clinical Psychology, 54,* 869–871.

Walks, D. M., Lavau, M., Presta, E., Yang, M. U., & Bjorntorp, P. (1983). Refeeding after fasting in the rat: Effects of dietary-induced obesity on energy balance regulation. *American Journal of Clinical Nutrition, 37,* 387–395.

Wellhöfer, P. R. (1981). *Selbstmord und Selbstmordverhütung.* Stuttgart: G. Fischer.

Williamson, D. H., & Mellonby, J. (1974). In H. U. Bermeyer (Ed.), *Methoden der enzymatischen Analyse* (pp 1883–1886). Weinheim: Verlag Chemie.

Winokur, A., Amsterdam, J. D., Oler, J., Mendels, J., Snyder, P. J., Caroff, S. N., & Brunswick, D. J. (1983). Multiple hormonal responses to protirelin (TRH) in depressed patients. *Archives of General Psychiatry, 40,* 525–531.

Witchy, J. K., Schlesser, M. A., Fulton, C. L., Orsulak, P. J., Giles, D. E., Fairchild, C., Crowley, G., & Rush, A. J. (1984). TRH-induced prolactin release is blunted in females with endogenous unipolar major depression. *Psychiatry Research, 12,* 321–331.

Wurtman, R. J., Hefti, F., & Melamed, E. (1981). Precursor control of neurotransmitter synthesis. *Pharmacological Review, 32,* 315–335.

Yerevanian, B. I., Baciewicz, G. J., Iker, H. P., & Prirtera, M. R. (1984). The influence of weight loss on the dexamethasone suppression test. *Psychiatry Research, 12,* 155–160.

Zerssen, D. v. (unter Mitarbeit von D. M. Koeller) (1976). *Klinische Selbstbeurteilungs-Skalen (KSb-S) aus dem Münchner Psychiatrischen Informationssystem. Paranoid-Depressivitätsskala und Depressivitätsskala.* Weinheim: Beltz.

Zimmerman, J., Pfohl, B. M., & Coryell, W. H. (1984). Appetite and weight change and the dexamethasone suppression test. *Biological Psychiatry, 19,* 923–928.

The Noradrenergic System in Anorexia and Bulimia Nervosa

K. M. Pirke

The activity of the noradrenergic system in the brain and in the periphery is reduced in anorexia and bulimia nervosa. These neurotransmitter changes are a consequence of starvation. Physical activity partly compensates this effect. The alterations in the noradrenergic system have numerous consequences for the regulation of cardiovascular functions, thermoregulation, endocrine regulations, etc. The most important influences concern the deterioration of mood and the development of depressive syndromes.

Norepinephrine is a neurotransmitter found in both the central and peripheral nervous system. The cell bodies of the central nervous system are located in the locus coeruleus and project from there to many areas of the brain. Of special interest for the understanding of the pathophysiology of eating disorders is the project of the ventral bundle into the hypothalamic area where many vegetative functions are regulated, for example, body temperature, cardiovascular function, metabolic regulation, hunger and satiety, neuroendocrine regulation, etc.

Norepinephrine is also the transmitter of the peripheral sympathetic nervous system, which innervates not only the vascular system, but many other organs and systems as well like the pancreas, the heart, the ovaries, the immune system, etc. The peripheral noradrenergic system is regulated by the central sympathetic system.

Norepinephrine is involved not only in the regulation of vegetative functions, but also in the control of human moods. Schildkraut's (1978) hypothesis assumes that reduced noradrenergic activity occurs in the brain of depressed persons. This hypothesis is mainly based on the depressiogenic effect of reducing central norepinephrine stores by reserpin and on the antidepressive effects of drugs stimulating the central noradrenergic activity by reuptake inhibition, monoamine oxidase inhibition, etc.

This chapter summarizes recent findings on noradrenergic function in eating disorders collected in our laboratory. Since anorexia nervosa is characterized by severe starvation and bulimic patients show intermittent dieting and starvation, the effects of reduced caloric intake in humans and animals are also discussed here. The effects of starvation on norepinephrine turnover in the starved rat are discussed here since this animal model provides insight into the mechanisms responsible for the reduced activity of the noradrenergic system and its consequences.

The Peripheral Noradrenergic System in Anorexia Nervosa and Bulimia Nervosa

In this chapter, anorexia nervosa and bulimia nervosa are defined according to DSM-III-R criteria, i.e., the bulimia nervosa group contains only normal-weight patients. Underweight patients with binging and vomiting behavior are classified as anorexia nervosa.

Max-Planck-Institut für Psychiatrie, Kraepelinstr. 10, D-8000 München 40.

Plasma concentrations of norepinephrine have been measured under resting conditions in patients with anorexia nervosa and bulimia (Gross, Lake, Ebert, Ziegler & Kopin, 1979; Pahl, Pirke, Schweiger, Warnhoff, Gerlinghoff, Brinkmann, Berger & Krieg, 1985; Pirke, Fichter & Pahl, 1985; Heufelder, Warnhoff & Pirke, 1985). Reduced to normal values were observed in both eating disorders. Basal concentrations have to be interpreted with caution as they are influenced not only by secretion, but also by the metabolism of the neurotransmitter and thus may not reflect the activity of the sympathetic nervous system (Kopin, 1978). The orthostatic test during which plasma norepinephrine is measured in supine and upright body position is considered a better indicator for noradrenergic activity (Kopin, 1978). When the orthostatic test is repeatedly performed during the course of treatment of anorexia nervosa, a clearer picture evolves (Kaye, Jimerson, Lake & Ebert, 1985): When anorectic patients in a state of starvation are admitted to the hospital, they either show low or normal or even elevated orthostatic norepinephrine responses. During treatment and weight gain, a more uniform picture develops: All anorectic patients now show reduced orthostatic norepinephrine increases. With continuous weight gain, there is a tendency toward normalization of the noradrenergic system. Weight-stabilized patients studied a year after the end of treatment, however, still show significantly lower norepinephrine responses than normal young women (Table 1). In order to understand this phenomenon, we have to consider the effects of starvation on norepinephrine in healthy subjects. Fichter and Pirke (1984) studied the orthostatic norepinephrine response in 5 normal-weight healthy young women before and during a 2-week starvation period. As can be seen in Figure 1, the orthostatic norepinephrine increase is totally suppressed by starvation. On the other hand (see below), the norepinephrine system in eating-disorder patients retains its ability to respond to stress with increases of plasma norepinephrine. The heterogeneity of the orthostatic norepinephrine response shortly after admission to the hospital may therefore be explained by the counteracting effects of starvation and stress.

The time course of delta-norepinephrine during weight gain indicates that the reduced activity of the peripheral noradrenergic system is normalized only very slowly.

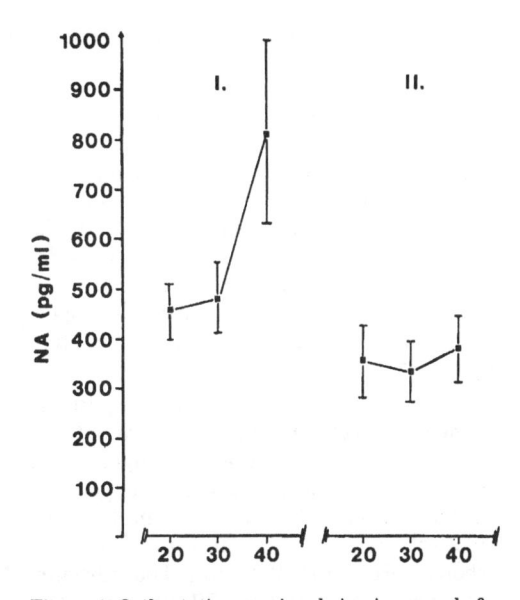

Figure 1. Orthostatic norepinephrine increase before (I.) and after (II.) 2 weeks of starvation in 5 healthy normal-weight women. 20, 30 = supine body position; 40 = standing.

Table 1. Orthostatic norepinephrine response in normal controls and in anorectic patients before and at two times after treatments.

	Anorectics on admission to hospital	Anorectics before release from hospital	Normal-weight anorectics 14 months later	Normal age- and sex-matched controls
NA supine (pg/ml)	226.9 ± 55.0	216.8 ± 44.0	84.6 ± 21.2	227.0 ± 12.9
Na standing (pg/ml)	346.7 ± 61.3	337.0 ± 68.3	185.7 ± 46.3	396.4 ± 17.8
Orthostatic NA increase	119.8 ± 45.3	120.2 ± 28.8	109.6 ± 27.3	169.4 ± 18.1

As in anorexia nervosa, we found a reduced orthostatic norepinephrine increase in normal-weight patients with bulimia nervosa (Heufelder et al., 1985). These patients show intermittent periods of starvation, which is reflected in weight fluctuations, elevated beta-hydroxybutyric acid and reduced serum T 3 values (Heufelder et al., 1985). Considering all these observations, there are several possibilities for explaining the impaired orthostatic norepinephrine response in anorectic patients after weight normalization:

1) The process of normalization of the noradrenergic system is so slow that normal values are not reached even after a year.
2) The weight-normalized anorectic patients still have a rather chaotic eating behavior characterized by intermittent periods of dieting, which in our experience is the case of many former anorectics.
3) The low norepinephrine activity is a trade-dependent variable of anorectic patients.

Whatever the mechanisms are, it must be considered that anorectic and bulimic patients retain their neurotransmitter abnormality for a long time. The consequences of this are discussed later.

Norepinephrine Response to Test Meals

Feeding stimulates the peripheral sympathetic nervous system (Landsberg & Young, 1978). This response is a complex one. The process of ingestion and digestion of food stimulates norepinephrine release. In the case of anorectic patients, we have to consider the fear and anxious resistance many patients show when confronted with the aspect of consuming calories and thus possibly gaining weight.

We studied anorectic and bulimic patients and healthy, age-matched women before and after the ingestion of either carbohydrate- or protein-rich test meals served as a pudding (volume 400 ml, 400 kcal). The protein-rich test meal contained 57% milk proteins, 17% carbohydrates, and 26% fat. The carbohydrate-rich meal contained 2% proteins, 98% carbohydrates, and no fat. All subjects consumed the meal in a supine body position in the morning between 8 a.m. and 10 a.m. Figure 2 shows the results: The protein-rich test meal elicited a rapid increase in plasma norepinephrine in all subjects studied. A similar response was observed after the carbohydrate meal (data not shown here). Baseline values were significantly lower in both groups of eating disorders. The area under the response curve was reduced in anorectic and bulimic patients. The anorectic patients had lower values than the bulimics at all points of time.

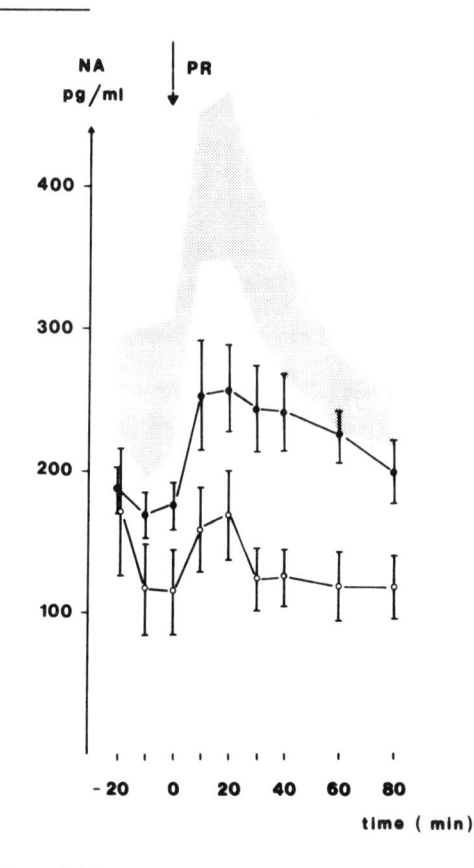

Figure 2. Norepinephrine in plasma before and after a protein-rich test meal in healthy controls (shaded area), in bulimic (●) and anorectic (O) patients.

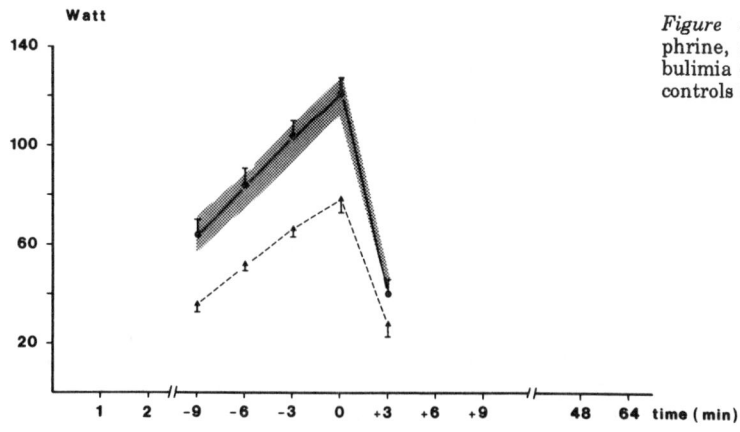

Figure 3. Power output, norepinephrine, and lactate in patients with bulimia (●), anorexia (▲), and normal controls (shaded area).

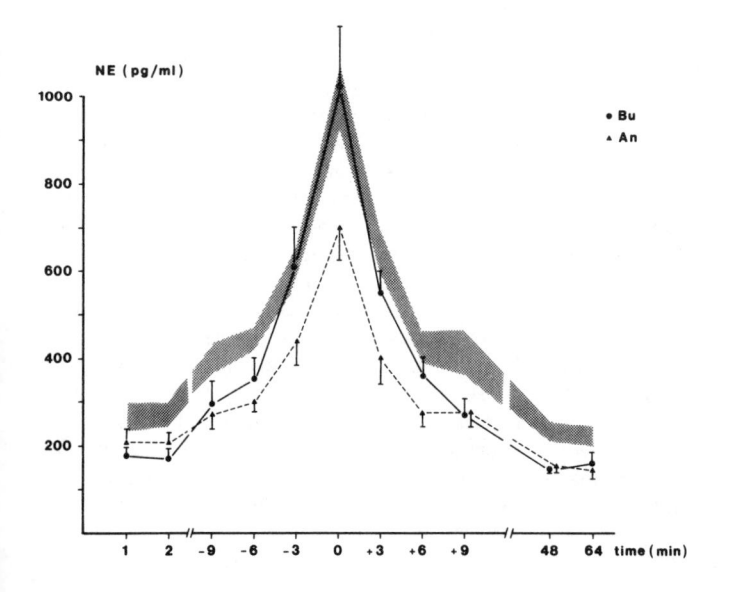

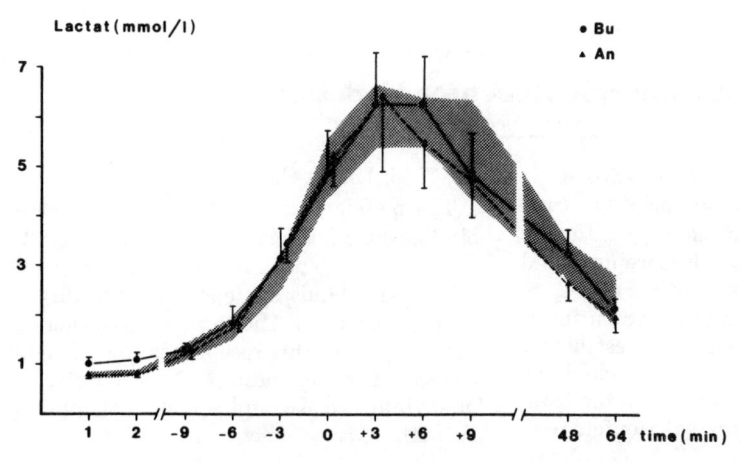

Norepinephrine secretion after test meals regulates diet-induced thermogenesis, which is responsible for a significant part of total energy consumption (for review, see Astrup, 1986). We can therefore speculate that the reduced norepinephrine release after test meals is responsible for a reduced thermogenesis in eating disorders (Pirke, Riedel, Tuschl, Schweiger, Schweiger, & Spyra, 1988).

Norepinephrine Response to Exercise

Norepinephrine plays an important role in the acute adaptation of muscular and cardiovascular function to exercise. Norepinephrine stimulates heart rate, systolic blood pressure, and anaerobic glycolysis, which results in the production of lactate.

We studied the effects of ergometric exercise performed in supine body position in anorectic and bulimic patients as well as in healthy, age-matched women. The exercise started at a level 100 W lower than the individual maximal power output determined in an electrocardiographic study on the day before the actual test. Blood was sampled every 3 minutes, and the power output was increased by 20 W.

Maximal power output of bulimic patients and normal controls did not differ and reached 130 ±5 W. The maximal power output of the anorectic patients was significantly lower and reached 75 ±8 W. Figure 3 shows norepinephrine values in all three groups. Basal norepinephrine was significantly reduced in both eating disorder groups. The maximal norepinephrine values were not different between bulimics and controls. They were, however, significantly lower in anorectic patients (Pirke, Eckert, Ofers, Goebl, Spyra, Schweiger, Tuschl & Fichter, 1989). The maximum heart rate as well as the maximum systolic blood pressure were significantly lower in the anorectic group compared with the bulimics and controls. Thus, a lower norepinephrine output during exercise corresponds to a lower activation of the cardiovascular system. Lactate values (Figure 3) were not different between groups. This does not, however, necessarily mean that lactate production in anorectic patients was as high as in controls. It could mean that the reabsorption of lactate into the muscle is reduced in anorectics as a consequence of reduced lean body mass. In interpreting our results and those of Nudel et al. (1984), it should be kept in mind that norepinephrine secretion during exercise is directly correlated with muscular mass, which means that the reduction of muscular mass contributes to the reduced activation of the noradrenergic system in anorectic patients during exercise.

Adrenergic Receptor Function

In order to understand the noradrenergic function, it is necessary not only to study norepinephrine release evoked by different stimuli, but also to study adrenoceptors and the second messenger systems coupled to them. Since adrenoceptors localized on internal organs and the brain are not accessible for biochemical studies in vitro, we studied the alpha-2 receptor of the platelets and the beta-2 receptor of the lymphocytes (Heufelder et al., 1985; Lonati-Galligani & Pirke, 1986).

The platelet adrenoceptor has complicated binding sites (Davies et al., 1982). One part of the receptor binds prostaglandin E 1, the other parts binds epinephrine and other adrenergic agonists. The second messenger system coupled to this receptor is the adenylate cyclase. Prostaglandin E 1 stimulates the adenylate cyclase and epinephrine inhibits this stimulating effect.

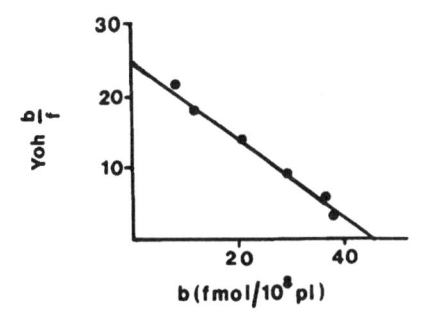

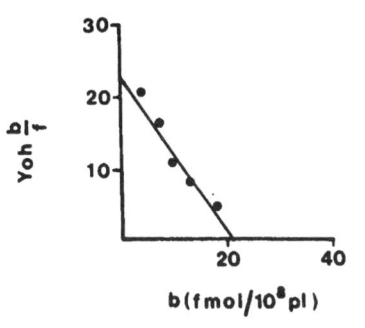

Figure 4. Scatchard plots of alpha-2-adrenoceptors on platelets of an anorectic patients (above) and a normal control (below).

We studied the adrenoceptor capacity and affinity using labeled yohimbine, an alpha-2 receptor antagonist. Figure 4 shows scatchard plots of an anorectic patient and a control. The increased intercept with the abscissa shows the increase of binding sites. When groups of anorectic patients were compared with bulimic patients and normal controls, significantly higher receptor capacity was observed in anorectics (506 ± 108 nmol/mg protein) and in bulimics (297 ±37 nmol/mg protein) than in controls (192 ±8 nmol/mg protein). This is partly a consequence of decreased catecholamine levels, since, for instance, patients with Shy Drager syndrome also show increased adrenoceptor capacity at the platelets (Davies et al., 1982). Other factors also seem to be involved in the up-regulation of the receptors. We observed significant correlations between receptor capacity and plasma cortisol. The low triiodothyronine found in patients with eating disorders may also contribute to the increase in receptor capacity as indicated by a highly significant inverse correlation between receptor capacity and triiodothyronine.

The second messenger system is also affected in eating disorders. As can be seen in Figure 5, the stimulatory and inhibitory effects are much greater in anorectic and bulimic patients. Luck, Mikhailidis, Dashwood, Barradas, Sever, Dandona and Wakeling (1983) have demonstrated hyperaggregability of platelets challenged with adrenergic agonists. When interpreting these findings, it has to be considered that the alpha-2 receptor is an autoreceptor that is located mainly presynaptically and that reduces the activity of the noradrenergic neuron. We can therefore speculate that the increase of alpha-2 receptor capacity may be one of the mechanisms responsible for the decrease of noradrenergic activity.

We studied the capacity and affinity of beta-2 receptors on circulating mononuclear leucocytes. The receptor capacity was significantly reduced in anorectic but not in bulimic patients. The receptor affinity was unchanged. Adenylate cyclase stimulation by isoproterenol was not statistically different between groups. These receptor changes further impair the function of the noradrenergic system.

Cortisol hypersecretion, found in anorectic though not in bulimic patients, is known to down-regulate beta-2 receptor capacity (Davies & Lefkowitz, 1980). This may be one of the reasons why anorectic but not bulimic patients show reduced beta-receptor capacity.

It is not clear whether these results can be generalized for other beta receptors found in the brain and in other organs. However, Stone (1983) found a reduction of receptor capacity in the brain of the starved rat, which favors the view that beta-receptor changes from starvation may generally occur in different organs and not only in lymphocytes.

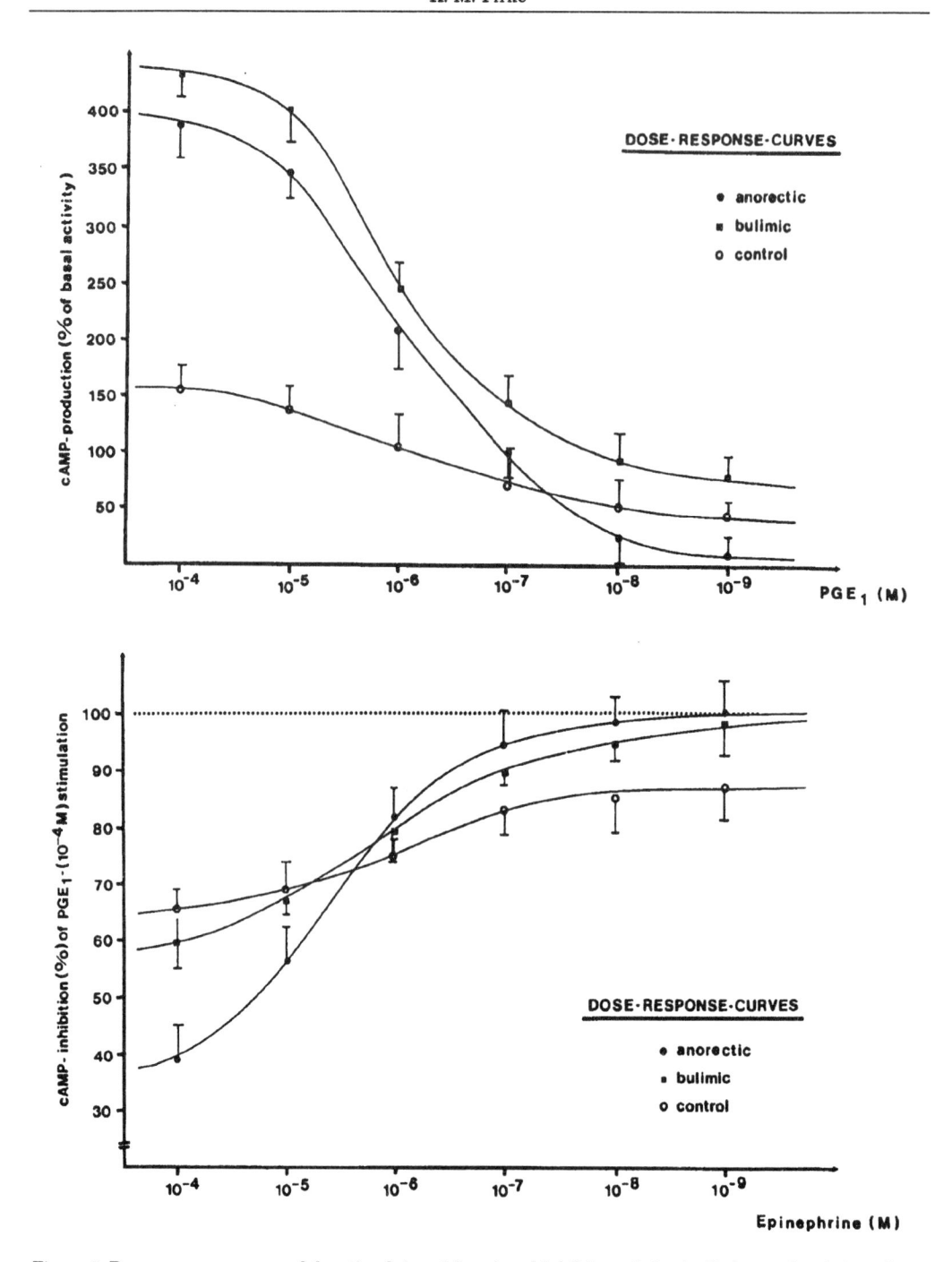

Figure 5. Dose-response curves of the stimulatory (above) and inhibitory (below) effects on adenylate cyclase.

Methoxy-hydroxy-phenylglycol (MHPG) in the Brain, Cerebrospinal Fluid, and Urine

Unconjugated MHPG is a major metabolite of norepinephrine in primates (for a review, see Roth, 1983). MHPG in brain tissue, cerebrospinal fluid, plasma, and urine reflects norepinephrine turnover and thus the activity of the noradrenergic system. Although no general agreement has been reached, it is assumed that about half of the MHPG measured in peripheral body fluids of humans is derived from norepinephrine produced in the brain (Kopin, 1978). Figure 6 shows the MHPG excretion in urine in patients with anorexia nervosa, bulimia nervosa, and healthy controls. The subjects collected three 24-hour portions of urine. Both groups of eating-disorder patients had significantly decreased MHPG levels.

These data reflect the decreased activity of the peripheral and the central noradrenergic system. They do not, however, allow determination of the extent to which the central norepinephrine turnover is reduced. Kaye, Ebert, Raleigh and Lake (1984) as well as Kaye et al. (1985) described reduced MHPG levels in the cerebrospinal fluid of anorectic patients. These results support the assumption that the activity of the central noradrenergic system is reduced in anorexia nervosa. Further evidence for this hypothesis comes from a Japanese group (Hirata, personal communication), which found reduced MHPG concentrations and reduced tyrosine hydroxylase activity in a postmortem study on the brain of an anorectic patient.

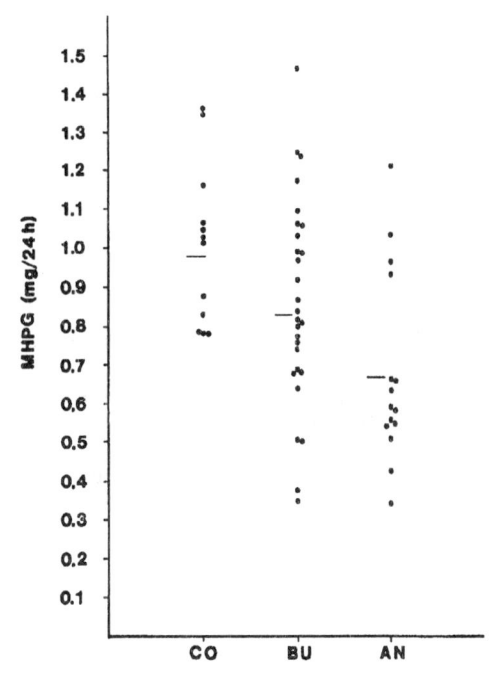

Figure 6. Excretion of methoxy-hydroxy-phenylglycol in anorexia, bulimia, and controls.

What Causes Reduced Norepinephrine Activity in Eating Disorders?

We have proposed the hypothesis that reduced caloric intake causes decreased activity of the peripheral and central noradrenergic system in anorexia and bulimia. In this section, we discuss evidence supporting the hypothesis and review tentative mechanisms causing reduced norepinephrine turnover.

As shown in Figure 1, the orthostatic response of plasma norepinephrine is significantly reduced after 2 weeks of starvation in healthy normal-weight subjects. This finding is in agreement with other reports in the literature (for review, see Pirke & Ploog, 1987).

Less severe forms of caloric restriction may also cause reduced noradrenergic activity, as we recently showed in a study on restrained eaters (Pirke, Tuschl, Spyra, Laessle, Schweiger, Broocks, Sambauer, & Zitzelsberger, in press). Restrained eaters are characterized by strict control over their caloric intake (Herman & Polivy, 1980). Restrained eaters who are otherwise healthy normal subjects consume about 300 kcal per day less than unrestrained eaters—although their body weight is not different (Tuschl, Platte, Laessle, Stichler & Pirke, in press). The plasma norepinephrine values before the protein-rich test meal were not different. After the test meal, restrained eaters had values about 15% lower than unrestrained eaters. These data indicate that even mild forms of caloric restriction can reduce noradrenergic activity. This is of special interest for the understanding of the noradrenaline changes in normal-weight bulimic patients. Restrained eating is thought to be a predisposing factor for the development of bulimia nervosa. Bulimia is characterized by intermittent periods of dieting and starvation, which are reflected in major fluctuations of body weight and in periodically elevated ketonbodies in plasma as well as by reduced plasma levels of triiodothyronine.

Landsberg and Young (1978) studied norepinephrine turnover in many peripheral organs of the starved rat. In all organ systems studied, they found significantly reduced norepinephrine turnover. This is a centrally mediated effect, since pharmacological ganglionic blockade eliminates the effects of starvation on peripheral noradrenaline.

We studied the central noradrenergic activity in the starved rat in a number of experiments. In our first set of experiments, we studied the effect of starvation in male Wistar rats. The animals were starved for 5 days and norepinephrine turnover was measured, using the DL-alpha-methyl-paratyrosine method. The drug (250 mg/kg) was injected i.p. and norepinephrine measured 3 h after injection of the drug or a saline solution. Turnover was calculated from the difference between the two groups. Figure 7 shows that norepinephrine turnover in the medial basal hypothalamus is significantly reduced after only 2 days of starvation and remains low thereafter (Pirke & Spyra, 1982).

Norepinephrine turnover in the cortex, pre-

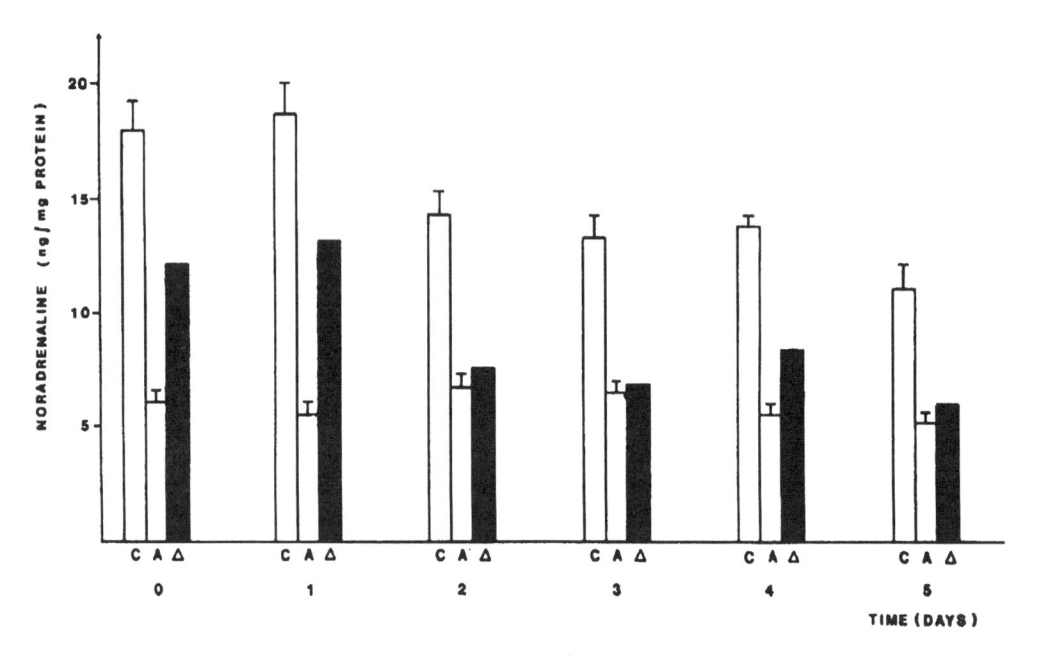

Figure 7. Effects of starvation on norepinephrine turnover in the basal medial hypothalamus of the rat. C = saline injection; A = alpha-methyl-paratyrosine; Δ = difference between C and A, representing norepinephrine turnover.

Figure 8. Methoxy-hydroxy-phenylglycol in the basal hypothalamus of starved (right columns) and fed (left columns) rats.

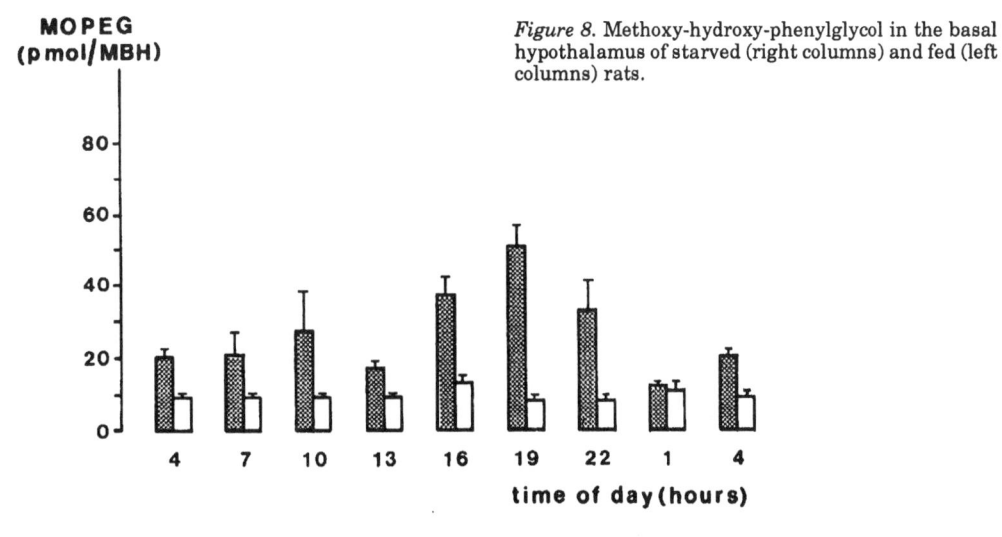

optic area, medial basal hypothalamus, and median eminence was also studied. It was significantly reduced in all areas after 5 days of starvation.

In further experiments, we studied the effect of semistarvation on hypothalamic norepinephrine turnover (Schweiger, Warnhoff & Pirke, 1985a). Wistar rats (200 g) were fed 4–8 g rat chow per day and lost, on average, 17% body weight over a 3-week period. During the same period, the control animals (fed ad libitum) gained 39.7% body weight. Animals were sacrificed during a 24-hour period at 3-hour intervals. Feeding time was 2:30 p.m. In these experiments, the concentration of 4-hydroxy-3-methoxy-phenylglycol (MOPEG) sulfate was measured as an indicator of norepinephrine turnover. Figure 8 shows the circadian rhythmicity of MOPEG sulfate in control animals (stippled columns). The peak is reached during the first half of the dark period. Semistarvation abolishes the circadian rhythm completely. The experiments reported here indicate that starvation of different intensity reduces norepinephrine turnover in the brain. This effect was demonstrated using different methods to measure norepinephrine turnover.

An impaired increase of norepinephrine turnover after exercise can be demonstrated in semistarved rats (Leifeld, Schweiger & Pirke, 1986): After a 3-week semistarvation period, during which the rats lost 20% of their body weight, individual animals ran in a motor-driven activity wheel (320 mm diameter) at 10 rpm for 1 h. Exercise increased the MOPEG sulfate in the medial basal hypothalamus from 8.7 pmol to 19.4 pmol in the semistarved group, and from 10.6 pmol to 30.1 pmol in the group fed ad libitum. MOPEG sulfate concentration was increased to a significantly smaller extent in the semistarved rats.

These results show again that the noradrenergic activity of the basal hypothalamus is reduced during conditions of semistarvation. When the noradrenergic system is activated by physiologic stimuli such as exercise, norepinephrine turnover is also increased during semistarvation. However, the effect of exercise is significantly smaller.

Forced wheel running is a considerable stress for rats. The effects of forced running may therefore not only reflect the influence of activity but also of stress. We therefore adopted the paradigm described by Routtenberg and Kuznesoff (1967), who showed that rats kept in running wheels increase their activity when their food intake is restricted. In our experiments, semistarved rats ran up to 18 km per day as compared to 2–3 km run by rats fed ad libitum.

Figure 9 shows the MOPEG sulfate concentration in the medial basal hypothalamus of semistarved running and sedentary rats, and in controls fed ad libitum (Broocks, Liu &

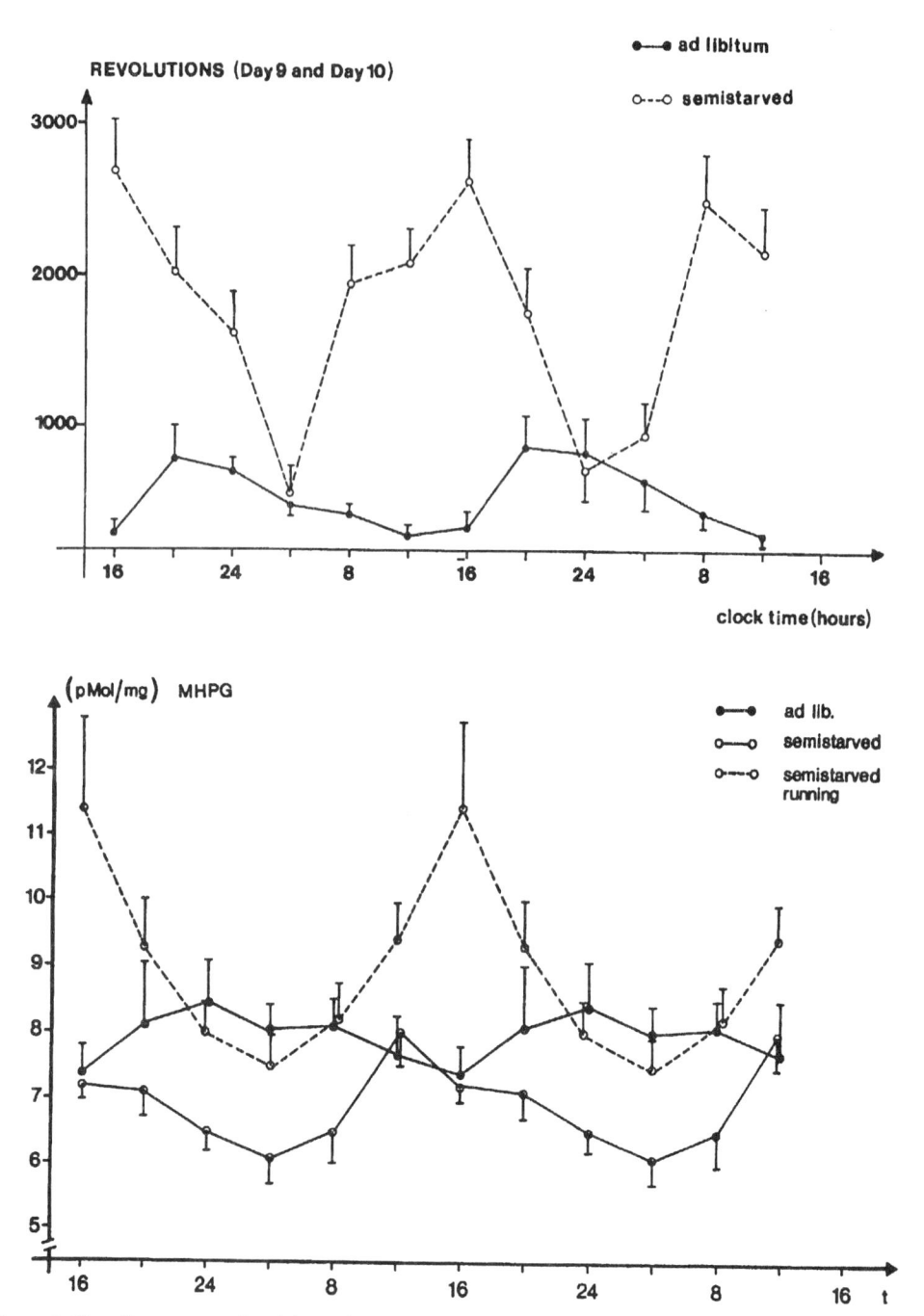

Figure 9. Circadian pattern of activity and methoxy-hydroxy-phenylglycol in the basal hypothalamus of the rat.

Pirke, in press). As in the other experiments described here, semistarvation reduced hypothalamic norepinephrine turnover. Running leads to an overcompensation of this effect. Studies in our laboratory are now underway to test the hypothesis that exercise-induced hyperactivity of the peripheral and central noradrenergic system may be involved in the development of hyperactivity so often observed in anorectic patients.

Changes in hypothalamic norepinephrine turnover during starvation are accompanied by changes in presynaptic alpha-adrenoceptors (Spyra & Pirke, 1982). The presynaptic receptor was studied with (3H)clonidine and the postsynaptic with (3H)WB4101. After 5 days of starvation, there was a highly significant increase in the capacity of the presynaptic alpha-2-adrenoceptor, whereas the postsynaptic alpha-1-adrenoceptor was unchanged. Thus, the starvation-induced changes in rat brain are identical with the findings on alpha-2-adrenoceptors on the platelets of anorectic patients. These observations suggest the hypothesis that the greatly increased capacity of presynaptic alpha-adrenoceptors causes the attenuated increase in norepinephrine turnover after exercise noted above.

Yohimbine was given 60 min before sacrifice. MOPEG sulfate concentrations, already elevated by exercise, can be further increased by blocking the presynaptic receptor. The increase is significant in control and semistarved rats. Since the maximum MOPEG sulfate concentration after exercise and yohimbine is significantly lower in semistarved animals, the increased capacity of the inhibitory presynaptic receptor cannot be the only cause of impaired norepinephrine turnover during exercise in semistarved rats.

In order to evaluate the mechanisms that cause the reduction of norepinephrine turnover in starvation, we followed two lines of research. Wurtman, Hefti, and Melamed (1981) found that, under certain conditions, the availability of tyrosine, the precursor of the catecholamines in the brain, regulates norepinephrine turnover. Rats underwent semistarvation for 3 weeks and lost 25% of body weight, while control animals gained 40%. Rats were fed either a carbohydrate-rich (58.0% carbohydrate, 14.5% protein, 3% fat) or a protein-rich (3.5% carbohydrate, 65.5% protein, 3% fat) diet. Large neutral amino acids, which compete for transport into the brain, were measured in plasma. Tyrosine and MOPEG sulfate were measured in brain tissue. Their concentrations were reduced under both conditions of starvation, although to a greater extent in the protein-rich group (Schweiger, Warnhoff & Pirke, 1985b). The tyrosine flow into the brain, calculated according to Wurtman, Hefti, and Melamed (1981), was significantly correlated with the MOPEG sulfate content of the brain ($r = 0.65$). These data indicate that reduced precursor (tyrosine) availability may contribute to reduced central norepinephrine turnover. The rather low correlation ($r = 0.65$) between tyrosine flow and MOPEG sulfate suggests that there may be other mechanisms as well.

Tyrosine hydroxylase is the rate-limiting enzyme in norepinephrine synthesis. We studied the effect of acute and chronic starvation on the activity of tyrosine hydroxylase (Philipp & Pirke, 1987). Acute starvation did not reduce enzyme activity after 20 h, but there was a significant reduction ($p<0.01$) after 4 days. Chronic starvation on a protein-rich but not on a carbohydrate-rich diet reduced tyrosine hydroxylase activity significantly. These data suggest that impaired activity of the enzyme may be one of the factors contributing to reduced catecholamine turnover during starvation.

In summary, norepinephrine turnover in the brain is reduced during starvation in the rat under baseline conditions. The severity and duration as well the quality of starvation (food composition) determine the norepinephrine turnover. Three factors involved have been noted: reduced precursor availability, reduced tyrosine hydroxylase activity, and increased autoreceptor (alpha-2-adrenoceptor) capacity.

Are the results of the animal studies reported here representative for the situation in anorectic and bulimic patients? The observations discussed here in detail support this assumption:

1) Starvation has identical effects on the peripheral noradrenergic system in humans and the rat.

2) The changes of the noradrenergic system observed in the starved rat are the same as

those observed in anorectic patients. This is true for norepinephrine secretion during exercise and for the regulation of alpha- and beta-adrenoceptors.

3) The limited information available on central norepinephrine turnover in anorectic and bulimic patients (MOPEG in cerebrospinal fluid and brain tissue) suggests a parallel reduction of central and peripheral norepinephrine turnover as with the starved rat.

Consequences of Reduced Noradrenergic Activity in Eating Disorders

Only few aspects of the consequences of reduced norepinephrine turnover have as yet been evaluated. It is clear that bradycardia is a consequence of reduced sympathetic activity. Silverman (1977) observed a heart rate of less than 60 in 80% of his anorectic patients. Fohlin (1977) recorded heart rates as low as 28, and an average heart rate of 53 on admission to the hospital.

Low blood pressure is a common finding in anorectic patients. Silverman (1977) found a resting systolic blood pressure of less than 70 mmHg in about half of his patients. Many other reports confirm these findings (review by Garfinkel & Garner, 1982). When bradycardia and hypotension are accompanied by reduced potassium concentrations, serious cardiovascular complications may occur.

Hypothermia and impaired temperature regulation are common in anorexia nervosa (Luck & Wakeling, 1980). It can be assumed that this disturbance is also a consequence of reduced noradrenergic activity. Other effects of reduced central noradrenergic activity on hypothalamic function in anorectic patients are less clear. Leibowitz (1984) emphasized the role of norepinephrine in feeding behavior in experimental animals. However, no data are available as yet on how norepinephrine turnover affects hunger and satiety in patients with eating disorders.

The neurotransmitter norepinephrine is known to participate in many neuroendocrine regulations; for instance, in the release of corticotropin-releasing factor (CRF) and gonadotropin-releasing hormone (GnRH). GnRH and CRF secretion are altered in anorexia nervosa: The hypothalamic pituitary adrenal axis is hyperactive, and the activity of the hypothalamic pituitary gonadal axis is suppressed (Pirke, Fichter, Lund & Doerr, 1979; Doerr, Fichter, Pirke & Lund, 1980). It is not clear at present which role the reduced noradrenergic activity plays in the development of these endocrine abnormalities. These are only two examples. We should keep in mind that almost all endocrine systems are altered in eating disorders, and that norepinephrine is involved in the hypothalamic regulation of most of these systems.

As mentioned above, norepinephrine is involved in the regulation of mood. Schildkraut (1978) has postulated that reduced noradrenergic activity causes depression.

Major depressive disorder is frequently diagnosed also in anorectic and bulimic patients. Laessle, Schweiger, Fichter, and Pirke (1988) have shown that depression develops secondary to the development of eating disorders. In most cases, major depression develops at least 1 year after the onset of the eating disorder.

We studied the relationship between mood and noradrenergic activity (as measured by the orthostatic norepinephrine response) in 24 patients with eating disorders (Laessle, Schweiger & Pirke, 1988). During an inpatient treatment, orthostatic tests and average mood ratings were evaluated every 3 weeks. At four of five points in time, a significant correlation was observed. The mood rating was worse, the lower the orthostatic norepinephrine response. These correlations suggest a causal relationship between low noradrenergic activity and depression.

Conclusions

It can be assumed that pathological eating behavior such as starvation and dieting as well as hyperactivity have a strong influence on the activity of the neurotransmitter system norepinephrine in the brain and in the periphery of the body. These secondary changes influence vegetative regulations as well as mood and possibly other brain functions as well. While many of these phenomena can be interpreted as adaptation to starvation, they nevertheless contribute significantly to the clinical picture of eating disorders. Without an understanding of the interaction of behavior and neurotransmitter activity, the syndromes of anorexia and bulimia nervosa cannot be understood. It is our firm belief that successful therapeutic strategies cannot be developed without knowledge of these interactions and the ability to interfere with them.

References

Astrup, A. (1986). Thermogenesis in human brown adipose tissue and skeletal muscle induced by sympathomimetic stimulation. *Acta Endocrinologica* (Suppl.), *112*, 1–32.

Bannister, R., & Sever. (1982). Increased numbers of alpha-receptors in sympathetic denervation supersensitivity in man. *J. Clin. Invest*, *69*, 779.

Broocks, A., Liu, J., & Pirke, K. M. (1989). Semistarvation-induced hyperactivity compensates for decreased norepinephrine and dopamine turnover in the mediobasal hypothalamus of the rat. *Journal of Neural Transmission*, in press.

Davies, A. O., & Lefkowitz, R. J. (1980). Corticosteroid-induced differential regulation of beta-adrenergic receptors in circulating human polymorphonuclear leukocytes and mononuclear leukocytes. *Journal of Clinical Endocrinology and Metabolism*, *51*, 599.

Doerr, P., Fichter, M. M., Pirke, K. M., & Lund, R. (1980). Relationship between weight gain and hypothalamic pituitary adrenal function in patients with anorexia nervosa. *Journal of Steroid Biochemistry*, *13*, 529–537.

Ebert, M. H., Kaye, W. K., & Gold, P. W. (1984). Neurotransmitter metabolisms in anorexia nervosa. In K. M. Pirke & D. Ploog (Eds.), *The psychobiology of anorexia nervosa* (pp. 58–72). Berlin: Springer-Verlag.

Fichter, M. M., & Pirke, K. M. (1984). Hypothalamic pituitary function in starving healthy subjects. In K. M. Pirke & D. Ploog (Eds.), *The psychobiology of anorexia nervosa* (pp. 124–135). Berlin: Springer-Verlag.

Fohlin, L., Freyschuss, U., Bjarke, B., Davis, C. T., & Thorén, C. (1978). Function and dimensions of the circulatory system in anorexia nervosa. *Acta Paediatr. Scand.*, *67*, 11–16.

Garfinkel, P. E., & Garner, D. M. (1982). *Anorexia nervosa—A multidimensional perspective* (pp. 302–326). New York: Brunner/Mazel.

Gross, H. A., Lake, C. R., Ebert, M. H., Ziegler, M. G., & Kopin, I. J. (1979). Catecholamine metabolism in primary anorexia nervosa. *J. Clin. Endocrinol. Metab.*, *49*, 805–809.

Herman, C. P., & Polivy, J. (1980). Restrained eating. In A. J. Stunkard (Ed.), *Obesity* (pp. 208–225). Philadelphia: Saunders.

Heufelder, A., Warnhoff, M., & Pirke, K. M. (1985). Platelet alpha$_2$-adrenoceptor and adenylate cyclase in patient with anorexia nervosa and bulimia. *J. Clin. Endocrinol. Metab.*, *61*, 1053–1060.

Kaye, W. H., Ebert, M. H., Raleigh, M., & Lake, C. R. (1984). Abnormalities in CNS monamine metabolism in anorexia nervosa. *Arch. Gen. Psychiatry*, *41*, 350–355.

Kaye, W. H., Jimerson, D. C., Lake, C. R., & Ebert, M. H. (1985). Altered norepinephrine metabolism following long-term weight recovery in patients with anorexia nervosa. *Psychiatry Research*, *14*, 333–342.

Kopin, I. J. (1978). Plasma levels of norepinephrine. *Annals of Internal Medicine*, *88*, 671–680.

Laessle, R. G., Schweiger, U., & Pirke, K. M. (1988). Mood and orthostatic norepinephrine response in anorexia nervosa. *Psychiatry Research*, *24*, 87–94.

Laessle, R. G., Schweiger, U., Fichter, M. M., & Pirke, K. M. (1988). Eating disorders and depression: Psychobiological findings in bulimia and anorexia nervosa. In K. M. Pirke, W. Vandereycken & D. Ploog (Eds.), *Psychobiology of bulimia nervosa* (pp. 90–100). Berlin: Springer-Verlag.

Landsberg, L., & Young, J. B. (1978). Fasting, feeding and regulation of the sympathetic nervous system. *N. Engl. J. Med.*, *298*, 1295–1301.

Leibowitz, S. F. (1984). Noradrenergic function in the

medial hypothalamus: Potential relation to anorexia nervosa and bulimia. In K. M. Pirke & D. Ploog (Eds.), *The psychobiology of anorexia nervosa* (pp. 35–45). Berlin: Springer-Verlag.

Leifeld, J., Schweiger, U., & Pirke, K. M. (1986). Exercise-induced increase of hypothalamic norepinephrine turnover in the rat is reduced by semistarvation. *Acta Endocrinologica* (Suppl. 274), 99–100.

Lonati-Galligani, M., & Pirke, K. M. (1986). Beta$_2$-adrenergic receptor regulation in circulating mononuclear leukocytes in anorexia nervosa and bulimia. *Psychiatry Research, 19*, 189–198.

Luck, P., Mikhailidis, D. P., Dashwood, R., Barradas, M. A., Sever, P. S., Dandona, P., & Wakeling, A. (1983). Platelet hyperaggregability and increased alpha-adrenoceptor density in anorexia nervosa. *J. Clin. Endocrinol. Metab., 57*, 911.

Luck, P., & Wakeling, A. (1980). Altered thresholds for thermoregulatory sweating and vasodilatation in anorexia nervosa. *Br. Med. J., 281*, 906–908.

Pahl, J., Pirke, K. M., Schweiger, U., Warnhoff, M., Gerlinghoff, M., Brinkmann, W., Berger, M., & Krieg, Ch. (1985). Anorectic behavior, mood, and metabolic and endocrine adaptation to starvation in anorexia nervosa during inpatient treatment. *Biol. Psychiatry, 20*, 874–887.

Philipp, E., & Pirke, K. M. (1987). Effect of starvation on hypothalamic tyrosine hydroxylase activity in adult male rats. *Brain Research, 413*, 53–59.

Pirke, K. M., Eckert, M., Ofers, B., Goebl, G., Spyra, B., Schweiger, U., Tuschl, R. J., & Fichter, M. M. (1989). Plasma norepinephrine response to exercise in bulimia, anorexia nervosa, and controls. *Biol. Psychiatry, 25*, 799–802.

Pirke, K. M., Fichter, M. M., & Pahl, J. (1985). Noradrenaline, trijod-thyronine, growth hormone and prolactine during weight gain in anorexia nervosa. *International Journal of Eating Disorders, 4*, 499–509.

Pirke, K. M., Fichter, M. M., Lund, R., & Doerr, P. (1979). Twenty-four hour sleep-wake pattern of plasma LH in patients with anorexia nervosa. *Acta Endocrinologica, 92*, 193–204.

Pirke, K. M., & Ploog, D. (1987). Biology of human starvation. In Beumont, Burrows & Casper (Eds.), *Handbook of eating disorders, Part 1* (pp. 79–102). Elsevier Science Publishers (Biomedical Division).

Pirke, K. M., Riedel, W., Tuschl, R., Schweiger, U., Schweiger, M., & Spyra, B. (1988). Effect of standardized test meals on plasma norepinephrine in patients with anorexia nervosa and bulimia. *Journal of Eating Disorders, 7* 369–373.

Pirke, K. M., & Spyra, B. (1982). Catacholamine turnover in the brain and the regulation of luteinizing hormone and corticosterone in starved male rats. *Acta Endocrinologica, 100*, 168–176.

Pirke, K. M., Tuschl, R. J., Spyra, B., Laessle, R. G., Schweiger, U., Brooks, A., Sambauer, S., & Zitzelsberger, G. (in press). Endocrine findings in restrained eaters. *Physiology and Behavior*.

Roth, R. H. (1983). Neuronal activity, impulse flow, and MHPG production. In *MHPG: Basic mechanisms and psychopathology*. New York: Academic Press.

Routtenberg, A., & Kuznesoff, A. W. (1967). Self-starvation of rats living in activity wheels on a restricted feeding schedule. *J. Comp. Physiol. Psychol., 64*, 414–421.

Schildkraut, J. J. (1978). Current status of the catecholamine hypothesis of affective disorders. In M. A. Liption, A. DiMascio & K. F. Killam (Eds.), *Psychopharmacology: A generation of progress*. New York: Raven Press.

Schweiger, U., Warnhoff, M., & Pirke, K. M. (1985a). Brain tyrosine availability and the depression of central nervous norepinephrine turnover in acute and chronic starvation in adult male rats. *Brain Research, 335*, 207–212.

Schweiger, U., Warnhoff, M., & Pirke, K. M. (1985b). Norephinephrine turnover in the hypothalamus of adult male rats: Alteration of circadian patterns by semistarvation. *J. Neurochem., 45*, 706–709.

Silverman, J. A. (1974). Anorexia nervosa: Clinical and metabolic observations in a successful treatment plan. *J. Pediatr., 84*, 68–73.

Spyra, B., & Pirke, K. M. (1982). Binding of (^{3}H)clonidine and (^{3}H)WB4101 to the pre- and postsynaptic alpha-adrenoceptors of the basal hypothalamus of the starved male rat. *Brain Research, 245*, 179–182.

Stone, E. (1983). Reduction in cortical-beta-adrenergic receptor density after chronic intermittent food deprivation. *Neuroscience Letters, 40*, 33.

Tuschl, R. J., Platte, P., Laessle, R. G., Stichler, W., & Pirke, K. M. (in press). Energy expenditure and everyday eating behavior in healthy young women. *Am. J. of Clin. Nutr.*

Wurtman, R. J., Hefti, F., & Melamed, E. (1981). Precursor control of neurotransmitter synthesis. *Pharmacol. Rev., 32*, 315–335.

Central Versus Peripheral Disturbances in the Norepinephrine Metabolism of Adolescents with Anorexia Nervosa

A. Rothenberger, H.-U. Müller and W. E. Müller

Studies concerning the central noradrenergic metabolism in anorexia nervosa have commonly used the strategy of measuring total MHPG in urine. Hence, measurement of total MHPG seems to be of questionable value as a marker for central norepinephrine turnover. Determination of different MHPG fractions (e.g., MHPG-glucoronide as a peripheral and MHPG-sulfate as a central marker) seems to be more adequate. We determined both MHPG-conjugates and total MHPG as well as VMA (as an additional marker for the peripheral norepinephrine metabolism) in a group of 10 adolescents when they had lost body weight and after weight gain. The design included a group of 10 emotionally disturbed psychiatric controls without eating disorders. The results suggest that (1) there seems to be mainly a disturbance of the peripheral norepinephrine metabolism in anorectic adolescents, which is related to starving; (2) this alteration of the peripheral norepinephrine metabolism is dominated by a metabolic shift of the peripheral norepinephrine pathways, probably in the liver; (3) the assumption of an additional increase of norepinephrine turnover in the CNS of anorectic patients needs further clarification.

The interest for investigating norepinephrine metabolism in patients with anorexia nervosa comes from two sources. Firstly, numerous endocrine abnormalities (e.g., hypercortisolism, suppression of gonadotropin secretion, elevation of growth hormone, decrease of triiodothyronine) and vegetative symptoms (e.g., problems in thermoregulation, low blood pressure and heart rate) as well as the control of appetite are closely related to the catecholamine metabolism in the hypothalamic region and the sympathetic nervous system. Secondly, many patients with anorexia nervosa also show depressive symptoms and there exists some evidence that disturbances of noradrenergic neurons are involved in the pathogenesis of depressive disorders (Pirke, Fichter & Pahl, 1985; Filser, Spira, Fischer, Gattaz & Müller, 1988; Peyrin, Pequignot, Chauplannaz, Laurent & Aimard 1985; Abraham, Beumont & Cobbin, 1981; Halmi, Dekirmenjian, Davis, Caspar & Goldberg, 1978).

Studies concerning the norepinephrine metabolism in anorexia nervosa have concentrated on different metabolites of norepinephrine (e. g., 3-Methoxy-4-hydroxyphenylethyleneglycol [MHPG], nor- metanephrine, metanephrine) or norepinephrine (NE) itself in cerebrospinal fluid, plasma or urine (Kaye et al., 1984). The main objective was to assess the activity of central noradrenergic neurons in patients with anorexia nervosa. The commonly used strategy to solve the problem was measuring total MHPG in urine assuming that it originates mainly from the brain. However, only about 20% of urinary MHPG originates from the CNS and the same holds true for plasma MHPG (Filser et al., 1986 and 1988). Hence, measurement of total MHPG seems to be of questionable value as a marker for central norepinephrine turnover. Determination of different MHPG fractions seems to be more adequate. Free MHPG represents only a small proportion (~10%) of total uri-

---

Central Institute of Mental Health, D-6800 Mannheim 1, West Germany
This research was supported by the German Research Society (Deutsche Forschungsgemeinschaft: SFB 258 Teilprojekt R/S, Universität Heidelberg and Mu 467/5-2). Parts of the work were presented at the XXI. Wissenschaftliche Tagung der Deutschen Gesellschaft für Kinder- und Jugendpsychiatrie, München, 1989.

nary MHPG. Most MHPG is excreted in conjugated form either as MHPG-glucuronide (~55%) or MHPG-sulfate (~35%). Some data indicate that urinary MHPG-glucuronide originates primarily from peripheral norepinephrine metabolism. In contrast, MHPG-sulfate is considered to derive mainly from central norepinephrine metabolism (see Filser et al., 1988 and 1989). Therefore, both the measurement of total MHPG and its fractions (free, glucuronide and sulfate) are of great importance to find out whether there exists a disturbance of the norepinephrine metabolism in the central nervous system of anorexia nervosa patients.

In general, the results of the cited MHPG studies in anorexia nervosa showed decreased total MHPG values in low weight anorexia nervosa patients compared with normals and an increase to normal values with weight gain. This could reflect a transient disturbance in central and/or peripheral NE metabolism. Even the important CSF NE findings in anorexia nervosa of Kaye et al. (1984) could not answer the question, since NE in CSF was normal at the beginning of the episode and decreased in anorectics, who had recovered weight for a relatively long time. Furthermore, it still has to be determined if NE in CSF originates mainly from the brain or the spinal cord (Post et al., 1973; Kopin, 1984).

Thus, we intended to shed some light on the above mentioned problem by determining both MHPG-conjugates and total MHPG in adolescents with anorexia nervosa on two separate occasions (a) at the first examination at a low body weight and (b) at the second examination a few weeks after weight restoration. In order to control for disorder specific results, the design included a group of psychiatric controls. Furthermore, besides MHPG-glucuronide, vanillylmandelic acid (VMA) was analyzed as an additional marker for the peripheral norepinephrine metabolism.

Method

We investigated two groups of adolescent inpatients. One group consisted of 10 patients with anorexia nervosa (8 females, 2 males, DSM-III criteria, ICD 307.1, normal intelligence, duration of weight loss till t_1 $\bar{x}$ = 13.4 ± 9.8 months, episodes of illness $\bar{x}$ = 1.7 ± 1.1, highest body weight before starving $\bar{x}$ = 49.7 ± 5.9 kg). As psychiatric controls, paralleled

Table 1. Basic group characteristics of emotionally disturbed (psychiatric controls) and anorectic adolescents.

	Emotional disturbance (n=10) (ICD 313)		Anorexia nervosa (n=10) (ICD 307.1)				
			t_1		t_2		
	$\bar{x}$	s	$\bar{x}$	s	$\bar{x}$	s	p
Body weight (kg)	55	13	36[b]	6	45[c]	6	<0.01+
Body weight (%IBW)*	112	22	72[a]	8	91[c]	8	<0.01+
Height (cm)	161	22	163	10	163	10	
Age (years)	14	3	14	2	15	2	
Controlled caloric diet (2000–2500 kcal/day)	—		10 Pat.		2 Pat.		

* % IBW = Percentage of ideal body weight: female (height in cm −100)–20%; male (height in cm −100) − 15%
Significant differences:
1) Anorectics vs. controls (Mann-Whitney U-Test):
a) p<0.001
b) p<0.01
c) p<0.05
2) Anorectics t_1 vs. t_2 (Wilcoxon-Test): +

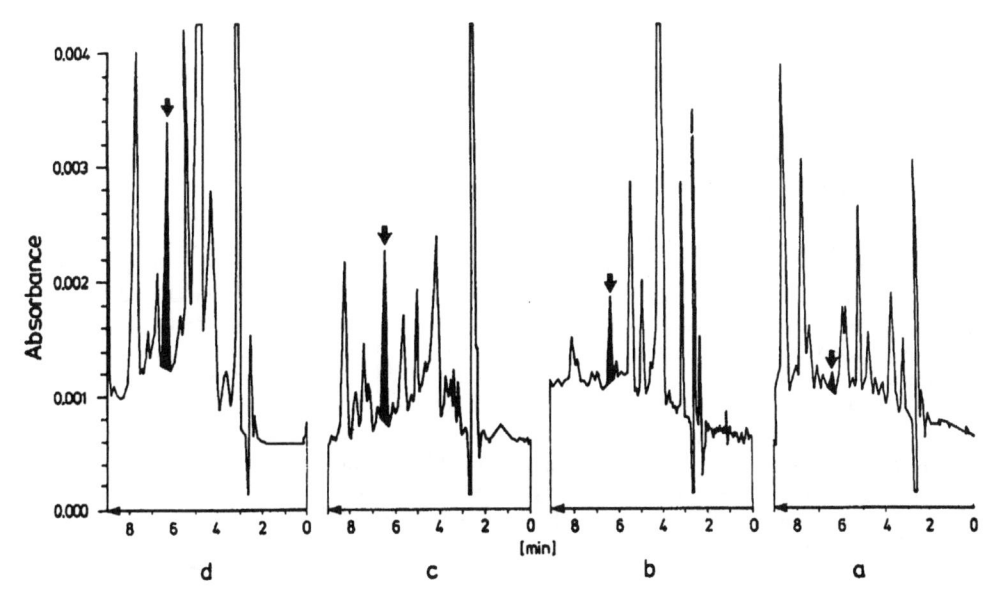

Figure 1. Chromatograms of MHPG detected with absorbance detection at 278 nm after extraction of urine. Marked peaks represent MHPG. (a) Determination of free MHPG after extraction of 1000 µl. (b) Determination of MHPG after treatment of 500 µl of urine with sulphatase and subsequent extraction. (c) Determination of MHPG after treatment of 500 µl of urine with glucuronidase and subsequent extraction. (d) Determination of MHPG after treatment of 500 µl of urine with glucuronidase/sulphatase and subsequent extraction. (Reproduced from Filser et al., 1989, with permission).

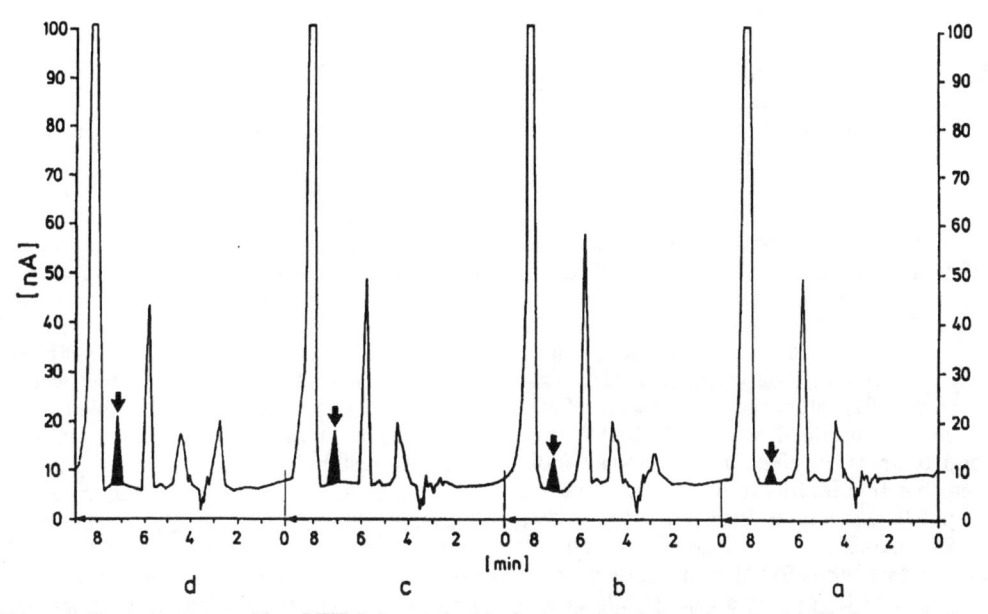

Figure 2. Chromatograms of free MHPG detected with electrochemical detection at +0.80V after extraction of 1000 µl of urine. Marked peaks represent MHPG. (a) No MHPG was added to urine. (b) 240 ng of MHPG were added to 1000 µl of urine. (c) 480 ng of MHPG were added to 1000 µl of urine. (d) 720 ng of MHPG were added to 1000 µl of urine. (Reproduced from Filser et al., 1989, with permission).

by age, sex and intelligence, we included 10 inpatients with emotional disturbances (8 female, 2 males, ICD-9 criteria, normal intelligence, no eating disorder) The anorexia nervosa group was investigated twice (i.e., within the first week of hospitalization, t_1, and after weight gain of at least 10% of their Ideal Body Weight as explained in Table 1, t_2). The controls were investigated only once. Neither anorectic patients nor psychiatric controls received a pharmacological treatment. There were no relevant depressive symptoms in both groups, evaluated by an experienced child psychiatrist.

Each patient collected three consecutive complete 24h urine samples. To control for adequate sampling only those samples which showed a level of mg creatinine/kg body weight ≥10 were accepted. The urine was filtered, stabilised with sodiummetabisulfite (0.5 mg/ml), and stored at −20°C until assayed. MHPG is stable under these conditions for at least 7 months. The analytical procedure for the determination of total MHPG, free MHPG and the two MHPG-conjugates has been described elsewhere (Filser et al., 1989). Briefly, after incubation and extraction the four parameters were analyzed by high pressure liquid chromatography (HPLC). For detection, an electrochemical detector was used. Four samples of each urine specimen were necessary to determine one MHPG value. To three of the specimens MHPG was added in increasing amounts before starting any other treatment. From the ratios of the HPLC peak height, a regression line was constructed to permit quantification of the amount of MHPG originally present in the sample without additional MHPG. VMA was also measured by HPLC with electrochemical detection using an assay supplied by Bio-Rad, Munich, FRG (Bio-Rad Instruction Manual VMA Test, 1987).

Statistical analyses, comparisons within or between groups, were performed with nonparametric tests (Wilcoxon-Test and Mann-Whitney U-test).

Results

There were no group differences of the daily excretion rates of creatinine and urine (Table 2). The excretion of the MHPG fractions as percentages of total MHPG are given in Figure 3.

The values for psychiatric controls (free MHPG 5%, MHPG-glucuronide 47%, MHPG-sulfate 48%) were within the range of values known from normal adults (Filser et al., 1988). Significant group differences (controls vs. anorectics) could be found for low-weight anorexia nervosa (t_1) only: free MHPG (5% vs. 10%, $p<0.01$) glucuronide (47% vs. 33%, $p<0.05$), but sulfate (48% vs. 57%, n.s.) Within group comparison of anorexia nervosa indicated that free MHPG decreased (t_1: 10%, t_2: 5%, $p<0.05$), glucuronide increased (t_1: 33%, t_2: 49%, $p<0.02$), and sulfate decreased (t_1: 57%, t_2: 46%, $p<0.05$). Also, in anorexia nervosa patients there was a remarkable difference at t_1 between glucuronide and sulfate (33% vs. 57%, $p<0.02$) not seen at t_2.

Besides these relative MHPG values we present also absolute values in µg/mg creatinine.

Table 2 states clearly that there are three main effects (a) MHPG-glucuronide in anorexia nervosa increased with weight gain (0.8 vs. 1.5, $p<0.02$), (b) VMA decreased with weight gain (3.9 vs. 3.1, $p<0,05$), and (c) the summation of peripheral norepinephrine markers (VMA plus MHPG-glucuronide) remained stable (4.7 vs. 4.5, n.s.). Furthermore, when controls and anorectics were compared only free MHPG was higher in low weight anorectics (0.1 vs. 0.2, $p<0.001$). Table 2 documents that there existed a high interindividual variability of the measured parameters. This can be seen also in Figure 4 (the extreme difference for a single pair of values in both MHPG-glucuronide and MHPG-sulfate does not belong to the same person). Hence, it seems to be justified that we first reported the percentages of MHPG fractions of total MHPG to smoothen this variability of absolute values.

Table 2. Results of urine analyses.

Parameter	Emotional disturbance (n=10) (ICD 313)		Anorexia nervosa (n=10) (ICD 307.1)				p
			t_1		t_2		
	$\bar{x}$	s	$\bar{x}$	s	$\bar{x}$	s	
Creatinine (mg/24h)	916	361	730	424	803	148	ns+
Urinevolume (ml/24h)	1063	632	1530	547	1358	1038	ns+
MHPG-glucuronide*	1.0	0.4	0.8	0.6	1.5	1.3	<0.02+
MHPG-sulfate*	1.0	0.6	1.3	0.4	1.4	1.2	ns+
MHPG-free*	0.1	0.04	0.2[a]	0.1	0.1	0.1	ns+
MHPG-total*	2.1	0.9	2.3	0.8	3.0	2.3	ns+
VMA*	3.8	1.3	3.9	1.0	3.1	0.9	<0.05+
VMA plus MHPG-glucuronide*	4.8	1.5	4.7	1.4	4.5	1.6	ns+

*) All values: µg/mg creatinine
+ Wilcoxon-Test: anorectics t_1 vs. t_2
[a] $p<0.001$ Mann-Whitney U-test: anorectics vs. controls

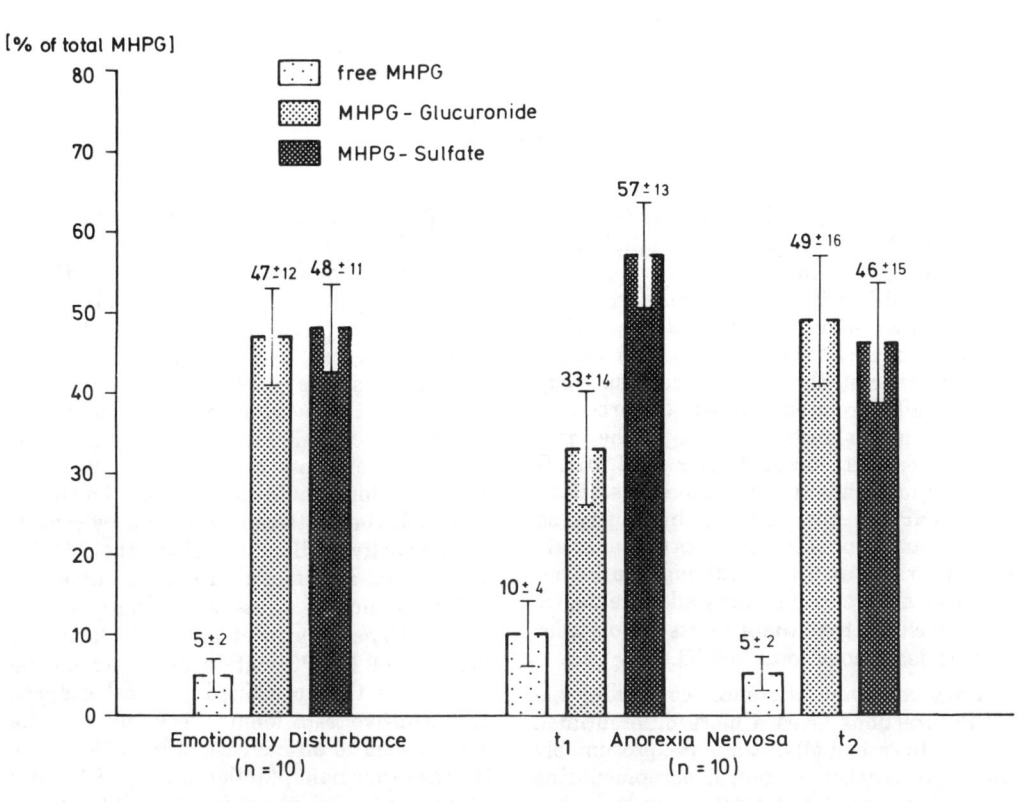

Figure 3. Percentages of MHPG fractions (free, glucuronide, sulfate) of total MHPG. Anorectics differ from controls only before weight gain. Statistics see text.

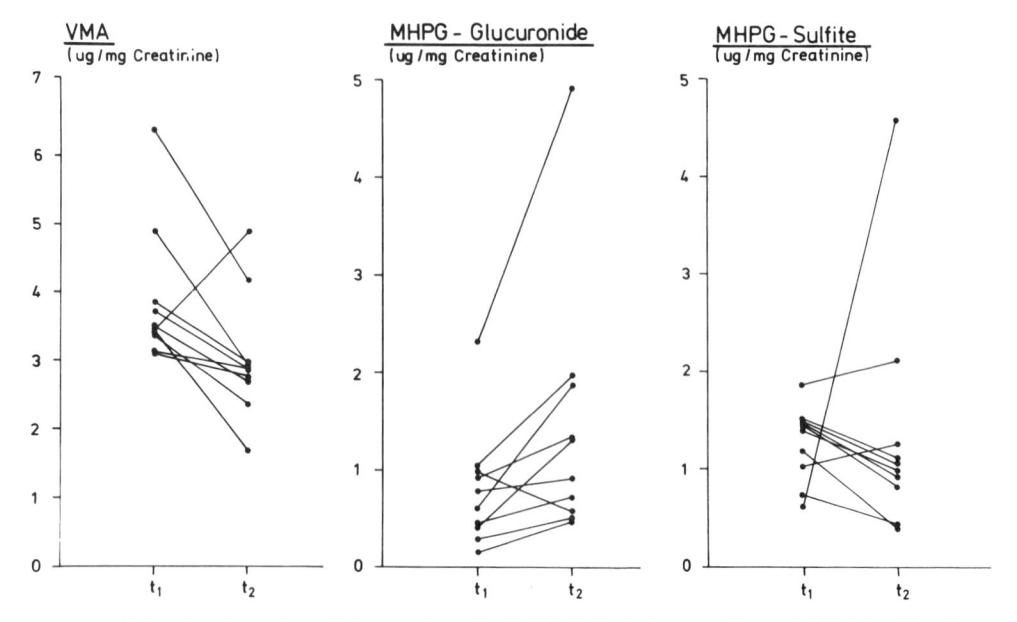

Figure 4. Individual values of vanillylmandelic acid (VMA), MHPG-glucuronide, and MHPG-sulfate for ten adolescent patients with anorexia nervosa before (t_1) and after (t_2) weight gain.

Discussion

As in studies with adult anorectics (Gross et al., 1979; Abraham et al., 1981; Halmi et al., 1978) we also found a trend to a decreased level of total MHPG in adolescents with anorexia nervosa when they were clearly underweight compared to their status after weight gain. In contrast, the anorexia nervosa group did not differ from emotionally disturbed inpatients in this respect, while in the cited studies normals showed higher total MHPG values than underweight anorectics. However, MHPG results did not differ between normals and depressive patients (Filser et al., 1988; Peyrin et al., 1985). Although we did not investigate a group of healthy adolescents, we may conclude, that there exists no disorder specific decrease of total MHPG.

A look at group differences concerning the MHPG fractions gives a more differentiated picture. In case of MHPG-sulfate, presumably the major marker of central norepinephrine metabolism, we found a tendency to higher NE turnover in low weight anorexia nervosa (t_1: 57% vs. t_2: 46.0%, $p<0.05$). If this holds true, it may be due to an increased arousal level in these patients (Herholz et al., 1987), i.e., it represents a state dependent alteration of the central noradrenergic metabolism in anorexia nervosa, probably as an expression of mental stress (hospitalization, psychopathology). However, such an interpretation has to be considered with caution. Until today, there exists no replicated study in humans which could demonstrate positively that MHPG-sulfate can be altered by central nervous activity. Bond and Howlett (1974) indicated that arithmetic calculation implicates sufficient mental stress to increase MHPG-sulfate alone. Peyrin et al. (1987) found an increase of MHPG-sulfate and epinephrine only when they combined physical exercise and cognitive tests. Mental performance alone did not lead to an increase of MHPG-sulfate. On the other hand, Müller et al. (1989) could demonstrate an increase of MHPG-sulfate after emotional stress (video of a stressful and

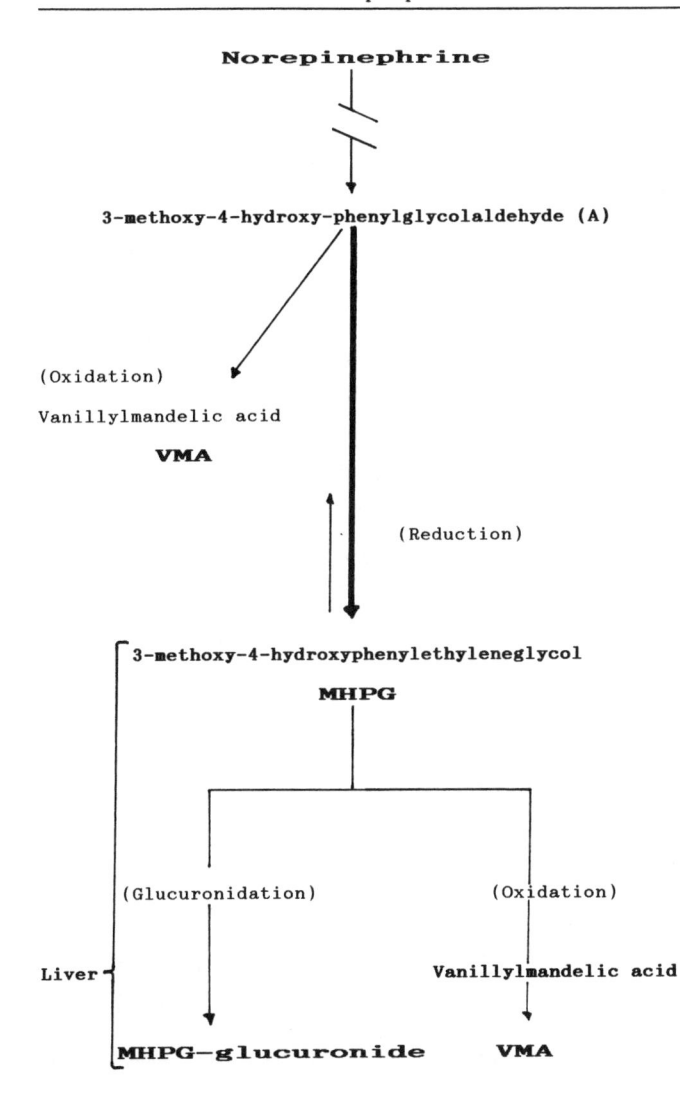

Figure 5. Scheme of of the peripheral noradrenergic pathways. The aldehyde (A) can be submitted either to a process of oxidation (VMA) or reduction (MHPG) depending on the enzymatic situation. In the liver, MHPG can be either oxidized to VMA or conjugated to MHPG-glucuronide. Anorectic patients excrete more VMA and less MHPG-glucuronide in the low weight status and the reverse holds true after weight gain (metabolic shift hypothesis). The combined value of both markers is not different at the two examinations.

upsetting film) in one group of normals, but it could not be replicated in a similar group. Most other studies (e.g., Peyrin & Pequignot 1983; Filser et al., 1988) presented only indirect evidence for the central origin of MHPG-sulfate.

In contrast to the small differences seen for MHPG-sulfate, MHPG-glucuronide, the peripheral marker of NE turnover, was significantly decreased in low weight anorectic adolescents compared with their status after weight gain. Contrary to MHPG-glucuronide, VMA, another marker of peripheral norepinephrine metabolism decreased when anorectic adolescents gained weight. To explain these at first glance contradictory results we have to refer to a certain step of the peripheral norepinephrine metabolism.

Filser et al. (1988) applied the fact that ethanol blocks the oxidation of free MHPG to VMA. This is presumed to occur by substrate competition for the enzyme alcohol dehydrogenase in the liver. As a consequence, the authors observed an increase of the glucuronide fraction of MHPG while the sulfate fraction remained unaltered. Obviously, by decreasing the magnitude of one metabolic pathway (oxidation), more free glycol became available peripherally for the other metabolic pathway (glucuronidation). Probably, a similar metabolic shift was responsible for the low VMA/MHPG-glucuronide ratio (2.1) in anorectics after weight gain. This ratio was high (4.9) when these patients were underweight. Since the summation of both markers remained about the same (t_1: 4.7; t_2: 4.5) it is likely that anorectic patients developed a shift of peripheral norepinephrine metabolism during weight gain: the balance between oxidation (VMA) vs. glucuronidation (MHPG-glucuronide) (Figure 5) seems to change with weight gain.

In conclusion, our data suggest only state dependent disturbances in norepinephrine metabolism of adolescent anorectics which seem to be related to starving. Our methodological approach, investigating besides total MHPG also its fractions, gives detailed insight into changes of norepinephrine metabolism in anorexia nervosa. We could differentiate central vs. peripheral NE turnover much better than it was possible in former studies. Thus, the reported increase of MHPG with restoration of weight seems to be due to MHPG-glucuronide and therefore a phenomenon of the peripheral norepinephrine metabolism. This alteration of the peripheral norepinephrine metabolism in anorectics is dominated by a metabolic shift, i.e., high VMA/MHPG-glucuronide ratio when the body weight is low and change to a low ratio after weight gain. If there might be, in addition, an increased norepinephrine turnover in CNS associated with a high level of arousal needs further clarification. In future studies we expect to get more insight into neurotransmitter metabolism of the CNS and its functional meaning in anorexia nervosa by combining neurochemical, neurophysiological, neuropsychological and psychopathological levels of investigation in the same patient.

References

Abraham, S. F., Beumont, P. J. V., & Cobbin, D. M. (1981). Catecholamine metabolism and body weight in anorexia nervosa. *British Journal of Psychiatry, 138*, 244–247.

Bond, P. A., & Howlett, D. R. (1974). Measurement of the two conjugates of 3-methoxy-4-hydroxyphenylglycol in urine. *Biochemical Medicine, 10*, 219–228.

Filser, J. G., Müller, W. E., & Beckmann, H. (1986). Should plasma or urinary MHPG be measured in psychiatric research? A critical comment. *British Journal of Psychiatry, 148*, 95–97.

Filser, J. G., Spira, J., Fischer, M., Gattaz, W. F., & Müller, W.E. (1988). The evaluation of 4-hydroxy-3-methoxyphenylglycol sulfate as a possible marker of central norepinephrine turnover. Studies in healthy volunteers and depressed patients. *Journal of Psychiatry Research, 22*, 171–181.

Filser, J. G., Koch, S., Fischer, M., & Müller, W.E. (1989). Determination of urinary 3-methoxy-4-hydroxyphenylethylene glycol and its conjugates by high-performance liquid chromatography with electrochemical and ultraviolet absorbance detection. *Journal of Chromatography, 493*, 275–286.

Gross, H. A., Lake, C. R., Ebert, M. H., Ziegler, M. G., & Kopin, I. J. (1979). Catecholamine metabolism in primary anorexia nervosa. *Journal of Clinical Endocrinolgy and Metabolism, 49*, 805–809.

Halmi, K. A., Dekirmenjian, H., Davis, J. M., Caspar, R., & Goldberg, S. (1978). Catecholamine metabolism in anorexia nervosa. *Archives of General Psychiatry, 35*, 458–460.

Herholz, K., Krieg, J. C., Emrich, H. M., Pawlik, G., Beil, C., Pirke, K. M., Pahl, J. J., Wagner, R., Wienhard, K., Ploog, D., & Heiss, W. D. (1987). Regional cerebral glucose metabolism in anorexia nervosa measured by positron emission tomography. *Biological Psychiatry, 22*, 43–51.

Kaye, W. H., Ebert, M. H., Raleigh, M., & Lake, R. (1984) Abnormalities in CNS monamine metabolism in anorexia nervosa. *Archives of General Psychiatry, 41*, 350–355.

Kopin, I. J. (1984). Avenues of investigation for the role of catecholamines in anxiety. *Psychopathology, 17* (suppl. 1), 83–97.

Müller, W. E., Gattaz, W. F., Rost, W., Berger, M., Riemann, D., & Jacobs, A. C. (1989). Untersuchungen zum peripheren und zentralen Noradrenalinstoffwechsel bei Depressiven mittels differentieller Bestimmung der MHPG-Konjugate. In B. Saletu (Ed.), *Biologische Psychiatrie, 2. Drei-Länder-Symposium für Biologische Psychiatrie, Innsbruck, September 1988* (354–357). Stuttgart, New York: Georg Thieme Verlag.

Peyrin, L., & Pequignot, J. M. (1983). Free and conjugated 3-methoxy-4-hydroxyphenylglycol in human urine: Peripheral origin of glucuronide. *Psychopharmacology, 79,* 16–20.

Peyrin, L., Pequignot, J. M., Chauplannaz, G., Laurent, B. & Aimard, G. (1985). Sulfate and glucuronide conjugates of 3-methoxy-4-hydroxyphenylglycol in urine of depressed patients: Central and peripheral influences. *Journal of Neural Transmission, 63,* 255–269.

Peyrin, L., Pequignot, J. M., Lacour, J. R., & Fourcade, J. (1987). Relationships between catecholamine or 3-methoxy-4-hydroxyphenylglycol changes and the mental performance under submaximal exercise in man. *Psychopharmacology, 93,* 188–192.

Pirke, K. M., Fichter, M. M., & Pahl, J. (1985). Noradrenaline, trijodthyronine, growth hormone and prolactin during weight gain in anorexia nervosa. *International Journal of Eating Disorders, 4,* 499–509.

Post, R. M., Goodwin, F. K., & Gordon, E. (1973). Amine metabolites in human cerebrospinal fluid: Effects of cord transection and spinal fluid block. *Science, 179,* 897–899.

Anorexia Nervosa and Urinary Excretion of Peptides and Protein-Associated Peptide Complexes

M. Råstam, C. Gillberg, O. Trygstad, I. Foss

A total population group of cases with anorexia nervosa were examined with respect to patterns of urinary excretion of peptides and protein-associated peptide complexes and contrasted with an age- and sex-matched group of school-mates. A further group of anorexia nervosa cases and their contrast cases were also examined. Altogether 31 cases and 31 school-mates were examined. No pattern typical of anorexia nervosa emerged. The results are discussed in relation to previous publications reporting on anorexia-nervosa-specific patterns.

In the late 1970s it was suggested that patients with anorexia nervosa and patients with certain other psychiatric disorders showed characteristic patterns of urinary excretion of peptides and protein-associated peptide complexes (Trygstad, Foss, Edminson, Johansen & Reichelt, 1978; Trygstad, Reichelt, Foss, Edminson, Saelid, Bremer, et al., 1980). In a study of 25 anorectic patients aged 12–19 years referred to the section of Pediatric Endocrinology at the Rikshospitalet, Oslo, Norway, 40% were said to have a characteristic excretion pattern in connection with classical "primary anorexia nervosa." Another 24% of the anorexia nervosa patients exhibited a pattern thought at that time to be common in schizophrenia and referred to as pattern B in later publications (Gillberg, Trygstad & Foss, 1982; Le Couteur, Trygstad, Evered, Gillberg & Rutter, 1988). This work seemed promising and worth following-up in strictly controlled ways. The preliminary studies, after all, could not serve as a basis for generalized conclusions for several reasons, the most important being the lack of a blindly examined comparison group of normal children.

We recently examined a population-based group of teenagers with anorexia nervosa as well as a group of consecutive referral cases with anorexia nervosa and their comparison cases. This paper reports on the results with respect to urinary peptide excretion in those cases.

Material and Methods

Anorexia Nervosa Population Group

The whole Göteborg population of children born in 1970 were meticulously screened for the occurrence of anorexia nervosa presenting before the child's 16th birthday. Overall, 20 cases of anorexia nervosa (18 girls and 2 boys) were found, corresponding to a population frequency of 0.5% of all Göteborg children under 16 years of age. The cases were clinically ex-

---

Department of Child and Adolescent Psychiatry, University of Gothenburg, Box 17113, S-40261 Göteborg, Sweden.
Supported by grants for Maria Råstam from the Swedish Ministry of Health and Social Affairs (grant no. F84/88) and for Christopher Gillberg from the Swedish Medical Research Council (grant no. 21X-07956).

amined in great detail by the first author. The detailed results as regards epidemiology have been reported in a separate paper (Råstam, Gillberg & Garton, 1989).

All except three of the anorexia nervosa cases in this group fulfilled DSM-III-R criteria for anorexia nervosa (APA, 1987). Of these, 70% also fulfilled DSM-III criteria for anorexia nervosa (APA, 1980), that is, they showed more than 25% weight loss relative to expected weight gain or level. The three "partial" anorexia nervosa" cases fulfilled DSM-III-R criteria except that in some cases real or projected weight loss was 15% or less, and in others anorectic behaviour, in spite of major weight loss, was not considered to be extreme.

Unfortunately, six of these 20 anorexia nervosa patients (30%) in the population group failed to participate in the present study for various reasons (1 refusal, 5 "forgot" to bring the urine sample to the clinical examination). The six patients who did not participate with a urine analysis were similar to the other anorexia nervosa cases with regard to clinical status as well as social and family background.

All 14 of the anorexia nervosa patients participating in the present study (12 girls, 2 boys) were of normal intelligence and free of major physical disorders, except in one case who suffered from diabetes mellitus. All of the children were 14–16 years old at the time of the study.

Anorexia Nervosa Referral Group

During and after the population screening study, doctors and nurses in Göteborg continued to refer children with anorexia nervosa to the first author. These new cases were 11–18 years of age. Altogether, 32 more anorexia nervosa cases fulfilling DSM-III and DSM-III-R criteria for anorexia nervosa were included in this "referral group." All the cases in this group underwent the same meticulous clinical examination procedure as the population group of cases. Of the 32 cases, 28 were asked to bring a urine sample for examination. One girl refused, and in another one the urine was judged by the laboratory personnel to be too diluted. Nine more cases "forgot" to bring a urine sample to the clinical examination.

Thus, 17 cases of anorexia nervosa in the referral group had their urine examined as described below.

Anorexia Nervosa Total Group

The two anorexia nervosa groups were similar with regard to age, clinical characteristics, degree of weight loss, associated psychiatric problems, and social and family background. They were therefore pooled for the purpose of the present study. Altogether 31 cases with anorexia nervosa (28 girls, 3 boys) participated in the study. Of these, 18 (15 girls, 3 boys) were still very emaciated at the time of the study. None of the remaining 13 cases (all girls) were free of anorectic symptoms, but a few had recovered with respect to weight and four had regained a normal pattern of menstruating.

Comparison of Groups

For each of the 31 anorexia nervosa cases, an age- and sex-matched schoolmate was chosen. All of these participated in the study. They too were all examined in great detail by the first author and were considered psychiatrically healthy.

Urinary Analysis

The early morning urine sample was collected in sterile bottles containing a few crystals of thymol. The procedure used was that described in previous studies (Trygstad et al., 1980; Gillberg, Trygstad & Foss, 1982). The specimens were then transferred to the laboratory in the frozen state. Once the samples had been thawed, a pH of 4.3 was obtained by adding 1N HCl. All urine samples were precipitated with 10% by volume ethanol saturated with benzoic acid at room temperature. Precipitation took place overnight at 4°C. After centrifugation (at 4000 g for 10 min.), repeating washing with ethanol removed the benzoic acid. The complete removal of the benzoic acid was assessed by checking the ultraviolet absorbency of the supernatant. The precipitate was then dissolved in 30 ml of 0.1M NH_4HCO_3 buffer at pH 8.5 and applied

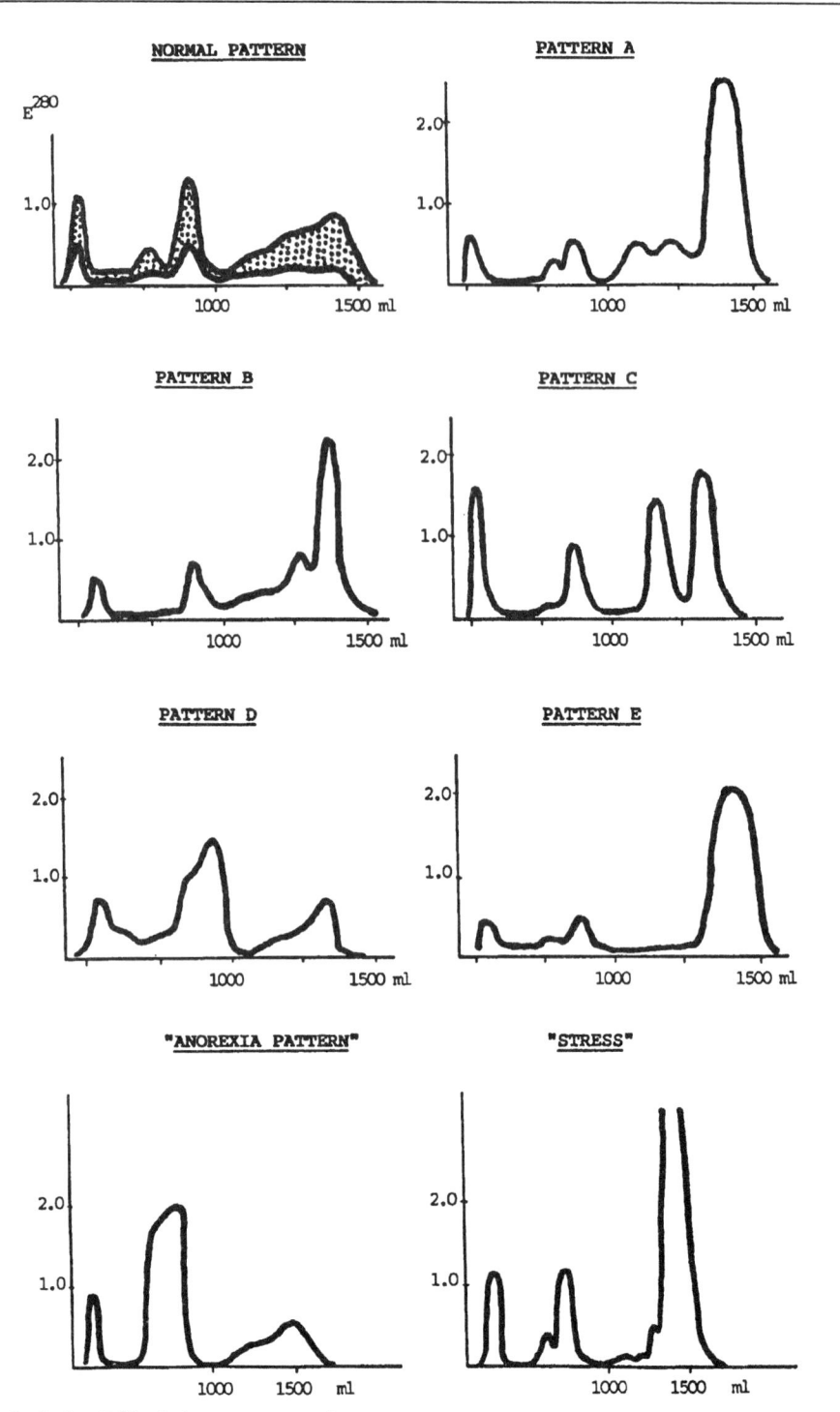

Figure 1. Sephadex G-25 gel chromatograms of peptide-protein complexes. Results obtained in previous studies by Trygstad et al. (1980) and Gillberg et al. (1982).

to a Sephadex G-25 gel filtration column. Fractions of 12 ml were collected and UV absorbency read at 280 nm. Precautions were also taken to ensure that the chromatographic patterns were not affected by contaminants of both benzoic acid and uric acid.

All urine samples were examined blind by the same laboratory technician.

Urinary Peptide Patterns

For all urine samples a urinary peptide chromatographic profile was produced, and the research team in Oslo ascribed a pattern from its shape and form to one of the eight characteristic patterns (see Figure 1) described in previous papers (Trygstad et al., 1980; Gillberg, Trygstad & Foss, 1982). One of these patterns has been said to be typical of "primary" anorexia nervosa.

Statistics

The sign test for matched pairs was used in the statistical analysis of the results.

Results

There were no major differences between the anorexia nervosa population group and the referral group with regard to urinary peptide patterns. Pattern B tended to be slightly more common in the latter group, but the difference was statistically nonsignificant.

Only one of the 31 cases (3%) with anorexia nervosa (a girl) showed the pattern said to be typical of anorexia nervosa, and even in this case there was doubt as to whether to classify it as abnormal or not. The results are shown comprehensively in Table 1. There were no significant differences between the anorexia nervosa and the comparison groups with regard to any of the seven different patterns seen.

Table 1. Urinary peptide patterns in anorexia nervosa (population and referral groups) and matched comparison cases.

Study group	Primary anorexia	A	B	C	D	E	Stress	Normal
Anorexia nervosa								
population group	1	0	1	0	0	2	4	6
referral group	0	1	6	0	0	2	0	8
all	1	1	7	0	0	4	4	14
	(1)	(0)	(4)			(1)	(4)	(8)
Comparison	0	3	12	5	0	1	2	8

Numbers in ( ) represent those case of anorexia nervosa who were extremely emaciated at the time of urinary analysis. All differences between "Anorexia nervosa" (all) cases and "Comparison" cases are statistically nonsignificant.

Discussion

We have been unable to replicate previously reported findings in this field. The number of anorexia nervosa patients included in this study was too small for generalized conclusions to be drawn. Nevertheless, the cases examined were possibly nearer to representativity than any other groups of anorexia nervosa cases reported in the literature (Råstam, Gillberg & Garton, 1989) and almost certainly much more typical of anorexia nervosa than the ones reported previously from Oslo. Also, this study made use of carefully matched comparison cases whose urine samples were blindly examined along with those of the anorexia nervosa group. Therefore, the results cannot be readily dismissed as atypical. Rather, even though it may be premature to decide definitely in this respect, it seems that the method holds little promise for the future when it comes to neurobiological research on anorexia nervosa. There was nothing at all to suggest even a trend with regard to urinary peptide patterns in anorexia nervosa. "Normal" patterns even tended to be more common in the deviant than in the blindly examined normal group, where indeed "normal" results occurred in only one of four cases. In a recent publication we presented additional evidence that urinary excretion of peptides as examined here does not differentiate normal from abnormal (autistic and mentally retarded) psychiatric cases (Le Couteur et al., 1988). However, those results pertained only to adults. The cases examined here were all in mid-puberty. We still lack experience with a (rigorously) blindly examined group of young normal children.

Overall, however, the present results together with those recently published do cast serious doubt as to the validity of this measure. It is our belief that the main reason for the discrepancy between these two later studies and the previous ones is that rigorous "blindness" and matched normal controls were not used in the early studies.

Only one case in this study may be suspected of showing the "typical" anorexia nervosa pattern (Trygstad et al., 1978). To be sure, this was the most severely emaciated case of all in the study. Even though it is difficult to attach much weight to a single case like this, it may be that it illustrates that the "specific" urinary pattern is associated with extreme weight loss in itself and has nothing to do with the primary deficit in anorexia nervosa.

References

American Psychiatric Association (1980). *Diagnostic and statistical manual of mental disorders. DSM-III* (3rd ed.). Washington, DC: APA.

American Psychiatric Association (1987). *Diagnostic and statistical manual of mental disorders. DSM-III-R* (3rd ed., rev.). Washington, DC: APA.

Gillberg, C., Trygstad, O., & Foss, I. (1982). Childhood psychosis and urinary excretion of peptides and protein-associated peptide complexes. *Journal of Autism and Developmental Disorders, 12,* 229–241.

Le Couteur, A., Trygstad, O., Evered, C., Gillberg, C., & Rutter, M. (1988). Infantile autism and urinary excretion of peptides and protein-associated peptide complexes. *Journal of Autism and Developmental Disorders, 18,* 181–190.

Råstam, M., Gillberg, C., & Garton, M. (1989). Anorexia nervosa in a Swedish urban region. A population-based study. *British Journal of Psychiatry, 155,* 642–646.

Trygstad, O., Foss, I., Edminson, P. D., Johansen, J. H., & Reichelt, K. L. (1978). Humoral control of appetite. A urinary anorexigenic peptide. Chromatographic patterns of urinary peptides in anorexia nervosa. *Acta Endocrinologica, 89,* 196–208.

Trygstad, O. E., Reichelt, K. L., Foss, I., Edminson, P. D., Saelid, G., Bremer, J., Hole, K., Örbeck, H., Johansen, J. H., Böler, J. B., Titlestad, K., & Opstad, P. K. (1980). Patterns of peptides and protein-associated peptide complexes in psychiatric disorders. *British Journal of Psychiatry, 136,* 59–72.

Genetic Vulnerability to Eating Disorders: Evidence from Twin and Family Studies

Janet Treasure and Anthony Holland

The syndrome of anorexia nervosa was delineated in the last century by Marcé in 1869 (Silverman, 1989), Gull (1873), and Lasègue (1873), whereas Russell described the syndrome of bulimia nervosa, which he considered to be an "ominous variant of anorexia nervosa" in 1979. Over the last decade, there has been a move to separate these two forms of eating disorder. DSM-III-R (APA, 1987) states that they are not mutually exclusive, so that both diagnoses can be given. The decision to consider anorexia nervosa and bulimia nervosa as discrete entities rather than part of a spectrum of eating abnormalities was based upon clinical features. Confirmation of this nosological distinction by aetiological features or clinical course is awaited. In this chapter we evaluate the role of familial factors in the development of anorexia nervosa and bulimia nervosa. We consider whether the aetiology of these conditions differs and in what way this information effects management.

Role of the Family in the Aetiology of Anorexia Nervosa: A Historical Perspective

Marcé, in 1860, considered that young subjects who were "predisposed to insanity from hereditary antecedents" were at risk of developing a disorder he termed hypochondriacal delirium (Silverman, 1989). We now recognise this as anorexia nervosa. His experience was that treatment was difficult if the subject remained within her family as the vivid emotion displayed by the sufferer prevented the physician from acting with "full liberty and moral ascendancy." He suggested that the patient should be entrusted to the care of strangers. This is remarkably similar to the later recommendations made by Gull (1873) and Lasègue (1873). An English physician, reporting 50 years later on his personal experience of 51 cases, also noted the higher incidence of nervousness in the immediate family and considered that parents may have contributed to the disorder (Ryle, 1936).

Psychiatric Disorders in Families of Probands with Eating Disorders

Genetic epidemiological studies have found that there is a clustering of psychiatric illnesses amongst the relatives of subjects with eating disorders. Affective disorders predominate (Winokur, March & Mendels, 1980; Gershon, Schreiber, Hamont, Dibble et al., 1984; Strober, 1982).

Bulimia nervosa is similarly associated

Institute of Psychiatry, De Crespigny Park, London SE5 8AF, United Kingdom.
We are grateful to the Mental Health Foundation and the Society for Research into Anorexia Nervosa for their support of this project. We are also grateful to all the centres in the United Kingdom who helped us recruit patients. Special thanks are due to Professor Gerald Russell and Professor Arthur Crisp.

with a coaggregation with affective disorders (Hudson, Pope, Jonas & Yorgelun Todd, 1983; Kassett, Gershon, Maxwell, Guroff et al., 1989). Alcoholism is also more common (Strober, Salkin, Burroughs & Morrell, 1982; Kassett et al., 1989).

Clinical features such as restriction, bingeing, or depression do not alter the morbid risk for affective disorder amongst their relations (Kassett et al., 1989; Logue, Crowe & Bean, 1989).

The Familial Nature of Eating Disorders

A history of anorexia nervosa within the family is occasionally seen in clinical practice. The family tree of one such subject who presented to our clinic is shown in Figure 1, and the affected relative of another patient is presented in Figure 2. The prevalence of anorexia nervosa in first-degree relatives is approximately 7% (Theander, 1970; Crisp, Hsu, Harding & Hartshome, 1980; Morgan & Russell, 1975).

Strober, Morrell, Burroughs, Salkin and Jacobs (1985) found that female relatives of 60 probands with anorexia nervosa (39 restricting and 21 bulimic) have a 5-fold greater risk for developing an eating disorder compared to control group of 95 psychiatric controls (45 with affective disorders, 22 with schizophrenia, 28 with conduct disorder). Eating disorders (typically bulimia nervosa) were more common amongst the relatives of the bulimic anorexic probands than those with restricting anorexia nervosa (13% vs. 8%). Severe restricting anorexia nervosa was confined to the relatives of restricting probands, and bulimia nervosa also appeared to be specifically distributed within families.

The morbid risk for an eating disorder amongst the first degree relatives of 40 probands with bulimia nervosa was higher than in the control group (11.8% vs. 3.5%), and again the predominant form was of bulimia nervosa (Kassett et al., 1989). There was no increased risk of anorexia nervosa, but the power of the study was probably too low.

Figure 1. A family with anorexia nervosa in several generations. (A) Presented to the eating disorders clinic aged 24 with primary amenorrhoea (39 kg, 158 cm); the onset of anorexia nervosa had been at 11 years. Her sister (B) developed anorexia nervosa age 15 with bulimic features but recovered 3 years later. The paternal aunt (C) developed anorexia nervosa aged 15 but recovered after 5 years and although married has no children. The paternal great-aunt (D) had anorexia nervosa at age 17 but never recovered from the illness; she never married, lived alone, and remained thin with eccentric eating habits until her death. Many of the male members of the family were physicians.

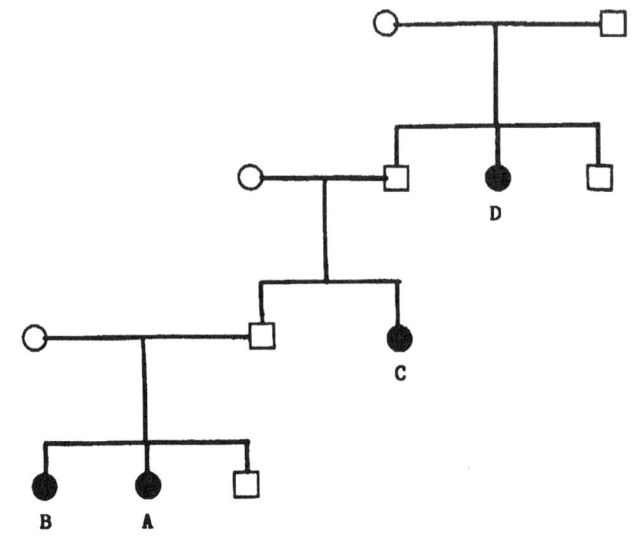

Figure 2. Photograph of the maternal grandmother of a current patient with anorexia nervosa. The photograph was taken when the grandmother was 15 in a seaside booth in which her weight was also recorded at 37 kg. The grandmother's weight loss led to admission to a nursing home for bed rest, the diagnosis of anorexia nervosa not being made at the time, although the family later recognized the similarity with the granddaughter's illness.

Family Forces

The concept that certain families foster the development of anorexia nervosa has persisted. There is little evidence for direct cultural passage. Abnormal attitudes toward weight or shape do not appear to be transmitted from mother to child (Garfinkel, Garner, Rose, Darby et al., 1983; Hall, Leibrich, Walkey & Welch, 1986). Interest has focussed on indirect forms of cultural pathogenesis.

The older literature generally described the mothers to be overprotective, intrusive, and dominating, and the fathers as distant and passive (Kaye & Leigh, 1954; King, 1963) Minuchin, Rosman and Baker (1978) hypothesised that the psychological and physiological regression produced by anorexia nervosa serves to generate harmony and closeness within the family by diverting attention away from the parents' vulnerabilities and marital strains. He considered that five types of interaction were thought to be characteristic of families with a child with anorexia nervosa: enmeshment, overprotectiveness, rigidity, conflict avoidance, and poor conflict resolution. Selvini-Palazzoli and Viaro (1988) also suggest that anorexia nervosa results when a girl becomes caught up in, and unable to cope with, a "family game."

Empirical studies of interpersonal attitudes and behaviours have revealed that there are differences between the families of origin of subjects with anorexia nervosa and bulimia nervosa. The families of bulimic probands have been found to be much more disturbed and less nurturing (Humphrey, 1986, 1987, 1988; Kog & Vandereycken, 1989; Humphrey & Stern, 1988). In contrast, subjects with classical anorexia nervosa and their parents were more positive about parent-child relationships and similar to controls. There was less congruency between the parents' views on the marriage, with the wives reporting that their husbands were withdrawn, sulky, and unaffectionate, and husbands blithely unaware of any difficulties (Humphrey, 1988). Families with a girl with anorexia nervosa also tend to deny or play down negative attitudes (Hall & Brown, 1983) and negate the daughter's self expression and development needs (Humphrey, 1989).

It is impossible to distinguish between primary pathogenic patterns and secondary reactions to the illness. As it is unusual for more than one sibling to be affected, these aetiological models must account for individual susceptibility.

Although the evidence that families have a role in the aetiology of anorexia nervosa is far from certain, disturbed interrelationships within the family do contribute to the prognosis. Poor outcome, or premature termination of treatment, has been noted to be associated with family dysfunction (Crisp et al., 1980; Hsu, Crisp & Harding, 1979; Morgan & Russell, 1975; Szmukler, Eisler, Russell & Dare, 1985).

Familiality: Genes or Environment?

Family studies do not discriminate between inherited factors and environmentally transmitted factors. Twins or adoption studies are needed for this. Problems arise when using these methods for disorders as rare as anorexia nervosa as it is difficult for any centre to build up a large enough consecutive series of twins, free from selection bias. Other forms of recruitment tend to bias the sample in favour of monozygotic and concordant pairs.

Reports of anorexia nervosa in twins have appeared (Garfinkel & Garner, 1982,; Vandereycken & Pierloot, 1981; Askevold & Heiberg, 1979; Nowlin, 1983; Scott, 1986). Often, the subjects are a mixture of twins seen by the authors and those reported in the literature. There is also a case report of monozygotic twins concordant for bulimia (Kaminer, Feingold & Lyons, 1988). It is difficult to draw conclusions from these idiographic studies and reviews because of possible reporting bias and in some cases lack of reliable methods of determining both zygosity and the co-twin's diagnosis.

In an earlier twin study by one of the authors, some of these methodological problems were minimised (Holland, Hall, Murray, Russell & Crisp, 1984; Crisp, Hall & Holland, 1985). Collaboration between two regional centres with specialised eating disorder units meant that a large sample of twins were recruited without gross selection bias. Thirty-four pairs of twins and a set of triplets were described. Of the 30 female-female pairs, 9 out of 16 (55%) MZ pairs were concordant for anorexia nervosa, whereas only 1 out of 14 (7%) DZ pairs was concordant. This significant difference in the concordance rate suggested that genetic factors contributed to anorexia nervosa. However, structured interviews to ascertain the form of the eating disorder were not used, and only in 18 pairs were both sisters seen. Of the possible environmental determinants, adverse perinatal events and nondominance in childhood were more often seen in the affected twin of discordant pairs.

Twin Study of Eating Disorders

The current authors embarked on a further twin study to investigate further some of the issues raised in this preliminary study (Holland, Sicotte & Treasure, 1988).

The Sample

Eighteen sets of twins were ascertained from the Maudsley twin register. Thirteen twins and their sisters were interviewed during the course of routine inpatient or outpatient management. The 5 male co-twins were not interviewed, since male/female twins were excluded from the study.

In addition, the authors personally contacted all the consultants in charge of the seven specialised eating disorder units within the UK, explaining the study and requesting permission to approach twins with eating disorders. All the twins from the previous study were also contacted. Twins were also recruited from the British self-help organisation, the Eating Disorder Association. Participants in the study came to the Institute of Psychiatry in London for interviews.

A total of 68 female-female twin pairs were seen. Each twin was separately given several structured interviews to document

- the lifetime eating disorder diagnosis (using a modified version of the *Eating Disorder Examination* (Cooper & Fairburn, 1987);
- lifetime psychiatric diagnosis (using the *Diagnostic Interview Schedule* (Robins, Helzer, Cronghan, Williams & Spitzer, 1981);
- a modified version of the Morgan and Russell (1975) assessment scales.

Eight blood groups were used to determine zygosity.

Analysis of the Twin Data

The methods available to determine the relative importance of inherited and environmentally transmitted factors require data from an unselected series of twins. For a condition as rare as anorexia nervosa, it is difficult to obtain such a series with enough power. In an attempt to overcome these mutually contradictory caveats, we decided to use data from the twins (31 MZ and 28 DZ, n=59) who had received hospital treatment for their eating disorder in this analysis. Seven MZ co-twins and one DZ co-twin had also received hospital treatment, so that these twin pairs were considered to be double probands.

The ratio of MZ:DZ pairs and the proportion of concordant pairs in the consecutive sample (the 13 Maudsley series) and the sample recruited from other sources did not differ. This suggests that the sample is not overtly selected. Monozygotic and concordant twin pairs are usually overrepresented in twins recruited voluntarily.

A comparison of the concordance rates between MZ and DZ twin pairs is shown in Table 1. The marked difference in the concordance rate for anorexia nervosa and restricting anorexia nervosa between MZ and DZ twins but not for bulimia nervosa suggests that genetic factors are more important in anorexia nervosa. However, a comparison of concordance rates for different types of a disorder (in which the population prevalence rates differs) does not give accurate quantitative information on heritability. The data was thus entered into the HERIT and THRESH programmes (Professor Peter McGuffin) in which population prevalences are added. The results are shown in Figure 3. Using this model, inherited factors account for approximately three quarters of the liability to develop anorexia nervosa, whereas the familial aggregation of bulimia nervosa probably results from environmental transmission.

This surprisingly high heritability for anorexia nervosa deserves comment. Firstly, it is an estimate of the variance within a population rather than an individual. Secondly, the models that have been used to derive these figures contain assumptions that may not be true for anorexia nervosa. The HERIT and THRESH programmes assume that genetic and environmental factors are additive. In obesity, an interactive rather than an addi-

Figure 3. A comparison of the partition of liability to develop either anorexia nervosa or bulimia nervosa. Data from 59 hospital case twins were analyzed using HERIT and THRESH.

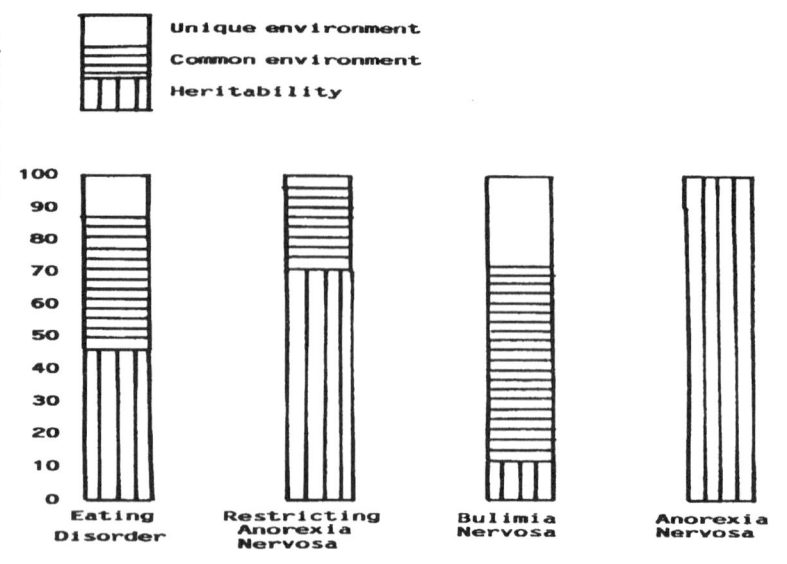

Table 1. Proband-wise concordance rates of the 59 hospital case twins.

Form of eating eating disorder (lifetime diagnosis)	Proportion of concordant pairs MZ	DZ
Eating disorder	21/38 (55%)	8/29 (27%)
Restricting anorexia nervosa	14/21 (66%)	0/10 (0%)
Bulimia nervosa ± anorexia nervosa	5/14 (35%)	5/17 (29%)
Anorexia nervosa	20/34 (68%)	2/26 (8%)

tive model appears to fit the data better (Bouchard, 1987). If this were also the case for anorexia nervosa, then estimates of the inherited component would be too high.

Although the exact size of the genetic component to anorexia nervosa remains uncertain, there is no doubt that it exceeds that of bulimia nervosa. The familiality observed in both conditions results from different mechanisms.

The clinical features of the familial form of anorexia nervosa differ from those of sporadic cases. The familial form had an earlier onset. Also, maximum weight, minimum weight, and current weight were lower than in the sporadic form.

This form of analysis is merely the starting point in the use of twins in the investigation of the putative aetiological factors in anorexia nervosa. Once it has been established that genetic factors are involved, then the discordant monozygotic twin model can be used to investigate aetiological factors more carefully. As monozygotic twins share the same genetic vulnerability and many external similarities, they can be used to focus on the specific environmental determinant that can lead to the development of anorexia nervosa.

Conclusions

Several conclusions can be tentatively drawn from these studies. Firstly, genetic factors contribute to the development of adolescent onset restricting anorexia nervosa. Secondly, eating disorders, especially bulimia nervosa, occurring in older women whose weight is above average, do not require a genetic predisposition and can develop in anyone exposed to the relevant pathogenic environmental factors.

What mechanisms could account for these findings? Our clinical experience leads us to consider a model in which weight loss (caused by physical or psychological illness or by dieting) uncovers the genetic vulnerability in body weight/appetite control. (One putative mechanism could be that weight loss in genetically vulnerable individuals could result in the release of endogenous opiates, which in turn could be reinforcing or addictive and result in the increased activity and alertness seen in patients with anorexia nervosa—which contrasts markedly to the apathy and retardation seen as a result of starvation in most people.)

These aetiological considerations must be evaluated against the known epidemiological and clinical features of the disorder: the much greater female prevalence, the preponderance in social classes 1 and 2, and the onset at the time of puberty. Anorexia nervosa has been recognised as a distinct illness for over a century (see above) and early descriptions of the disorder date from the 17th century (Morton, 1694), as would be consistent with a condition with a biological aetiology.

The female/male ratio is readily explained by a biological model. The control of weight and reproduction in females is intertwined, although the exact mechanisms are ill-understood (Unvas-Moberg, 1988). The nutritional cost of pregnancy and lactation is large, and it is probable that the physiological strategies to cover this involve changes in appetite and/or metabolism driven by hormonal signals. Such changes have also been observed during the menstrual cycle (Bisdee, James & Shaw, 1989; Lissner, Stevens, Levitsky, Rasmussen & Strupp, 1988). In animals, there are often periods of anorexia and weight loss even when food is present when the animal is involved in other important activities which interfere with feeding; these are usually activities important in reproduction (Mrosovsky & Sherry, 1980).

Reciprocally, reproductive function is markedly affected in the female by changes in weight (Frisch, 1988). Dieting can rapidly interrupt the menstrual cycle (Pirke, Schweiger & Lemmel, 1985). Central neurotransmitter function is altered during dieting (Goodwin, Fairburn & Cowen, 1987); serotonergic function is more affected in women. It is possible that the hormonal fluxes at puberty disturb the weight set-point or control of appetite in certain vulnerable individuals, which leads to a further disturbance in the hypothalamic function. This would explain the sex ratio and the time of onset of the disorder.

If weight loss does uncover the genetic vulnerability, this also could explain the onset in adolescence and social class distribution as these are associated with dieting behaviour (Nylander, 1971). In others, the emergence of sexual feelings with the weight-related pubertal changes may reawaken memories of earlier sexual abuse (Oppenheimer, Howells, Palmer & Chaloner, 1985) and lead to avoidance by weight loss.

It is unlikely that any psychiatric disorder can be explained solely on the basis of a genetic vulnerability, although this may be a necessary condition. It is probable that the reaction of the family to a daughter's weight loss alters the course of the illness. For example, conflict between the parents may render them impotent to change their daughter's behaviour, or disengagement within the family may result in the weight loss proceeding unheeded. In Western society, numerous secondary gains accrue from weight loss that is deemed fashionable, attractive, and an outward sign of self-discipline and control. Later, the consequences of starvation such as depression, obsessiveness, social withdrawal, and sexual regression serve to perpetuate the disorder.

Implications for management arise. The concept of an inherited predisposition should neither provoke, on the one hand, therapeutic nihilism nor, on the other hand, unrealistic expectations from genetic engineering! More usefully, parents can be absolved from the guilt of assuming that their behaviour "caused" their daughter to develop anorexia nervosa and can be mobilised to combat a less shameful threat. Our interaction model would explain why weight restoration is needed to promote recovery. Nevertheless, skilled psychotherapeutic support is also required to minimise the cascade of secondary disabilities that arise once the illness becomes entrenched. Anorexia nervosa occurs at a critical period in psychosexual development, leading to problems ranging from the physiological (prolonged amenorrhoea, infertility, and osteoporosis) to the social (how does one behave on the first date, aged 30, when peers are already settled with families or negotiating a second marriage?).

Preventative measures should warn of the dangers of weight loss, especially for those who may be constitutionally vulnerable to developing anorexia nervosa.

In contrast, there is no genetically vulnerable group at more risk of developing bulimia nervosa. This behaviour is contagious (Chiodo & Latimer, 1983; Crandall, 1988). Glamourised descriptions of eating disorders in the popular press with revelations about the secret methods of weight loss have probably contributed to its increasing prevalence. The symptoms of bulimia nervosa can be explained on the basis of homeostatic mechanisms utilised to restore weight to its set point (Lancet Editorial, 1988; Treasure, 1988). Although weight loss is probably the final common pathway in the aetiology of bulimia nervosa, the factors that lead to this behaviour becoming so highly valued are diverse. Many studies have found that a "nervosa" element underpins the development of bulimia nervosa (Patton, 1988; Steel, Young, Lloyd & Macintyre, 1989; Crandall, 1988). This reinforces the hypothesis that bulimia may have replaced depressive symptoms as a primary pathway of expressing psychological distress amongst younger women (Russell, 1985; Crandall, 1988).

In conclusion, the answer to the question frequently posed jokingly to those who treat patients with eating disorders, "How can I catch anorexia nervosa for a few weeks?" is that, probably, you cannot. But you can all too easily acquire the behaviours and become immersed in the hazardous habits of bulimia nervosa.

References

American Psychiatric Asociation (1987). Diagnostic and statistical manual of mental disorders (3rd ed. rev.). Washington, DC: APA.

Askevold, F., & Heiberg, A. (1979). Anorexia nervosa: Two cases of discordant MZ twins. *Psychotherapy and Psychosomatics, 32*, 223–228.

Bisdee, J. T., James, W. P. T., & Shaw, M. A. (1989). Changes in energy expenditure during the menstrual cycle. *British Journal of Nutrition, 61*, 187–199.

Bouchard, C. (1987). Genetics of body fat, energy expenditure and adipose tissue metabolism. In E. M. Berry, S. H. Blondheim, H. Eliahou & E. Shafrir (Eds.), *Proceedings of the 5th International Congress on Obesity. Recent advances in obesity research* (pp. 16–25). London: John Libby.

Chiodo, J., & Latimer, P. R. (1983). Vomiting as a learned weight control technique in bulimia. *Journal of Behaviour Therapy and Experimental Psychiatry, 14*, 131–135.

Cooper, Z., & Fairburn, C. G. (1987). The Eating Disorder Examination: A semi-structured interview for the assessment of the specific psychopathology of eating disorders. *International Journal of Eating Disorders, 6*, 1–8.

Crandall, C. S. (1988) Social contagion of binge eating. *Journal of Personality and Social Psychology, 55*, 588–598.

Crisp, A. H., Hsu, L. K. G., Harding, B., & Hartshome, J. (1980). Clinical features of anorexia nervosa: A study of consecutive series of 102 female patients. *Journal of Psychosomatic Research, 24*, 179–191.

Crisp, A. H., Hall, A., & Holland, A. J. (1985). Nature and nurture in anorexia nervosa: A study of 34 pairs of twins, one pair of triplets, and an adoptive family. *International Journal of Eating Disorders, 4*, 5–27.

Editorial (1988). *Lancet, i*, 629.

Frisch, R. E. (1988). Fatness and fertility. *Scientific American, 258*, 70–77.

Garfinkel, P. E., & Garner, D. M. (1982). *Anorexia nervosa: A multidimensional perspective.* New York: Brunner/Mazel.

Garfinkel, P. E., Garner, D. M., Rose, J., Darby, P. L., Brandes, J. S., O'Hanlon, J., & Walsh, N. (1983). A comparison of characteristics in the families of patients with anorexia nervosa and normal controls. *Psychological Medicine, 13*, 821–828.

Gershon, E. S., Schreiber, J. L., Hamont, J. R., Dibble, E. D., Kaye, W., Nurnberger, J. L., Andersen, A. E., & Ebert, M. (1984). Clinical findings in patients with anorexia nervosa and affective illness in relatives. *American Journal of Psychiatry, 141*, 1419–1422.

Goodwin, G. M., Fairburn, C. G., & Cowen, P. J. (1987) Dieting changes serotonergic function in women, not men: Implications for the aetiology of anorexia nervosa? *Psychological Medicine, 17*, 839–842.

Gull, W. (1873). Proceedings of the Clinical Society of London. *British Medical Journal, 1,* 527–529.

Hall, A., & Brown, L. B. (1983). A comparison of the attitudes of young anorexia nervosa patients and non-patients with those of their mothers. *British Journal of Medical Psychology, 56,* 39–48.

Hall, A., Leibrich, J., Walkey, F. H., & Welch, G. (1986). Investigation of "weight pathology" of 58 mothers of anorexia nervosa patients and 204 mothers of schoolgirls. *Psychological Medicine, 16,* 71–76.

Holland, A. J., Hall, A., Murray, R., Russell, G. F. M., & Crisp, A. H. (1984). Anorexia nervosa: A study of 34 pairs of twins and one set of triplets. *British Journal of Psychiatry, 145,* 414–419.

Holland, A.J., Sicotte, N., & Treasure, J. (1988). Anorexia nervosa: evidence for a genetic basis. *Journal of Psychosomatic Research, 32,* 561–571.

Hsu, L.K.G., Crisp, A. H., & Harding, B. (1979). Outcome of anorexia nervosa. *Lancet, i,* 62–65.

Hudson, J. I., Pope, H. G., Jonas, J. M., & Yorgelun Todd, D. (1983). A family study of anorexia nervosa and bulimia. *British Journal of Psychiatry, 142,* 133–138.

Humphrey, L. L. (1986). Structural analysis of parent-child relationships in eating disorders. *Journal of Abnormal Psychology, 95,* 395–402.

Humphrey, L. L. (1987). A comparison of bulimic-anorexic and nondistressed families using structural analysis of social behaviour. *Journal of American Academy of Child and Adolescent Psychiatry, 26,* 248–255.

Humphrey, L. L. (1988). Relationships within subtypes of anorexic, bulimic, and normal families. *Journal of the American Academy of Child and Adolescent Psychiatry, 27,* 544–551.

Humphrey, L. L. (1989). Observed family interactions among subtypes of eating disorders using structural analysis of social behaviour. *Journal of Consulting and Clinical Psychology, 57,* 206–214.

Humphrey, L. L., & Stern, S. (1988). Object relations and the family systems in bulimia: A theoretical integration. *Journal of Marital and Family Therapy, 14,* 337–350.

Kaminer,Y., Feingold, M., & Lyons, K (1988). Bulimia in a pair of monozygotic twins. *Journal of Nervous and Mental Disease, 176,* 246–248.

Kassett, J. A., Gershon, E. S., Maxwell, M. E., Guroff, J. J., Kazuba, D. M., Smith, A., Brandt, H. A., & Jimerson, D. C. (1989). Psychiatric disorders in first degree relatives of probands with bulimia nervosa. *American Journal of Psychiatry, 146,* 1468–1471.

Kaye, D. W. K., & Leigh, D. (1954). The natural history of treatment and prognosis of anorexia nervosa based on a study of 38 patients. *Journal of Mental Science, 100,* 411–431.

King, A. (1963). Primary and secondary anorexia nervosa. *British Journal of Psychiatry, 109,* 470–479.

Kog, E., & Vandereycken, W. (1989). Family interaction in eating disorder patients and normal controls. *International Journal of Eating Disorders, 8,* 11–23.

Lasègue, E. C. (1873). On hysterical anorexia. *Medical Times Gazette, 2,* 265–269.

Lissner, L. Stevens, J., Levitsky, D. A., Rasmussen, K. M., & Strupp, B. J. (1988). Variation in energy intake during the menstrual cycle: Implications for food intake research. *American Journal of Clinical Nutrition, 48,* 956–962.

Logue, C. M., Crowe, R. R., & Bean, J. A. (1989). A family study of anorexia nervosa and bulimia. *Comprehensive Psychiatry, 30,* 179–188.

Minuchin, S., Rosman, B. L., & Baker, L. (1978). *Psychosomatic families, anorexia nervosa in context.* London: Harvard University Press.

Morgan, H. G., & Russell, G. F. M. (1975). Value of family background and clinical features as predictors of long-term outcome in anorexia nervosa: Four year follow-up study of 41 patients. *Psychological Medicine, 5,* 355–371.

Morton, R. (1694). *Phthisiologia: or, a Treatise of Consumptions.* London: Smith and Walford.

Mrosovsky, N., & Sherry, D. (1980). Animal anorexias. *Science, 207,* 837–842.

Nowlin, N. S. (1983). Anorexia nervosa in twins: case report and review. *Journal of Clinical Psychiatry, 44,* 101–105.

Nylander, I. (1971). The feeling of being fat and dieting in a school population: epidemiologic interview investigation. *Acta Sociomedica Scandinavia, 3,* 579–584.

Oppenheimer, R., Howells, K. Palmer, R.L., & Chaloner, D. A. (1985). Adverse sexual experience in childhood and clinical eating disorders: A preliminary description. *Journal of Psychiatric Research, 19,* 357–363.

Patton, G. C. (1988). The spectrum of eating disorder in adolescence. *Journal of Psychosomatic Research, 32,* 579–584.

Pirke, K. M., Schweiger, J., & Lemmel, W. (1985). The influence of dieting on the menstrual cycle of healthy young women. *Journal of clinical Endocrinology and Metabolism, 60,* 1174–1179.

Robins, L. N., Helzer, J., Cronghan, J., Williams, J. B. W., & Spitzer, R. L. (1981). *NIMH Diagnostic Interview Schedule.* Washington University School of Medicine.

Russell, G. F. M. (1979). Bulimia nervosa: An ominous variant of anorexia nervosa. *Psychological Medicine, 9,* 429–448.

Russell, G. F. M. (1985). Premenarchal anorexia nervosa and its sequelae. *Journal of Psychiatric Research, 19,* 363–370.

Ryle, J. A. (1936). Anorexia nervosa. *Lancet, ii,* 893–899.

Scott, D. W. (1986). Anorexia nervosa: A review of possible genetic factors. *International Journal of Eating Disorders, 5,* 1–20.

Selvini-Palazzoli, M., & Viaro, M. (1988). The anorectic process in the family: A six-stage model as a guide for individual therapy. *Family Process, 27,* 129–148.

Silverman, J. A. (1989). Louis-Victor Marcé, 1828–1864: Anorexia nervosa's forgotten man. *Psychological Medicine, 19,* 833–835.

Steel, J. M., Young, R. J., Lloyd, G. G., & Macintyre, C. C. A. (1989). Abnormal eating attitudes in young insulin dependent diabetics. *British Journal of Psychiatry, 155,* 515–521.

Strober, M., Morrell, W., Burroughs, J., Salkin, B., & Jacobs, C. (1985) A controlled family study of anorexia nervosa. *Journal of Psychiatric Research, 19,* 239–246.

Strober, M., Salkin, B., Burroughs, J., & Morrell, W. (1982) Validity of the bulimia-restrictor distinction in anorexia nervosa. *Journal of Nervous and Mental Disease, 170,* 345–351.

Szmukler, G. I., Eisler, I., Russell, G. F. M., & Dare, C. (1985). Parental "expressed emotion," anorexia nervosa and dropping out of treatment. *British Journal of Psychiatry, 147,* 265–271.

Theander, S. (1970). Anorexia nervosa: A psychiatric investigation of 44 female cases. *Acta Psychiatrica Scandinavia* (Suppl), *214,* 1–194.

Treasure, J. (1988). Psychopharmacological approaches to anorexia nervosa. In D. Scott (Ed.), *Anorexia and bulimia nervosa. Practical approaches* (pp. 123–134). London: Croom Helm.

Unvas-Moberg, K. (1989). Neuroendocrine regulation of hunger and satiety. In P. Bjomtorp & S. Rossner (Eds.), *Obesity 1988. Proceedings of the 1st European Congress on Obesity* (pp. 1–21). London/Paris: John Libby.

Vandereycken, W., & Pierloot, R. (1981). Anorexia nervosa in twins. *Psychotherapy and Psychosomatics, 35,* 55–63.

Winokur, A., March, V., & Mendels, J. (1980). Primary affective disorder in relatives of patients with anorexia nervosa. *American Journal of Psychiatry, 137,* 695–698.

Anorexia Nervosa and Depression: A Continuing Debate

Beate Herpertz-Dahlmann and Helmut Remschmidt

In the following review, recent findings on the relationship between anorexia nervosa and affective disorders are summarized. Topics such as elevated familial load with affective disorders in families with an anorectic child, weight dependence of depressive symptoms in anorexia nervosa, and neuroendocrinological findings in both disorders including the role of starvation are discussed. In addition, the predictive potential of the dexamathasone suppression test (DST) in anorexia nervosa is investigated. Weight-restored patients who did not normalize their DST responses during inpatient treatment were at greater risk for poor outcome. It appears that reversion to a positive DST result might reflect a stress response in anorexia nervosa patients who failed to recover completely through weight stabilization. Although anorexia nervosa and affective disorder might overlap in some individuals, most depression-like phenomena in anorexia nervosa are at least in part starvation-induced changes and do not point to a common etiology of both disorders.

In 1883, 10 years after the first characterization of anorexia nervosa by Sir William Gull and Lasègue, Franz Kafka was born. This famous poet exhibited symptoms of an eating disorder resembling anorexia nervosa as well as a severe depressive psychopathology (for details see Fichter, 1987). His story "A Hunger Artist" (1922) reminds us of the proudness and conflicts, but also of the resignative sadness expressed by many of our anorectic patients.

In the history of anorexia nervosa, similarities to affective disorders have been discussed by several authors like Kraepelin (quoted in Thomae, 1967) and Zutt (1948). Even Sigmund Freud (1916) pointed out the common etiology of anorexia nervosa and melancholia.

In current literature, a nosological link between these disorders has become the subject of a continuing debate. While some authors argue that eating disorders (anorexia nervosa and bulimia nervosa) are subgroups (variants) of affective disorders, others refer to depressive states in anorectic and bulimic patients as consequences, not causes, of the eating disorder.

The following observations and arguments might suggest an overlap between both conditions:

1) There is a high frequency of affective disorders in the families of anorectic patients (Gershon, Schreiber, Hamovit, Dibble, Kaye, Nurnberger et al., 1984; Herpertz-Dahlmann, 1988; Hudson, Pope, Jonas & Yurgelun-Todd, 1983; Rivinus, Biederman, Herzog, Kemper, Harper, Harnatz et al., 1984).

2) Depressive symptomatology in anorexia nervosa and primary affective disorder is similar: about 40% to 60% of all anorectic patients fulfill the DSM-III criteria of major depressive disorder (MDD) (Hendren, 1983; Herzog, 1984; Laessle, Kittle, Fichter, Wittchen & Pirke, 1987; Piran, Kennedy, Garfinkel & Owens 1985).

3) Corresponding neuroendocrinological findings underline the relationship (Weiner, 1985; Newman & Halmi, 1988; Hudson & Hudson, 1984).

4) In longitudinal studies, a higher frequency of affective disorders during later life peri-

---

Department of Child and Adolescent Psychiatry, Philipps University, Hans-Sachs-Str. 6, D-3550 Marburg, West Germany.

ods of anorectic patients could be demonstrated (Hall, Slim, Hawker & Salmond, 1984; Toner, Garfinkel & Garner, 1986; Willi, Limacher, Helbing & Nussbaum, 1989).

5) There is evidence of effective treatment with antidepressants in both conditions (Halmi, Eckert & LaDu, 1986).

But there are also arguments against a close relationship of both disorders:

1) A high familial load with affective illness was found only in the families of those anorectic patients who suffered from depression themselves (Biederman, Rivinus, Kemper, Hamilton, MacFayden & Harmatz, 1985).

2) Depressive symptoms were also found in other states of starvation (Keys, Brozek, Henschel, Mickolsen & Taylor, 1950; Schiele & Brozek, 1948) and in healthy women under the condition of voluntary starvation (Fichter, 1985).

3) A great proportion of the neuroendocrinological disturbances normalize parallel to weight gain (Pahl, Pirke, Schweiger, Warnhoff, Gerlinghoff, Brinkmann et al., 1985).

4) A remarkable improvement of depressive symptoms was observed with increase of body weight (Channon & DeSilva, 1985; Eckert, Goldberg, Halmi, Casper & Davis, 1982; Herpertz-Dahlmann & Remschmidt, 1987b; Laessle, Schweiger & Pirke, 1988).

These considerations form the basis for this report, in which we summarize recent findings on the relationship between anorexia nervosa and affective disorders, some of which were collected in our department.

Methodology

All inpatients fulfilling DSM-III-R criteria for anorexia nervosa who had been consecutively admitted to our inpatient ward during 1985–1988 were included in different studies. The age of the patients was between 10 and 19 years with a mean age of 15;8 years (range 10–21 years). Normal-weight patients with bulimia nervosa (according to DSM-III-R) were excluded. The earliest onset of disease was 8 years, and in all cases at least 4 months before admission. The patients' weight loss was determined by comparing their body weight to their ideal weight. The latter was calculated according to the Broca formulae (for girls: {height [in cm]–100} kg minus 20%, for boys minus 15%). For patients under 14 years of age, we had recourse to pediatric charts (Kunze, 1977). At admission, the mean weight was between 75–80% of ideal body weight depending on the patients participating in the respective study. Further details are given below.

Affective Disorders in the Families of Patients with Anorexia Nervosa

Family history information about first-, second-, and third-degree relatives of 45 anorectic patients (38 females, 7 males) was compared to that of 38 age-, sex- and IQ-matched control subjects with different kinds of neurosis (except depressive neurosis, MAS 300.4) or specific emotional disorder of childhood according to MAS (except MAS 313.1) (Remschmidt & Schmidt, 1986). We chose inpatient controls to presume similar psychosocial stress for the families provoked by their child's admission to a psychiatric ward.

Data were obtained by interviewing parents of patients and control subjects; only four fathers could not be interviewed (three from the patients' group and one from the control group). Familial load for psychiatric disorder was only counted when diagnosis

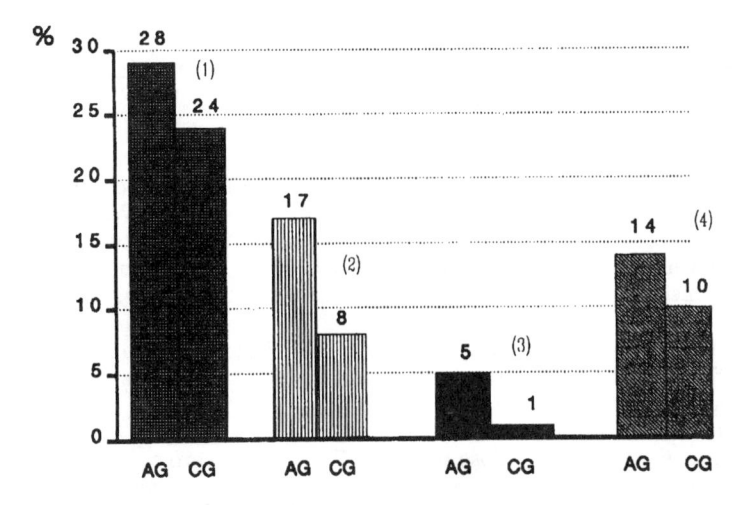

Figure 1. Psychiatric disorders in first and second degree relatives of anorexia nervosa patients and inpatient controls (AG: anorectic group; CG: Control group). (1) includes first and second degree relatives with any psychiatric disorder; (2) includes first and second degree relatives with affective disorders; (3) includes first and second degree relatives with eating disorders; (4) includes first and second degree relatives with alcohol abuse.

had been made by a medical doctor (for exact description of methodology, see Herpertz-Dahlmann, 1988).

Our data reveal nearly the same prevalence of psychiatric disorders in general for both groups. The rate of alcohol abuse was higher in the anorectic group without attaining significance. Families with anorectic children showed significantly more affective disorders ($\chi^2 = 4,518$; $p<0.035$) and eating disorders ($\chi^2 = 4,072$; $p<0.044$) than control families. 10.3% of the parents (n=9) of our anorectic patients were diagnosed as having affective disorders. In comparison, new data by Propping (1989) show that first-degree female relatives of a female subject with recurrent major depression have a life-long morbidity risk for affective disorder of 14.5%, male first-degree relatives of 7,8%.

Family data from other studies are in close agreement with our results in demonstrating an increased expectancy of affective disorders among relatives of anorectic patients (Rivinus et al., 1984; Gershon et al., 1984). Some authors suggest that only anorexia nervosa patients who suffer from depression themselves are more likely to have relatives with affective disorder (Biederman et al., 1985; Strober & Katz, 1987), whereas this was denied by others (Gershon et al., 1984). In our study, anorectic patients with or without MDD according to DSM-III did not differ in the risk for depressive disorders among their relatives.

On the other hand, there are strong arguments against a simple common genetic link between affective and eating disorders. Strober and his group (Strober & Katz, 1987) did not find a higher prevalence of eating disorders in first-degree female relatives of patients with major depression. There are also profound differences between affective disorder and anorexia nervosa in sex and socioeconomic distribution (Altshuler & Weiner, 1985). While major depressive disorders have a female:male ratio of 2:1, anorexia nervosa has a female:male ratio ranging from 25:1 to 7:1 (Leichner & Gentler, 1988). Major depression is not limited to persons with high intelligence upper-level socioeconomic status, which is typical for patients with anorexia nervosa.

Obviously, studies have to take into account that families with an anorectic child are prone to severe psychosocial stress evoked by the disorder which might probably be followed by a higher rate of depressive reactions. Vice versa, the vulnerability of a girl for developing anorexia nervosa could be enhanced by a depressive disorder of her father or mother. In our study, 6 of 45 mothers and 3 of 42 fathers suffered from different kinds of mood disorders.

To define the issue more clearly, more studies with raters blind to the diagnosis of the patient have to be done. Prospective studies could elucidate whether anorectic patients with a high familial load for affective disorders exhibit a greater morbidity for life-long depression than patients without such a risk.

Symptomatology and Psychopathology of Anorexia Nervosa— A Correlate of Weight Deficit?

As depressive symptoms were also found in other states of starvation and in healthy volunteers, we wanted to find out whether depressive states in anorexia nervosa might be weight dependent and thus a consequence of starvation.

The sample comprised 41 females and 7 males; 42 patients were classified as so-called restricters and 6 as bulimic subtype of DSM-III-R anorexia nervosa (see above). Within 3 days after admission, all patients were investigated by means of a semistandardized interview and a standardized psychiatric examination to assess DSM-III criteria of MDD (further methodological data are described elsewhere: Herpertz-Dahlmann & Remschmidt, 1989). In addition, the *Hamilton Depression Scale* (HAMD) (Hamilton, 1960) was filled out by the therapists and the *Zung Self-Depression Rating Scale* (SDS) (Zung, 1972) by the patients. According to extreme weight loss and to special therapeutic interventions (nasogastrial tube, bed rest), items No. 7, 12 and 16 of the HAMD could not be considered, as they are connected directly or indirectly to weight loss, eating behavior, and body activity. For 29 patients, the ratings of depression were repeated after 3 months (t2) and at discharge (t3) after approximately 6 months.

In order to investigate the weight dependency of depression, an extreme group comparison was done. Patients with high scores on the HAMD (>14, n=19) and SDS-scores (>51, n=15) at the beginning of inpatient treatment (t1) were compared with those who scored very low on the HRS (<8, n=15) and SDS (<39, n=13). Testing was performed throughout t1–t3 by t-test or by the Wilcoxon-test if there was no normal distribution.

Another comparison was carried out including patients whose weight at admission was below 72% of their ideal body weight (n=14) as opposed to those whose weight at admission was beyond 82.5% of their ideal weight (n=14).

Anorectic patients with MDD (n=28) and those without MDD (n=20) were significantly different with respect to their body weight (t=2.43; df=46; p<0.019). This result means that patients with MDD revealed a significantly lower weight at intake (in percent of ideal body weight) than patients without MDD.

The frequency of depressive symptoms according to the DSM-III criteria for MDD is demonstrated in Table 1.

As the table shows, a high loading of depressive symptoms can be found within the group of anorectic patients, also if poor appetite and significant weight loss that may be looked upon as typical for anorexia nervosa are put aside. The extreme group comparison between patients who scored high on the depression rating scales (HAMD, SDS) and those who scored low demonstrated that the more depressed group showed a significantly lower body weight. The difference between both extreme groups is no more present after normalization of body weight (between t2 and t3) (Table 2).

Patients with high weight loss had a trend toward higher depression scores at admission

Table 1. Frequency of depressive symptoms according to DSM-III criteria for major depressive disorder in patients with anorexia nervosa (n=48).

Poor appetite or significant weight loss	98.0%
Dysphoric mood/depressed	74.5%
Feelings of worthlessness, self-reproach	66.7%
Psychomotor agitation or retardation	54.9%
Insomnia or hypersomnia	51.0%
Loss of energy, fatigue	41.0%
Loss of interest or pleasure in usual activities	31.4%
Diminished ability to concentrate	31.4%
Recurrent thoughts of death, suicidal ideation	27.5%

Table 2. Extreme group comparison for patients with high and low depression scores (HAMD and SDS). t₁, t₂, t₃ = control dates during inpatient treatment; HAMD = Hamilton Depression Scale; SDS = Self-Rating Depression Scale; %IBW = body weight in % of ideal weight; max./min. = maximal and minimal depression scores by HAMD and SDS.

		n	t-value	df	p	%IBW	t-value	df	p
t₁ HAMD	min. 4.5 ± 2.4	15	−10.33	29.26	≤0.0001	82.7 ± 8.13	2.69	32	≤0.011
	max. 16.4 ± 4.2	19				74.5 ± 9.37			
t₂ HAMD	min. 3.5 ± 2.2	11	−4.55	21.36	≤0.0001	96.6 ± 5.4	1.51	26	≤0.14 (n.s.)
	max. 10.13 ± 5.3	16				93.6 ± 5.3			
t₃ HAMD	min. 4.5 ± 3.5	8	−0.93	20	n.s.	99.9 ± 3.0	1.07	22	n.s.
	max. 5.9 ± 3.1	14				98.1 ± 4.3			
t₁ SDS	min. 29.5 ± 6.0	13	−13.48	17.16	≤0.0001	81.4 ± 9.8	2.64	26	≤0.014
	max. 54.5 ± 3.0	15				71.7 ± 9.5			
t₂ SDS	min. 31.6 ± 11.9	7	−2.06	17	≤0.06 (n.s.)	93.6 ± 6.5	0.59	21	n.s.
	max. 42.9 ± 11.3	12				92.1 ± 5.7			
t₃ SDS	min. 31.4 ± 6.4	7	−2.16	14.93	≤0.05	98.1 ± 6.4	−0.04	18	n.s.
	max. 42.0 ± 14.1	11				98.2 ± 5.3			

(HAMD: t-value: 1.94; df=26; p<0.064; SDS: t-value: 1.91; df=26; p<0.067). Table 3 shows the results concerning body weight, HAMD and SDS throughout the three dates during inpatient treatment (multivariate analysis). Parallel with weight gain, a highly significant decrease in the scores on both scales of depression was registered.

After the first testing, 31% (n=15) of our sample received tricyclic antidepressants, in most cases amitryptiline.

Both groups with or without medication ameliorated in a similar range and time, e.g., weight gain and improvement of depressive symptoms was independent of pharmacological treatment. (The statistical procedure was carried out by testing the linear trend of the contrast variables with the two-tailed one-sample Wilcoxon (signed-rank) test; method see below.)

Of our anorectic patients, 58.3% met DSM-III criteria for MDD. This result is in line with the findings of other investigators (Hendren, 1983; Herzog, 1984), while Laessle et al. (1987) found fewer numbers (44%). Our results underline a close relationship between severity of starvation and intensity of depression in anorectic patients, which is true also for intraindividual and interindividual comparisons. Our study, however, gives no clear answer to the question whether the depressive state of eating disorder patients during extreme weight loss is a consequence of an acute metabolic disorder during the state of starvation or merely a consequence of low body weight. Laessle et al. (1988) state that patients with high β-hydroxy-butyric acid plasma levels (BHBA)—which they found to be a reliable indicator of acute malnutrition—displayed higher mean depression scores than patients with low BHBA values. Pirke (in this volume) and Morley (for a review, see Morley & Blundell, 1988) point to starvation-dependent changes of neurotransmitters, which might—according to Schildkraut's hypothesis—be one reason for the development of depression in eating disorders.

Our results show at least very clearly that the diagnosis "MDD" is to some extent dependent on low body weight. This means that the DSM-III and DSM-III-R criteria for MDD do not discriminate sufficiently between de-

Table 3. Comparison of weight and depression scores at three control dates (t_1, t_2, and t_3) during inpatient treatment. HAMD = Hamilton Depression Scale; SDS = Self-Rating Depression Scale (multivariate analysis).

	t_1	t_2	t_3	F-value	p
Weight in % of ideal weight	78.6 ± 7.62	92.56 ± 5.98	97.66 ± 4.66	120.67	<0.000001
HAMD score (n=29)	12.34 ± 6.30	8.62 ± 5.19	5.34 ± 3.05	19.35	<0.000001
SDS score (n=24)	45.00 ± 9.32	40.41 ± 10.37	37.16 ± 12.00	7.75	<0.001

pressive states with and without remarkable weight loss. Bearing in mind our results, it seems a little confusing to mix the symptoms poor appetite and significant weight loss in a single criterion for MDD, as it is done in DSM-III. Poor appetite may not only be a cause, but also a consequence of weight loss (Ceaser, 1979; Garfinkel, 1974). In recent literature, delayed gastric emptying was found in anorectic patients resulting in poor appetite (Robinson, 1989; Rigaud, Bedig, Merrouche, Vulpillat, Bonfils & Apfelbaum, 1988).

Disturbances of sleep rhythms resembling those of depression appear to correlate with weight deficit (Levy, Dixon & Schmidt, 1988). Lauer, Krieg, Zulley, Riemann and Berger (1989) demonstrated even qualitative differences in polysomnographic studies of anorectic and young depressive patients.

Concentration disorders seen in anorectic patients and in the test subjects of the experiment by Keys and his group (1950) might be a result of pseudoatrophia cerebri, which is partly weight dependent as well (Krieg, Pirke, Lauer & Backmund, 1988; Hoffman, Ellinwood, Rockwell, Herfkens, Nishita & Guthrie, 1989).

Loss of libido is to a certain degree a consequence of starvation-induced endocrinological disturbances.

Hence, typical symptoms of anorexia nervosa, such as depressive mood, impaired appetite, loss of libido, sleep and concentration disorders, which are to a high degree dependent on weight loss, lead to the fulfillment of five criteria for DSM-III MDD.

Some of our anorectic subjects went on to score high in the SDS (Table 2). It is possible that in some anorectic patients a depressive symptomatology continues at follow-up while body weight is maintained in a normal range. This could be a special subgroup of anorexia nervosa with long-lasting depressive states, where weight loss could be looked upon as a kind of trigger mechanism for the manifestation of a major depressive disorder.

The Endocrinology of Anorexia Nervosa: Comparison to Affective Disorders

Biological studies of anorexia nervosa and depression have contributed to the hypothesis that both disorders share a common etiology. In the following we review endocrine disturbances in anorexia nervosa; briefly, two types of hormonal changes can be observed:

1) hormones showing an obvious relationship to malnutrition and weight loss,

2) hormones in which weight loss alone does not appear sufficient to explain the changes.

To assess the influence of weight restoration, we analyzed endocrinological data at different times of inpatient treatment: at admission, upon reaching certain weight marks (e.g., 70%, 80%, 90%, and 100% of ideal body weight) and at discharge. In addition, we tried to check the influence of depressive mood on hormonal variables. Every time blood levels were taken, the level of current depression was measured with the *Hamilton Rating Scale for Depression* (HAMD) and with the *Zung Self-Depression Rating Scale* (SDS) (method see above).

Basal TSH, Prolactin, LH, FSH, estradiol,

estrone, T3 and T4 were drawn between 8.00 and 9.00 a.m. prior to a bolus injection of 200 µg TRH, followed by a second TSH collection 30 minutes later. The TRH test always preceded the dexamethasone suppression test (DST).

Hormone concentrations were analyzed by immunradiometric assays (IRMA) (FSH, LH, prolactin, TSH) and radioimmune methods (RIA) (T3, T4, estradiol, estrone). All patients were amenorrheic. At admission and discharge assays, all patients were medication free for at least 2 weeks. In between 5 patients received a tricyclic antidepressant (amitryptiline), none of them neuroleptics.

Statistical Procedure

In order to test the null hypothesis that the linear trend component of hormone levels viewed as a function of body weight is zero, a linear contrast for each patient was computed from the sequence of hormonal data. Noting that the number and location of measurements differed from patient to patient, special attention was paid to the standardization of the contrasts: They were standardized under the null hypothesis that the contrast variable for each patient had mean zero and the same variance irrespective of the differing number and location of the measurements. Only data of patients who participated in the testing at least once at a weight mark ≤85% IBW and at least once ≥95% IBW were computed. Testing was carried out applying the two-tailed one-sample Wilcoxon (signed-rank) test to the contrast variables.

Hypothalamo-Pituitary-Ovarian (HPO) Axis

For FSH, LH, and estradiol (E2) plasma levels, a high correlation with the degree of weight loss is found (Figure 2). During weight restoration, gonadotropin and estradiol levels increase; often the rise in FSH precedes secretion of LH and estradiol. There is also a distinct increase of estrone (E1) indicating gain of adipose tissue which is a major site of estrone production from androstendione (Vigersky & Loriaux, 1977; Kiriike, Nishiwaki, Izumiya, Maeda & Kawakita, 1988).

Prolactin secretion remained unchanged throughout weight restoration. These results are in line with those of other investigators (Isaacs, Leslie, Gomez & Sir Bayliss, 1980; Lemaire, Ardaens, Lepretre, Racadot, Buvat-Herbot & Buvat, 1983; Beumont, George, Pimstone & Vinik, 1976).

However, menstrual dysfunction is only partially accounted for by low body weight since amenorrhea precedes significant weight loss in about 20% of anorectic patients, and gonadotropin levels and ovarian function do not always respond to weight restoration. Figure 3 demonstrates an increase of LH in patient 1, while LH levels in patients 2 and 3 remain low though normal weight.

In a current longitudinal study, 5 of 14 former anorectic patients who had been weight stable for more than a year suffered from continuing amenorrhea and corresponding low gonadotropin levels. In contrast to those with normal menstrual function, they scored much higher in the ANIS (Fichter & Keeser, 1980), a German eating attitudes test. This observation is in agreement with that of Katz, Boyar, Roffwarg, Hellman and Weiner, (1978), who illustrated that an adult circadian LH-secretory pattern was not present in women who had achieved ideal body weight but otherwise remained "symptomatic."

According to Unden, Ljunggren, Beck-Friis, Kjellman and Wetterberg (1988), we found no correlation between hormonal data and depression measured by HAMD and SDS.

There are only few studies with controversial results about gonadotropin levels in depression. While some report low levels (Brambilla, Smeraldi, Sacchetti, Negri, Cocchi & Mueller, 1978), others found normal FSH and LH indices (Amsterdam, Winokur, Caroff & Snyder, 1981; Winokur, Amsterdam, Caroff, Snyder & Brunswick, 1982). There is, however, no doubt about the influence of stress on menstrual cycle (Meyer, 1985).

Hypothalamo-Pituitary-Thyroid (HPT) Axis

In 8 patients, serum thyrotropin was measured before and 30 minutes after stimulation with thyrotropin-releasing hormone (TRH test). Despite the small number of patients,

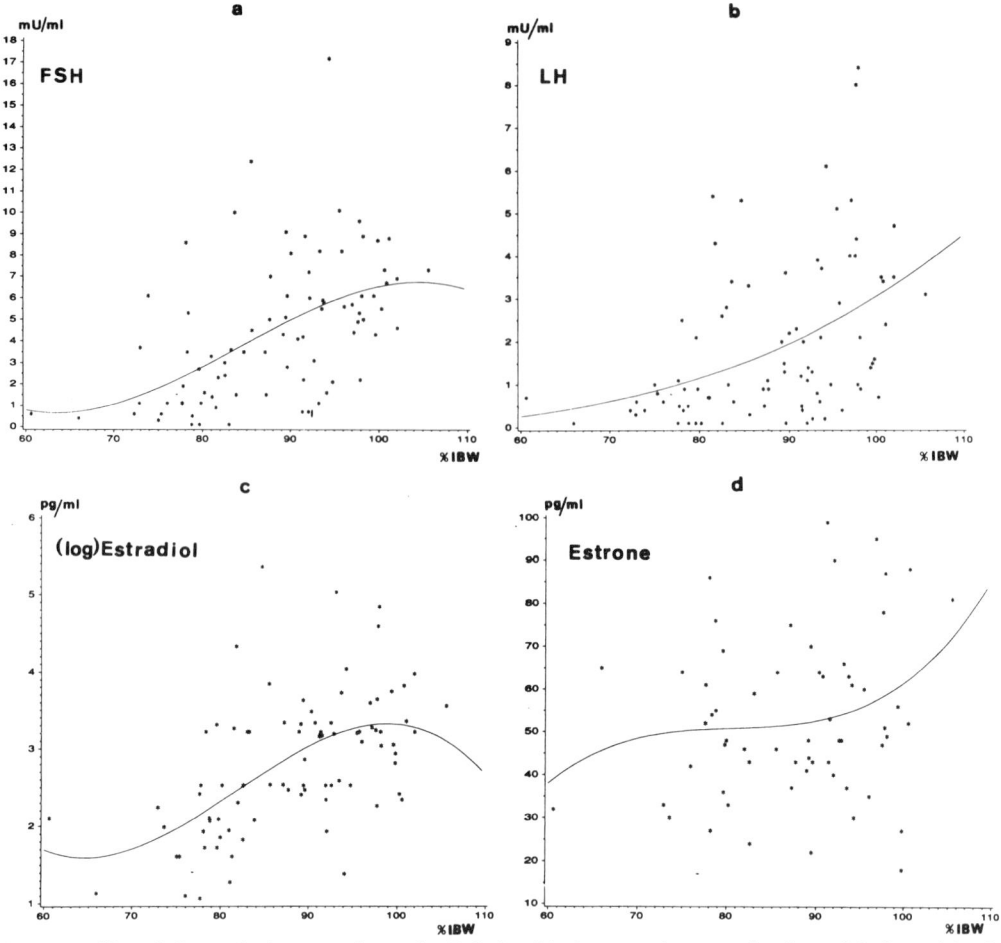

Figure 2. Hypothalamo-pituitary-ovarian axis. Relationship between hormone levels and body weight (in percent of ideal body weight = %IBW) in anorexia nervosa patients. (a) FSH (n=16; p<0.001) (b) LH (n=16; p<0.001) (c) (log)estradiol (n=16; p<0.0006) (d) estrone (n=10; p<0.05).

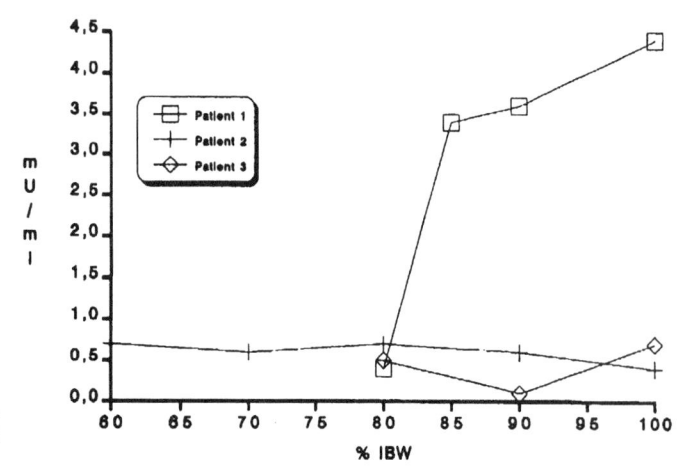

Figure 3. LH-pattern in three anorexia nervosa patients at different marks of body weight.

there was a trend toward an increase in TSH response (TSH) during weight recovery (Figure 4a).

We have no information whether the lower TSH response at admission was due to a delayed or blunted (less than 5 units change) TSH rise after TRH injection, because we did not want to take more than two blood samples from our rather young patients. Some studies report a delayed peak (Kiriike, Nishiwaki, Izumiya, Maeda & Kawakita, 1987), others a blunted one (Kiyohara, Tamai, Karibe, Kobayashi, Fujii, Fukino et al., 1987). Low response often, though not always, normalizes with weight gain (Casper & Frohman, 1982; Kiyohara et al., 1987). In Figure 4b, TSH responses in patient 2 and patient 3 continue to be abnormal although both subjects attained target weight. These findings clarify that abnormalities in weight loss are not due solely to weight loss. Our number of patients was too small to estimate any correlation between depressive mood and TSH response. Kiriike et al. (1987) reported no association with depressive symptoms, but Kiyohara et al. (1987) suggested that abnormal TSH response is due to the eating disorder itself.

An abnormal TSH response to TRH is also observed in 25% of patients with affective disorders, in many of them even in full remission periods (Holsboer, 1988). But there are also blunted TSH responses in adolescent patients with conduct disorders or substance or alcohol-abuse disorders (Khan, 1988). In some investigations on affective disorders, TSH responses to TRH correlate significantly with post-dexamethasone-cortisol levels (Roy, Koroum, Linnoila & Pickar, 1988; Loosen, Prange & Wilson, 1978), suggesting a contribution of stress or stress-related hypercortisolism (v. Zerssen, Berger & Doerr, 1986). According to other studies (Leslie, Isaacs, Gomez, Raggatt & Bayliss, 1978), we could not establish any correlation between weight deficit and T4, but in most of the patients T4 was in the low normal range.

Low triiodothyronine levels in anorexia nervosa (the so-called low T3-syndrome) are often described in literature (Buvat, Lemaire, Buvat-Herbaut, Lepretre & Fourlinnie, 1983; Althoff, Schifferdecker & Neubauer, 1986). We found a highly significant increase of T3 with weight gain (Figure 4c).

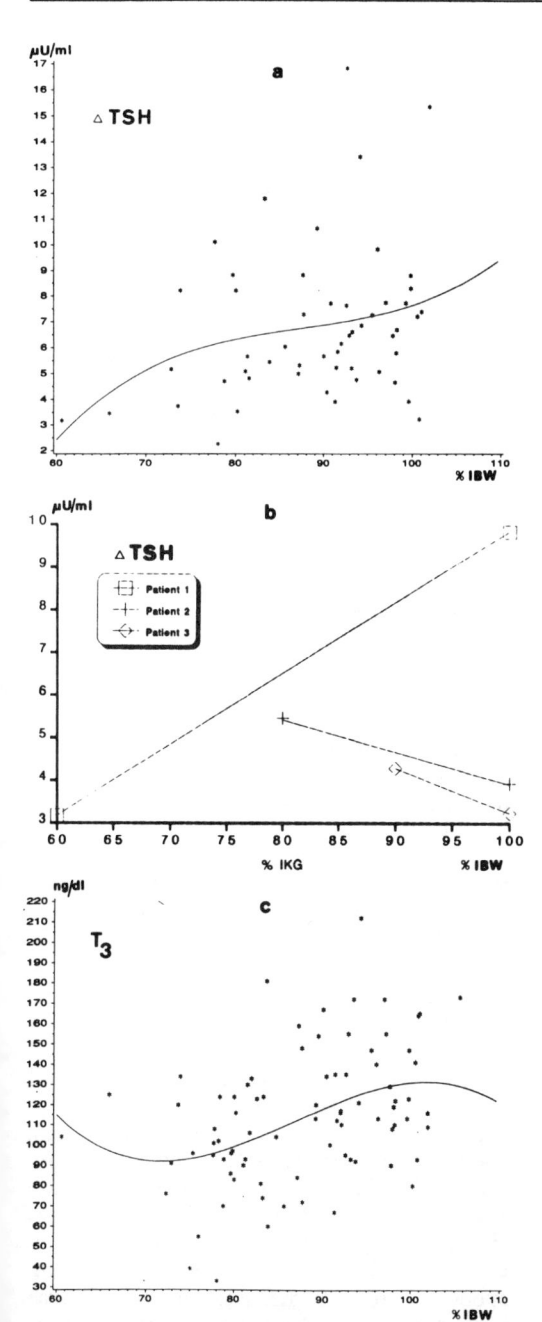

Figure 4. Hypothalamo-pituitary-thyroid axis. (a) TSH response (ΔTSH) in relationship to ideal body weight (in percent of ideal body weight = %IBW) (n=8; p<0.1). ΔTSH = TSH response to TRH stimulation after 30 minutes minus TSH basal level. (b) TSH pattern in three anorexia nervosa patients at different marks of body weight. (c) Relationship between T3 levels and body weight (n=16; p<0.002).

77

Table 4. Short-term follow-up of 31 anorexia nervosa patients according to the Morgan and Russell outcome score one year after discharge.

	No. of patients	Outcome criteria
Category 1 "good outcome"	16 (52%)	body weight within 15% of ideal weight (IBW), at most residual symptoms of anorectic behavior, at least three regular menstrual cycles
Category 2 "intermediate outcome"	2 (6%)	body weight within 15% of ideal body weight, but severe feeding difficulties, irregular menstrual cycles
Category 3 "poor outcome"	4 (13%)	low body weight (<85% IBW) and/or amenorrhea
Category 4	9 (29%)	new admission to hospital because of deterioration of anorexia nervosa

Investigations of peripheric thyroid hormones in affective disorder present an increase in T4 and FT4 indices in depressed patients and reduced levels of T3 (Müller & Böning, 1988; Holsboer, 1988).

In our anorectic patients no relationship was found between any hormone concerning the thyroid and HAMD and SDS depression scales.

Hypothalamo-Pituitary-Adrenal (HPA) Axis

Most anorectic patients show elevated plasma cortisol levels after administration of dexamethasone, which is also true for 45% of patients with MDD (Arana, Baldessarini & Ornsteen 1985). Some authors thought that the disturbance of the HPA axis found in patients of both disorders referred to a common etiology (Gwirtsman & Gerner, 1981; Hudson et al., 1983; Piran et al., 1985). Recently, it has been elucidated that weight loss and intermittent starvation undoubtedly play an important role in nonsuppression of the DST in eating disorders. In most anorectic patients the post-DST-cortisol value rapidly returns to normal range after weight gain (Kuhs & Mester, 1985; Halmi, 1985; Abou-Saleh, Oleesky, Crisp & Lacey, 1986; Herpertz-Dahlmann & Remschmidt, 1987b). In our sample, the sharpest decrease in plasma-cortisol levels was observed after a weight gain of approximately 15% (Herpertz-Dahlmann & Remschmidt, 1987a). Healthy individuals also exhibit a nonsuppression of the DST during experimental starving conditions.

Besides weight changes, HPA axis is also affected by acute stress (Baumgartner, Gräf & Kürten, 1985).

We could not find a causal relationship between DST response and depression scores assessed by HAMD and SDS, although depression is alleviated parallel to body weight (see above).

Yet weight loss alone is not sufficient to explain all the findings. Cortisol production rate is elevated in anorexia nervosa (Walsh, Katz, Levin, Kream, Fukushima, Hellman et al. 1978), but diminished in other forms of malnutrition. In protein-caloric malnutrition, all subjects suppress post-DST-cortisol levels after weight recovery (Smith et al., 1975), while some of the anorectic patients do not through weight stabilization.

In the light of studies in affective disorders, we set out to investigate the predictive potential of the DST in anorexia nervosa. These studies (Holsboer, 1983a, b; Maes, De Ruyter, Hubin & Suy, 1986) demonstrated that patients who did not normalize their DST responses were at higher risk for early relapse into depression. According to these experiences we wanted to find out whether normalization of the hypothalamo-pituitary-adrenal axis is also necessary for beneficial outcome in anorexia nervosa.

One year after discharge the follow-up was conducted in those patients who had partici-

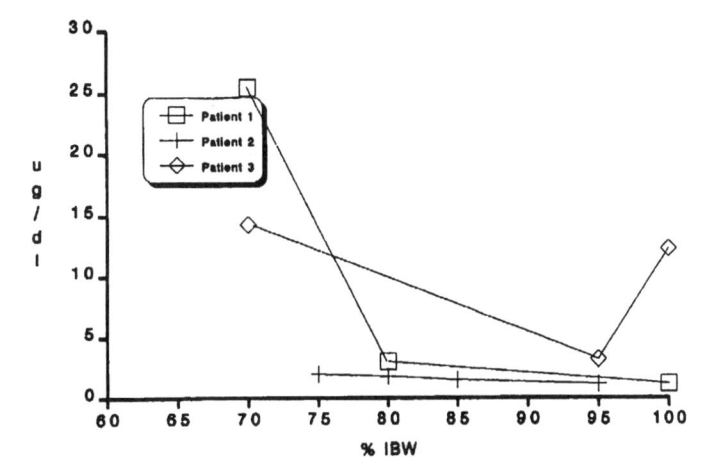

Figure 5. DST patterns in relationship to ideal body weight (in percent of ideal body weight = %IBW). Patient 1: 14-year-old female, illustration of DST type 1 "decreasing"; Patient 2: 13-year-old girl, illustration of type 2 "non-reacting"; Patient 3: 17 year-old boy, illustration of type 3 "increasing."

pated in the DST at three times during inpatient treatment. Before the last assessment they had to be weight-stable for at least 3 weeks. To rule out intermittent starvation, blood sugar and ketone bodies were measured. The DST was performed as described by Caroll et al. (1981) (for methodological details see Herpertz-Dahlmann & Remschmidt, in press). Information according to the Morgan and Russell outcome score (1975) could be obtained from 31 patients. In 15 patients information was available by an outpatient service therapist, in 6 cases we talked to the patient on the phone, and 5 patients answered a questionnaire.

Patients were categorized into four subgroups on the basis of Morgan's and Russell's outcome score: "good," "intermediate," "poor," and an additional fourth category for new admission to hospital because of deterioration of anorexia nervosa (Table 4).

During inpatient treatment, we found three types of DST-profiles:

1) The most common profile was a decrease in post-DST-cortisol levels according to weight gain (Type 1, n=18).

2) Few anorectic patients exhibited similar (mostly normal) post-DST-cortisol levels independent of body weight (Type 2, n=5).

3) Some anorectic patients returned to non-suppression of DST, although they had already presented a normal DST-result after a smaller increase in body weight (Type 3, n=8) (Figure 5).

Relationship between General Outcome Scores and post-DST-cortisol levels at discharge (maximum and mean value of 8.00 a.m., 4 p.m. and 11 p.m. cortisol indices) was tested by use of Spearman's rank correlation.

After weight differences between both groups had been ruled out (U-test by Mann-Whitney-Wilcoxon), the follow-up of patients with DST-profile "Type 1" was compared to those with "Type 3." Because of the small

Table 5. Dexamethasone suppression test (DST) and short-term follow-up (one year) in anorexia nervosa.

Spearman's rank correlation between post-DST cortisol level (in μg/dl) and outcome criteria

a) mean cortisol value (from values at 8 a.m., 4 p.m. and 11 p.m.)
r = 0.4911
n = 31
p ≤ 0.003

b) maximum cortisol value (from values at 8 a.m., 4 p.m. and 11 p.m.)
r = 0.4142
n = 31
p ≤ 0.01

Table 6. DST "profile" and prognosis (1 year) in anorexia nervosa.

No. of patients n=31	Category 1 ("good")	Category 2 ("intermediate")	Category 3 ("poor")	Category 4 (readmission to hospital)
Type 1 "descending" n=18	13 (50%)	1 (3.8%)	2 (7.7%)	2 (7.7%)
Type 3 "ascending" n=8	1 (3.8%)	1 (3.8%)	2 (7.7%)	4 (15.4%)
U-test (Mann-Whitney-Wilcoxon): U = 26.0, $p \leq 0.005$				
Type 2 "nonreacting" n=5	2			3

sample size, testing was carried out by nonparametric methods (U-test by Mann-Whitney-Wilcoxon).

There was a highly significant association between the post-DST-cortisol plasma value in weight-restored patients at discharge and the 1-year follow-up (Table 5).

Patients who failed to suppress cortisol at discharge had a poorer short-term prognosis. Consequently, the comparisons of the DST profiles revealed a highly significant difference concerning the 1-year follow-up. Of 18 patients with DST profile "type 1," 13 were assigned to the outcome score "good," but only 1 of 8 subjects with "type 3" (Table 6).

These results demonstrated that weight-restored anorexia nervosa patients who fail to suppress cortisol at discharge seem to be at higher risk for a poor short-term outcome than those whose DST results were normal.

Although the results of our study are limited by the small sample size and indirect methods of follow-up (no personal interview), it appears that reversion to a positive DST result might reflect a stress response in patients who failed to recover completely though weight stabilization. HPA activation is more pronounced in situations in which threatening events (e.g., in our sample being afraid to live in the family again or to go back to school) are anticipated and is also related to type and effectiveness of psychological defences against anxiety factors (Mason, 1975). Adolescents and adults hospitalized for psychiatric and physical illness and who had low social support or poor coping skills had more pronounced hypercortisolism than those with high social support and good coping skills (Levine quoted in Abou-Saleh et al., 1985).

Several authors demonstrated that the mean level of CRH in the cerebrospinal fluid of anorectic patients was higher than in control subjects. According to the current literature, hypersecretion of CRH is the cause of nonsuppression in the DST (for a review see Kathol, Jaeckle, Lopez & Meller, 1989).

Stress might lead to a new rise of CRH in vulnerable weight-corrected anorectics. CRH is known to be a potent anorectic agent that appears to be responsible for some of the typical disturbances seen in anorexia nervosa, like increased physical activity and decrease of libido (Gold, Gwirtsman & Gerner, 1986; Hotta, Shibash & Masurd, 1986; Morley & Blundell, 1988). We presume that stress at discharge followed by an elevation of CRH might start the anorectic circle again.

Although CRH is also elevated in CSF of depressive patients and reversion to nonsuppression is a predictive tool in affective illness, we do not think that the present study points to a common etiology of both conditions. Nonsuppression in the DST might rather be an unspecific response to stress-related factors that probably play an important role in the origin of both disorders.

Conclusions

Although at first view there seem to be many similarities between anorexia nervosa and depression, many of them do not hold up to a second glance or even rise more questions:

1) As described above, there is a high rate of affective disorders in the families of anorexia nervosa patients, but no familial loading for eating disorders in adolescent depression could be found. Thus, these findings do not point to a simple genetic kinship. Further studies should concentrate on anorexia nervosa patients with an elevated rate of depressive conditions in their families. It would be important to know whether this subgroup has a poorer prognosis and is more likely to develop major depressive disorder.

2) Psychopathological phenomena in anorexia nervosa that proved to be characteristic of primary affective disorder are at least in part weight-dependent symptoms. From this point of view, especially weight-restored anorexia nervosa patients who still suffer from depression seem to be interesting for follow-up studies.

3) Neuroendocrinological disturbances in anorexia nervosa are often the result of starvation, although some of them did not improve with weight gain. Perhaps starvation-linked neuroendocrinological and neurotransmitter changes might serve as a trigger mechanism for development of depression in those patients who have an elevated genetic vulnerability for affective disorder.

4) On the other hand, in affective disorders a lot of patients suffer from weight loss, which might induce neuroendocrinological changes similar to those found in anorexia nervosa. Further, there seems to be an important role for stress-provoked alterations in both conditions.

As far as we know today, differences in both disorders appear to be more important than congruences. With respect to therapy, each of the two diseases needs a specialized treatment approach—in anorexia nervosa weight gain seems to be the most potent antidepressive drug. In some patients anorexia nervosa and affective disorder may overlap, and one disorder might exacerbate the other. Further studies will clarify these interrelations.

References

Abou-Saleh, M. T., Oleesky, D., Crisp, A. H., & Lacey, J. H. (1983). Dexamethasone suppression test and energy balance in eating disorders. *Acta Psychiatrica Scandinavica, 732,* 242–251.

Abou-Saleh, M. T. (1985). Dexamethasone suppression tests in psychiatry: Is there a place for an integrated hypothesis? *Psychiatric Developments, 3,* 275–305.

Althoff, P.-H., Schifferdecker, E., & Neubauer, M. (1986). Anorexia nervosa—endokrine Veränderungen. *Medizinische Klinik, 81,* 795–803.

Altshuler, K. Z., & Weiner, M. F. (1985). Anorexia nervosa and depression: A dissenting view. *American Journal of Psychiatry, 142,* 328–332.

Amsterdam, J. D., Winokur, A., Caroff, S., & Snyder, P. (1983). Gonadotropin release after administration of GnRH in depressed patients and healthy volunteers. *Journal of Affective Disorders, 3,* 367–380.

Arana, G. W., Baldessarini, R. J., & Ornsteen, M. (1985). The dexamethasone suppression test for diagnosis and prognosis in psychiatry. *Archives of General Psychiatry, 42,* 1193–1204.

Baumgartner, A., Gräf, K. J., & Kürten, I. (1985). The dexamethasone suppression test in depression, in schizophrenia, and during experimental stress. *Biological Psychiatry, 20,* 675–679.

Beumont, P. J. V., George, G. C. W., Pimstone, B. L., & Vinik, A. I. (1976). Body weight and the pituitary response to hypothalamic releasing hormones in patients with anorexia nervosa. *Journal of Clinical Endocrinology and Metabolism, 43,* 487–496.

Biederman, J., Rivinus, T., Kemper, K., Hamilton, D., MacFayden, J., & Harmatz, J. (1985). Depressive disorders in relatives of anorexia nervosa patients with and without a current episode of nonbipolar major depression. *American Journal of Psychiatry, 142,* 1495–1497.

Brambilla, F., Smeraldi, E., Sacchetti, E., Negri, F., Cocchi, D., & Mueller, E. E. (1978). Deranged anterior pituitary responsiveness to hypothalamic hormones in depressed patients. *Archives of General Psychiatry, 35,* 1231–1238.

Buvat, J., Lemaire, A., Buvat-Herbaut, M., Lepretre, P., & Fourlinnie, J. C. (1983). Psychoneuroendocrine investigations in 115 cases of female anorexia nervosa at the time of their maximum emaciation. *International Journal of Eating Disorders, 2,* 117–128.

Carroll, B. J., Feinberg, M., Greden, J. F., Tarika, J., Albala, A. A., Haskett, R. F., James, N. M., Kronfol, Z., Lohr, N., Steiner, M., Vigne, J. P. de, & Young, E.(1981). A specific laboratory test for the diagnosis of melancholia. *Archives of General Psychiatry, 38,* 15–22.

Casper, R. C., & Frohman, L. A. (1982). Delayed TSH release in anorexia nervosa following injection of thyrotropin-releasing hormone (TRH). *Psychoneuroendocrinology, 7,* 59–68.

Ceaser, M. (1979). Hunger in anorexia nervosa. *American Journal of Psychiatry, 136,* 979–980.

Channon, S., & DeSilva, W. P. (1985). Psychological correlates of weight gain in patients with anorexia nervosa. *Journal of Psychiatric Research, 19,* 267–271.

Eckert, E. D., Goldberg, S. C., Halmi, K. A., Casper, R. C., & Davis, J. M. (1982). Depression in anorexia nervosa. *Psychological Medicine, 12,* 115–122.

Fichter, M. M. (1985). *Magersucht und Bulimia.* Berlin, Heidelberg, New York, Tokyo: Springer-Verlag.

Fichter, M. M. (1987). The anorexia nervosa of Franz Kafka. *International Journal of Eating Disorders, 6,* 367–377.

Fichter, M. M., & Keeser, W. (1980). Das Anorexia-Inventar zur Selbstbeurteilung (ANIS). *Archives of Psychiatry and Neurological Sciences, 228,* 67–89.

Freud, S. (1916). Trauer und Melancholie. *Gesammelte Werke X.* London: Imago.

Garfinkel, P. E. (1974). Perception of hunger and satiety in anorexia nervosa. *Psychological Medicine, 4,* 309–315.

Gershon, E. S., Schreiber, J. L., Hamovit, J. R., Dibble, E. D., Kaye, W., Nurnberger, J. I., Andersen, A. E., & Ebert, M. (1984). Clinical findings in patients with anorexia nervosa and affective illness in their relatives. *American Journal of Psychiatry, 141,* 1419–1422.

Gold, P. W., Gwirtsman, H., Avgerinos, P. C., Nieman, L. K., Gallucci, W. T., Kaye, W., Jimerson, D., Egbert, M., Rittmaster, R., Loriaux, L., & Chrousos, G. P. (1986). Abnormal hypothalamic-pituitary-adrenal function in anorexia nervosa. *New England Journal of Medicine, 314,* 1335–1342.

Gwirtsman, H. E., & Gerner, R. H. (1981). Neurochemical abnormalities in anorexia nervosa: Similarities to affective disorders. *Biological Psychiatry, 16,* 991–995.

Hall, A., Slim, E., Hawker, F., & Salmond, C. (1984). Anorexia nervosa: Long-term outcome in 50 female patients. *British Journal of Psychiatry, 145,* 407–413.

Halmi, K. A., Eckert, E., & LaDu, T. J. (1986). Anorexia nervosa: Treatment efficacy of cyproheptadine and amitriptyline. *Archives of General Psychiatry, 43,* 177–181.

Hamilton, M. (1960). A rating scale of depression. *Journal of Neurology, Neurosurgery and Psychiatry, 23,* 56–62.

Hendren, R. L. (1983). Depression in anorexia nervosa. *Journal of the American Academy of Child Psychiatry, 22,* 59–62.

Herpertz-Dahlmann, B., & Remschmidt, H. (1989). Anorexia Nervosa und Depression. *Der Nervenarzt, 60,* 490–495.

Herpertz-Dahlmann, B., & Remschmidt, H. (1987b). Der Aussagewert des Dexamethason-Suppressions-Testes bei Anorexia Nervosa. *Monatsschrift Kinderheilkunde, 135,* 758–762.

Herpertz-Dahlmann, B., & Remschmidt, H. (1987a). Depressive Symptomatik und Dexamethason-Suppressions-Test im stationären Behandlungsverlauf der Anorexia Nervosa. *Der Nervenarzt, 58,* 610–616.

Herpertz-Dahlmann, B., & Remschmidt, H. (in press). Die prognostische Aussagekraft des Dexamethason-Suppressions-Testes für den Verlauf der Anorexia Nervosa im Vergleich mit depressiven Erkrankungen. *Zeitschrift für Kinder- und Jugendpsychiatrie.*

Herpertz-Dahlmann, B. (1988). Familiäre Belastungen mit affektiven Erkrankungen von Patienten mit Anorexia Nervosa. *Zeitschrift für Kinder- und Jugendpsychiatrie, 16,* 14–19.

Herzog, D. B. (1984). Are anorexic and bulimic patients depressed? *American Journal of Psychiatry, 141,* 1594–1597.

Hoffman, G. W., Ellinwood, E. H., Rockwell, W. J. K., Herfkens, R. J., Nishita, J. K., & Guthrie, L. F. (1989). Cerebral atrophy in anorexia nervosa: A pilot study. *Biological Psychiatry 26,* 321–323.

Holsboer, F., Steiger, A., & Maier, W. (1983a). Four cases of reversion to abnormal dexamethasone suppression test response as indicator of clinical response: A preliminary report. *Biological Psychiatry, 18,* 911–912.

Holsboer, F. (1983b). Prediction of clinical course by dexamethasone suppression test (DST) response in depressed patients: Physiological and clinical construct validity of the DST. *Pharmacopsychiatry, 16,* 186–191.

Holsboer, F. (1988). Neuroendokrine Regulation bei affektiven Störungen. In D. v. Zerssen & H. J. Möller (Eds.), *Affektive Störungen* (pp. 165–180). Berlin, Heidelberg, New York, Tokyo: Springer-Verlag.

Hotta, M., Shibash, T., & Masurd, A. (1986). The response of plasma adrenocorticotropin and cortisol to corticotropin-releasing hormone (CRH) and cerebrospinal fluid immunoreactive CRH in anorexia nervosa patients. *Journal of Clinical Endocrinology and Metabolism, 62,* 319–324.

Hudson, J. I., & Hudson, M. S. (1984). Endocrine dysfunction in anorexia nervosa and bulimia: Comparison with abnormalities in other psychiatric disorders and disturbances due to metabolic factors. *Psychiatric Developments, 4,* 237–272.

Hudson, J. I., Pope, H. G. Jr., Jonas, J. M., & Yurgelun-Todd, D. (1983a). Phenomenologic relationship of eating disorders to major affective disorder. *Psychiatry Research, 9,* 345–354.

Hudson, J. I., Pope, H. G. Jr., Jonas, J. M., & Yurgelun-Todd, D. (1983b). Family history study of anorexia nervosa and bulimia. *British Journal of Psychiatry, 142,* 133–138.

Isaacs, A. J., Leslie, R. D. G., Gomez, J., & Sir Bayliss, R. (1980). The effect of weight gain on gonadotropins and prolactin in anorexia nervosa. *Acta Endocrinologica, 94,* 145–150.

Kathol, R. G., Jaeckle, R. S., Lopez, J. F., & Meller, W. H. (1989). Pathophysiology of HPA axis abnormalities in patients with major depression: An update. *American Journal of Psychiatry, 146,* 311–317.

Katz, J. L., Boyar, R., Roffwarg, H., Hellman, L., & Weiner, H. (1978). Weight and circadian luteinizing hormone secretory pattern in anorexia nervosa. *Psychosomatic Medicine, 40,* 549–567.

Keys, A., Brozek, J., Henschel, A., Mickolsen, O., & Taylor, H. L. (1950). *The biology of human starvation.* Minneapolis: University of Minneapolis Press.

Khan, A. (1988). Sensitivity and specificity of TRH stimulation test in depressed and nondepressed adolescents. *Psychiatry Research, 25,* 11–19.

Kiriike, N., Nishiwaki, S., Izumiya, Y., Maeda, Y., & Kawakita, Y. (1987). Thyrotropin, prolactin and growth hormone responses to thyrotropin-releasing hormone in anorexia nervosa and bulimia. *Biological Psychiatry, 22,* 167–176.

Kiriike, N., Nishiwaki, S., Nagata, T., Maeda, Y., & Kawakita, Y. (1988). Gonadotropin response to LH-RH in anorexia nervosa and bulimia. *Acta Psychiatrica Scandinavica, 77,* 420–427.

Kiyohara, K., Tamai, H., Karibe, C., Kobayashi, N., Fujii, S., Fukino, O., Nakagawa, T., Kumagai, L. F., & Nagataki, S. (1987). Serum thyrotropin (TSH) responses to thyrotropin-releasing hormone (TRH) in patients with anorexia nervosa and bulimia: Influence of changes in body weight and eating disorders. *Psychoneuroendocrinology, 12,* 21–28.

Krieg, J.-C., Pirke, K.-M., Lauer, C., & Backmund, H. (1988). Endocrine, metabolic and cranial computed tomographic findings in anorexia nervosa. *Biological Psychiatry, 23,* 377–387.

Kuhs, H., & Mester, H. (1985). Der Dexamethason-Suppressions-Test bei Anorexia Nervosa. *European Archives of Psychiatry and Neurological Sciences, 234,* 335–340.

Kunze, D. (1977). Alters/Größen- und Größen/Gewichtsbeziehung dargestellt als neue Perzentilenkurve. *Kinderarzt, 8,* 979.

Laessle, R. G., Kittl, S., Fichter, M. M., Wittchen, H.-U., & Pirke, K. M. (1987). Major affective disorder in anorexia nervosa and bulimia: A descriptive diagnostic Study. *British Journal of Psychiatry, 151,* 785–789.

Laessle, R. G., Schweiger, U., & Pirke, K. M. (1988). Depression as a correlate of starvation in patients with eating disorders. *Biological Psychiatry, 23,* 719–725.

Lauer, Ch., Krieg, J. Ch., Zulley, J., Riemann, D., & Berger, M. (1989). Der Schlaf bei Anorexia nervosa, Bulimia nervosa und depressiven Erkrankungen. Eine polysomnographische Vergleichsstudie. *Fortschritte der Neurologie und Psychiatrie, 57,* 403–410.

Leichner, P., & Gentler, A. (1988). Prevalence and incidence studies of anorexia nervosa. In B. J. Blinder, B. F. Chaitin & R. S. Goldstein (Eds.), *The eating disorders* (pp. 131–150). New York: PMA Publishing Corp.

Lemaire, A., Ardaens, K., Lepretre, J., Racadot, A., Buvat-Herbaut, M., & Buvat, J. (1983). Gonadal hormones in male anorexia nervosa. *International Journal of Eating Disorders, 2,* 135–144.

Leslie, R. D. G., Isaacs, A. J., Gomez, J., Raggatt, P. R., & Bayliss, R. (1978). Hypothalamo-pituitary-thyroid function in anorexia nervosa: Influence of weight gain. *British Medical Journal, 2,* 526–528.

Levy, A. B., Dixon, K. N., & Schmidt, H. (1988). Sleep architecture in anorexia nervosa and bulimia. *Biological Psychiatry, 23,* 99–101.

Loosen, P. T., Prange, A. J., & Wilson, I. C. (1978). Influence of cortisol on TRH-induced TSH response in depression. *American Journal of Psychiatry, 135,* 244–246.

Maes, M., De Ruyter, M., Hobin, P., & Suy, E. (1986). Repeated dexamethasone suppression test in depressed patients. *Journal of Affective Disorders, 11,* 165–172.

Mason, J. W. (1975). A historical view of the stress field. *Journal of Human Stress, 196,* 12–20.

Meyer, J. K. (1985). Disorders in sexual function. In J. Wilson & D. Foster (Eds.), *Textbook of endocrinology* (pp. 476–491). Philadelphia: Saunders.

Morgan, H. G., & Hayward, A. E. (1988). Clinical assessment of anorexia nervosa: The Morgan-Russell outcome assessment schedule. *British Journal of Psychiatry, 152,* 367–371.

Morgan, H. G., & Russell, G. F. M. (1975). Value of family background and clinical features as predictors of long-term outcome in anorexia nervosa: Four-year follow-up study of 41 patients. *Psychological Medicine, 5,* 355–371.

Morley, J. E., & Blundell, J. E. (1988). The neurobiological basis of eating disorders: Some formulations. *Biological Psychiatry, 23,* 53–78.

Müller, B., & Böning, J. (1988). Changes in the pituitary-thyroid axis accompanying major affective disorders. *Acta Psychiatrica Scandinavica, 77,* 143–150.

Newman, M. M., & Halmi, K. A. (1988). The endocrinology of anorexia nervosa and bulimia nervosa. *Endocrinology and Metabolism Clinics of North America, 17,* 195–212.

Pahl, J., Pirke, K. M., Schweiger, U., Warnhoff, M., Gerlinghoff, M., Brinkmann, W., Berger, M., & Krieg, C. (1985). Anorectic behavior, mood, metabolic and endocrine adaptation to starvation in anorexia nervosa during inpatient treatment. *Biological Psychiatry, 20,* 874–887.

Piran, N., Kennedy, S., Garfinkel, P. E., & Owens, M. (1985). Affective disturbances in eating disorders. *The Journal of Nervous and Mental Disease, 173,* 395–400.

Propping, P. (1989). *Psychiatrische Genetik.* Berlin, Heidelberg, New York, Tokyo: Springer-Verlag.

Remschmidt, H., & Schmidt, M. (1986). *Multiaxiales Klassifikationsschema für psychiatrische Erkrankungen im Kindes- und Jugendalter nach Rutter.* Bern, Stuttgart, Wien: Huber.

Rigaud, D., Bedig, G., Merrouche, M., Vulpillat, M., Bonfils, S., & Apfelbaum, M. (1988). Delayed gastric emptying in anorexia nervosa is improved by completion of a renutrition program. *Digestive Diseases and Sciences, 33,* 919–925.

Rivinus, T. M., Biederman, J., Herzog, D. B., Kemper, K., Harper, G. P., Harmatz, J. S., & Houseworth, S. (1984). Anorexia nervosa and affective disorders: A controlled family history study. *American Journal of Psychiatry, 141,* 1414–1418.

Robinson, P. H. (1989). Perceptivity and paraceptivity during measurement of gastric emptying in anorexia and bulimia nervosa. *The British Journal of Psychiatry, 154,* 400–421.

Roy, A., Karoum, F., Linnoila, M., & Pickar, D. (1980). Thyrotropin releasing hormone test in unipolar depressed patients and controls: Relationship to clinical and biological variables. *Acta Psychiatrica Scandinavica, 77,* 151–159.

Schiele, B. C., & Brozek, J. (1948). "Experimental neurosis" resulting from semistarvation in man. *Psychosomatic Medicine, 10,* 31–50.

Schildkraut, J. J. (1978). Current status of the catecholamine hypothesis of affective disorders. In M. A. Lipton, A. DiMascio & K. F. Killam (Eds.), *Psychopharmacology. A generation of progress.* New York: Raven.

Smith, S. R., Bledsoe, T., & Chetri, M. K. (1975). Cortisol metabolism and the pituitary adrenal axis in adults with protein calorie malnutrition. *Journal of Clinical Endocrinology and Metabolism, 49,* 43–52.

Strober, M., & Katz, J. L. (1987). Do eating disorders and affective disorders share a common etiology? A dissenting opinion. *International Journal of Eating Disorders, 6,* 171–180.

Thomä, H. (1967). *Anorexia nervosa.* New York: International Universities Press.

Toner, B. B., Garfinkel, P. E., & Garner, D. M. (1986). Long-term follow-up of anorexia nervosa. *Psychosomatic Medicine, 48,* 520–529.

Unden, F., Ljunggren, J. G., Beck-Friis, J., Kjellman, B. F., & Wetterberg, L. (1988). Hypothalamic-pituitary-gonadal axis in major depressive disorders. *Acta Psychiatrica Scandinavica, 78,* 138–146.

Vigersky, A., & Loriaux, D. L. (1977). Anorexia nervosa as a model of hypothalamic dysfunction. In R. A. Vigersky (Ed.), *Anorexia nervosa* (pp. 109–115). New York: Raven.

Walsh, B. T., Katz, J. L., Levin, J., Kream, J., Fukushima, D. K., Hellman, L. D., Weiner, H., & Zumoff, B. (1978). Adrenal activity in anorexia nervosa. *Psychosomatic Medicine, 40,* 499–505.

Weiner, H. (1985). The physiology of eating disorders. *International Journal of Eating Disorders, 4,* 347–388.

Willi, J., Limacher, B., & Nussbaum, P. (1989). 10-Jahres-Katamnese der 1973–1975 im Kanton Zürich erstmals hospitalisierten Anorexia-Fälle. *Schweizer medizinische Wochenschrift, 119,* 147–155.

Winokur, A., Amsterdam, J., Caroff, S., Snyder, P. J., & Brunswick, D. (1982). Variability of hormonal responses to a series of neuroendocrine challenges in depressed patients. *American Journal of Psychiatry, 139,* 39–44.

Zerssen, D. von, Berger, M., & Doerr, P. (1987). Neuroendocrinological studies on depression with special reference to research at the Max-Planck-Institute of Psychiatry. *Pharmacopsychiatry, 20,* 8–22.

Zung, W. W. K. (1972). The Depression Status Inventory: An adjunct to the Self-Rating Depression Scale. *Journal of Clinical Psychology, 28,* 539–543.

Zutt, J. (1948). Das psychiatrische Krankheitsbild der Pubertätsmagersucht. *Archiv für Psychiatrie und Nervenkrankheiten, 180,* 776–849.

Self-Perception of Anorectic and Normal-Weight Adolescents

G. Lehmkuhl*, H. Flechtner*, I. Woerner**, W. Woerner**, J. Masberg**

Aspects of self-perception and appraisal of the body are of great importance for symptomatology, course of diseasse, and therapy of anorexia nervosa. Two empirical studies were used to investigate whether anorexia nervosa patients differ from a normal-weight control group regarding body image; and to what extent variables like weight, age, and attitudes toward food influence the subjective assessment of the body. Using a specially designed procedure consisting of 12 distorted pictures of the same person, only in 20% of the patients were ideal and real image identical. A comparable result, however, was found within the control group. After inpatient treatment, patients rated themselves in the mean more attractive and experienced their body image as less divergent from their ideal image found at the beginning of treatment.

Self-perception and self-appraisal play important roles in the symptoms, course of disease, and therapy of anorexia nervosa. The particular significance of body image is reflected, for instance, in body-oriented therapeutic concepts, like the one suggested by Vandereycken, Depreitere and Probst (1987). The aim of these interventions is to reduce hyperactive behavior, to obtain a realistic self-concept, to gain pleasure in one's body, and to develop social competences. According to Wooley and Wooley (1985), the main goal is to attain greater awareness of the distortion in body image, thereby lessening the distortion and clarifying the relationship between negative body image and disordered eating. Though distortion in body image belongs to the cardinal symptoms of anorexia nervosa—among other such as a disturbed perception of affective and visceral stimuli and a piercing feeling of ineffectiveness, as described by Bruch (1973)—numerous studies have led to very divergent results (Fichter & Meermann, 1981; Meermann & Fichter, 1982; Garfinkel, Moldofsky & Garner, 1979; Niebel, 1987; Cash & Brown, 1987). Challenging these in part contradictory results, Hsu (1982) asked whether there is any specific distortion of body image in anorectic patients. The critical objections are related to the methodological difficulties in determining distortions of body image. According to Meermann and Fichter (1982), on the one hand, these difficulties concern the various methods of investigation, like photography, video pictures, mirror images, marker method, and special questionnaires. On the other hand, these difficulties result from the often heterogeneous and hardly comparable samples of patients and controls. Body image is influenced mainly by age at onset of symptoms and by the time of measurement during the course of disease (Halmi, Goldberg & Cunningham, 1977; Garner, Garfinkel, Stancer & Moldofsky, 1976; Button, Fransella & Slade, 1977). While Garfinkel, Moldofsky and Garner (1979) found—independent of weight gain—no change in anorectic patients in overestimating own body size over a period of 1 year, Proctor and Morley (1986) were able to identify in these patients at the same time very differently disturbed perceptions, depending on the respective test instructions. Thompson and Dolce (1989) and Thompson, Dolce, Spana and Register (1987) showed that different test instructions led to differences in estimating own body even in women without eating disorders. The authors distinguish between emotional ratings based on how one

---

*Department of Child and Adolescent Psychiatry, University of Cologne, West Germany.
**Department of Child and Adolescent Psychiatry, Central Institute for Mental Health, Mannheim, West Germany.

"felt" about the body and elicited ratings that were larger than actual and larger than ideal size measures. Size ratings based on rational instructions were no different from actual sizes, though they were larger than ideal ratings. These empirical findings suggest that clear specification of experimental procedures in body-image research is very important.

Taking reference to the statement of Shonz (1974), that the concept of a disturbed body image can only be of significance if it contributes to the understanding of etiology, course of disease, and prognosis of anorexia nervosa, we tried to clarify the following questions in two empirical studies:

- Do adolescent patients with anorexia nervosa have, besides the eating disorder, a different estimation of their own body compared to a healthy control group?
- Do significant relationships exist between weight, age at start of treatment, and attitude toward food, on the one hand, and the subjective perception of one's own body on the other?
- Do disturbances in body image persist in patients with anorexia nervosa after a catamnestic time interval of several years?

Patients and Methods

Trial I

Sample I comprised 27 girls who were recruited to the study within 14 consecutive months. All had come for inpatient treatment because of anorectic symptoms. They fulfilled the Feighner criteria as well as the diagnostic criteria of DSM-III, including the required weight loss. Duration of symptoms before admission was a mean of 15.3 months. In most cases, a few treatment attempts on an outpatient basis had already failed, and 7 patients had already been treated as inpatients. The mean weight loss was 15.7 kg, and the mean weight at admission was 38.7 kg (Table 1).

The control group was recruited from a high school and comprised 61 girls without any eating disorders. We used whole school classes (no refusals) from A and B courses to have cognitive abilities comparable to those in the patient group. From this sample we drew a control group of the same size as the patient group, using age and height as matching criteria (Table 1).

Trial II

The second sample consisted of 20 patients who had been treated as inpatients for anorexia nervosa a mean of 5.5 years ago. The catamnestic time interval was 3 to 7.8 years. At the time of reexamination, they were a mean 20;11 years old and had a mean weight of 55 kg with a mean height of 165 cm. Only 4 patients weighed less than 85% of their ideal weight. Results from these patients were compared to a control group of normal weight, corresponding age, and without psychiatric disorders (Table 1).

Table 1. Trial I and Trial II—Sample characteristics (Mann-Whitney u-test). *p≤0.001.

Group n		Trial I Anorexia nervosa 27	Trial I Control group 27	Trial II Anorexia nervosa 20	Trial II Control group 20
Age (years)	x	15;4	15;1	20;11	20;9
	s	1;2	1;2	2;1	0;11
Weight (kg)	x	38.7	57.6*	55.5	59.1
	s	6.4	10.4	9.6	9.2
Height (cm)	x	162	163	165	167
	s	8.5	8.7	8.8	4.7
Weight/height × 100	x	23.9	35.1*	33.4	35.2
	s	3.5	5.4	5.2	4.9

Instruments

Trial I

Within a week after admission, a structured interview was carried out, covering symptoms, self-assessment, and family relations (Sian-Ex, Fichter & Meermann, 1981). As instrument for self-rating of eating habits, anorectic symptoms, and attitudes, we employed the *Eating Attitude Test* (EAT-26) of Garner and Garfinkel (1979). Factor analysis yielded three scales: *Dietary Habits, Bulimia and Obsession by Eating,* and *Oral Control*. The authors published psychometric and clinical standardization data from large samples of female anorectic patients and controls.

As standardized method to inquire about attitudes toward one's own body, we used an appropriate questionnaire developed by Strauss and Appelt (1983). It consists of 52 items forming 3 scales: *Insecurity/Dysesthesia, Attractiveness/Self-Confidence,* and *Accentuation of the Body/Sensitivity*. The factor *Insecurity/Dysesthesia* comprises expression of lack of sensitivity as well as insecurity and refusal of appearance and bodily reactions. The items of the scale *Attractiveness/Self-Confidence* describe a positive view of one's own body. Among expressions of satisfaction and identification, statements about one's own attractiveness, confidence in one's own body and its reactions belong to that factor. The third scale, *Accentuation of the body/Sensitivity,* deals with the significance of body appearance and personal hygiene as well as with "judgements about the appeal of one's own body to others, sensitivity toward appearance and body changes as well as concern about one's health and bodily function" (Strauss & Appelt, 1983), in the sense of a hypochondriac-depressive, conscious concern with one's own body. No validity data have been published for the questionnaire of Strauss and Appelt (1983). The authors report on a negative correlation of the scale *Insecurity/Dysesthesia* with a self-confidence questionnaire. Investigations regarding differential validity yielded a good discriminant function for separating groups with eating disorders and healthy controls. According to Strauss and Appelt (1983), reliability coefficients (internal consistency, Cronbach alpha) for scales 1, 2, and 3 are .82, .75, and .74 (n = 527). The corresponding values for girls between 10 and 16 years of age are .63, .74, and .59 (n = 61) (Rauch, 1984).

Data on the course of disease are available from 12 anorectic patients investigated with the described instruments within the first week of admission and in the last week before discharge. The time interval between test and retest was 26.4 weeks. Because of the small sample size, statistical analyses of the mean values comparisons were carried out with nonparametric procedures (U-test, Wilcoxon, Spearman rank correlations).

Trial II

Patients were asked to select their body image from 12 pictures of the same person, showing images ranging from 75% up to 130% body size, in 5% increments. They had to estimate their real and their ideal size. In addition to different clinical parameters, a structured interview for symptoms, self-assessment, and family relations (Sian-Ex, Fichter & Meermann, 1981) was carried out as well as an assessment of prognosis using the criteria of Morgan and Russell (1975).

Results

Trial I

A summary of the results concerning the specific anorectic symptoms, obtained by the structured interview on anorexia nervosa symptoms of Fichter and Meermann (1981), is given in Table 2. Supervalent thoughts about food, a marked ideal of slenderness, deliberate fasting, and hyperactivity were striking in almost all patients, whereas vomiting and laxative abuse were less frequent as means of weight reduction. Given equal height, the mean difference in body weight between anorexia nervosa patients and the control group was 18.9 kg. No significant differences were present with regard to age and height (Table 1).

On the questionnaire, patients with anorexia nervosa attain significantly higher scores (i.e., are more disturbed) on all three scales of the EAT-26 than the controls (Table 3). On the instrument of Strauss and Appelt (1983) for body attitudes, patients show an increased insecurity and more physical unwellness than nonanorectic adolescents, whereas attractiveness, self-confidence, and satisfaction with appearance are rated significantly lower. Concern about physical health in the sense of a hypochondriac-depressive concern with appearance is significantly more promi-

Table 2. Trial I—Results from the structured interview regarding specific symptoms of anorexia nervosa (SIAN-EX, n = 27).

	Not or low pronounced	Clear or strong pronounced
Supervalent thoughts about food	2	25
Marked ideal of slenderness	3	24
Deliberate fasting	1	26
Bulimia	13	14
Deliberate vomiting	17	10
Abuse of laxatives	19	8
Hyperactivity	5	22
Disturbances in the perception of internal stimuli (hunger, fatigue, temperature)	8	19

Table 3. Trial I—Mean values comparisons of EAT-26 and questionnaire for body attitudes, anorectic versus normal-weight adolescents, and comparison with data from the literature (U-test, unilateral).

		Adolescents Own study		Steinhausen 1985	Adults Garner et al. 1982	
Instrument scale	Item numbers	Anorexia nervosa n=27	Normal-weight control groups n=27	Anorexia nervosa n=18	Anorexia nervosa n=160	Control group n=140
EAT-26						
Diet	13	13.1	5.1***	11.1	19.9	7.1***
Bulimia	6	5.1	0.9***	2.6	8.0	1.0***
Eating control	7	8.7	1.8***	8.6	8.3	1.9***
					Strauss & Appelt 1983	
Questionnaire for Body Attitudes		n=27	n=27		n=27	n=27
Insecurity/ dysesthesia	19	7.4	4.9**		8.7	4.4***
Attractiveness/ self-confidence	13	3.9	6.4**		5.0	9.9***
Accentuation/ sensitivity	20	12.4	10.8*		11.9	12.2

*p<0.05, **p<0.01, ***p<0.001

Table 4. Trial I—Correlation of scores (EAT-26 and Questionnaire for Body Attitudes) with weight and age (Spearman r, bilateral).

Instrument		Weight/height quotient		Age	
		Anorexia nervosa n=27	Normal-weight adolescents n=27	Anorexia nervosa n=27	Normal-weight adolescents n=27
EAT-26	Diet	.43*	.65***	.18	−.13
	Bulimia	.14	.03	.44*	.19
	Eating control	.08	−.37*	.39*	.10
Questionnaire for Body Attitudes	Insecurity/ dysesthesia	.07	.28	.29	−.09
	Attractiveness/ self-confidence	.10	−.35*	.01	.19
	Accentuation/ sensitivity	.12	−.03	.31	.02

Table 5. Trial I—Mean values comparisons (EAT-26 and Questionnaire for Body Attitudes) in anorexia nervosa patients: Time to admission to hospital versus time at discharge from hospital.

Variable		Time at admission n=12	Time at discharge n=12
Weight (kg)		36.4	46.7***
EAT-26	Diet	13.1	8.3*
	Bulimia	5.0	2.1
	Eating control	8.8	5.3
Questionnaire for Body Attitudes	Insecurity/ dysesthesia	7.9	6.2*
	Attractiveness/ self-confidence	3.3	4.9
	Accentuation/ sensitivity	13.3	13.3

*p<0.05, ***p<0.001

nent in anorectic girls than in the control group (Table 3). In order to obtain a comparison with data from other clinical samples of adolescents and adult anorexia nervosa patients, results from Steinhausen (1985), Garner and Garfinkel (1979), and Strauss and Appelt (1983) have been added to our own results in Table 3.

The correlation between weight/height quotient and age as well as the data from EAT-26 and the questionnaire for body attitudes are shown in Table 4. In both groups higher weight/height quotient run parallel to enhanced dietary behavior, but only in the control group is the own eating pattern simultaneously regarded as less controlled. In the control group there is a relationship between attractiveness and lower weight in the questionnaire for body attitudes. But only in anorectic adolescents does age have a significant influence on the results from the questionnaires. Older patients more often show bulimic behavior and increased eating control.

As to the questionnaire for body attitudes, neither for the patients with anorexia nervosa nor for the adolescents of the control group were further distinct influences of weight and age found.

Subsample patients, reexamined at discharge from the hospital, had achieved a median increase in weight of 10.3 kg. At their second examination, the patients rated their eating behavior as significantly less disturbed

Table 6. Trial II—Assessment of body perception.

	Anorexia nervosa n=20	Control group n=20
Real = ideal image	5 (26%)	8 (31%)
Real > ideal image	13 (61%)	12 (69%)
Real < ideal image	2 (13%)	–

on all three scales of the EAT-26, although the scores obtained were still clearly above those of a healthy control group (Table 5). Similar results were derived from the questionnaire for body attitudes: A decrease in insecurity and dysesthesia in experiencing one's own body is accompanied by an increase in ratings of the one's own attractiveness and self-confidence. At the end of the inpatient treatment, however, these scores still differ markedly from those of the control group, whereas the hypochondriac-depressive concern with one's own appearance remains unchanged over the time of treatment (Table 5).

Trial II

Of the catamnestically reexamined patients, 35% had a good, 56% an average, and 9% an unfavorable prognosis according to the criteria of Morgan and Russell (1975). Fifty percent of the girls reported an improvement of symptoms, 27% experienced no change, and 23% had a deterioration of symptoms. In 10 cases a further period of anorexia nervosa occurred, 5 of which took place in the first year.

In assessing the body image, real and ideal image were in accordance in only 20%. A comparable result, however, was obtained from the normal weight control group (Table 6). Extreme differences between real and ideal image were clearly seen more often in anorectic patients, but no significant differences in mean values were found (Table 7).

The large interindividual differences and their significance for the course of disease are demonstrated below by two examples (Figures 1 and 2). Assessment of body image and the EAT-26 (Garner & Garfinkel, 1979) were carried out repeatedly during the course of disease. Both patients showed a very different course: While in the one case weight, body image, and eating behavior had stabilized after a catamnestic time period of 3.3 years (Figure 2), the other patient was able to normalize her weight during a stay in the hospital, whereas body image and eating behavior remained disturbed, and at the time of reexamination 3.7 years later, a pronounced anorectic symptomatology was present (Figure 1).

Table 7. Trial II—Extent of difference between real and ideal image.

Difference (%)	5%	10%	15%	20%	25%	30%
Anorexia nervosa (n=20)	5	4	3	4	2	2
Control group (n=20)	8	7	4	1	–	–

Discussion

Our results indicate that in adolescent patients with anorexia nervosa, attitudes toward and perception of one's own body as well as estimation of one's own attractiveness and self-confidence are significantly altered and distorted, compared to a normal-weight control group of the same age. The extent of anorectic symptomatology in our samples, derived from the EAT-26, is in accordance with the data of Steinhausen (1985b), whereas the adult population of Garner, Olmstedt, Born and Garfinkel (1982) show markedly higher scores in the areas diet and bulimia. In comparison with the investigation of Strauss and Appelt (1983), it can be stated that the differences in the subjective assessment of one's own body between anorectic patients and normal-weight controls are similar in adults and adolescents. It is remarkable that a distinct relationship between weight or age

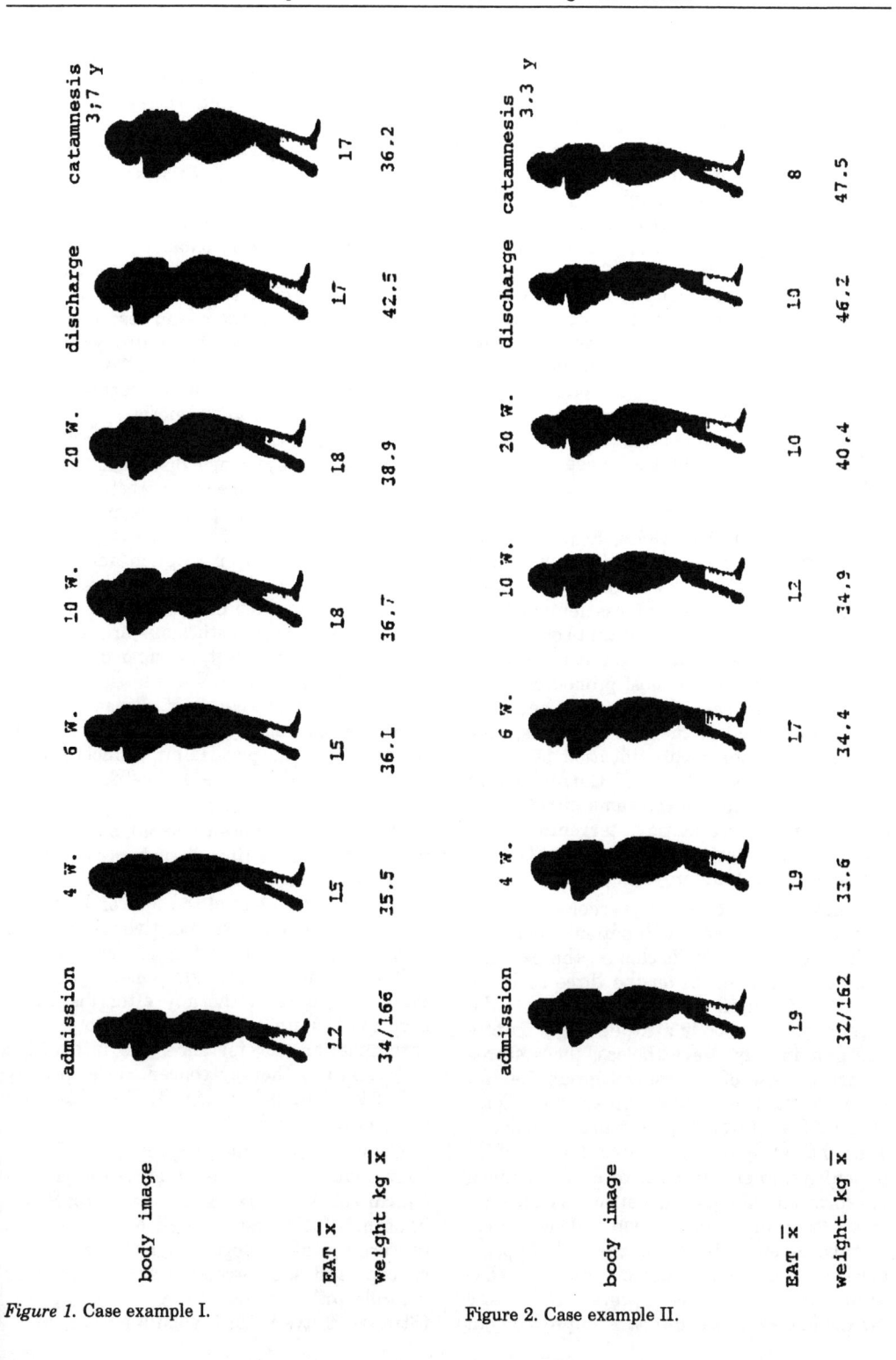

Self-Perception of Anorectic and Normal-Weight Adolescents

	admission	4 w.	6 w.	10 w.	20 w.	discharge	catamnesis 3;7 y
body image							
EAT $\bar{x}$	12	15	15	18	18	17	17
weight kg $\bar{x}$	34/166	35.5	36.1	36.7	38.9	42.5	36.2

Figure 1. Case example I.

	admission	4 w.	6 w.	10 w.	20 w.	discharge	catamnesis 3.3 y
body image							
EAT $\bar{x}$	19	19	17	12	10	10	8
weight kg $\bar{x}$	32/162	33.6	34.4	34.9	40.4	46.2	47.5

Figure 2. Case example II.

and the ratings in the questionnaire for body attitudes was seen neither in the patient nor in the control group, meaning that the actual weight does not directly correlate with the assessment of one's own body. These findings can thus be interpreted as meaning that also with anorectic symptomatology, the subjective assessment is not related to the actual loss of weight (Woerner, Lehmkuhl & Woerner, 1989). Rauch (1984), who also studied a normal-weight sample, was not able to demonstrate the presumed relationship between body perception and subjective assessment of the body. Her interpretation is that the more unconscious body perception and the conscious attitude toward the body are perhaps largely independently functioning areas of body experience, in the sense of Shonz (1974).

Very similar results were obtained by Thompson and Dolce (1989), Schulze et al. (1989), Thompson and Psaltis (1988), and Thompson et al. (1987), who compared different instructions for the assessment of body image. Our data, too, suggest that body image distortion is not specific for anorexia nervosa. On the other hand, the most pronounced disturbances were seen in anorectic patients, and as illustrated by the case examples, they can be related to a chronification of symptoms. The investigations of Garfinkel and Garner (1982) point in the same direction, so that specific therapeutic interventions are necessary for altering this symptom (Garner & Bemis, 1985; Vandereycken, 1988).

Which changes occur in psychological variables during the course of inpatient treatment with weight gain? At discharge, the patients rated their difficulties on the three scales of the EAT-26 and in two of three factors of the questionnaire for body attitudes significantly less prominently. Nevertheless, these scores lie above those of the control group, i.e., an increased control of food intake and a pronounced fear of weight gain continue to determine the eating behavior after the end of inpatient treatment. In spite of a clear clinical improvement, the psychometric variables are only partially normalized. The hypochondriac-depressive concern with appearance also did not change. *Insecurity/Dysesthesia* was less pronounced and *Attractiveness/Self-confidence* improved, but the results were still clearly different from a normal-weight control group. Garner et al. (1982) reported abnormal scores in EAT and a disturbed body perception, low satisfaction with one's own appearance, and somatic complaints. According to Strauss and Ryan (1987), in these patients this sort of insecurity about body perception indicates their central problem of lacking autonomous competence. Patients exhibiting bulimic or restrictive eating behavior show, according to this report, an unstable self-concept and less developed autonomy than comparable control groups. So far, however, no data are available on the significance of these findings regarding the course of therapy and prognosis.

Our catamnestic results also indicate that pronounced body image distortions further persist in a fair number of anorectic patients, which seems to accompany a poorer prognosis. Investigations of the relationship between disturbances of body perception and psychopathological and clinical parameters can be summarized in that overestimation of body image—and thus dysesthesias—are related to a lower weight at onset, a longer duration of therapy, more frequent stays in the hospital, a poorer understanding of disease, and a poorer prognosis (Garfinkel, Moldofsky & Garner, 1977; Casper, Halmi, Goldberg, Eckert & Davis, 1979; Slade, 1984; Touyz & Beumont, 1987).

Whereas Steinhausen (1985a), using an instrument for detecting disturbances of body perception, observed clear changes in body image in all variables at the time of discharge (in the sense of increased positive relationship toward one's own body), this phenomenon occurred to a much lesser extent in our patients. Thus, a long-term therapy after discharge from the hospital seems necessary to prevent chronification, for instance, the integrative in-/outpatient therapy concept developed by Bossert, Schnabel, Krieg, Molitor, Kemper and Berger (1987).

The divergent results regarding stability of body image disturbances in anorexia nervosa (Garfinkel, Moldofsky & Garner, 1979; Steinhausen, 1985b) and the still open questions concerning the etiological significance of self-concept and self-perception as well as their possible influence on therapy and prognosis (Strauss & Ryan, 1987) should encourage investigations to examine in more detail the course of these psychological variables during treatment and their consequences for development, as we have attempted with the illustration of the courses of two patients, in order to develop more suitable therapeutic concepts for these patients (Vandereycken, Depreitere & Probst, 1987).

References

Bossert, S., Schnabel, E., Krieg, J. C., Molitor, P., Kemper, J., & Berger, M. (1987). Integratives stationär-ambulantes Therapiekonzept bei Patienten mit Anorexia nervosa: Ein revidierter Therapieansatz. *Psychotherapie Psychosomatik Medizinische Psychologie, 37*, 331–336.

Bruch, H. (1973). *Eating disorders.* New York: Basic Books.

Button, E. J., Fransella, F., & Slade, P. D. (1977). A reappraisal of body perception disturbance in anorexia nervosa. *Psychological Medicine, 7*, 235–243.

Cash, T. T., & Brown, T. A. (1987). Body image in anorexia nervosa. A review of the literature. *Behavior Modification, 11*, 487–521.

Casper, R. C., Halmi, K. A., Goldberg, S. C., Eckert, E. D., & Davies, J. M. (1979). Disturbances in body image estimation as related to other characteristics and outcome of anorexia nervosa. *British Journal of Psychiatry, 134*, 60–66.

Eckert, E. D., Goldberg, S. C., Halmi, K. A., Casper, R. C., & Davis, J. M. (1979). Behavior therapy and anorexia nervosa. *British Journal of Psychiatry, 134*, 55–59.

Feighner, J. P., Robins, E., Guze, S. B., Woodruff, R., Winokur, G., & Munoz, R. (1972). Diagnostic criteria for use in psychiatric research. *Archives of General Psychiatry, 26*, 57–63.

Fichter, M., & Meermann, R. (1981). Zur Psychopathometrie der Anorexia nervosa. In R. Meermann (Ed.), *Anorexia nervosa* (pp. 17–31). Stuttgart: Enke.

Fichter, M., Meister, J., & Koch, H. J. (1986). The measurement of body image disturbances in anorexia nervosa: Experimental comparison to different methods. *British Journal of Psychiatry, 148*, 453–461.

Garfinkel, P. E., Moldofsky, H., & Garner, D. M. (1977). The outcome of anorexia nervosa: Significance of clinical features, body image and behavior modification. In Vigersky (Ed.), *Anorexia nervosa* (pp. 315–329). New York: Raven Press.

Garfinkel, P. E., Moldofsky, H., & Garner, D. M. (1979). The stability of perceptual disturbances in anorexia nervosa. *Psychological Medicine, 9*, 703–708.

Garfinkel, P. E., & Garner, D. M. (1982). *Anorexia nervosa: A multidimensional perspective.* New York: Brunner/Mazel.

Garner, D. M., Garfinkel, P. E., Stancer, H. C., & Moldofsky, H. (1976). Body image disturbances in anorexia nervosa and obesity. *Psychosomatic Medicine, 38*, 327–336.

Garner, D. M., & Garfinkel, P. M. (1979). The Eating Attitude Test: An index of symptoms for anorexia nervosa. *Psychological Medicine, 9*, 273–279.

Garner, D. M., Olmstedt, P. M., Bohr, Y., & Garfinkel, P. E. (1982). The Eating Attitude Test: Psychometric features and clinical correlates. *Psychological Medicine, 12*, 871–878.

Garner, D. M., & Bemis, K. M. (1985). Cognitive therapy for anorexia nervosa. In D. M. Garner & P. E. Garfinkel (Eds.), *Handbook of psychotherapy for anorexia nervosa and bulimia* (pp. 107–146). New York: Guilford Press.

Halmi, K. A., Goldberg, S., & Cunningham, S. (1977). Perceptual distribution of body image in adolescent girls: Distortion of body image in adolescence. *Psychological Medicine, 67*, 253–257.

Hsu, K. G. (1982). Is there a disturbance in body image in anorexia nervosa? *Journal of Nervous and Mental Disease, 170*, 305–307.

Meermann, R., & Fichter, M. (1982). Störungen des Körperschemas (body image) by psychischen Krankheiten—Methodik und experimentelle Ergebnisse bei Anorexia nervosa. *Psychotherapie Psychosomatik Medizinische Psychologie, 32*, 162–169.

Morgan, H. G., & Russell, G. F. N. (1975). A value of family background and clinical features as predictors of long-term outcome in anorexia nervosa: 4-year follow-up of 41 patients. *Psychological Medicine, 5*, 355–371.

Niebel, G. (1987). Psychopathologische Aspekte gestörten Eßverhaltens bei Frauen. *Zeitschrift für Psychotherapie Medizinische Psychologie, 37*, 317–330.

Proctor, L., & Morley, S. (1986). "Demand characteristics" in body-size estimation in anorexia nervosa. *British Journal of Psychiatry, 149*, 113–118.

Rauch, I. (1984). *Die Wahrnehmung der eigenen Körpermaße bei 10- bis 16-jährigen Mädchen: Altersunterschiede und mögliche Einflußfaktoren.* Diplomarbeit, Psychologisches Institut der Universität Mannheim.

Remschmidt, H., & Stutte, H. (1989). Neurologische, psychische und psychosoziale Folgen von Schädel-Hirn-Traumen im Kindes- und Jugendalter. In H. Remschmidt & H. Stutte (Eds.), *Neuropsychiatrische Folgen nach Schädel-Hirn-Traumen bei Kindern und Jugendlichen*. Bern: Huber.

Schulze, C., Rees, U. M., Thoma, W. & Lehmkuhl, G. (1989). Die Bedeutung neuropsychologischer Testbatterien für die Diagnostik der Hirnfunktionsstörungen im Kindesalter. *Zeitschrift für Kinder- und Jugendpsychiatrie, 17,* 23–30.

Shonz, F. C. (1974). Body image and its disorders. *International Journal of Psychiatry in Medicine, 5,* 461–472.

Slade, P. D. (1984). A review of body image studies in anorexia nervosa and bulimia nervosa. *Proceedings of the International Conference of Anorexia nervosa and Related Disorders,* Swansea, Wales.

Steinhausen, H. C. (1985a). Das Körperbild bei jungen Mädchen und Frauen im Vergleich zu anorektischen Patientinnen: Prüfung eines Meßinstrumentes. *Nervenarzt, 56,* 270–274.

Steinhausen, H. C. (1985b). Eating attitudes in adolescent anorectic patients. *International Journal of Eating Disorders, 29,* 145–164.

Strauss, B., & Appelt, H. (1983). Ein Fragebogen zur Beurteilung des eigenen Körpers. *Diagnostica, 29,* 145–164.

Strauss, B., & Ryan, R. M. (1987). Autonomy disturbances in subtypes of anorexia nervosa. *Journal of Abnormal Psychology, 96,* 254–258.

Thompson, J. K., Dolce, J. J., Spana, R. E., & Register, A. (1987). Emotionally versus intellectually based estimates of body size. *International Journal of Eating Disorders, 6,* 507–513.

Thompson, J. K., Psaltis, K. (1988). Multiple aspects and correlates of body figure ratings: A replication and extension of Fallon and Rozin (1985). *International Journal of Eating Disorders, 7,* 813–818.

Thompson, J. K., & Dolce, J. J. (1989). The discrepancy between emotional vs. rational estimates of body size, actual size, and ideal body ratings: Theoretical and clinical implications. *Journal of Clinical Psychology, 45,* 473–478.

Touyz, S. W., & Beumont, P. J. V. (1987). Body image and its disturbance. In P. J. V. Beumont & R. C. Casper (Eds.), *Handbook of eating disorders, Part 1: Anorexia and bulimia nervosa* (pp. 171–187). Amsterdam, New York, Oxford: Elsevier.

Vandereycken, W. (1988). Organization and evaluation of an inpatient treatment program for eating disorders. *Behavioral Residential Treatment, 3,* 153–165.

Vandereycken, D. A., Depreitere, L., & Probst, R. (1987). Body-orientated therapy for anorexia nervosa patients. *American Journal of Psychotherapy, 61,* 252–259.

Woerner, I., Lehmkuhl, G., & Woerner, W. (1989). Zur Beziehung von Körperwahrnehmung, Eßverhalten und Körpergewicht bei anorektischen und normalgewichtigen Jugendlichen. *Zeitschrift für Klinische Psychologie, 18,* 319–331.

Wooley, S. C., & Wooley, W. (1985). Intensive outpatient and residential treatment for bulimia. In D. M. Garner & P. E. Garfinkel (Eds.), *Handbook of psychotherapy for anorexia nervosa and bulimia* (pp. 391–430). New York: Guilford Press.

The Assessment of Body-Image Distortion Using a Semantic Differential: A Methodological Study

Hans-Christoph Steinhausen

A semantic differential for the assessment of disturbances in the perception of body image in patients with anorexia nervosa is presented. This method was used to evaluate four different samples: 109 adolescent secondary-school pupils, 60 nursing school students, and two clinical groups of adolescent female patients with anorexia nervosa. One of the clinical groups consisted of prospectively evaluated patients during the course of inpatient treatment. The other clinical group consisted of former inpatients who were studied for their long-term outcome. Besides the utility and economy of the method, the validity for discriminating between the clinical groups and the control groups of healthy subjects was proven. Reliability was also ascertained through retest examinations. Factor analysis revealed four dimensions that may be used as subscales. The evaluated body image was shown to be independent of age, socioeconomic status, and weight. Finally, it was possible to demonstrate the sensitivity of the method for evaluating changes in body image in an inpatient treatment setting.

Body-image distortion is an essential criterion of diagnosis in anorexia nervosa. According to the DSM-III-R, it is defined as a disturbance in the way in which one's body weight, size, or shape is experienced. In a recent paper, Slade (1988) distinguished two aspects of body image: (a) accuracy of body size estimation, and (b) feelings toward the body and body parts, which he called body dissatisfaction.

Body image has been studied experimentally in anorectics in a fairly large number of studies (Bell, Kirkpatrick, & Rinn, 1986; Ben-Tovim, Hunter, & Crisp, 1977; Buree, Papageorgis, & Solyom, 1984; Button, 1986; Casper, Halmi, Goldberg, Eckert, & Davis, 1979; Collins, Beumont, Touyz, Krass, Thompson, & Philips, 1987; Crisp & Kalucy, 1974; Fichter, Meister, & Koch, 1986; Freeman, Thomas, Solyom, & Koopman, 1985; Gardner & Moncrieff, 1988; Garfinkel, Moldofsky, Garner, Stancer, & Coscina, 1978; Huon & Brown, 1986; Kalliopuska, 1982; Norris, 1984; Russel, Campbell, & Slade, 1975; Slade, & Russel, 1973; Strober, 1981; Thompson, 1987; Touyz, Beumont, Collins, 1988; Touyz, Beumont, Collins, McCabe, & Jupp, 1984; Whitehouse & Freeman, 1988; Wingate & Christie 1978). The major conclusions of the earlier studies were that

1) anorectics, as compared to controls, markedly overestimate their own body widths;

2) patients show an improvement in their accuracy of body-size judgement as they gain weight, although

3) they, on the average, still overestimate their body widths at the time of discharge, and

4) the extent of overestimation at the time of discharge from hospital treatment was found to predict future relapse (Slade, 1988).

More recent studies, however, have led to a revision and specification of these conclusions.

Not only anorectics, but pregnant women (Slade, 1977) as well as normal subjects (Crisp & Kalucy, 1974) also tend to overestimate their body dimensions and, in this respect, do not differ from anorectics (Buree,

Department of Child and Adolescent Psychiatry, University of Zurich, Switzerland.

Papageorgis & Solyom, 1984; Gardner & Moncrieff, 1988). Furthermore, adolescents not only express concerns and dissatisfaction regarding body shape (Davies & Furnham, 1986; Salmons, 1988), but they also tend to distort body image as well (Halmi, Goldberg & Cunningham, 1977). But one must conclude that anorectics overestimate their body widths significantly more than the other groups mentioned above (Slade, 1985).

The last conclusion may be specified even further. Body-image distortion is observed only in some anorectic patients, especially during the very early phase of inpatient treatment (Button, 1986; Button, Fransella & Slade, 1977). This includes bulimic patients with previous anorexia (Freeman et al., 1985) as well as patients displaying vomiting and early relapse (Button, Fransella & Slade, 1977). A recent study by Touyz, Beumont and Collins (1988) indicates that overestimation of body shape does not appear to have an adverse influence upon weight gain during inpatient treatment.

The main experimental methods used for measuring body image are image-distortion techniques or size-estimation techniques. While the former are increasingly based on recent video technology, the latter also include movable caliper techniques in which the image-marking procedure requires the subject to face a wall and mark the perceived body widths on a sheet of paper attached to the wall. Empirical findings based on these methods have been reviewed by Slade (1985) and by Garner and Garfinkel (1981).

While such methods as those used in experimental studies often rely to a certain extent upon sophisticated technological equipment, there are other measures that are more easily incorporated into clinical practice. Such measures include scales in questionnaires (i.e., Garner et al., 1983), clinical interviews, draw-a-person tests, or even projective tests. The present study introduces one such instrument for evaluating the course and outcome of body-image distortion in anorexia nervosa which was especially designed for easy use in the clinical setting. According to Slade's (1988) distinction cited above, this semantic differential deals with body dissatisfaction rather than with body-size estimation.

A number of objectives converged in the present study. First of all, it was tested whether or not the method used in this study differentiated between patients with anorexia nervosa and controls (i.e., young women and female adolescents). Besides testing discriminant validity, both reliability and factorial structure were analyzed. In addition, another part of the study considered to what extent age, socioeconomic status, and body weight influenced the body image of the control subjects. In a final section, sensitivity to change, i.e., to changes during the course of the disorder, was assessed.

Samples

A total of 169 female adolescents and young adult women participated in the study: 109 adolescent pupils of a local secondary school in West Berlin ranging in age from 14 to 18 years (Sample A); and 60 nursingschool students ranging in age from 18 to 27 years (Sample B). The assessment was repeated 36 days later with 37 of the nursing-school students to test the retest reliability of the method. The sample characteristics, including height and weight, are presented in Table 1.

For the purpose of comparison, two series of patients with anorexia nervosa comprised the clinical groups: a prospectively evaluated series of N=24 adolescent patients with acute anorexia nervosa (Sample C) and a series of N=21 former anorexia nervosa inpatients who were evaluated with regard to long-term outcome (Sample D). The findings concerning the last series of patients were presented elsewhere (Steinhausen & Glanville, 1983). In both series only those patients who developed anorexia nervosa during either childhood or adolescence were evaluated.

Table 1. Population characteristics.

Population	N	Age M	Age SD	Height (cm) M	Height (cm) SD	Weight (kg) M	Weight (kg) SD	Deviation from standard weight (%) M	Age at onset (y) M	Socioeconomic status (%) LC	Socioeconomic status (%) MC/UC
A Secondary-school pupils	109	15.1	1.0	164.3	6.4	53.9	6.2	− 0.1		33.0	67.0
B Nursing-school students	60	20.7	2.5	166.5	7.1	58.5	5.1	+ 4.4		20.0	80.0
C Adolescent anorectic inpatients at admission	24	13.9	1.5	161.8	5.1	34.2	4.3	−34.1	13.9	36.4	63.6
D Former anorectic inpatients at follow-up	21	24.6	8.5	n.d.		52.8	9.2	− 8.8	14.0	14.0	86.0

n.d. = not determined; LC = lower class; MC = middle class; UC = upper class

Method

The study is based upon a questionnaire developed by a collaborative study group in the United States for the purpose of evaluating a subject's attitude toward her body. Preliminary findings resulting from studies based on the original instrument have been reported by Eckert et al. (1982). The questionnaire was constructed according to the model of the semantic differential and requests a self-description of the body in terms of 16 bipolar adjectives. The questionnaire was translated into German by the author for use in a German-speaking population.

The examination of the control subjects took place in groups during classroom time. Height and weight were also measured at that time. The data concerning the clinical groups were collected from individual interviews. The subjects belonging to the follow-up series were interviewed at their place of residence while the acutely ill patients were interviewed in the clinic.

Findings

The profiles of the four groups resulting from the questionnaire were compared using a multivariate variance analysis (MANOVA). As can be seen from Table 2, the two groups were significantly different from each other. With the exception of two pairs of attributes—"large/small" and "firm/flabby"—there were individual attributes which consistently produced highly significant differences. Figure 1 reveals that the control groups and the clinical groups share respectively quite similar profiles. The control groups and the clinical groups, however, are clearly distinguishable from each other.

Both internal consistency (Cronbach's alpha) as well as retest stability were determined in order to test reliability. Internal consistency amounted to $r_{tc}=0.44$ for the combined samples of secondary-school pupils and nursing school students (N=169), which suggests multidimensionality. The stability coefficient amounted to $r_{tt}=0.75$ based on retests of 37 control subjects.

The presumed multidimensionality was examined by performing a factor analysis. Only the combined control groups (Samples A and B) provided the requisite sample size for this data analysis. The findings of this analysis

Table 2. Comparison of body image in the four groups.

Paired Attributes	Samples A M	SD	B M	SD	C M	SD	D M	SD	F	p
1. Fat/Thin	4.3	1.3	4.4	1.3	5.5	1.2	4.5	1.4	5.39	0.001
2. Beautiful/Ugly	2.6	0.9	3.1	0.9	4.1	1.3	4.1	1.3	15.22	0.00001
3. Desirable/Undesirable	2.6	1.3	2.9	1.2	3.9	1.9	4.4	1.9	11.55	0.00001
4. Dirty/Clean	6.3	1.2	6.6	1.0	6.0	1.5	5.5	1.5	4.38	0.005
5. Soft/Hard	2.8	1.3	3.4	1.3	4.3	1.9	3.9	1.9	7.68	0.0001
6. Proportioned/Unproportioned	2.9	1.5	3.0	1.2	4.1	2.3	3.3	1.6	4.26	0.006
7. Light/Heavy	3.5	1.6	3.7	1.5	2.3	1.6	3.4	1.6	4.53	0.004
8. Powerful/Weak	3.0	1.4	3.2	1.2	4.9	1.8	4.2	1.9	11.27	0.00001
9. Pleasant/Unpleasant	2.3	1.1	2.8	1.2	3.7	1.9	3.7	1.7	9.93	0.00001
10. Fragile/Massive	4.2	1.2	4.7	1.3	3.0	1.5	3.5	1.5	11.88	0.00001
11. Attractive/Repulsive	2.5	1.0	3.0	1.0	4.0	1.7	3.6	1.4	10.30	0.00001
12. Large/Small	3.6	1.7	3.5	1.5	3.8	1.7	4.0	1.4	0.92	n.s.
13. Inactive/Active	5.2	1.4	5.1	1.4	3.9	2.1	4.0	2.2	5.94	0.001
14. Firm/Flabby	2.7	1.4	2.9	1.3	2.4	1.2	2.8	1.2	1.14	n.s
15. Bad/Good	5.6	1.3	5.3	1.3	4.0	2.0	4.1	1.9	10.70	0.00001
16. Uncomfortable/Comfortable	5.3	1.4	4.7	1.3	3.8	1.8	4.7	1.5	7.16	0.00001

MANOVA (df = 48; 575)
A = Secondary-school pupils; B = Nursing-school students; C = Adolescent anorectic inpatients at admission; D = Former anorectic inpatients at follow-up

Table 3. Factor analysis of the data of the normal subjects (N = 169)[a].

Paired attributes	F1	F2	F3	F4	h^2
1. Fat/Thin	−0.76				0.66
2. Beautiful/Ugly		0.77			0.65
3. Desirable/Undesirable			−0.45		0.43
4. Dirty/Clean			0.51		0.27
5. Soft/Hard					0.10
6. Proportioned/Unproportioned					0.20
7. Light/Heavy	0.68				0.57
8. Powerful/Weak				0.43	0.43
9. Pleasant/Unpleasant			−0.43		0.41
10. Fragile/Massive				−0.94	0.97
11. Attractive/Repulsive		0.57			0.47
12. Large/Small					0.03
13. Inactive/Active			0.41		0.17
14. Firm/Flabby	0.63				0.48
15. Bad/Good			0.64		0.55
16. Uncomfortable/Comfortable					0.19
Eigenwert	3.9	2.3	1.3	1.2	
% Variance	24.4	14.3	8.0	7.3	
% Total Variance	24.4	38.7	46.7	54.0	

[a] Only loadings >0.40 have been included in the tables.

are summarized in Table 3. Using the ScreeTest four factors were extracted that accounted for a total of 54% of the variance. The four factors are described by the following labels:

- Factor 1—Shapeless
- Factor 2—Unattractive
- Factor 3—Valued
- Factor 4—Fragile.

The effect of age, socioeconomic status, and weight were not found to relate in any significant way with body image. Finally, the instrument's sensitivity to change was tested by comparing the profiles of the 24 adolescent

MY BODY RIGHT NOW

	1	2	3	4	5	6	7	
Fat								Thin
Beautiful								Ugly
Desirable								Undesirable
Dirty								Clean
Soft								Hard
Proportioned								Unproportioned
Light								Heavy
Powerful								Weak
Pleasant								Unpleasant
Fragile								Massive
Attractive								Repulsive
Large								Small
Inactive								Active
Firm								Flabby
Bad								Good
Uncomfortable								Comfortable

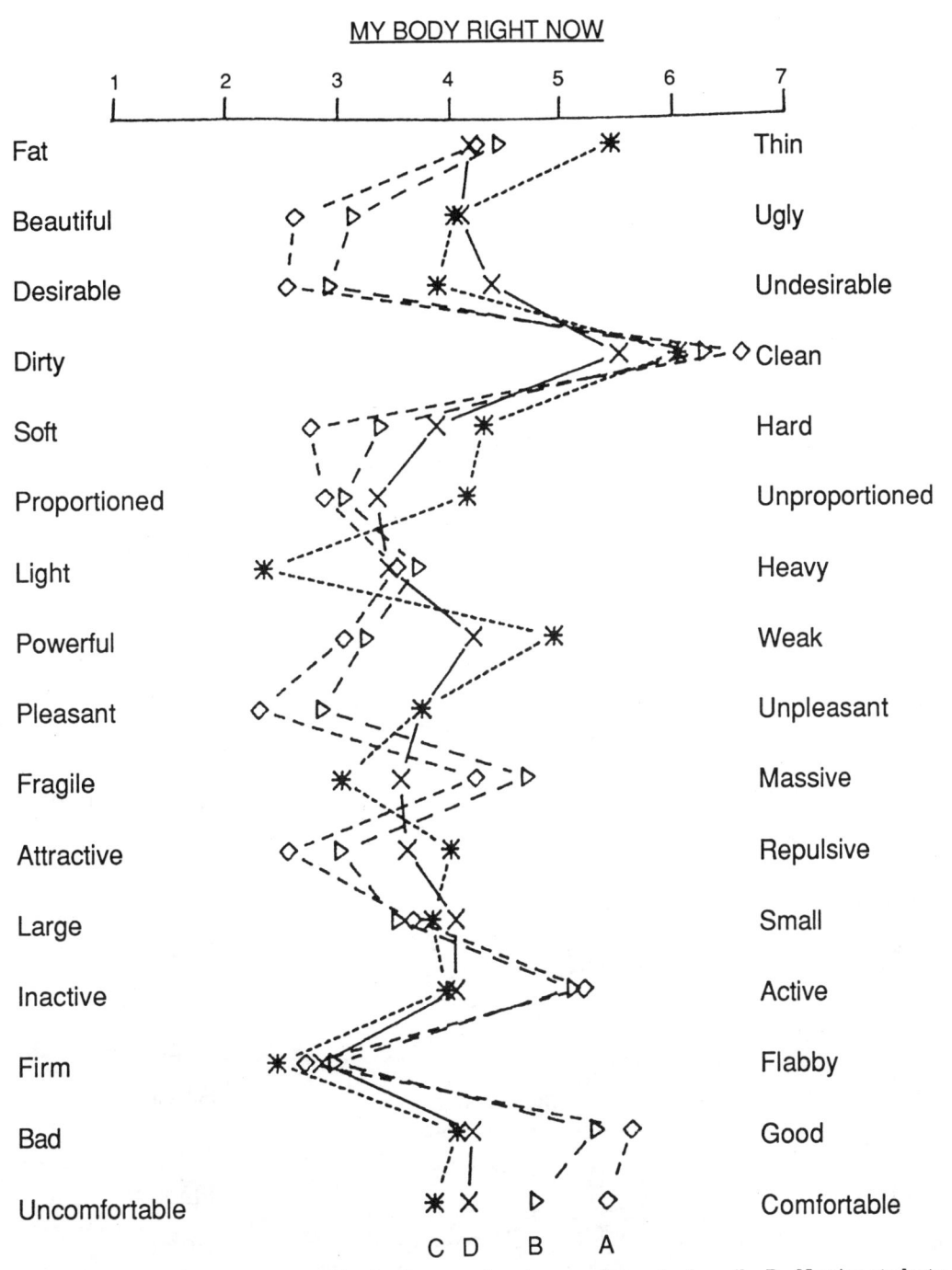

Figure 1. Comparison of body image in the four samples: A—secondary-school pupils; B—Nursing students; C—Anorectic inpatients at admission; D—Former anorectic patients at followup.

Table 4. Comparison of body image in 21 adolescent anorectic inpatients at admission and discharge.

Paired attributes	Admission M	SD	Discharge M	SD	t	p (df = 20)
1. Fat/Thin	5.5	1.5	4.3	1.1	2.64	0.016
2. Beautiful/Ugly	3.9	1.6	3.2	1.4	1.85	n.s
3. Desirable/Undesirable	3.9	1.9	2.8	1.4	2.20	0.04
4. Dirty/Clean	6.2	1.1	6.1	1.3	0.15	n.s
5. Soft/Hard	4.3	2.0	3.5	1.5	1.55	n.s
6. Proportioned/Unproportioned	3.6	2.3	2.9	1.9	1.25	n.s
7. Light/Heavy	2.2	1.3	3.4	1.2	−2.67	0.015
8. Powerful/Weak	4.7	1.8	3.0	1.4	4.46	0.000
9. Pleasant/Unpleasant	3.7	1.7	2.7	1.6	2.07	0.05
10. Fragile/Massive	3.0	1.2	4.6	1.2	−4.74	0.000
11. Attractive/Repulsive	3.9	1.6	3.0	1.5	1.99	n.s.
12. Large/Small	4.0	1.7	3.9	1.5	0.29	n.s.
13. Inactive/Active	4.2	2.1	5.7	1.4	−3.24	0.004
14. Firm/Flabby	2.4	1.2	2.7	1.4	−0.65	n.s.
15. Bad/Good	4.3	2.0	5.4	1.4	−2.77	0.012
16. Uncomfortable/Comfortable	3.8	1.8	5.7	2.0	−6.13	0.000

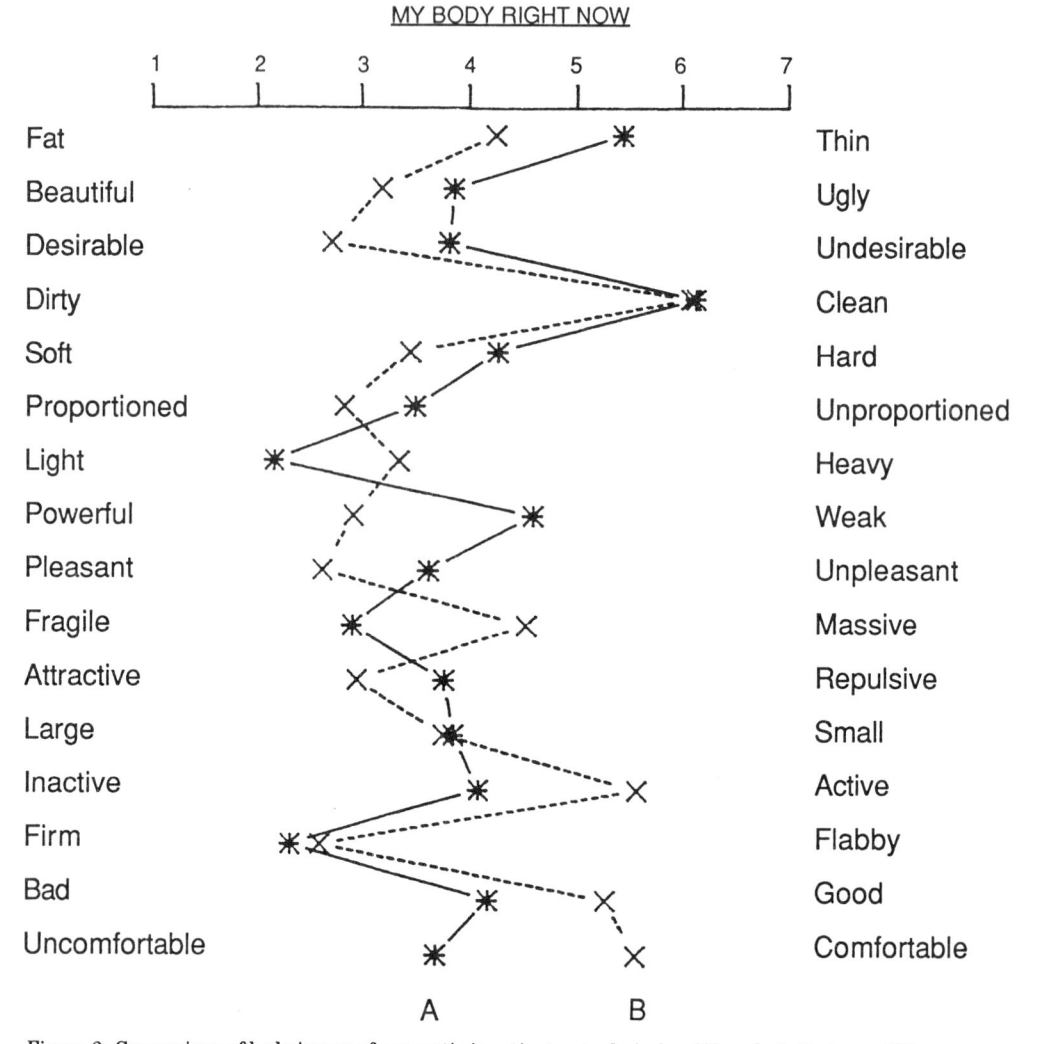

Figure 2. Comparison of body image of anorectic inpatients at admission (A) und at discharge (B).

patients suffering from anorexia nervosa at the beginning as well as at the end of the inpatient treatment. As one can see from Table 4 and Figure 2, there are indeed considerable changes in the profile at the time of admission as compared with the profile at the time of discharge. This change is expressed at almost all levels of attribution in the direction of a more positive attitude toward one's own body.

Discussion

A number of expectations arose and were for the most part met in connection with the presented method of evaluating body image as perceived by patients with anorexia nervosa as well as by normal control subjects. This assessment instrument, founded upon the semantic differential model, is not only practical and economic, but exhibits a number of attributes that are prescriptive of psychological methods of evaluation. To begin with, it was determined that the data collected with the questionnaire allowed adequate differentiation between the control groups of normal subjects and the clinical patients with anorexia nervosa. This condition fulfills the criteria for discriminant validity and was only insignificantly reduced by the lack of discriminating potential in two of the attribute pairs ("Large/Small" and "Firm/Flabby"). These attribute pairs could eventually be eliminated in future studies.

The reliability test resulted in satisfactory stability for a small sample of normal subjects and, as expected for a semantic differential, a moderate degree of internal consistency. This last measure was found to be determined by the multidimensionality of the instrument. The four isolated factors could be taken as subscales for use in both individual evaluations as well as in comparing groups. It is, however, necessary to qualify this last statement in that these factors are based on data of the normal subjects. In the future, analogous analyses of the data of patients with anorexia nervosa will have to determine the extent to which identical or deviating dimensions of body image in this clinical population need to be considered.

Interestingly, it was demonstrated that the construct of body image among the normal subjects was not affected by age, socioeconomic status, or weight. This evidence further supports the abovementioned criteria of discriminant validity.

Finally, the utility of the method is also apparent in its sensitivity to change. The presented data, originating in the pretests and posttests during the course of inpatient treatment of patients with anorexia nervosa, elucidate the special application of this method for studies evaluating factors influencing course of the disease and effects of therapy.

References

Bell, C., Kirkpatrick, S. W., & Rinn, R. C. (1986). Body image of anorexic, obese, and normal females. *Journal of Clinical Psychology, 42*, 431–439.

BenTovim, D. I., Hunter, M., & Crisp, A. H. (1977). Discrimination and evaluation of shape and size of anorexia nervosa. An exploratory study. *Research Communications in Psychology, Psychiatry and Behavior, 2*, 241–258.

Buree, B, Papageorgis, D., & Solyom, L. (1984). Body image perception and preference in anorexia nervosa. *Canadian Journal of Psychiatry, 29*, 557–563.

Button, E. (1986). Body size perception and response to inpatient treatment in anorexia nervosa. *International Journal of Eating Disorders, 5*, 617–630.

Button, E. J., Fransella, F., & Slade, P. D. (1977). A reappraisal of body perception disturbance in anorexia nervosa. *Psychological Medicine, 7*, 235–243.

Casper, R. C., Halmi, K. A., Goldberg, S. C., Eckert, E. D., & Davis, J. M. (1979). Disturbances in body image estimation as related to other characteristics and outcome in anorexia nervosa. *British Journal of Psychiatry, 134,* 60–66.

Collins, J. K., Beumont, P., Touyz, S., Krass, J., Thompson, P., & Philips, T. (1987). Accuracy of body image with varying degrees of information about the face and body contours. *International Journal of Eating Disorders, 6,* 67–74.

Crisp, A. H., & Kalucy, R. (1974). Aspects of the perceptual disorder in anorexia nervosa. *British Journal of Medical Psychology, 47,* 349–361.

Davies, E., & Furnham, A. (1986). The dieting and body shape concerns of adolescent females. *Journal of Child Psychology and Psychiatry, 27,* 417–428.

Eckert, E. D., Goldberg, S. C., Halmi, K. A., Casper, R. C., & Davis, J. M. (1982). Depression in anorexia nervosa. *Psychological Medicine, 12,* 115–122.

Fichter, M. M., Meister, I., & Koch, H. J. (1986). The measurement of body image disturbances in anorexia nervosa-experimental comparison of different methods. *British Journal of Psychiatry, 148,* 453–461.

Freeman, R. J., Thomas, C. D., Solyom, L., & Koopman, R. F. (1985). Clinical and personality correlates of body size overestimation in anorexia nervosa and bulimia nervosa. *International Journal of Eating Disorders, 4,* 439–456.

Gardner, R. M., & Moncrieff, C. (1988). Body image distortion in anorexics as a non-sensory phenomenon: A signal detection approach. *Journal of Clinical Psychology, 44,* 101–107.

Garfinkel, P. E., Moldofsky, H., Garner, D. M., Stancer, H. C., & Coscina, D. V. (1978). Body awareness in anorexia nervosa: Disturbances in "body image" and "satiety." *Psychosomatic Medicine, 40,* 487–499.

Garner, D. M., & Garfinkel, P. E. (1981). Body image in anorexia nervosa: Measurement, theory and clinical implications. *International Journal of Psychiatry and Medicine, 11,* 263–284.

Halmi, K. A., Goldberg, S. G., & Cunningham, S. (1977). Perceptual distortion of body image in adolescent girls: distortion of body image in adolescence. *Psychological Medicine, 7,* 253–257.

Hsu, L. K. G. (1982). Brief communication. Is there a disturbance in body image in anorexia nervosa? *Journal of Nervous and Mental Disease, 170,* 305–307.

Huon, G. F., & Brown, L. B. (1986). Body images in anorexia nervosa and bulimia nervosa. *International Journal of Eating Disorders, 5,* 421–440.

Kalliopuska, M. (1982). Body-image disturbances in patients with anorexia nervosa. *Psychological Reports, 51,* 715–722.

Norris, D. L. (1984). The effects of mirror confrontation on selfestimation of body dimensions in anorexia nervosa, bulimia and two control groups. *Psychological Medicine, 14,* 835–842.

Russel, G. F. M., Campbell, P. G., & Slade, P. D. (1975). Experimental studies on the nature of the psychological disorder in anorexia nervosa. *Psychoneuroendocrinology, 1,* 45–56.

Slade, P. D. (1977). Awareness of body dimensions during pregnancy: An analogue study. *Psychological Medicine, 7,* 245–252.

Slade, P. D. (1985). Review: A review of body-image studies in anorexia nervosa and bulimia nervosa. *Journal of Psychiatric Research, 19,* 255–265.

Slade, P. D. (1988). Body image in anorexia nervosa. *British Journal of Psychiatry, 153* (suppl. 2), 20–22.

Slade, P. D., & Russel, G. F. M. (1973). Awareness of body dimensions in anorexia nervosa. *Psychological Medicine, 3,* 188–199.

Steinhausen, H. C., & Glanville, K. (1983). A long-term follow-up of adolescent anorexia nervosa. *Acta Psychiatrica Scandinavica, 68,* 1–10.

Strober, M. (1981). The relation of personality characteristics to body image disturbances in juvenile anorexia nervosa: A multivariate analysis. *Psychosomatic Medicine, 43,* 323–330.

Thompson, J. K. (1987). Body size distortion in anorexia nervosa: reanalysis and reconceptualization. *Journal of Eating Disorders, 6,* 379–384.

Touyz, S., Beumont, P., & Collins, J. (1988). Does over- or under-estimation of body shape influence response to treatment in patients with anorexia nervosa? *International Journal of Eating Disorders, 7,* 687–691.

Touyz, S. W., Beumont, P. J. V., Collins, J. K., & McCabe, M. (1984). Body shape perception and its disturbance in anorexia nervosa. *British Journal of Psychiatry, 144,* 167–171.

Vandereycken, W., & Vanderlinden, J. L. (1983). Denial of illness and the use of self-reporting measures in anorexia nervosa patients. *International Journal of Eating Disorders, 2,* 101–107.

Whitehouse, A. M., Freeman, C. P. L., & Annandale, A. (1988). Body size estimation in anorexia nervosa. *British Journal of Psychiatry, 153* (suppl. 2), 23–26.

Wingate, B. A., & Christie, M. J. (1978). Ego strength and body image in anorexia nervosa. *Journal of Psychosomatic Research, 22,* 201–204.

Construction of a Questionnaire on the Body Experience of Anorexia Nervosa

H. Van Coppenolle*, M. Probst*, W. Vandereycken*, M. Goris*, R. Meermann**

In the literature on anorexia nervosa, a disturbed body experience is widely acknowledged. However, there is no typical instrument available to evaluate the body experience of this particular group. To this end, an experimental questionnaire was constructed containing 39 items that refer to the most commonly cited views about how anorectic patients experience their bodies. The questionnaire was given to 124 subjects: 28 female anorectic patients, 20 female psychiatric patients with other disorders, and 76 "normals." From the data, 12 factors were abstracted representing global dimensions of body experience. The three groups of subjects could be discriminated by four of these factors: frightening body estrangement, body shyness, body denial, and an urge for slimness. The first and second discriminating factors are in keeping with the generally accepted views on anorexia nervosa, while the third and fourth show little correspondence. As a result of critical observation and awareness of the most discriminating items in the questionnaire, a revision is proposed.

Anorexia nervosa is mostly diagnosed on the basis of the criteria of the *Diagnostical and Statistical Manual of Mental Disorders* (DSM): an outspoken fear of putting on weight, a disturbed body image (the feeling one is fat, although one has a normal weight), and emaciation (25%) because of reduction of food or the use of laxatives and/or extreme body movement, amenorrhea, and an excessive preoccupation with one's body (frequent looks in the mirror). First, however, any possible organic cause that could explain the weight reduction should be excluded.

All theories of anorexia nervosa agree on the central importance of the body experience of anorectic patients. They are proud of their emaciated bodies and consider them ideal. Even such extreme estrangement from one's own body can occur that the patient is completely indifferent to extreme emaciation and its consequences. Patients would rather not have bodies anymore (Van de Loo, 1981a). This disturbed body experience is often expressed as a rejection of the body—a refusal to grow up, an attempt to stop time, not to grow up but to return to the way a child functions in the latency period (Lafeber, 1971).

Because the disturbed body experience is central to the diagnosis and symptomatology, it is logical that equal importance be attached to turn the negative body experience into a more positive one. Acquiring a realistic body image and recovering the "lost body" is considered a vital prerequisite to recovery (Bruch, 1971) and a cornerstone of therapy (Van de Loo, 1981b). How this can be realized in practice still remains an open question. Most often, individual and group forms of psychomotor therapy are used in which confrontation with, and an awareness of, the body is emphasized in order to change the negative body experience into a more positive attitude (Depreitere, Van Wouwe & Vandereycken, 1983).

Considering the importance of the body experience of such patients, it is not surprising that attempts are being made to evaluate it. Generally, methods are used that demand the patients to estimate their measures, after which the estimates are compared with their real measures. From this it can be deduced to

---

*University Psychiatric Center Kortenberg and Institute of Physical Education, Catholic University, Leuven, Belgium.
**Psychosomatic Hospital, D-3280 Bad Pyrmont, West Germany.

what extent anorexia nervosa patients over- or underestimate their measures in comparison with a control group (for a survey of these studies, see Garfinkel & Garner, 1982; Meermann, Napierski & Vandereycken, 1988).

In addition, the questionnaire method is used, such as Fisher's (1970) *Body-Distortion Questionnaire*. Here, the subjects are asked to respond to 82 statements (with "yes," "no," or "undecided") relating to 7 categories of body distortion (feeling taller, smaller, loss of body boundaries, feeling one is loathsome and dirty, blocked body openings, abnormal skin sensations, and feelings of depersonalization).

Another technique applied in studies of anorexia nervosa patients is Witkin's (1962) body-concept scale. This consists of a 5-degree scale that purports to evaluate the degree of differentiation of the body concept, inasmuch as it manifests itself in a drawing of the human body. Scores range from 1 ("very sophisticated drawings") to 5 ("primitive and infantile drawings"). Results from these studies do not unanimously support the proposition that anorexia nervosa patients have a disturbed body experience (Slade & Russell, 1973; Crisp & Kalucy, 1974; Halmi, 1977; Garner, 1975; Fries, 1977; Goldberg, 1979; Button, 1977; Pierloot & Houben, 1978; Casper, 1979; Askevold, 1975; Strober et al., 1979; Garfinkel, 1979).

An explanation is perhaps that the most commonly used technique is the estimation of the body measures, which can only be considered a limited aspect of the body-experience concept. Fisher's body-distortion questionnaire and Witkin's concept scale are also susceptible to criticism: With the former, one could question the construction of the items, which are formulated in a rather vague and direct, threatening way. As examples we cite the following items: "My body feels dull"—"My anus feels strange"—"My genitals feel strange." Furthermore, it is unclear how the author ended up with 7 categories. In a study of psychically undisturbed female students (Thys, 1981), relatively high correlations were found between the 7 dimensions put forward by Fisher as independent. His classifications seem to overlap to some extent. Nor can Witkin's scale, in which drawings are interpreted in a rather subjective way, be considered a scientifically sound method.

In order to eliminate these shortcomings, we devised a *specific* questionnaire to inform us about the body experience of anorexia nervosa patients, specific because—as will be shown later—the items were collected on the basis of data found in the literature on the body experience of anorexia nervosa patients.

Method

Subjects

The test group that took part in the study consisted of 124 subjects: 28 anorexia nervosa patients hospitalized in St. Joseph's University Psychiatric Center in Kortenberg, 20 female psychiatric patients from the same institution with diverse disorders (with the exception of psychotic and borderline patients), and 76 female "normals." The latter were selected from a group of 150 subjects (male and female) with different study levels, who functioned as subjects in a preliminary study (Van Troos, 1982). The group of 76 were selected on the basis of equality to the anorexia subgroups compared with one another as to age distribution (average 21.2 years).

As to the study level, the subjects were divided into 8 categories used by the Ministry of Education, varying from 1 (primary education) to 8 (university degree). The average study level of the anorexia nervosa patients was 5.7 and the level of the normals 6.

Procedure

In order construct a questionnaire to assess the body experience of anorexia nervosa patients, Goldberg's (1970) three construction strategies were used. In that model, the first step is to start with an intuitive construction of the scales. Subsequently, the scales are made homogeneous by means of factor and item analysis, and in a third move the potential of the scale for discrimination between the groups is examined.

In the literature on anorexia nervosa, the following general characteristics of the body experience of patients are mentioned by several authors:

- general dissatisfaction with own body (practically all authors),
- a deindividualization, depersonalization of the body; the body is experienced as a strange, passive, numb, dead object (Bruch, 1973; Brinks, 1977; Amir, 1977),
- a permanent feeling one is too fat (Lafeber, 1971),
- a lack of trust in one's own body, a lack of feeling secure physically (Van de Loo, 1981),
- hyperactivity and restlessness (Vandereycken, 1978).

For each of these 5 characteristics, items were compiled on the basis of data from the literature. We opted for two kinds of questions: dichotomic questions and questions with multiple-choice response—the first because the subjects' attention is more easily kept if different types of questions are used, the second because multiple-choice questions supply more information.

The experimental questionnaire shown in Table 1 was drawn up along these lines (Van Troos, 1982).

Some of the items are repeated in a negative formulation in order to get information about the reliability of the responses. Thus, item 13 "My hips seem too narrow for me" is a control item for item 3 "My hips seem too broad to me." Items 1 to 24 were scored dichotomically (right/wrong), whereas items 25 to 39 were scored on a 5-point scale. The lower the score, the more problematic the body experience was considered to be. The questionnaire was given the subjects individually.

Table 1. Body attitudes questionnaire (experimental version).

NAME: SEX:
AGE:

The purpose of this questionnaire is to find out how you experience your own body. The data will remain strictly confidential. Please indicate whether the following statements are right or wrong to you, by putting an X in the appropriate column.

	Right	Wrong

1) When I compare myself with my peers, I feel dissatisfied with my body.
2) My body appears to be a numb object.
3) My hips seem too broad to me.
4) I feel comfortable within my own body.
5) My body looks too male to me.
6) I have an urge to be slimmer.
7) I think my breasts are too large.
8) My shoulders seem too narrow to me.
9) I am inclined to hide my body (e.g., under loose clothing).
10) When I look at myself in the mirror, I am dissatisfied with my appearance.
11) It is easy for me to relax physically.
12) I think I am too thin.
13) My hips seem too narrow to me.
14) I experience my body as a burden.
15) It is as if my body is not mine.
16) When I am in company, I feel embarrassed with my appearance.
17) My body is a numb object.
18) Some parts of my body look as if swollen.
19) My body seems too female to me.
20) My body is a threat to me.

21) My shoulders seem too broad to me.
22) I am indifferent to my appearance.
23) I find my growth of hair is too male.
24) I look as if I am pregnant.

Table 1 continued

There are 5 response options with the following statements. Please indicate the appropriate response by putting an X in the appropriate column.

	Always	Often	Sometimes	Rarely	Never

25) I envy others their physical appearance.
26) Things go on in my body which frighten me.
27) I am obsessed with the idea that there is fat on my body.
28) I compare my appearance with that of others.
29) I feel swollen after a meal.
30) I feel a nervousness in my body.
31) My appearance embarrasses me during contacts with others.
32) I prefer tight clothes.
33) I have an urge to be slim.
34) I observe my looks in the mirror.

	Quite dissatisfied	Dissatisfied	Indifferent	Satisfied	Very satisfied

35) With, or to, the size of my breast I feel
36) With, or to, my height I feel
37) With, or to, my growth of hair I feel

	Very important	Important	Of some importance	Secondary	Completely unimportant

38) To me the width of my shoulders is
39) To me the width of my hips is

Results

Factor Analysis

An explorative factor analysis was carried out on the responses from the total test group (Nunnally, 1967) to reduce the 39 items to more homogeneous dimensions. If we follow Nunnally's guidelines, a number of factors equal to one-third of the number of variables should be selected, in our case 13 factors. According to Knippenberg (1980), those factors can be isolated without an eigenvalue higher than 1 or whose total percentage of explained variance amounts to 70%.

As Table 2 shows, 12 factors have an eigenvalue higher than 1. These factors taken together account for 72% of the total variance of the 39 items. These factors can be interpreted and named on the basis of the items that are loading high on each of them (min. 40).

Factor 1 has a high positive loading on
- Things go on in my body which frighten me (.79)
- It is as if my body is not mine (.76)
- I feel a nervousness in my body (.72)
- I experience my body as a burden (.68)
- My body is a threat to me (.68)
- My body is a numb object (.65),

and a high negative loading on
- It is easy for me to relax physically (−.59)
- I feel comfortable in my own body (−.58).

Meaning: frightening body estrangement.

Table 2. Explained variance per (rotated) factor.

Factor	Eigenvalue	Variance percentage	Cumulative percentage
1	6.28	16.10	16.10
2	2.84	7.28	28.38
3	2.24	5.74	29.12
4	2.23	5.71	34.83
5	2.19	5.62	40.45
6	2.19	5.62	46.07
7	2.02	5.17	51.24
8	1.83	4.69	55.93
9	1.75	4.48	60.40
10	1.67	4.28	64.60
11	1.59	4.07	68.60
12	1.25	3.20	71.80

Factor 2 has a high positive loading on
- I am inclined to hide my body (.80)
- When I am in company I feel embarrassed with my appearance (.53)

Meaning: body shyness.

Factor 3 has a high positive loading on
- The width of my hips is (more or less un-) important to me (.85)
- The width of my shoulders is (more or less un-) important to me (.82)

Meaning: importance of body width (see factor 8).

Factor 4 has a high positive loading on
- I have an urge to be slimmer (.80)
- My hips seem too broad to me (.52),

and a high negative loading on
- I think I am too slim (−.56).

Meaning: urge for slimness.

Factor 5 has a high positive loading on
- I am (more or less dis-) satisfied with my growth of hair (.81)
- I find my growth of hair is too female (.85).

Meaning: growth of hair.

Factor 6 has a high positive laoding on
- I observe my appearance in the mirror (.80)
- I compare my appearance with that of others (.59)
- I envy others their physical appearance (.53).

Meaning: exaggerated body self-consciousness.

Factor 7 has a high positive loading on
- I am indifferent to my appearance (.75)
- My body is a numb object (.63).

Meaning: body denial.

Factor 8 has a positive loading on
- My shoulders seem too narrow to me (.83)
- My hips seem to narrow to me (.69).

Meaning: feeling of frontal narrowing (cf. factor 3).

Factor 9 has a high positive loading on
- I am (more or less dis-) satisfied with my height (.72),

and a high negative loading on
- My body seems too male to me (−.55).

Meaning: dissatisfaction with one's own body (cf. factor 12).

Factor 10 has a high positive loading on
- My breasts seem too large to me (.83)
- I am (more or less dis-) satisfied with the size of my breasts (.72).

Meaning: breast size.

Factor 11 has a high positive loading on
- My shoulders seem too broad to me (.73),

and a high negative loading on
- My body seems too female to me (−.55).

Meaning: dissatisfaction with one's body (cf. factor 9).

On the basis of this factor analysis, 5 items could be eliminated because they do not score high on any factor:

- I look as if I am pregnant
- I am obsessed with the idea that there is fat on my body
- During contacts with others my appearance embarrasses me
- I have an urge to be slimmer
- When I look in the mirror, I feel dissatisfied with my appearance.

The 39 items could be reduced to 12, which would then correspond to the 12 factors. We do not propose such a reduction, though, because a relatively long questionnaire is a means of distracting attention from more direct questions that may restrain subjects from responding truthfully.

Discriminant Analysis

Because this questionnaire is meant to be used as a diagnostic means (e.g., for early identification and secondary prevention), it is important to analyze the discriminatory power of the different factors and items of the anorexia patients on the one hand, and the normal subjects and other psychiatric patients on the other.

Table 3. Means and standard deviations of the factor scores of the "normal" group per factor.

Factors	Means	Standard deviations
1	0.520	0.603
2	0.157	0.807
3	−0.040	0.904
4	−0.120	0.885
5	0.082	0.805
6	−0.064	0.986
7	0.159	0.564
8	−0.007	0.707
9	0.009	0.851
10	0.013	1.000
11	−0.004	0.844
12	0.021	−0.955

Table 4. Means and deviations of the factor scores of the anorexia nervosa patients group per factor.

Factors	Means	Standard deviations
1	−1.104	0.897
2	−0.562	1.263
3	−1.149	1.066
4	0.370	1.291
5	−0.250	1.310
6	0.204	1.007
7	0.163	1.048
8	−0.031	1.286
9	0.056	1.103
10	0.035	0.838
11	−0.021	1.027
12	0.111	0.958

Table 5. Means and standard deviations of the factor scores of the psychiatric patients.

Factors	Means	Standard deviations
1	−0.430	0.904
2	0.190	1.015
3	0.363	1.205
4	−0.059	0.863
5	0.036	1.163
6	−0.043	1.052
7	−0.834	1.667
8	0.073	1.461
9	−0.113	1.364
10	−0.100	1.228
11	0.048	1.469
12	−0.239	1.217

To this end, discriminant analysis was used, which can be applied both for the interpretation and classification. Interpretation involves gaining insight into the nature of the differences between the groups. With classification, we want to make future predictions of group classification possible. First, the factor scores for the three groups were computed (means and standard deviations).*

Subsequently, the computer selects from the 12 factors those that best express the difference between the groups. This occurs step by step. Thus, the discriminant scores of a factor that are determined first will discriminate best between the groups studied. After

---

*The negative means in Tables 3, 4, 5 express the fact that these factors do exist since the affirmative responses to the items constituting these factors are scored lower than a negative response.

Table 6. Discriminant analysis on the basis of factor scores.

Step no.	Variable entered	F-value to enter included	No. of variables	U-statistic	Approx. F-statistic	Degrees of freedom
1	factor 1	54.7753	1	0.5248	54.775	2.00	121.00
2	factor 2	10.9160	2	0.4440	30.041	4.00	240.00
3	factor 3	10.0242	3	0.3800	24.679	6.00	238.00
4	factor 4	5.4708	4	0.3478	20.523	8.00	236.00

having deducted the common variance with the discriminant scores from the original data, the computer searches for the remaining best discriminant function of the remaining variance.

From the 12 factors, 4 were successively selected:

- factor 1: frightening body estrangement
- factor 2: body shyness
- factor 7: body denial
- factor 4: urge for slimness.

Now we can ask ourselves if the three groups differ significantly on these 4 factors. If the obtained F-value is higher than the critical F-value, H_0 can be rejected. Since the computed F-values for the three groups (12.91, 9.92, and 10.17, respectively) are higher than the critical F-value (for df 4 and 102: 3.48 at the 1% level), the null hypothesis can be rejected.

So the three groups differ significantly on these four factors. Other factors do not contribute to further differentiation.

From the point of view of the anorexia patients, we can interpret these differences as follows:

- The anorexia patients say they are suffering from a marked frightening body estrangement, the normal subjects do not, and the psychiatric patients do so to a lesser extent.
- The anorexia patients say they are clearly embarrassed about their bodies, the normal subjects and the psychiatric patients do not.
- The anorexia patients and the normal subjects say they do not have body denial, but the psychiatric patients do.
- The anorexia patients say they do not have an urge for slimness, but the normal subjects do, and the psychiatric patients to a lesser extent.

If we compare these findings with data from the literature, we must conclude that the data with regard to body estrangement and body shyness fit (Bruch, 1973; Brinks, 1977; Lefeber, 1971; Amir, 1977). The data on body denial and urge for slimness appear to be inconsistent with the accepted views (Van de Loo, 1982; Lafeber, 1971). A possible explanation might be sought in the fact that the items on these two factors may have been put too bluntly, so that the anorexia patient—if she is to be truthful—would have to admit rationally that her body has an important function, and that she should normalize it ("I know I must put on weight, but I'd rather be or remain slim"). It could also constitute a tactic to divert attention from the psychic aspect. It could also mean that the patient conforms to social reality, a characteristic that can be found in this group.

Thus, the questionnaire is shown to be able to discriminate sufficiently between the different groups. This is even more evident if the reverse procedure is followed and the subjects are divided into three groups on the basis of the factor scores of the 12 factors. This shows that 89.1% of all subjects were correctly classified, indicating that the responses to most items are typical of anorexia patients.

Discriminant Analysis of the Item Scores

To find the most discriminant items, we also carried out a discriminant analysis on the mean item scores. Step by step those items are selected from the 39 items that discriminate most between the three groups. In this way, 6 items were selected:

- My body seems to be a dead object to me
- I think I am too thin
- Some parts of my body seem swollen to me
- I am indifferent to my appearance
- Things happen in my body that frighten me
- I observe my appearance in the mirror.

Differences on Basis of Total Scores

Differences in body experience between the three groups can also be analyzed on the basis of the total score on the questionnaire. This procedure attributes the same importance to each item. The mean score on the 39 items then expresses the body experience. A high score corresponds with a positive body experience and vice versa. If the mean scores of each group are compared, it shows that (in keeping with the data in the literature) the anorexia patients obtain the lowest score (85.7), the normal subjects 95, and the psychiatric patients 91.1. These means differ significantly (at the 0.001 level) between the anorectic patients and the normal group. So the anorexia patients have a significantly more negative body experience than the normal subjects. There is no difference, however, between anorexia patients and psychiatric patients.

Influence of Age and Study Level

Age and study level could influence the response pattern of the subjects. Therefore, the null hypothesis that there is no correlation between age and the responses was tested. The responses were shown not to have been influenced by age.

A possible correlation between study level and the responses was also analyzed. Here, the null hypothesis of no correlation was rejected for 7 of the 39 items. We can summarize the influence of the study level as follows:

- At the lower study levels, there are more subjects who declare they do not feel comfortable in their bodies, and who experience their bodies as strange and frightening.
- At the higher study levels, there are more subjects who state that they are concerned about their experience, that they feel comfortable in their bodies, that they often compare their appearance with that of others and feel embarrassed about it.

The interpretation of these findings is not easy because, for example, the subjects with a low study level chiefly belonged to the category of psychiatric patients. A lower study level could also imply that subjects in that category understand less well more abstractly formulated items or interpret them in a different way than intended.

The Truthfulness of the Responses

Finally, we tried to find out if there were any correlations between the control items. A control item is an item that is formulated differently or whose formulation is the negative of another item. Responses to both items can indicate whether the items are responded to in a reliable way. If this is the case, responses to an item and its control item must correlate positively or negatively.

The expected correlation between the control items was not always found. Of the 11 control items, there were six with the anorexia patients, five with the normal subjects, and five with the psychiatric patients which didn't correlate. On first sight, one could doubt whether the questionnaire was responded to in a truthful way. But other explanations for the not always consistent responses to the control items appear to be acceptable. An example may clarify this: With items 5 and 19, it is acceptable if someone experiences her body as neither too male or too female, so the fact that responses to both items are negative still doesn't imply a contradiction. Some items, like the one on feeling as if one is pregnant, may be too direct or may offend feelings of decency.

Another explanation may lie in the fact that some subjects lack self-knowledge, are unaware of certain aspects of their personalities, and hence respond to control items unexpectedly. On the other hand, the number of unreliable responses to control items from anorexia patients is not higher than that from normal subjects, from which could be deduced that both groups responded equally reliably.

Proposal for a Revised Questionnaire and Discussion

Taking into account critical observations on the experimental questionnaire, we propose a revised version (Appendix) containing 20 items scored on a 6-point scale (0–5). The maximum score is 100. The higher the score, the more disturbed the body experience. We decided to keep only those items on the list that sufficiently discriminate between anorexia nervosa patients and normal subjects or psychiatric patients. Some items, though, have been formulated in a less probing way. A shorter questionnaire is also more convenient and more reliable. In addition to the items with a high discrimination potential, we have also kept some related items that serves as control items. The revised questionnaire must be used not only as a diagnostic instrument, but also as an evaluation of body experience and its possible evolution during and after treatment. For that, dichotomic questions are hardly suitable because they do not enable gradation or differentiation. Thus, we decided to make the revised version one with uniformly multiple-response options. This revised version is now being used for comparative analysis, which is still imperative, as we mention below.

In contrast to methods that often only refer to estimating the body measures, the *Body Attitudes Questionnaire* discussed here clearly shows the disturbed body experience of the anorexia patients. And so we take the view that this questionnaire, in addition to other observational data, can provide a valuable contribution to the diagnosis and therapy of the body experience of anorexia nervosa patients.

One must always bear in mind, though, that all questionnaires asking about self-evaluation have weak points (Crombach, 1970). The patients often do not know themselves sufficiently well to respond reliably to such questions. The disease-denial factor can seriously affect the response pattern of anorexia patients (Vandereycken & Vanderlinden, 1983). Sometimes, the responses are deliberately false, sometimes the meaning of an item or response category is ambiguous. A further objection against the use of questionnaires is that many real-life situations or subtle observational data cannot be fit into test items. Some of these objections were raised when the correlations between control items were analyzed.

The experimental phase of the test construction has now been completed, but the clinical usefulness and validity of the revised *Body Attitudes Questionnaire* needs to be examined further: a test-retest reliability study, research into the value of the instrument during therapy and follow-up, validation on the basis of analogous questionnaires, and a cross-validation on other anorexia nervosa patients and on larger subject groups. We therefore invite anyone interested to use our *Body Attitudes Questionnaire* (subject to source quotation) and to inform us about their experiences.

APPENDIX

	Always Usually Often Sometimes Rarely Never

1) When I compare myself with others (peers), I'm dissatisfied with my own body.
2) My body appears to be a numb object.
3) My hips seem too broad to me.
4) I feel comfortable within my own body.
5) I have a strong desire to be thinner.
6) I think my breasts are too large.
7) I am inclined to hide my body (e.g., under loose clothing).
9) It's easy for me to relax physically.
10) I think I am too fat.
11) I feel my body as a burden.
12) My body is a threat to me.
13) Some parts of my body look swollen.
14) My body appears as if it's not mine.
15) My bodily appearance is very important.
16) My belly looks as if I'm pregnant.
17) I feel tense in my body.
18) I envy others for their physical appearance.
19) Things go on in my body that frighten me.
20) I observe my appearance in the mirror.

NOTE: With the exception of the negatively keyed items (4, 9), items are scored as follows: Always = 5, Usually = 4, Often = 3, Sometimes = 2, Rarely = 1, Never = 0. The maximum score is 100, and the lower the score, the more "normal" the response pattern.

References

Askevold, F. (1975). Measuring body image. *Psychotherapy and Psychosomatics, 26,* 71–77.

Amir, A. P. (1977). Anorexia nervosa. Blijf van mijn lijf. *Tijdschrift Psychomotorische Therapie, 5,* 198–207.

Brinks, M. J. (1977). Behandeling van een anorexia nervosa. *Tijdschrift Psychomotorische Therapie, 5,* 208–226.

Bruch, H. (1973). *Eating disorders. Obesity, anorexia nervosa and the person within.* London: Routledge, Kegan & Paul.

Bruch, H. (1979). *Als een mus in een gouden kooi.* Baarn: In de Toren.

Button, E. J., Fransella, F., & Slade, P. O. (1977). A reappraisal of body perception disturbance in anorexia nervosa. *Psychological Medicine, 7,* 235–243.

Casper, A. M. et al. (1979). Disturbances in body image estimation as related to other characteristics and outcome in anorexia nervosa. *British Journal of Psychiatry, 134,* 60–66.

Crisp, A. M., & Kalucy, R. S. (1974). Aspects of the perceptual disorder in anorexia nervosa. *British Journal of Medical Psychology, 47,* 349–361.

Crisp, A. H. (1980). *Anorexia nervosa. Let me be.* London: Academic Press.

Cronbach, L. J. (1970). *Essential of psychological testing.* New York: Harper & Row.

Dally, P. (1969). *Anorexia nervosa.* London: Heinemann.

Depreitere, L., & Vandereycken, W. (1977). Een psychomotorisch oefenprogramma voor anorexia nervosa patiënten. *Tijdschrift Psychomotorische Therapie, 12,* 121–128.

American Psychiatric Association (1980). *Diagnostical and statistical manual of mental disorders* (3rd ed.). Washington, DC: APA.

Fisher, S. (1970). *Body experience in fantasy and behavior.* New York: Appleton-Century-Croft.

Fisher, S., & Cleveland, S. E. (1969). *Body image and personality.* New York: Dover Publications.

Fries, H. (1977). Studies on secondary amenorrhea, anorectic behavior and body perception: Importance for the early recognition of anorexia nervosa. In R. A. Vigersky (Ed.), *Anorexia nervosa.* New York: Raven Press.

Garfinkel, P. E., & Garner, D. M. (1982). *Anorexia nervosa: A multidimensional perspective.* New York: Brunner/Mazel.

Garfinkel, P. E., Moldofsky, H., & Garner, D. M. (1979). The stability of perceptual disturbances in anorexia nervosa. *Psychological Medicine, 9,* 703–708.

Garner, D. M. et al. (1976). Body image disturbances in anorexia nervosa and obesity. *Psychosomatic Medicine, 38,* 327–336.

Goldberg, D. et al. (1977). A standardized interview of use in community surveys. *British Journal of Preventive and Social Medicine, 24,* 18–23.

Hallstein, E. A. (1965). Adolescent anorexia nervosa treated by desensitization. *Behavior Research and Therapy, 3,* 87–91.

Halmi, K. A., Goldberg, S. C., & Cunnigham, S. (1977). Perceptual distortion of body image in adolescence. *Psychological Medicine, 7,* 253–257.

Jacques, I. (1983). *Een vragenlijst over lichaamsbeleving; vergelijkend onderzoek tussen anorexia nervosa patiënten, psychiatrische patiënten en normale proefpersonen.* Niet gepubliceerde licentiaatsverhandeling Motorische Revalidatie en Kinesitherapie, Instituut voor Lichamelijke Opleiding, Katholieke Universiteit Leuven.

Lafeber, C. (1971). *Anorexia nervosa.* Stafleu: Leiden.

Meermann, R., Napierski, C., & Vandereycken, W. (1988). Experimental body image research in anorexia nervosa patients. In Blinder et al. (Eds.), *The eating disorders* (pp. 177–194). Jamaica: PMA Publishing Corp.

Nunnally, J. C. (1967). *Psychometric theory.* New York: McGraw-Hill.

Pierloot, R., & Houben, M. E. (1978). Estimation of body dimensions in anorexia nervosa. *Psychological Medicine, 8,* 317–324.

Reitman, E. E., & Cleveland, S. E. (1964). Changes in body image following sensory deprivation in schizophrenic and control groups. *Journal of Abnormal and Social Psychology, 68,* 170.

Slade, P. D., & Russel, G. F. M. (1973). Experimental investigation of bodily perception in anorexia nervosa and obesity. *Psychotherapy and Psychosomatics,* 359–363.

Strober, M. et al. (1979). Body image disturbance in anorexia nervosa during the acute and recuperative phase. *Psychological Medicine, 9,* 685–701.

Thijs, P. (1981). *Lichaamsbeleving nagegaan met behulp van de Body Distortion Questionnaire: Literatuuronderzoek en experiment.* Niet gepubliceerd seminariewerk, aangeboden tot het behalen van het getuigschrift van specialisatie in de psychomotorische therapie voor psychisch gestoorden. Instituut voor Lichamelijke Opleiding, Katholieke Universiteit, Leuven.

Van Coppenolle, H., & Laenen, P. (1975). Psychomotorisch onderzoek buj anorexia nervosa patiënten. *Tijdschrift Psychomotorische Therapie, 4,* 177–179.

Van de Loo, K. J. M. (1981a). Anorexia nervosa: Belichaamde onmacht. In K. J. M. Van de Loo, W. Vandereycken & L. Eyckman (Eds.), *Anorexia nervosa, diagnostiek, behandeling, en onderzoek.* Nijmegen: Dekker & Van de Vegt.

Van de Loo, K. J. M. (1981b). Hoekstenen voor een komplexe therapie van anorexia nervosa. In K. J. M. Van de Loo, W. Vandereycken & L. Eyckman (Eds.), *Anorexia nervosa, diagnostiek, behandeling, en onderzoek.* Nijmegen: Dekker & Van de Vegt.

Vandereycken, W. (1978). Magerzucht en bewegingsdrang. De betekenis van hyperactiviteit bij anorexia nervosa (deel 1). *Tijdschrift voor Psychiatrie, 20,* 61–78.

Vandereycken, W., & VanderLinden, J. (1983). Denial of illness and the use of self-reporting measures in anorexia nervosa patients. *International Journal of Eating Disorders, 2,* 101–107.

Van Knippenberg, A., & Siero, F. (1980). *Multivariate analyse.* Deventer: Van Loghum Slaterus.

Van Troos, H. (1982). *De lichaamsbeleving bij anorexia nervosa patiënten.* Niet gepubliceerde licentiaatsverhandeling. Instituut voor Lichamelijke Opleiding, Katholieke Universiteit, Leuven.

Wallet, H. (1964). Anorexia nervosa: A paradigm. In M. R. Kaufman (Ed.), *Evolution of psychosomatic concepts.* New York: International Universities Press.

Williams, P., Tarnepolsky, A., & Hand, O. (1980). Case definition and case identification in psychiatric epidemiology review and assessment. *Psychological Medicine, 10,* 101–114.

Witkin, H. A. et al. (1962). *Psychological differentiation. Studies of development.* New York, London: Wiley.

Ziemer, R. R., & Rosse, J. L. (1970). Anorexia nervosa: A new approach. *American Corrective Therapeutical Journal, 24,* 34–42.

Behavioral and Self-Report Methods in the Study of Family Interaction Concepts

W. Vandereycken*, H. Vertommen*, E. Kog*, R. Meermann**

In psychosomatic families, especially those with an eating disorder patient, certain interactional patterns seem to be characteristic. The interaction concepts "cohesion," "adaptability," and "conflict" were studied by means of two behavioral methods (direct observation and behavioral products) and one self-report method. Structural equation modeling, as a confirmatory factor analysis technique, gave uninterpretable estimations of the parameters, so that no definite conclusions could be drawn. An explanatory factor analysis revealed three latent variables: (1) positive/negative evaluation, which is best measured with a self-report scale; (2) boundaries, which is best measured by means of direct observation; (3) emotional overinvolvement, which is uniquely measured with a direct observation scale.

Since Minuchin and coworkers (1975, 1978) stressed the importance of interactional features in the families of psychosomatic patients, many clinicians and family therapists have become familiar with the transactional characteristics that would typify the psychosomatic family organization: enmeshment, rigidity, overprotectiveness, and lack of conflict resolution. We have questioned, however, Minuchin's conceptualizations on theoretical and epistemological grounds (Kog, Vandereycken & Vertommen, 1985a). An attempt to verify the psychosomatic family model in anorexic or bulimic patients (Kog, Vandereycken & Vertommen, 1985b) turned out to necessitate a large concept-validation study using a multitrait-multimethod approach (Kog, Vertommen & Vandereycken, 1987). We tested the convergent and discriminant validity of both behavioral (coded observation) and self-report (questionnaire) operationalizations of three major concepts in eating disorder families: cohesion, adaptability, and conflict. In a following step, we carried out a controlled investigation of 30 families with an eating-disorder patient versus 30 normal control families, which revealed many interesting differences in interactional patterns (Kog & Vandereycken, 1988). But during the whole project we were increasingly faced with essential methodological questions especially regarding the use of insider's perspective (the family's own viewpoint as assessed by a self-report measure) versus outsider's perception (trained observers coding a videotape for the family interactions). This issue has important practical implications because a behavioral observation method is rather complex and time consuming. In order to find an economically acceptable but also scientifically justified procedure for more routine assessment of families, we compared the self-report and behavioral operationalizations in a large group of both eating disorder and normal families. The objective was to find the best method of measuring each of the three concepts (cohesion, adaptability, conflict) by means of a confirmatory and exploratory factor analysis of the multitrait-multimethod correlation matrix. Moreover, this study would allow us to test the internal relationships between these family concepts.

*Department of Psychology, Catholic University Leuven, Belgium.
**Psychosomatic Hospital, D-3280 Bad Pyrmont, West Germany.

Method

Subjects

A total of 83 families with children between 7 and 25 years served as subjects in this study. In addition to 30 "normal" families, i.e., without any member in psychiatric treatment, we included 53 families with an anorexia nervosa or bulimia patient. Detailed characteristics of this population are described elsewhere (Kog & Vandereycken, 1988). The families came from all social classes, with a slight overrepresentation of the higher social class.

Operationalizations

Each concept is measured with two behavioral methods (a direct observation and a behavioral product measure) and one self-report method. Behavioral data are based on semistructured tasks: a decision-making task and a conflict-resolution task. The final outcome of each interaction task (the behavioral product measure) as well as the interaction process (direct observation) are studied. The self-report measures are based on the answers of the child (eating disorder child or normal control child) on the *Leuven Family Questionnaire* (Kog, Vertommen & Degroote, 1985), which had to be filled out by each family member separately, immediately after the interaction tasks were finished (for a detailed discussion of the procedure, see Kog, Vandereycken & Vertommen, 1985b; Vandereycken, Kog & Vanderlinden, 1988).

Assessment of Cohesion

This concept is defined as the degree of togetherness or differentiation within the family. Table 1 gives an overview of the three operationalizations for this concept.

The direct observation measure (see Table 1) is a scale of 10 behavioral categories that measure the degree of differentiation of subsystems within the family (individual family members, parents/children) in order to carry out the tasks. The behaviors are reliably scored (percentage agreement = 87.8 and the kappa-coefficient = 0.81 for the 10 items), and Cronbach's alpha of the scale is 0.78.

The behavioral product measure (see Table 1) focuses on the degree of differentiation of individually chosen preferences. The split-half reliability of this measure is 0.50.

The self-report measure (see Table 1) comprises 21 items, measuring cohesion and a feeling of loyalty toward other family members. The Cronbach's alpha of this scale is 0.83.

Assessment of Adaptability.

This concept is defined as the degree of organization and flexibility in organization toward new situations or tasks. The three operationalizations for this concept are discussed in Table 2.

The direct observation measure (see Table 2) consists of five behavioral categories that are all scored during the interest-task. This task is subdivided in an individual and an interactional part. First, family members have to choose their preferences individually (see Appendix); then, they have to deliberate about "who likes to do what with whom." The interactions that are scored refer to a lack of task orientation and an orientation toward one another. The interobserver reliability of the five codes in percentage agreement = 84.7 and kappa-coefficient = 0.71. The internal consistency of the scale is Cronbach's alpha = 0.71.

The behavioral product measure (see Table 2) focuses on the degree of stability of the family organization pattern in six hypothetical situations, by comparing the final outcome of the deliberation about "who likes to do what with whom."

The self-report measure (see Table 2) comprises 22 items about a lack of organization and separateness in the family. This refers to extreme adaptability or "chaos." The internal consistency of this scale is 0.89.

Table 1. Cohesion: Three operationalizations.

Direct observation measure	Behavioral product measure	Self-report measure
-1) Does one talk?[1] (decision making task: individual part) 2) Do the parents talk together? (preparation part: disagreement task) 3) Do the children talk together? (preparation part: disagreement task) -4) Do the parents talk to the children? (preparation part: disagreement task) -5) Do the children talk to the parents? (preparation part: disagreement task) 6) How long does one discuss the subject? (discussion of the problem of the parents/children in the negotiation? 7) What is the contribution of parents/children in the negotiation? 8) How long does one discuss the subject? (discussion of the problem of the parents) 9) Do the children support one another? (discussion of the problem of the children) 10) What is the contribution of the parents/children in the negotiation? (discussion of the problem of the parents)	During the interest-task (see Appendix), each family member has to choose two alternatives he/she likes the most and the least for each of the twelve items. The questionnaires of all possible dyads in the family are compared with respect to spontaneous agreements, i.e., similarity in choices without consulting together. Inspired by Ferreira and Winter (1965) we use the following scoring system for each of the twelve items: 1) Conformity in choices is scored positively, i.e. +1 point for each response alternatives similarly chosen by each member of the dyad. Thus, the maximum conforming score for a single item is +4. 2) Difference in choices is scored negatively, i.e. −1 point if the members of a dyad disagree about response alternatives. As above, this yields a maximum difference score for −4 for any individual item. The scores for the 12 items are added, and may thus theoretically vary between −48 and +48 for each dyad. The difference between the highest and the lowest spontaneous agreement score reflects the degree of differentiation of preferences among dyads within the family.	1) Family members are completely involved in each other's lives. 2) We defend our family, regardless of what has happened. 3) I do not know any family that is closer than ours. 4) We weigh our words carefully while discussing, because we are all very sensitive. 5) We easily take the blame. 6) I feel more comfortable within our family than outside of it. 7) I feel guilty when I do my own way. 8) I feel responsible for the other family members. 9) When we are having a pleasant time, we do not keep track of time. 10) Without the support of the family, it would be difficult to undertake anything. 11) The parents always side with each other and so do the children. 12) In a discussion, parents and children are able to reach an agreement. 13) Our family life is so well-organized that everything goes smoothly (e.g. fixed mealtimes, fixed weekend activities and weekly menu). 14) Our family hates quarrelling and shouting. 15) We comfort each other when one of us is in trouble. 16) We hate tensions and quarrelling in our family. 17) We spend the evenings together. 18) We always agree on major issues. 19) Family ties are more important to us than friendships. 20) We try to avoid quarrelling at all costs. 21) The parents worry a lot about the children.

[1] The interaction task during which the behavioral category has to be scored is mentioned between brackets. A negative item refers to the cohesion pole of the dimension, the positive items refer to the differentiation pole of the dimension.

Table 2. Adaptability: Three operationalizations.

Direct observation measure	Behavioral product measure	Self-report measure
1) Does one give comments on the task? (individual part interest-task)	The family members have to decide what they prefer to do on the first six questions of the interest-task (appendix) and have to add with whom they like to do this. We examine to what extent the family organizes itself identically or differently in the six situations. For intact families, we differentiate six organization patterns: (1) the whole family; (2) each family member separately; (3) parents together and children separately or together; (4) parents separately and children separately or together; (5) one parent with one or more children, and (6) both parents with one or more other children (not all of them). In one-child families, only patterns 1, 2, 3, 4 and 5 are available. In one-child, one-parent families only patterns 1 and 2 are available. Each of the six situations is compared with each other (a total of 15 comparisons). The number of identical organizations determines the degree of organizational stability: this may be 0, 1, 2, 3, 4, 5, 6, 7, 10 or 15. Because of nonlinearity, we transfer 10 to 8 and 15 to 9. So, the absolute score may vary between 0 and 9, but this score has to be corrected for the degree of stability by change, depending upon the number of available organization patterns which varies for intact and broken families (see above). The percentage stability is expressed according to the following formula: $$\left(I - \frac{D}{A-1}\right) \times \frac{100}{9}$$ where I = number of identical patterns D = number of different patterns A = number of available patterns This score is comparable between families of different size. Families may score negatively because of a slight overcorrection (min. = −20; no organizational stability; and max. = 100; strong organizational stability).	1) In our family, everybody has to solve his own problems.
2) Does attention-seeking behavior occur? (individual part interest-task)		2) The parents let the children live their own lives without interfering a lot.
3) Does attention-giving behavior occur? (individual part interest-task)		-3) There is a lot of friendship in our family.
4) Does one interrupt each other? (interactional part interest-task)		4) It seems there is no room to be alone in our house.
5) Did one move towards each other? (interactional part interest-task)		5) In our family, there is no regularity.
		6) We feel more comfortable with friends than at home.
		7) In our family decisions are made without consultations.
		8) We do not feel friendship for each other.
		-9) Before we make a decision, we ask for the approval of the other family members.
		10) Each of us lives his own life.
		11) Our parents do not agree on the education of the children.
		-12) We feel very close to each other.
		13) When the parents quarrel, they both try to get the children on their side.
		14) We do not have meals together.
		15) We do not feel responsible for the other family members.
		16) We feel little love for each other.
		17) The parents decide together without consulting the children.
		18) We do not know whether we can count on each other.
		19) We do not appreciate the advice and support that are given by the family.
		20) We bottle up all tensions.
		21) Family members decide on the basis of their own judgments.
		22) Family members do not cling together.

Table 3. Conflict: Three operationalizations.

Direct observation measure	Behavioral product measure	Self-report measure
1) Does one openly disagree? (interactional part: interest-task) 2) Are coalitions formed? (interactional part: interest-task) 3) Do the parents support one another? 4) Do the parents support one another? (discussion of the problem of the parents) 5) Does one of the parents take sides with the children? (discussion of the problem of the children)	This measure is based on the outcome of the disagreement task. This is a conflict management task, to be carried out between the subsystems "parents" and "children," separated in the room. The preparing phase of this task is carried out by each of the subsystems directly. Each subsystem has to choose one subject (problem) on which they disagree with the other subsystem and write it down on a card. They have to put the card on the table, so that the other subsystem may read the problem without discussing it already. Then, each subsystem has to write down on a separate list their proposal for resolution of their own problem and of the problem formulated by the other subsystem. Once this is done, the negotiation may start. First, the parents explain the problem they have chosen, the children say what they think about it, and finally parents and children try to achieve resolution. The parents write this agreement on their card. Afterwards, the children explain their problem, and a similar negotiation follows. The final outcome of the negotiation of the problem of the parents and the children is categorized as follows: 1) Conflict avoidance (score = 1): no problem. 2) Spontaneous agreement (score = 2): parents and children have the same proposal for resolution of the problem. 3) Compromise solution (score = 3): parents and children have a different proposal for resolution of the problem but agree upon a new solution. 4) Convincing process (score = 4): parents and children have a different proposal for resolution and the final solution is identical to the proposal for resolution of one of them. 5) Conflict escalation (score = 5): the discussion ends without reaching an agreement. The scores of the two problems are added and may then theoretically vary between 2 (extreme conflict avoidance) and 10 (extreme conflict escalation).	1) It is very clear who likes or dislikes each other in our family. 2) If in our family something has to be decided, each parent has his supporters among the children. 3) Some physical complaints reoccur in our family. 4) The same family members usually take sides with each other. 5) We easily blame other family members. 6) Parents and children regularly quarrel with each other. 7) Each family wants to have his own say, so we usually cannot reach a decision. 8) We talk a lot about our conflicts but do not reach an agreement. 9) Our parents always agree. 10) In our family, opinions regularly differ. 11) Physical complaints are merely an expression of all tensions within our family. 12) When the parents quarrel, the children take sides with one of them. 13) When we are angry with each other, there can be great turmoil. 14) Family members have conflicts that cannot be talked out. 15) Most of the time we have to agree with those who criticize our family. 16) The least cause can greatly upset our family. 17) In family interactions, we always return to the same habits. 18) Tensions between family members are inevitable. 19) Major conflicts exist in our family. 20) Some children always support one particular parent. 21) A discussion easily results in reproaches. 22) The same persons always decide for the whole family. 23) We easily take out our problems on the family, even if they have nothing to do with the family. 24) A tense atmosphere sometimes lasts several days. 25) Some members of our family interfere with one another. 26) Parents and children are unable to reach an agreement on certain issues. 27) The atmosphere in our house can change from one moment to the next. 28) When the children quarrel, each of them tries to get the parents on his side. 29) We easily take out tensions on our family. 30) Conflicts do not occur in our family.

Assessment of Conflict

This concept refers to the extent to which divergent opinions are discussed, coalitions are formed and to the existence of tension in the family. Table 3 gives an outline of the three operationalizations for this concept.

The direct observation measure (see Table 3) comprises five categories, focusing on disagreements and coalition formation in the family. The percentage agreement of this scale is 80.0 and the kapa-coefficient is 0.66. Cronbach's alpha is 0.58. This scale is somewhat less reliably scored and less consistent, probably because of the combination of two items referring to disagreements in the family and three items referring to disagreements between the parents.

The behavioral product measure (see Table 3) focuses on the degree of discussion of divergent opinions between parents and children. The split-half reliability of this measure is 0.67.

The self-report measure (see Table 3) comprises 30 items with an internal consistency of 0.92. The items refer to the existence of tension as well as coalition formation (generational and intergenerational).

Results

Multitrait-Multimethod Matrix

Because of missing observations for two families, the correlation matrix is based upon the results of 81 families (Table 4).

According to Campbell and Fiske (1959), the convergent as well as the discriminant validity of the operationalizations can be determined by a qualitative investigation of the correlations in the multitrait-multimethod matrix. There has to be a significant correlation between different measures of the same dimension *(convergent validity)*, but these correlations also have to be higher than the correlations between measures of different dimensions, even if the same method was used *(discriminant validity)*. Miller, Rollins and Thomas (1982) mention the problem of methods that are not independent in the multitrait-multimethod matrix. When measurements share method variance, then part of the correlation between traits may result from systematic error, which may be interpreted erroneously as evidence for convergent validity. The parameter fitting statistical analysis "structural equation modeling" is a confirmatory factor analysis that makes it possible, among other things, to control for this problem as it is able to determine the concept variance and error variance in each measure. We apply this data-analysis method to our multitrait-multimethod matrix.

Table 4. Multitrait-multimethod matrix.

		Behavioral products			Direct observations			Self-ratings		
		A_1	B_1	C_1	A_2	B_2	C_2	A_3	B_3	C_3
Behavioral products										
Cohesion	A_1	X								
Adaptability	B_1	−0.046	X							
Conflict	C_1	0.179	−0.185*	X						
Direct observations										
Cohesion	A_2	0.252**	−0.136	0.168	X					
Adaptability	B_2	0.110	−0.102	0.134	−0.125	X				
Conflict	C_2	0.095	−0.068	0.115	−0.104	0.027	X			
Self-ratings										
Cohesion	A_3	−0.310***	0.177	−0.315***	−0.150	−0.094	−0.302***	X		
Adaptability	B_3	0.090	−0.078	0.232**	−0.031	0.087	0.330***	−0.651***	X	
Conflict	C_3	0.081	−0.031	0.353***	−0.050	−0.111	0.218**	−0.418***	0.580***	X

*** $p<0.01$, ** $p<0.05$, * $p<0.01$; significance levels for r when population correlation coefficient is zero.

Confirmatory Factor Analysis

One can test the difference of fit between various models with more or less restrictions on the latent variables (see Table 5). Jöreskog and Sörbom (1981) developed the computer program LISREL (Analysis of Linear Structural Relationships) to carry out a confirmatory analysis of covariance matrices (Jöreskog, 1984).

Table 5. Goodness-of-fit between latent models and empirical data.

Model	χ^2	d.f.	p
1. Three trait factors	30.79	24	0.160
2. Three trait factors Three method factors	8.53	12	0.742
3. Two trait factors Two method factors	15.89	16	0.460
1 versus 2	22.26	12	<0.025
3 versus 2	7.36	4	<0.25

We first tested a model with three trait factors, because it seems natural to begin with the hypothesis that all methods are equivalent in measuring each trait. This hypothesis implies that all variation and covariation in the multitrait-multimethod matrix is due to trait factors only. The fit of this model with the empirical data was $\chi^2_{24} = 30.79$ (prob. level = 0.160). The χ^2-measure is sensitive to sample size and very sensitive to departure from multivariate normality of the observed variables. Large sample sizes and departures from normality tend to increase χ^2 over and above what can be expected from specification error in the model. So, our relatively small sample size (N = 82) could have decreased the χ^2 and thus elevated the probability level in favor of the acceptance of the model (a nonsignificant χ^2 indicates that the model fits with the data). The goodness-of-fit index is another measure for judging the fit of the model. It is a measure of the relative amount of variances and covariances jointly accounted for by the model. Unlike χ^2, the goodness-of-fit index is independent of the sample size and relatively robust against departures from normality. Unfortunately, however, its statistical distribution is unknown, so there is no standard to compare it with. Nevertheless, we can compare the goodness-of-fit indices of various models which refer to the same set of data. The goodness-of-fit index, adjusted for degrees of freedom, for this model is 0.850. Because of the relatively poor fit, we relaxed the model to a model with three trait and three method factors (one method factor for each method). In this model, it is assumed that trait factors may correlate and method factors may correlate too, but trait and method factors are uncorrelated. This results in a fit of $\chi^2_{12} = 8.53$ (prob. level = 0.742) and an adjusted goodness-of-fit index = 0.909. This is a better model than the previous one because the reduction in $\chi^2 = 22.26$ (30.79–8.53), compared to the difference in degrees of freedom = 12 (24–12) is significant (p<0.025). The estimated correlation between the direct observation and behavioral product method was, however, quite high (0.821), as was the estimated correlation between the trait factors adaptability and conflict (0.422). Thus, we tested a slightly more restricted model with two trait factors (cohesion and adaptability/conflict) and two method factors (behavioral methods and self-report method). This proved to explain the data slightly better: $\chi^2_{16} = 15.89$ (prob. level = 0.460) and the adjusted goodness-of-fit = 0.869. The increase in $\chi^2 = 7.36$ (15.89–8.53), compared to the gain in degrees of freedom = 4 (16–12) was just barely non-significant (p between 0.10 and 0.25). So, we conclude that the most economic model (see Table 5) with a satisfying fit is the one that states that all variances and covariances in the matrix are due to two concepts—cohesion and conflict/adaptability—which are measured in a different way by means of behavioral methods compared to self-report.

We do not, however, discuss the estimations of the variance components because there was one serious problem in the estimations of the parameters. The program sometimes gave unreasonable values. For example, the result was negative or higher than one, while the parameter had to vary between zero and one. According to Jöreskog and Sörbom (1981), none of the estimations are reliable in this case. The program is not able to estimate the parameters reliably because the sample is not large enough or the model is fundamentally wrong. The nonsignificant χ^2 of our analysis could thus be an artefact of the relatively small sample size, which decreases the χ^2 and

Table 6. Rotated factor pattern of the nine measures.

		Factor 1 Pos./neg. evaluation	Factor 2 Boundaries	Factor 3 Emotional overinvolvement
Behavioral product	Cohesion	0.11772	0.40306	0.10944
	Adaptability	−0.08225	−0.23606	−0.12745
	Conflict	0.32027	0.32663	0.10118
Direct observation	Cohesion	−0.15086	0.73990	−0.26641
	Adaptability	0.00876	0.07983	0.66429
	Conflict	0.38574	0.00657	0.08606
Self-report	Cohesion	−0.68078	−0.40220	−0.12740
	Adaptability	0.82691	0.09554	0.05950
	Conflict	0.69783	0.04500	−0.16460
		1.929037	1.0511649	0.605984

thus makes it more quickly nonsignificant. So, we could not draw any definite conclusions out of this confirmatory factor.

Explanatory Factor Analysis

We extracted nine factors out of the intercorrelation matrix, using iterated principal factor analysis. The first three factors accounted for 100% of the common variance. So, the first three factors were rotated in orthogonal simple structure, using the normalized varimax criterion. Table 6 gives the rotated factor pattern. The first factor, which explains 60% of the common variance (eigenvalue 2.131), has five measures with a factor loading higher than 0.30; these are the three self-report measures and the two behavioral measures for conflict. The self-report measure for adaptability has the highest loading on this factor (0.83). Thus, we prefer not to use the term "conflict" to characterize this factor. We should rather call it *positive/negative evaluation* because the three measures for conflict and the self-report measure for adaptability have a clear negative connotation, while the self-report measure for cohesion, with also a high but negative factor loading, has a clear positive connotation. It is obvious that this factor is best measured by a self-report method, but the behavioral measures also show convergent as well as discriminant validity (the other behavioral measures have a low loading on this factor).

The second factor has four measures with a loading higher than 0.30: the three cohesion measures and the behavioral product measure for conflict. The direct observation measure for cohesion, which has the highest loading on this factor, refers to the intensity of boundaries between subsystems (especially parents and children) in order to carry out its tasks. The behavioral product measure for cohesion also focuses on the degree of differentiation of dyads within the family, as to their preferences. The self-report measure for cohesion, with a similar but negative loading, operationalizes the other pole of cohesion—togetherness or lack of differentiation. The behavioral product measure for conflict finally focuses on disagreements between parents and children. We prefer to label this factor *boundaries* as a common denominator in all these loadings.

The third factor has only one high-loading measure: the direct observation measure for adaptability. There is another moderate-loading measure (−0.27): the direct observation measure for cohesion. The five behavioral categories for adaptability refer to a lack of task orientation and a high degree of concern for each other. The ten behavioral categories for cohesion refer to an efficient task orientation and a differentiation between parents and children, to carry out the task as expected. This latter scale has a negative loading, and the previous scale has a high positive loading. We label this factor *emotional overinvolvement*, with lack of task orientation and differentiation as a possible correlate.

In conclusion, we characterize the latent variables that explain the correlations between the nine operationalizations as positive/negative evaluation, boundaries, and emotional overinvolvement.

Discussion

We first mention the advantages and disadvantages of the use of the structural equation modeling for concept-validation studies in the field of family interaction research at this stage. Afterwards, we discuss the results of our concept validation and compare these with the findings of other authors.

With regard to the use of *structural equation models* in family research, Miller, Rollins and Thomas (1982) hold that confirmatory methods of data analysis are one of the advances in statistical literature that are waiting for their application by marriage and family researchers. Indeed, the relative contribution of trait and method variance can be weighed more rigorously by a parameter fitting statistical analysis than with the heuristic guidelines of Campbell and Fiske (1959). Jackson (1975) also mentions this problem and proposes a multimethod factor analysis, which is, however, exploratory rather than confirmatory. Up until now, there was still one serious problem with the use of structural equation models in marriage and family research. As discussed above, a theoretical model can seem to fit well with the empirical data, but further investigation may reveal that the estimations are unreliable. Our test of the model (see confirmatory analysis above) has failed in this sample either because of the inappropriateness of the model or because of the limited amount of data. As to sample size, 81 subjects are not that few: Jöreskog and Sörbom (1981) consider a sample of at least 100 subjects to be large enough to use the structural analysis of covariance matrices as a definite test for a model. So, probably, the model is wrong, though the heteromethod correlations for cohesion and conflict are not that low, taking into account that two totally independent methods are included: self-report and behavioral methods. Previous systematic comparisons of self-report and behavioral measures of similar interaction concepts by Oliveri and Reiss (1984), Olson (1981), and Sigafoos et al. (1985) did not prove the predicted association. Nevertheless, totally independent methods are the best tests for convergent and discriminant validity according to Campbell and Fiske (1959). In multimethod family research, it will thus frequently be the case that the data are not so "nice": First, because small sample sizes are the artefact of the time-consuming behavioral observation; second, because behavioral and self-report methods correlate to a low degree; and third, because self-report measures intercorrelate highly (Haynes, 1984)—which is bad for discriminant validity. So, in this stage of family interaction concept building, when using smaller samples or when the model as a whole fails to explain the data, the heuristic guidelines of Campbell and Fiske (1959) and an exploratory factor analysis seem to offer an adequate framework for hypothesis testing and further hypothesis building as to the separate concepts of the model. We hope to be able to carry out a confirmatory data analysis later on.

With regard to the *results of our concept-validation study*, we found convergent validity for two concepts, which we redefined as positive/negative evaluation and boundaries. Moreover, the original direct observation measure for adaptability had an exclusive high loading on a third factor we characterized as emotional overinvolvement.

We concluded that a global positive/negative evaluation is best collected by means of self-report, though this method is not able to measure other concepts with discriminant validity. Even the self-report measure for cohesion, which loads 0.40 on the boundary factor, loads almost twice as high on the positive/negative evaluation factor. Forgatch, Patterson and Skinner (1985, p. 16) also reported that "A total reliance on parent-self-report data creates a situation in which it is extremely difficult to separate methods from (construct) structure . . . While it is possible to obtain a good convergence in measuring structures, the magnitude of the interconstruct correlations (path coefficients) suggests a bipolar dimension of negative (e.g., 'I'm living an awful life and everything in it is awful')." In a more restricted sample of 53 families with an eating disorder patient (Kog, Vertommen & Vandereycken, 1987), we ourselves also reported a significant correlation between a self-report and two behavioral measures for conflict and even a higher significant intercorrelation between the various self-report measures.

The behavioral measures for boundaries show convergent as well as discriminant validity. The direct observation measure is the best operationalization for this concept. These and previous reported findings (Kog, Vertommen & Vandereycken, 1987) suggest that this concept is best measured with a behavioral method because it is slightly different from the self-report operationalization for cohesion, which refers more to a positive/negative evaluation of family interaction. Reiss and coworkers reported even a nonsignificant correlation between their behavioral measure of coordination in the *Card Sort Procedure* (CSP) and the self-report measures of cohesion in the *Family Adaptability and Cohesion Evaluation Scales* (FACES) (Sigafoos, Reiis, Rich & Douglas, 1985) and the *Family Environment Scale* (FES) (Oliveri & Reiss, 1984). Nor did Hannum and Mayer (1984) find a significant correlation between the same cohesion scale of the FES and their behavioral observation scale for cohesion. However, Russell (1979) noted a relatively high correlation ($r = 0.41$) between the cohesion scale of FACES and his behavioral measure for cohesion, which was also based on the degree of coordination while carrying out the problem-solving task SIMFAM. The relationships between the associated concepts cohesion, coordination, and boundaries thus has to be further explored in order to draw more definite conclusions.

The third concept, emotional overinvolvement, is uniquely measured with direct observation. It is comparable to Minuchin's concept of "overprotectiveness" (Minuchin et al., 1978) and Bowen's concept of "stuck togetherness." It refers to a great deal of attention for each other and a lack of task orientation. This concept can hardly be associated with the original concept "adaptability," because of a low loading of two of the three operationalizations. In a previous study (Kog et al., 1987) of eating-disorder families, however, we did find a significant correlation between two behavioral measures for adaptability but not between a self-report and any of the behavioral measures. Sigafoos et al. (1985) reported a nonsignificant correlation between the degree of closure in their behavioral task CSP and the degree of adaptability as measured with the self-report scale FACES. However, Russell (1979) again found a high correlation ($r = 0.50$) between the same self-report scale and his behavioral scales for adaptability. These partly contradictory findings suggest that this concept is not clearly demarcated and needs further investigation.

To summarize, the explorative study of various operationalizations for the concepts conflict, adaptability and cohesion suggest that a self-report scale measures a global positive/negative evaluation. This latter evaluation can also be done by means of behavioral methods, though these are most valuable to judge more specific concepts, such as boundaries and emotional overinvolvement. These findings have to be further explored before we can arrive to the stage of confirmatory analysis of conceptual models.

References

Bowen, M. (1978). *Family therapy in clinical practice*. New York: Jason Aronson.

Campbell, D. T., & Fiske, D. W. (1959). Convergent and discriminant validation by the multitrait-multimethod matrix. *Psychological Bulletin, 56*, 81–105.

Ferreira, A. J., & Winter, W. (1965). Family interaction and decision making. *Archives of General Psychiatry, 13*, 214–223.

Forgatch, M. S., Patterson, G. R., & Skinner, M. L. (1985). *A mediational model for the effect of divorce on antisocial behavior in boys*. Paper presented to the NICD-sponsored conference on The Impact of Divorce, Single Parenting and Stepparenting on Children.

Hannum, J. W., & Mayer, J. M. (1984). Validation of two assessment approaches. *Journal of Marriage and the Family*, (August), 741–748.

Haynes, S. (1984). Behavioral assessments of adult. In G. Goldstein & M. Hersen (Eds.), *Handbook of psychological assessment.* Oxford, Paris: Pergamon.

Jackson, D. N. (1975). Multimethod factor analysis: A reformulation. *Multivariate Behavioral Research, 10,* 259–76.

Jöreskog, K., & Sörbom, D. (1981). *Lisrel V. User's guide.* Chicago: National Educational Resources.

Kog, E., & Vandereycken, W. (1988). Family interaction in eating disorder patients and normal controls. *International Journal of Eating Disorders, 7,* in press.

Kog, E., Vandereycken, W., & Vertommen, H. (1985a). The psychosomatic family model: A critical analysis of family interaction concepts. *Journal of Family Therapy, 7,* 31–44.

Kog, E., Vandereycken, W. & Vertommen, H. (1985b). Toward a verification of the psychosomatic family model: A pilot study of 10 families with an anorexia/bulimia nervosa patient. *International Journal of Eating Disorders, 4,* 525–38.

Kog, E., Vertommen, H., & Degroote, T. (1985). Family interaction research in anorexia nervosa: The use and misuse of a family questionnaire. *International Journal of Family Psychiatry, 6,* 227–43.

Kog, E., Vertommen, H., & Vandereycken, W. (1987). Minuchin's psychosomatic family model revised: A concept-validation study using a multitrait-multimethod approach. *Family Process, 26,* 235–253.

Miller, B. C., Rollins, B. C., & Thomas, D. L. (1982). On methods of studying marriages and families. *Journal of Marriage and the Family, 44,* 851–75.

Minuchin, S., Baker, L., Rosman, B. L., Liebman, R., Milman, L., & Todd, T. C. (1975). A conceptual model of psychosomatic illness in children: Family organization and family therapy. *Archives of General Psychiatry, 32,* 1031–1038.

Minuchin, S., Rosman, B., & Baker, L. (1978). *Psychosomatic families: Anorexia nervosa in context.* Cambridge, MA: Harvard University Press.

Oliveri, M., & Reiss, D. (1984). Family concepts and their measurement: Things are seldom what they seem. *Family Process, 23,* 33–48.

Olson, D. H. (1969). The measurement of family power by self-report and behavioral methods. *Journal of Marriage and the Family, 31,* 545–50.

Russel, C. S. (1979). Circumplex model of marital and family systems. III: Empirical evaluation with families. *Family Process, 18,* 29–45.

Sigafoos, A., Reiss, D., Rich, J., & Douglas, E. (1985). Pragmatics in the measurement of family functioning: An interpretative framework for methodology. *Family Process, 24,* 189–203.

Vandereycken, W., Kog, E. & Vanderlinden, J. (1988). *The family approach to eating disorders: Assessment and treatment of anorexia nervosa and bulimia.* New York: PMA Publications.

APPENDIX

Interest Task

1) What do you like to do the most and the least in leisure time? sports, carpentering, visiting friends, watching TV, engaging in corporate life, going to the movies, reading

2) Which type of movie do you like the most and the least? science fiction, historical film, psychological film, thriller, cartoon, comedy, western

3) Where do you like to dine out the most and the least? hamburger house, fish restaurant, vegetarian restaurant, sandwich bar, chinese restaurant, gastronomic restaurant, self-service

4) In what way do you like to become engaged the most and the least? nature, Third World, your neighborhood, sports, theater, encounter group, hobby club

5) In which way do you like to travel or spend your holidays the most and the least? in house trailer, in tent, in bungalow, in hotel, in apartment, on cruise, hitchhike with rucksack

6) Which type of work do you like the most and the least? housework, lacework, trade, taking care of patients, research activities, giving guidance, handicrafts

7) Which dish do you like to eat the most and the least? Jacob's shell, steak, tonguelet, rabbit, asparagus shamroll, lamb, turkey

8) Which values do you find the most and the least important? liberty, honesty, equality, friendliness, forgiveness, responsibility, willpower

9) Which color do you like the most and the least? blue, yellow, green, red, white, black, brown

10) Which kind of profession do you like the most and the least? craftsman, self-employed, teacher, athlete, researcher, medical assistant, artist

11) Which animal do you like the most and the least? dog, hot-water fish, cat, rabbit, monkey, lamb, canary

12) In what type of residence do you like to live the most and the least? apartment, gentleman's house, country house, farm, community, welfare house, an isolated house

The Long-Term Course of Anorexia Nervosa

Helmut Remschmidt, Franz Wienand, Christoph Wewetzer

Reported are the results of a follow-up study on 103 inpatients with anorexia nervosa. Reliable information could be gathered for 81 patients, 5 patients refused to participate in the study, for 12 patients only insufficient information from relatives were available, 3 patients had died, and 2 could not be retraced. From the follow-up sample of 81 patients, 69% (n=58) showed a good prognosis (according to the criteria of Morgan and Russell), 11% (n=9) an intermediate, and 17% (n=14) an unfavorable prognosis. The probability for a favorable long-term outcome was worse for patients with premorbid eating disorders and better for those without premorbid eating disorders. Other important variables for long-term prognosis were age at the onset of the disorder and some weight parameters during inpatient treatment.

With the increase of anorectic patients in outpatient and inpatient institutions the question of the long-term course of this disease has become increasingly important. A number of follow-up investigations exist (reviewed by Hsu 1980, 1988; Steinhausen & Glanville 1983, 1984; Herzog, Keller & Lavori, 1988). Many studies cannot be compared with each other, though, either because the diagnosis of anorexia nervosa was not based on the same standardized criteria (in addition, bulimic courses were not differentiated earlier), or because the criteria for the assessment of the course were very different. A number of further problems pertaining to catamnestic investigations have to be added: rate of refusal, shrinking of the samples through relocation or death, differences in the follow-up interval, nonconsideration of different types of the disease, etc.

In the last 10 years, the criteria introduced by Morgan and Russell (1975) have won recognition in several comparable follow-up studies. These criteria are defined in three steps:

1) *Good prognosis:* This category applies if the actual weight is between 85% and 115% of the ideal weight at the time of reexamination and if menstruation is regular.

2) *Intermediate prognosis:* This category is applied if the body weight varies between 85% and 115% at reexamination, but possibly fluctuating even more and/or menstrual disturbances exist.

3) *Unfavorable prognosis:* This exists only if the actual body weight lies under 85% at reexamination and/or if the menstruation has not returned.

Table 1 shows the results of four follow-up studies employing the above-mentioned criteria. Our own study is added as a fifth. The table shows that after a follow-up interval of at least 4 years, approximately 53% can expect a good prognosis, 24% an average, and 20% an unfavorable prognosis. The last category includes those patients who succumb to the disease in the long run. The mortality rate of anorexia nervosa in the five studies of Table 1 varies between 1% and 5%. In their review on outcome in anorexia nervosa and bulimia nervosa Herzog, Keller and Lavori (1988) mention a mortality rate ranging from 0% to 22%, with over half of the studies reporting 4% or less. Eight studies with follow-up periods between 4 months and 43 years reported a mortality rate of 0%. The authors analyzed also the causes of death in 88 cases of the different studies: In about half of the cases, the cause was the anorexic disorder itself and its complications, whereas in 24% it was suicide; in the rest of the cases lung diseases (6%) and other causes were reported. It

Department of Child and Adolescent Psychiatry, Philipps-University, Hans-Sachs-Str. 6, D-3550 Marburg, West Germany

Table 1. Results of follow-up studies according to the outcome categories of Morgan and Russell (1975).

	N	Good	Intermediate	Poor	Mortality
Morgan & Russell (1975)	41	16 (39%)	12 (27%)	11 (29%)	2 (5%)
Hsu et al. (1979)	100	48 (48%)	30 (30%)	20 (20%)	2 (2%)
Morgan et al. (1983)	76	45 (59%)	15 (20%)	15 (19%)	1 (1%)
Hall et al. (1984)*	49	18 (36%)	18 (36%)	12 (24%)	1 (1%)
Present study	84	58 (69%)	9 (11%)	14 (17%)	3 (3%)
	352	185 (53%)	84 (24%)	72 (20%)	9 (3%)

* 2% not assessed

is interesting that the mortality rates vary in relation to the follow-up interval. So Theander (1983) reported a mortality rate of 6.4% after a 5-year follow-up, but mortality rates of 11.7% and 14.9% after a follow-up interval of up to 10 or 20 years, respectively.

These surveys show only the global result, not the type of course the disease can take. One can also criticize the criteria of Morgan and Russell as being very general and do not sufficiently take psychopathologic findings into consideration.

Two studies exist that consider the type of course of the disease (Ziolko 1978; Steinhausen & Glanville 1984). Despite the small size of the sample, the consideration of the type of course is highly important and allows differentiated considerations of the long-term perspective. According to Ziolko (1978), an *acute course* means complete disappearance of symptoms within a few months. A *simple chronic course* means a duration of several years with a more or less marked subsidence of the disease. A *chronic-relapsing* or *intermitting course* means that symptoms can relapse acutely after symptom-free phases over many years, and a *chronic-persistent course* finally is marked by unchanged or increased symptoms without remission.

The results of Ziolko (1978), Steinhausen and Glanville (1984) and our study are given in Table 2. The results are discussed later.

The psychosocial adaptation of patients at reexamination was objectified in different studies (Morgan & Russell 1975; Hsu, Crisp & Harding, 1979). It could be shown that approximately 35% to 55% had difficulties in their family relationships even later, and one-fourth to one-half of patients endured social anxieties.

Finally, premorbid conspicuities (Cantwell, Sturzenberger, Borroughs, Salkin & Green, 1977) and psychiatric diagnoses at reexamination (Tolstrup, 1985) were considered in long-term follow-up studies. The results of the studies are shown in Tables 3 and 4.

Table 3 shows that a large number of patients suffered from anxiety, depression, somatic complaints, and compulsive symptoms prior to the manifestation of the disease. Phobias existed relatively frequently as well.

As Table 4 shows, half of the patients in the to date largest sample of Tolstrup, Brinch, Isager, Nielsen, Nystrup, et al. (1985) were inconspicuous after 12.5 years, one-fourth suffered from an anorexia nervosa, and nearly one-fourth suffered from other psychiatric diagnoses.

According to the results of outcome studies, the following factors have to be viewed as prognostically unfavorable (HERZOG et al. 1988; Hsu 1988): bulimic type, self-induced

Table 2. Type of course in anorexia nervosa.

	Ziolko, 1978		Steinhausen & Glanville, 1984		Present study	
	n	%	n	%	n	%
Acute	1	3.6	0	0	16	20.3
Simple chronic	20	71.4	9	42.8	38	48.1
Chronic-relapsing	5	17.4	6	28.6	20	25.3
Chronic-persistent	2	7.1	6	28.6	5	6.3
	28		21		79	

Table 3. Premorbid psychiatric symptomatology (from Cantwell et al., 1977).

Symptoms	Patient report (%)	Parent report (%)
Depressive		
Dysphoric mood	61	30
Sleep difficulty	22	7
Loss of energy	11	7
Agitation	6	15
Cries easily	22	11
Feels worthless	22	7
Feels guilty	11	0
Feels sorry for self	22	0
Difficulty making decisions	17	11
Difficulty starting tasks	11	0
Difficulty finishing tasks	17	11
Worries	44	15
Death wishes	6	0
Inability to concentrate	0	7
Anxiety attacks	16	0
Phobic		
Fearful	72	56
Phobias	22	37
School phobia	6	26
Obsessive-compulsive		
Obsessive	39	19
Perfectionistic	33	37
Compulsive	28	11
Somatic complaints	44	56
Learning difficulties	6	11
Behavioral problems	0	11

Table 4. Psychiatric diagnoses at follow-up.

Diagnoses	Tolstrup et al. (1985)	Present study
Restrictive anorexia nervosa	37 (25%)	13 (18%)
Bulimia	— —	7 (10%)
"Neuroses"	15 (11%)	4 (5%)
Psychotic depression	9 (6%)	— —
Schizophrenia	3 (2%)	2 (3%)
Personality disorder	2 (1%)	2 (3%)
Borderline personality	4 (3%)	1 (1%)
No psychiatric diagnosis	61 (47%)	44 (60%)
Total	131 (100%)	73 (100%)

vomiting, misuse of laxatives, extreme weight loss, disturbed attitude toward sexuality, pronounced disturbance of the body-pattern, premorbid conspicuities, psychiatric disease of parents, pronounced pathological relationships in the family.

Sample and Methods

Sample

All patients treated as inpatients at the Hospital for Child and Youth Psychiatry, Philipps University, Marburg, from 1952 to 1982, were included in the investigation. There were a total of 103 patients (99 female and 4 male) whose age at the beginning of the disease was an average of 13.3 years (range 9 to 19.2 years). The age at the first admittance to hospital was an average of 14.5 years, the average duration of treatment 4.9 months (median 4 months), the duration to follow-up 11.7 years (median 8.3), the age of patients at reexamination 26.0 years (median 23 years). Reliable data were obtained from 81 patients (78.6%). In 12 cases (11.7%), the information was insufficient, and no information was obtained on 7 patients (6.8%): Two (1.9%) could not be retraced, and 5 (4.9%) refused to partake in the examination. Three patients (3%) had died within the follow-up interval, all from their disorders or its complications.

Classification

For those patients admitted since 1980, the diagnosis was made according to the multiaxial classification scheme on the basis of ICD-9 (German edition by Remschmidt & Schmidt, 1986) as well as according to the DSM-III (APA, 1980). All patients were, if necessary, classified retrospectively according to the criteria of the multiaxial classification scheme, the DSM-III, and the criteria of Feighner, Robins, Guze, Woodruff, Winokur and Munoz (1972). All 103 patients fulfilled the criteria of the MAS (100%), 88 the criteria of DSM-III (85.4%), and 74 patients (71.8%) met Feighner's criteria.

Methods

A number of methods were utilized in the catamnestic examination: among others, an interview for the long-term course of anorexia nervosa developed at our hospital, the "Anorexia-nervosa-Inventory for Self-Assessment (ANIS)" by Fichter and Keeser (1980), the *Freiburg Personality Inventory* (Fahrenberg, Hampel & Selg, 1984), the MMPI, the *Child Behavior Checklist* of Achenbach and Edelbrock (1983), and a psychiatric exploration.

Further, a special evaluation of the weight curves of the 36 first reexamined patients was undertaken with the goal to predict the long-term prognosis from the weight curves during the inpatient treatment (Remschmidt & Müller, 1987; Müller & Remschmidt, 1988). A further paper using weight curve parameters as predictors of outcome based on two different samples is part of this volume (Remschmidt, Schmidt & Gutenbrunner).

This paper refers only to the global results of the catamnestic examination to the long-term course, derived from the psychiatric exploration and our own interview. The other results will be reported elsewhere.

Results

Course of the Disease

In Table 1, the results of our study according to the criteria of Morgan and Russell (1975) are contrasted with the results of four other studies employing the same criteria. It is shown that the results of our study are markedly more favorable than those of the other studies. This could be because our follow-up interval was longer (average 11.7 years—median 8.3 years) than that of the other studies (around 4 years). A longer follow-up interval means that there is a greater chance in the development of the patients to lose the symptoms of the disease. A further reason for the relatively favorable results of our study may lie in the fact that our patients are decisively younger on average than those of the other studies: The onset of disease was at an average of 13.3 years among our patients, the age at admittance 14.5 years.

A similar result is found in comparing the criteria of Ziolko with his examination (Ziolko, 1978) and the study of Steinhausen and Glanville (1984). It is astonishing that the patients in our study belong more frequently to the acute type, and that the chronic-persistent types occur relatively seldom (see Table 2).

Even if the global clinical score of Garfinkel et al. (1977) is utilized, our results are remarkably good compared to those of Garfinkel. The reasons are probably to be found in the arguments mentioned above. The global clinical score of Garfinkel is based on an evaluation considering weight, eating behavior, menstruation, social and occupational adaptation.

Table 5 shows a comparison of our results with those of Garfinkel et al. (1977). According to the global clinical score, 50 out of 70 patients of our sample (71%) could be rated as "excellent," 14 (20%) as "much improved," 2 (3%) as "symptomatic," and 4 (6%) as "poor."

Table 5. Comparison of our sample with the sample of Garfinkel, Modolfsky and Garner (1977) in terms of the global clinical score.

	Garfinkel et al. (1977)	Present study
Excellent	7 (17%)	50 (71%)
Much improved	14 (33%)	14 (20%)
Symptomatic	13 (31%)	2 (3%)
Poor	8 (19%)	4 (6%)

Table 6. Frequency of psychiatric symptoms at follow-up.

	n	%
Psychosomatic complaints	31	43.1
Depressed mood	15	20.8
Disturbed self-esteem	15	20.8
Compulsive symptoms	12	16.7
Hypochondric symptoms	6	8.3
Lack of initiative	6	8.3
Abuse of alcohol and drugs	4	5.6
Social isolation	4	5.6
Ideas of reference	2	2.8

It should be mentioned in this context that the patients of Garfinkel et al. (1977) were much older (age at manifestation of the disorder: 17 years), and that the follow-up interval was only 2.7 years.

On the other hand, 20 patients out of 81 from whom we received reliable information suffered at follow-up from anorexia or bulimia nervosa: 13 of them were classified as anorexic and 7 as bulimic.

The incidence of psychic disturbances at reexamination for 72 patients can be deduced from Table 6.

Despite the generally good results concerning the anorectic symptoms, 43% of patients still had psychosomatic complaints, 20.8% depressive emotions, a similar percentage disorders of self-esteem, and 16.7% compulsive symptoms.

Table 4 gives an overview over the psychiatric diagnoses in comparison to the study of Tolstrup et al. (1985). The diagnoses of our study had been rated according to DSM-III. But in order to make a comparison possible a compromise concerning the term "neuroses" was necessary. The comparison reveals several similarities. Differences concern the frequency of neuroses, psychiatric depression, and the frequency of psychiatric diagnoses as such. They are more frequent in Tolstrup's study.

Results of Psychosocial Adaptation

Results of psychosocial adaptation are reproduced in Table 7, again comparing the results of our study with those of Morgan and Russell (1975) and of Hsu, Crisp and Harding (1979). Approximately 45% of our patients had difficulties in family relationships. Compared to the results of the two other investigations, this lies well within average. Concerning full occupation, the rate of 64.8% among our patients is lower than that in the other investigations. One has to consider that the patients were younger on average. At reexamination, 57 of our patients (63.3%) were living alone, 9 patients (10%) had a stable partner, and 24 (26.7%) were married. Twenty-six of our patients had a total of 46 children. The children will be reexamined in a separate study.

Table 7. Psychosocial adaptation.

	Morgan & Russell (1975) n=41	%	Hsu et al. (1979) n=105	%	Present study n=71	%
Difficulties in family relationships	22	55	39	37	32	45.1
Full-time job	28	73	82	78	46	64.8

The contact behavior could be evaluated in 77 patients according to the exploration and the interview: 47 of them (61%) were normal for their age, among 14 (18.2%) difficulties in their contact behavior were ascertainable (tendencies toward withdrawal, fear of social contacts), and among 16 (20.8%) the contact behavior was very disturbed.

Concerning the attitude toward sexuality, a normal attitude for their age could be found among 66 patients (74.2%), among 13 (14.6%) the attitude toward sexuality was evaluated as indifferent, while 10 patients (11.2%) showed a marked rejection of the sexual realm.

Prediction of Long-Term Prognosis from Premorbid Characteristics and Variables During Inpatient Treatment

Several variables were used in order to predict long-term success. Among them were amount of weight loss at intake, duration of the disorder until intake, number of inpatient treatments before intake in our department, duration of inpatient treatment, weight at discharge, IQ, social class, personality structure at intake, artificial nourishment, and length of the follow-up interval. None of these variables was a reliable predictor on long-term outcome.

But there were three other variables of high predictive validity: age at onset of the disorder, presence or absence of premorbid eating disorders, and characteristics of weight curves during inpatient treatment.

Age at Onset of the Disorder

There was a clear relationship between a relatively low age at onset of the disorder and a good or at least intermediate outcome. This result is in line with several other investigations (Frazier, 1985; Theander, 1970; Halmi et al., 1973, 1975; Morgan & Russell, 1975; WILLI & Hageman, 1976; Sturzenberger et al., 1977; Hsu, Crisp & Harding, 1979). There are also other studies that do not confirm this correlation; but these studies deal as a rule with patients who are much older.

Premorbid Eating Disorders

We have already mentioned the existence of a correlation between a relatively good outcome and the length of the follow-up interval. Within a special analysis, we tried to evaluate this connection by calculating the probability for good outcome in relation to the follow-up interval for patients who did or did not have premorbid eating disorders. By a very thorough interview that included several questions on premorbid eating disorders, the following items were checked by inquiry of the parents and the patients themselves: eating disorders during the first year of life or premorbid eating disorders during childhood and adolescence, premorbid adipositas at any age before starting of anorexia nervosa. With respect to the presence or absence of these "premorbid eating disorders," the group of 81 patients for whom we had reliable information was broken down into two subgroups:

- a subgroup that had such premorbid eating disorders in their history (group A),
- a second group that did not (group B).

For both of the groups, the probability for good success was calculated using the criteria defined by Morgan and Russell (1975). A good success in this definition was represented by stage I of Morgan and Russell, whereas an unfavorable outcome was defined by stages II and III (intermediate and poor outcome).

Figure 1 shows the probability of a good success in relation of follow-up interval and a

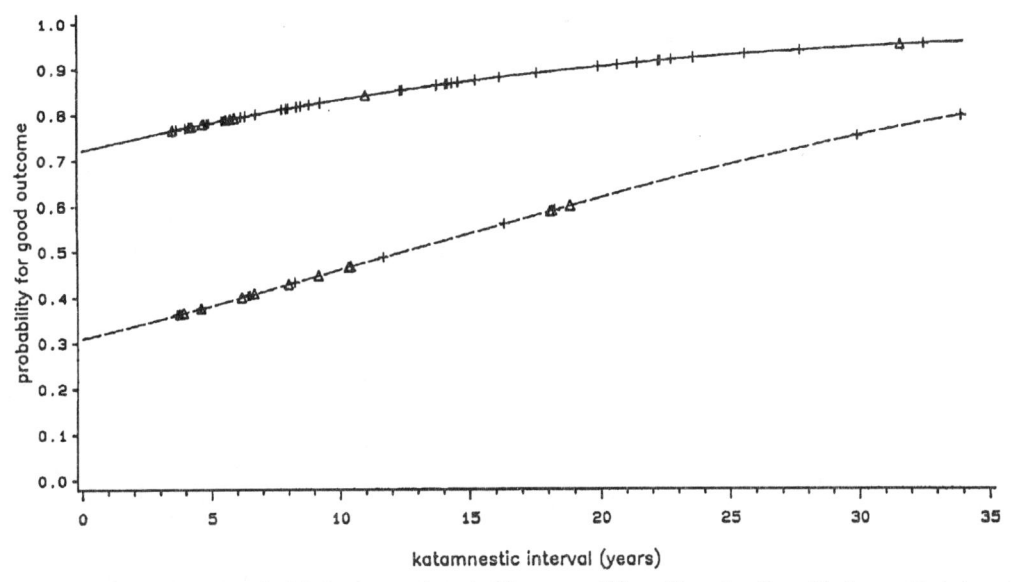

Figure 1. Probability of good global outcome (acc. to Morgan and Russell) as function of katamnestic interval and premorbid eating disorders (sample size n=81). +++ = good outcome; Δ = intermediate and poor outcome; —— = no premorbid eating disorders; ----- = premorbid eating disorders.

premorbid loading with eating disorders. The figure exemplifies several interesting results:

- First, it shows in general that there exists a connection between the probability for a good success and the length of the follow-up interval. This relationship applies to both groups of patients.
- Secondly, it becomes clear that the group without premorbid eating disorders has a higher probability for a good success in relation to the length of the follow-up interval. This group starts already with a probability rate of 0.7 and reaches a probability of nearly 1.0 after a follow-up interval of about 30 years. However, the group of patients who suffered from premorbid eating disorders has a much lower probability for a good outcome in relation to the follow-up interval.

Weight Curve Parameters as Predictors of Long-Term Outcome

In a study of a subsample of 36 patients (age at onset: 14.5 ± 1.9 years), an attempt was made to predict long-term outcome (follow-up interval: 7.8 ± 3.77 years) from weight changes during inpatient treatment (duration of treatment: 156 ± 76 days). Several statistical methods appropriate for the use with longitudinal data were applied. The long-term course could be predicted correctly for 96% of the patients with good or intermediate outcome (prognostic criteria of Morgan and Russell), and for 89% of those with poor outcome. The most important factors predictive of a good outcome were a relatively long time to stabilization of weight (>47 days), a stabilized weight of at least 64% of ideal weight, a low age at onset (<13 years), and a high variability in weight during inpatient treatment compared with patients who had a poor prognosis (Remschmidt & Müller, 1987). This analysis was carried out using the classification and regression trees (CART) by Breiman et al. (1984). As the CART program has an built-in cross-validation, it was possible to test also the predictive results by using this procedure. In this case, the predictive power was not as impressive. For the category "good prognosis" (putting together the two categories "good" and "intermediate outcome"), 86% of the cases could be predicted correctly, while in 14% of the cases a misclassification was registered. Concerning poor outcome, a correct prognosis was only possible in 44% of the cases, a misclassification, however, in 56% (Remschmidt & Müller, 1987).

The whole issue of prediction of long-term outcome from inpatient longitudinal weight data is discussed in detail in another article of this volume (Remschmidt, Schmidt & Gutenbrunner).

Comparison of the Follow-Up Sample with the Sample of Refusers

All follow-up studies have to face the problem of refusers. Within this study, reliable information was collected from 81 patients. Of these, 69 were investigated personally, 9 further patients filled in questionnaires and the interview form, and we received reliable information on 3 further patients through their therapists. Five patients refused to participate in the study, and for 12 patients we received only insufficient information by family members. Only 2 patients could not be retraced, and 3 had died. Thus, the sample of refusers comprises 17 patients (5 who refused and 12 from whom we had insufficient information).

For the generalizability of the results, it is very important to compare the follow-up sample with the sample of the refusers. Such a comparison is shown in Table 8. As the table demonstrates, there are not many substantial differences between the two samples. Statistically significant differences can only be found concerning hyperactivity (more frequent in the follow-up sample) and self-induced vomiting (more frequent in the group of the refusers). Besides these differences, further ones were observed only concerning the mean frequency of inpatient treatments (1.06 for the follow-up sample versus 0.41 for the refusers) and the mean duration of inpatient treatment (5.1 months for the follow-up sample and 3.4 months for the refusers).

In summary, the group of the refusers does not seem to be very different from the follow-up sample, though some differences can be registered. On the whole, it seems to be unlikely that the differences mentioned might restrict the generalization of the results.

Table 8. Comparison of the follow-up sample with the sample of refusers.

	Follow-up sample n=81	%*	Refusers n=17	%*	p-value (two-tailed Fisher's exact test)
Female	78	96.3	16	94.1	0.54
Male	3	3.7	1	5.9	
Lower social classes	25	30.9	7	41.2	0.40
Middle class	56	69.1	10	58.8	
Disturbed eating behavior and eating attitudes	81	100	17	100	—
Disturbed body scheme	62	100	9	100	—
Amenorrhea	46	59.7	10	62.5	1.00
Premenarche	31	39.7	5	31.3	0.58
Hyperactivity	56	72.7	4	30.8	0.008**
Bulimic attacks	25	33.8	3	37.5	1.00
Self-induced vomiting	25	34.25	8	72.7	0.02*
Abuse of laxatives	31	41.3	4	44.4	1.00
Premorbid eating disorders during first year of life	10	12.5	3	17.6	0.69
Premorbid eating disorder during childhood and adolescence	9	11.7	1	6.3	1.00
Premorbid social or psychopathological disturbances	37	47.4	7	43.8	1.00

* Percentage of cases with nonmissing values

Discussion

Follow-up studies of patients with anorexia nervosa have to deal with a number of difficulties, as discussed at the beginning of this paper. With the introduction of standardized diagnostic criteria (MAS, DSM-III, criteria according to Feighner et al. (1972)) and with the introduction of standardized criteria for the course and prognosis (Morgan & Russell, 1975; Ziolko, 1978; Garfinkel, Modolfsky & Garner, 1977) as well as through the introduction of standardized methods of examination (e.g., *Anorexia Nervosa Inventory for Self-Evaluation*, Fichter & Keeser, 1980), methods are now available which enable the comparison of different follow-up studies. These methods were utilized in our own study of 103 patients.

We were able to obtain relatively favorable results in our sample with an average interval up to reexamination of 11.7 years. This is surely because our patients were markedly younger and the follow-up time period was markedly longer than in most studies referred to. Several studies have found a positive correlation between favorable outcome and the follow-up interval (Niskanen, Jääskäläinen & Achte, 1974; Vandereycken & Pierloot, 1983). On the other hand, there is also a relationship between the mortality rate and the follow-up interval.

It is difficult to determine the role of treatment. All our patients were treated by individual psychotherapy, two-thirds temporarily took psychopharmaceutical medication (antidepressive or neuroleptic drugs), two-thirds were further treated by behavior therapy, one-third by family therapy, 21.3% were fed by naso-gastric tubes. For the subsample of the 36 patients examined according to their weight curves, we could not show an influence of the naso-gastric feeding toward long-term success; rather, some weight parameters concerning weight changes during inpatient treatment were found to be significant for the long-term course. So it turned out that the long-term course was likely to be unfavorable if the time to stabilization of the weight curve at a weight curve plateau was too short and at a low level.

The results of our studies on the prognostic value of the weight course during inpatient treatment (Remschmidt & Müller, 1987; Müller & Remschmidt, 1988; Remschmidt, Schmidt & Gutenbrunner, this volume) suggest that one should ascribe a great importance to the weight gain up to stabilization, and that one should pay careful attention to the weight dynamics during treatment. It seems unjustifiable to us to neglect the weight data in favor of other priorities during the course of the treatment. The psychotherapy of anorexia nervosa must consider the problems of individuation, the familiar context, and the weight parameters as equally important, and include these in the therapeutic process.

The results of the social adaptation of the patients were basically congruent with those of the other examiners.

References

Achenbach, T. M., & Edelbrock, C. (1983). *Manual for the Child Behavior Checklist and Revised Child Behavior Profile*. Burlington, VT: University of Vermont Press.

American Psychiatric Association (1980). *Diagnostic and statistical manual for mental disorders* (3rd ed). Washington, DC: APA.

Cantwell, D.P., Sturzenberger, S., Borroughs, J., Salkin, B., & Green, J. K. (1977). Anorexia nervosa: an affective disorder? *Archives of General Psychiatry, 34*, 1087-1093.

Fahrenberg, J., Hampel, R., & Selg, H. (1984). *Das Freiburger Persönlichkeits-Inventar (FPI)* (4th rev. ed.). Göttingen: Hogrefe.

Feighner, J. P. E., Robins, E., Guze, S. B., Woodruff, R. A., Winokur, G., & Munoz, R. (1972). Diagnostic criteria for the use in psychiatric research. *Archives of General Psychiatry, 26*, 57–63.

Fichter, M. M., & Keeser, W. (1980). Das Anorexia-nervosa-Inventar zur Selbstbeurteilung (ANIS).

Archiv für Psychiatrie und Nervenkrankheiten, 288, 67–89.

Garfinkel, P. E., Modolfsky, M., & Garner, D. M. (1977). Prognosis in anorexia nervosa as influenced by clinical features, treatment and self-perception. *Canadian Medical Association Journal, 117,* 1041–1045.

Hall, A., Slim, E., Hawker, F., & Salmone, C. (1984). Anorexia nervosa: long-term outcome in 50 female patients. *British Journal of Psychiatry, 145,* 407–413.

Herzog, D. B., Keller, M. B., & Lavori, P. W. (1988). Outcome in anorexia nervosa and bulimia nervosa. A review of the literature. *Journal of Nervous and Mental Disease, 176,* 131–143.

Hsu, L. K. G. (1980). Outcome of anorexia nervosa. A review of the literature (1954–1978). *Archives of General Psychiatry, 37,* 1041–1046.

Hsu, L. K. G. (1988). The outcome of anorexia nervosa: a re-appraisal. *Psychological Medicine, 18,* 807–812.

Hsu, L. K. G., Crisp, A. H., & Harding, G. B. (1979). Outcome of anorexia nervosa. *Lancet, I,* 61–65.

Morgan, H. G., & Russell, G. F. M. (1975). Value of family background and clinical features as predictors of long-term outcome in anorexia nervosa: 4 year follow-up study of 41 patients. *Psychological Medicine, 5,* 355–371.

Morgan, H. G., Pungold, J., & Wellbourne, J. (1983). Management and outcome study in anorexia nervosa. A standardised prognostic study. *British Journal of Psychiatry, 143,* 282–287.

Müller, H.G., Remschmidt, H. (1988). Nonparametric methods for the analysis of longitudinal medical data, with an application to the prognosis of anorectic patients from longitudinal weight measurements. In Société Adolphe Quetelet (Ed.), *Proceedings of invited papers. XIVth International Biometric Conference at Namur/Belgium, July 18–22, 1988* (pp. 229–240). Gembloux/Belgium: Société Adolphe Quetelet.

Niskanen, P. J., Jääskäläinen, J., & Achte, K. (1974). Anorexia nervosa, treatment, results, and prognosis. *Psychiatrica Fennica, 5,* 257–263.

Remschmidt, H., & Schmidt, M. H. (Eds.) (1986). *Multiaxiales Klassifikationsschema für psychiatrische Erkrankungen im Kindes- und Jugendalter nach Rutter, Shaffer und Sturge* (2nd ed.). Bern-Stuttgart-Toronto: Huber.

Remschmidt, H., & Müller, H. G. (1987). Stationäre Gewichts-Ausgangsdaten und Langzeitprognose der Anorexia nervosa. *Zeitschrift für Kinder- und Jugendpsychiatrie, 15,* 327–341.

Remschmidt, H., Wienand, F., & Wewetzer, C. (1988). Der Langzeitverlauf der Anorexia nervosa. *Monatsschrift für Kinderheilkunde, 136,* 726–731.

Remschmidt, H., Wienand, F., & Wewetzer, C. (1990). Langzeitprognose bei der Anorexia nervosa. Eine Verlaufsuntersuchung an 103 Patientinnen und Patienten. *Münchner Medizinische Wochenschrift, 132,* 29–32.

Steinhausen, H. Ch., & Glanville, K. (1983). Follow-up studies of anorexia nervosa—A review of research findings. *Psychological Medicine, 13,* 239–249.

Steinhausen, H. C., & Glanville, K. (1984). Der langfristige Verlauf der Anorexia nervosa. *Nervenarzt, 55,* 236–248.

Tolstrup, K., Brinch, M., Isager, T., Nielsen, S., Nystrup, J., Severin, B., & Olesen, N. S. (1985). Long-term outcome of 151 cases of anorexia nervosa. *Acta Psychiatrica Scandinavica, 71,* 380–387.

Vandereycken, W., & Pierloot, R. (1983). Long-term outcome research in anorexia nervosa: The problem of patient selection and follow-up duration. *International Journal of Eating Disorders, 2,* 237–242.

Ziolko, H. U. (1978). Zur Katamnese der Pubertätsmagersucht. *Archiv für Psychiatrie und Nervenkrankheiten, 225,* 117–125.

Anorectic Psychopathology in Young Women

Fredrik Almqvist

The material consists of 41 former anorectic patients and an equal number of matched gynecological patients. Roughly 75% of both groups answered a mailed questionnaire including, among other things, two standardized sets of questions. The same questionnaire was answered by 115 females students, matched for age. Since the former anorectic patients still had significantly more psychiatric and anorectic symptoms than the others, it was possible to analyze different aspects and anorectic symptoms, also in relation to family factors. Because tréated anorectic patients later show a significant overload of psychiatric symptoms, the great majority of anorectic adolescents require psychotherapy. The study identifies some specific psychopathological features of anorexia nervosa.

Thorough clinical examination using basic measures and growth standards as well as anamnestic interview usually provide a sufficient basis for establishing or excluding the diagnosis of anorexia nervosa. Possible physical causes of weight loss are readily identifiable (Russell, 1985). A sudden change or exceptionally severe loss of body weight may, however, indicate a psychological imbalance, personality disorder, or family crisis. Assessing the patient's mental status and need for psychiatric treatment is more difficult. This is partly because there are neither sufficient data nor a general consensus concerning the significance of various symptoms for the psychodynamics and pathogenesis of anorexia nervosa (Miller & Carlton, 1985; Bryant & Bates, 1985; Almqvist, 1985).

Aims

Clinical experience with anorectic patients has created a need for empirical systematic studies on the psychological phenomenology of eating disorder and weight reduction in young women. It is important to gain a better understanding of the problems in order to improve the examination and treatment of anorectic patients.

This study describes and analyzes the spectrum of symptoms as well as attitudes and behavior of anorectic patients by comparison with normal subjects.

Material

The material consisted originally of 41 female patients treated for anorectic problems in an outpatient clinic for adolescent medicine in Helsinki between 1978 and 1986. The essential anorectic features according to DSM-III criteria for anorexia nervosa of the patients are documented in Table 1. The frequencies of other physical symptoms and behavioral features are summarized in Table 2. A detailed description of the material has been pub-

---

Department of Child Psychiatry, University of Helsinki, Lastenlinnantie 2, SF-00250 Helsinki, Finland.

Table 1. Frequency of anorectic symptomatology modified according to DSM-III among anorectic patients (N=41) and distribution of the material according to an anorectic symptom index based on the same criteria.

		Frequency (%)	Index points*
1.	Fear of becoming obese	54	1
	+ which does not diminish as weight loss progresses	22	2
2.	Disturbance of body image	44	1
	+ e.g., claiming to feel fat even when emaciated	44	2
3.	Weight loss:		
	10–24%	54	1
	+25%	41	2
4.	Inability to maintain weight	44	1
	+ refusal to maintain weight	22	2
5	Physical illness	0	

Distribution (%) according to sum of points:
2 points: 27
3–4 points: 39
5–6 points: 20
7–8 points: 15
Total 101
Mean 3.9

*Index point 1 indicates a mild form of the symptoms and 2 indicates a severe form of the symptom.

Table 2. Frequencies of physical symptoms and behavioral features among the anorectic patients.

	Frequency (%) (N=41)
Actively reduced intake of food	90
Amenorrhea	85
primary	12
secondary	73
Ambivalent attitude toward food and eating	78
Physical overactivity	74
Aversion to food and eating	63
Hypothermia	61
Regards herself as having normal weight though much too thin	51
Irregular menstruation (before or after amenorrhea)	46
Fear of not being able to stop eating	44
Bradycardia	39
Bulimic features	34
Excessive interest in food and eating	32
Signs of dehydration	27
Lanugo	27
Vomiting	27
Regards her abnormal eating habits as normal	24
Fear of not being able to eat	17
Painful menstruation	5
Use of laxatives	2

lished elsewhere (Almqvist, 1987).

Controls were selected among gynecological patients attending the same clinic, matched for age and date of admission. Most of these girls had come for family planning advice and possibly for contraceptives.

A third group consisted of female students in two nursing schools (B and F), matched for age at the time of the follow-up study. The three materials are presented in Table 3.

Table 3. Characteristics of the materials. Response rate in each of the three groups. Representativeness of the answers according to age and severity of anorectic symptoms* and total number of visits to the clinic during treatment.

		Anorectic patients		Gynecol. patients		Students B	F
Original material (O)	N	41		41		112	32
Number of respondents (R)	N	30		31		89	26
Response rate	%	73		76		79	81
Age structure:		O	R	O	R		
Mean		20	20	21	21	21	21
Lowest		15	15	16	16	17	17
Highest		27	27	25	25	25	29
STD		2.2	2.3	1.7	1.7	1.7	2.5
*Severity of psychopathology when visiting the clinic:**							
Respondents		O	R	O	R		
Mean		12.3	12.6	2.9	2.8		
Lowest		3	3	2	2		
Highest		22	22	6	5		
STD		4.3	4.4	1.0	0.9		
Total number of visits:							
Respondents		O	R	O	R		
Mean		43	46	4	4		
Lowest		1	3	1	1		
Highest		306	306	15	15		
STD		92	65	4	4		

*Index based on anorectic and other psychological symptoms.

Methods

The results presented in this report were based on a questionnaire mailed to the patients 1–6 years after the end of treatment and given to the students. All returned the questionnaire anonymously. The response rate (73–81%) is acceptable. The respondents represent the original materials fairly well. Some other features of the material are also shown in Table 3. The questionnaire contains two standardized scales and other sets of questions. The first scale was based on the *Cornell Medical Index* (Brodman, Erdman & Wolff, 1949). Factor analysis has previously been used to identify factors that best describe psychiatric symptoms in young women (Almqvist, 1986). The scale comprised five questions for each of five factors, totaling 25 questions. The results thus obtained are referred to as *psychiatric symptoms*.

The other scales was based on the *Eating Disorder Inventory* (EDI) (Garner, Olmsted & Polivy, 1983), which the author has translated into Finnish and adapted to local conditions. The results are referred to as anorectic symptoms and factors. Statistical data processing was carried out using the BMDP software.

Table 4. Distribution (%) of background variables used in the present study in the three subject groups and the total material.

Background variable	Anorectic patients	Gynecol. patients	Students	Total material
Social status of father:	n=28	n=30	n=106	n=164
3 highest = high	64	63	44	51
2 lowest = low	36	37	56	49
χ^2=5.683, D.F.=2, p=0.06				
Social status of mother:	n=28	n=28	n=109	n=165
High	50	43	25	32
Low	50	57	75	68
χ^2=8.286, D.F.=2, p=0.02				
Marriage status of parents:	n=30	n=31	n=115	n=176
Married	77	68	84	80
Divorced/deceased	23	32	16	20
χ^2=4.496, D.F.=2, p=0.1				
Relationship with mother:	n=30	n=31	n=114	n=175
Good	60	87	88	83
Poor	20	13	12	17
χ^2=13.324, D.F.=2, p=0.001				
Relationship with father:	n=30	n=30	n=110	n=170
Good	50	70	78	72
Poor	50	30	22	28
χ^2=9.295, D.F.=2, p=0.01				
Mother happy:	n=29	n=31	n=115	n=175
Yes	45	52	63	58
No	55	48	37	42
χ^2=3.575, D.F.=2, p=0.17				
Father happy:	n=29	n=30	n=111	n=170
Yes	34	47	60	54
No	66	53	40	4
χ^2=6.879, D.F.=2, p=0.03				
Relationship between parents:	n=30	n=30	n=30	n=172
Good	43	40	60	54
Poor	37	60	40	46
χ^2=5.243, D.F.=2, p=0.07				

Results

Family Characteristics

In the anorectic group, the social status of the parents, especially that of the mother, was almost significantly higher than in the control and student groups (Table 4). There were no significant differences between the groups in divorce or death of parents, the relationship between parents, or the happiness of the mother (as perceived by the child). In the anorectic group, the child's relationship to the parents was significantly poorer and the father almost significantly more frequently unhappy than in the other groups.

Table 5. Nature and severity of psychiatric symptoms in different subject groups according to sets of questions based on factor analysis of the questions in the *Cornell Medical Index*, parts I-R (Almqvist, 1986).

Factors		Anorectic patients	Gynecological patients	Students
N		30	31	114
All 5 factors				
—Mean		7.3	3.6	3.9
—STD		5.6	3.9	2.8
—Highest		21	15	11
—Lowest		0	0	0
F=11.3, p<0.001				
T-test		T (pooled)	p	
	Anor./Gyn.	4.0	<0.001	
	Anor./Stud.	4.6	<0.001	
	Gyn./Stud.	−0.37	=0.7	
—More than 7 yes answers (%)		37	13	10
I. Uncertainty, weak ego				
—Mean		1.9	0.7	1.3
—STD		1.6	0.9	1.2
—Highest		5	3	5
—Lowest		0	0	0
F=6.72, p<0.001				
T-test		T (pooled)	p	
	Anor./Gyn.	3.7	<0.001	
	Anor./Stud.	2.2	=0.03	
	Gyn./Stud.	−2.4	=0.02	
—More than 2 yes answers (%)		43	3	17
Fisher's exact				
	Anor./Gyn.		<0.001	
	Anor./Stud.		=0.003	
	Gyn./Stud.		=0.04	
II. Sickliness				
—Mean		0.7	0.4	0.2
—STD		1.2	1.1	0.6
—Highest		4	5	3
—Lowest		0	0	0
F=3.20, p=0.04				
T-test		T (pooled)	p	
	Anor/Gyn.	1.5	=0.14	
	Anor./Stud.	2.5	=0.01	
	Gyn./Stud.	0.7	=0.48	
—More than 1 yes answers (%)		17	10	6
Fisher's exact:			p	
	Anor./Gyn.		=0.33	
	Anor./Stud.		=0.08	
	Gyn./Stud.		=0.35	
III. Depression				
—Mean		1.3	0.3	0.1
—STD		1.8	0.8	0.4
—Highest		5	3	2
—Lowest		0	0	0
F=23.3, p<0.001				

Table 5 continued

Factors	Anorectic patients	Gynecological patients	Students
N	30	31	114
T-test		T (pooled) p	
Anor./Gyn.		4.7 <0.001	
Anor./Stud.		6.8 <0.001	
Gyn./Stud.		0.9 =0.34	
—One or more yes answers (%)	47	13	10
Fisher's exact:		p	
Anor./Gyn.		=0.004	
Anor./Stud.		<0.001	
Gyn./Stud.		=0.04	
IV. Sensitivity, lability			
—Mean	2.4	1.6	1.5
—STD	1.6	1.5	1.4
—Highest	5	5	5
—Lowest	0	0	0
F=5.0, p=0.008			
T-test		T (pooled) p	
Anor./Gyn.		2.2 =0.03	
Anor./Stud.		3.1 =0.002	
Gyn./Stud.		0.4 =0.6	
—More than 3 yes answers (%)	20	16	10
Fisher's exact:		p	
Anor./Gyn.		=0.48	
Anor./Stud.		=0.14	
Gyn./Stud.		=0.28	
V. Fearfulness			
—Mean	1.0	0.6	0.7
—STD	1.2	1.1	0.8
—Highest	4	4	3
—Lowest	0	0	0
F=1.0, p=0.36			
T-test		T (pooled) p	
Anor./Gyn.		1.3 =0.18	
Anor./Stud.		1.2 =0.2	
Gyn./Stud.		–0.4 =0.66	
—More than 2 yes answers (%)	13	10	3
Fisher's exact: more than 2 yes		p	
Anor./Gyn.		=0.48	
Anor./Stud.		=0.06	
Gyn./Stud.		=0.17	

Psychiatric Symptoms

All 25 Symptoms

In the anorectic group, the mean total score describing psychiatric disorder was almost twice as high as in the control and student groups, and the frequency of respondents giving eight or more yes responses was three times higher in the anorectic group than among the nonanorectic respondents (p<0.001). Table 5 displays also the following information on the five separate factors:

– Factor: Uncertainty and Weak Ego

Symptoms reflecting uncertainty and a weak ego were most frequent in the anorectic group and least frequent in the student group. The differences are statistically highly significant, both as mean values and as frequencies. The

Table 6. Dependence of psychiatric symptoms on study group and on social status, separation in relation to the parents, and poor relationship between parent and child. Two-way variance analysis.

Factors	Social status of father high/low p	Separation from parents no/yes p	Relationship with mother good/poor p	Relationship with father good/poor p
All factors				
Antecedent[1]	n.s.	n.s.	***	***
Material[2]	***	**	***	***
Interaction[3]	n.s.	n.s.	*	n.s.
I. Uncertainty, weak ego				
Antecedent	n.s.	n.s.	**	***
Material	**	**	*	**
Interaction	n.s.	n.s.	n.s.	n.s.
II. Sickliness				
Antecedent	n.s.	*	***	***
Material	*	n.s.	**	n.s.
Interaction	n.s.	n.s.	***	n.s.
III. Depression				
Antecedent	n.s.	n.s.	*	*
Material	***	***	***	***
Interaction	n.s.	n.s.	n.s.	*
IV. Sensitivity, lability				
Antecedent	n.s.	*	***	**
Material	***	*	n.s.	n.s.
Interaction	n.s.	n.s.	n.s.	n.s.
V. Fearfulness				
Antecedent	n.s.	n.s.	**	***
Material	n.s.	n.s.	n.s.	n.s.
Interaction	n.s.	n.s.	n.s.	n.s.

[1] Statistical significance of the difference between classes of respective background variable when the variable study group (former anorectic patients, gynecological patients, students) is standardized.
[2] Statistical significance of the differences between the anorectic and control groups when the influence of respective background variable is standardized.
[3] Statistical significance of possible interaction between two variables (study groups and respective antecedent).

assurance and strong ego among the controls are probably related to an advanced sexual identity. Since they were seeking contraceptives, they had obviously been dating and felt mature enough for sexual intercourse.

For all other symptom factors, the students scored the least and the anorectic group the most.

– Factor: Sickliness

The differences in mean and frequency of sickliness between the groups are almost statistically significant.

– Factor: Depression

The anorectic patients were clearly more depressed than either the controls or the students. The role of depression in anorexia nervosa has been amply discussed in the literature. It has not been established, however, to what extent this is normative depression characteristic of adolescence, or to what extent it is specifically related to the clinical picture of anorexia nervosa. Simply put, the 10–13% depression rate and mean score of 0.1–0.3 among gynecological patients and the students are normative. Among the anorectics the overall depression rate was 50% and the mean score 1.3.

– Factor: Sensitivity

The mean score for sensitivity was significantly higher for the anorectics and also twice as common in the anorectic group as in the student group. This difference was, however, not statistically significant.

– Factor: Fearfulness

Fearfulness, indicating rather severe symptoms, is the only one of the five factors that does not differentiate the three groups from each other.

Social Background

There was no significant difference in psychiatric symptoms between subjects with high and low social background (Table 6). When social status is standardized, the three study groups differ very significantly with respect to total symptomatology, with the highest mean of 2.5 for the anorectics. Depression and sensitivity were present among the anorectics to a very significantly higher degree than among the controls and students. Although the highest proportion (75%) of depressed subjects was noted for anorectics with low social status, there was no statistically significant interaction between the two variables social status and study group.

Separation in Relation to Parents

Sensitivity/lability and sickliness are categories of symptoms that were (almost significantly) related to experience of separation. In each study group sickliness was highest among those who had not experienced separation or loss. This applies particularly to the anorectic group ($p \leq 0.015$). Sensitivity/lability was highest among those in the anorectic group who had experienced separation or loss. There was no significant interaction between the two variables separation and study group.

Relationship with Mother

A poor relationship with the mother was significantly or higher significantly related to a high load of psychiatric symptoms. There was a clear interaction between a poor maternal relationship and belonging to the anorectic group, especially for sickliness, resulting in a significantly higher ($p<0.0001$) proportion and mean of sickliness in these subjects than among the controls whose maternal relationship had been good or among students irrespective of the nature of the relationship.

Relationship with Father

A poor relationship with the father was as strongly related to a high degree of psychiatric symptoms as a poor relationship with the mother. As far as uncertainty, sickliness, and fearfulness are concerned, this connection was even stronger than in the case of a poor relationship with the mother. Behind depression, a significant interactional effect is found between poor relationship and anorexia nervosa.

In the anorectic group, a poor relationship with the father was most strongly associated with depression, uncertainty, and sensitivity.

Anorectic Symptoms

The total score for anorectic symptoms on the EDI inventory was highest for the anorectic group (Table 7). The anorectic group rated very significantly ($p<0.001$) more symptoms in the factors measuring different psychopathological aspects of anorexia nervosa than the other groups. The two exceptions were the factors describing negative experiences related to one's own body and fear of growing up. Here, the differences were only almost statistically significant. This suggests that negative body image and fear of growing up are not so characteristic of anorexia nervosa. There is, of course, the possibility that this finding is a positive reflection of treatment.

The selection of gynecological patients probably accounts for their stronger desire to be lean, greater perfectionism, and lower tendency toward inhibitions than in the student group.

Anorectic Symptoms and Family Characteristics

Two-way variance analysis was used to determine how the antecedents—social background, divorce or death of the parents, and the perceived nature of the relationship between the parents and the child—were related to psychiatric "disorder" and to different "syndromes" (factors) in each of the three materials.

Variance analysis showed (Table 8) that, irrespective of the study group to which the

Table 7. Mean values of total scores and scores on different factors in the standardized questionnaire (EDI) measuring anorectic symptoms in the three study groups.

	Mean value	STD	Max	Min	N
Total score:					
Total material	24.3	21.8	117	0	173
Anorectic group	48.2	32.7	117	7	29
Gynecological group	20.7	16.1	81	2	31
Student group F	21.1	13.7	58	5	25
Student group B	18.7	14.9	74	0	88
F=18.3, p<0.001					
I. Desire to be lean:					
Total material	3.3	4.8	20	0	173
Anorectic group	7.5	6.9	20	0	29
Gynecological group	3.4	4.1	16	0	31
Student group F	1.9	3.6	15	0	25
Student group B	2.3	3.7	18	0	88
F=10.9, p<0.001					
II. Bulimia:					
Total material	1.5	2.8	18	0	173
Anorectic group	4.3	4.8	18	0	29
Gynecological group	1.3	1.6	7	0	31
Student group F	0.6	1.7	8	0	25
Student group B	1.0	1.8	9	0	88
F=14.4, p<0.001					
III. Dissatisfaction with own body:					
Total material	7.3	6.6	27	0	173
Anorectic group	9.9	7.2	25	0	29
Gynecological group	6.6	6.7	25	0	31
Student group F	8.2	7.6	27	0	25
Student group B	6.4	6.0	25	0	88
F=2.34, p=0.08					
IV. Feelings of being ineffective:					
Total material	2.6	4.3	26	0	173
Anorectic group	7.1	7.7	26	0	29
Gynecological group	1.4	2.5	12	0	31
Student group F	1.6	2.0	6	0	25
Student group B	1.8	2.3	11	0	88
F=16.4, p<0.001					
V. Perfectionism					
Total material	2.1	2.6	12	0	173
Anorectic group	4.6	3.4	12	0	29
Gynecological group	2.6	2.2	7	0	31
Student group F	1.3	1.8	7	0	25
Student group B	1.4	2.0	10	0	88
F=15.3, p<0.001					
VI. Inhibitions:					
Total material	2.0	2.8	14	0	173
Anorectic group	4.1	4.3	14	0	29
Gynecological group	1.3	2.8	13	0	31
Student group F	2.6	1.9	5	0	25
Student group B	1.4	2.0	9	0	88
F=8.8, p<0.001					

Table 7 continued

	Mean value	STD	Max	Min	N
VII. Mixed feelings:					
Total material	2.0	3.4	17	0	173
Anorectic group	5.5	6.1	17	0	29
Gynecological group	1.2	2.0	7	0	31
Student group F	1.4	2.3	8	0	25
Student group B	1.3	1.8	9	0	88
$F=15.0, p<0.001$					
VIII. Fear of growing up:					
Total material	3.5	3.2	22	0	173
Anorectic group	5.3	4.6	22	0	29
Gynecological group	3.3	3.3	17	0	31
Student group F	3.4	1.5	6	0	25
Student group B	3.1	2.9	19	0	88
$F=3.6, p<0.05$					

subjects belonged, anorectic symptoms were more manifest among those whose mothers had a higher social status (p = 0.02) and among those who perceived their relationship to their parents as poor. Irrespective of these background variables, anorectic patients had significantly more (p<0.001) anorectic symptoms, attitudes, and behaviors than females in the other two groups.

High social status of the mother probably reflects certain attitudes related to success, profession, and occupation. That the female child identified with these attitudes may be associated with the perfectionism and feelings of ineffectiveness so characteristic of the anorectic group. It may also be that in some cases excessive devotion of the parents—in this case the mother—to their work limits the possibilities of maintaining a relationship that the child would perceive as good and supportive.

Risk Group

The median of the total score (36) on the EDI in the anorectic group can preliminarily be suggested as a cut-off point above which young women are considered at risk. Thus, 13% (4/31) of those in the gynecological group and 8% (9/113) of those in the student group are at risk of developing anorexia nervosa.

Quality of Life

Casual (p = 0.012) and steady dating (p = 0.01) were less frequent among the anorectic

Table 8. Dependence of total score for anorectic disorder on social status, separation or loss experienced in relation to the parents and poor relationship between parent and child. Two-way variance analysis.

	Social status Comparison between groups		Separation from parents No/yes	Perceived relationship with mother Good/poor	with father Good/poor
	Father p	Mother p	p	p	p
Total score:					
—Antecedent[1]	n.s.	*	n.s.	**	***
—Material[2]	***	***	***	***	***
—Interaction[3]	n.s.	n.s.	*	n.s.	*

[1] Statistical significance of the difference between classes of respective background variable when the variable study group (former anorectic patients, gynecological patients, students) is standardized.
[2] Statistical significance of the differences between the anorectic and the control groups when the influence of respective background variable is standardized.
[3] Statistical significance of possible interaction between two variables (study groups and respective antecedent).

group than among the others. The selection of gynecological patients clearly explains the higher frequency of dating in this group. Although those in the anorectic group experienced themselves as more lonely ($p<0.001$) and unhealthier ($p<0.001$) and tended to enjoy life less ($p<0.02$) than the others, many of them had friends. Over 50% of them felt healthy, and 80% said they enjoyed life (Table 9), which again is probably a positive outcome of treatment.

Table 9. Distribution (%) of variables describing the life of subjects such as dating, health, and satisfaction in the different study groups.

Variable N		Anorectic group 30	Gynecological group 31	Students 115
Steady dating $\chi^2=9.08$, D.F.$=2^*$	%	40	77	61
Casual dating $\chi^2=8.880$, D.F.$=2^*$	%	77	94	94
Has friends $\chi^2=17.878$, D.F.$=2^{***}$	%	77	98	97
Enjoys life $\chi^2=8.114$, D.F.$=2^{**}$		80	90	96
Feels healthy $\chi^2=18.463$, D.F.$=2^{***}$		55	94	86

Discussion and Conclusions

The study design, in which anorectic patients are compared with two control groups, makes it possible to draw reliable conclusions from the observations made. Although treatment is not complete in the anorectic group and the majority (76%) have reported feeling well or at least better, it is possible to examine anorexia nervosa and its related phenomena further. The assumption can be made that the typical features of anorexia nervosa remain characteristic of the patient's personality later in life, even after treatment. The results show this assumption to be at least partly true. Some of the former anorectic patients, however, no longer manifest strong anorectic features, probably as the result of the treatment.

Personality features characteristic of anorexia nervosa were clearly more distinguishable among the anorectic group than among the gynecological patients and students.

The mean EDI scores obtained in this study are slightly lower than those published by Garner, Olmsted and Polivy (1983), especially for the anorectic group. This may partly result from the Finnish anorexia group having been less disturbed initially. Another probable explanation is the positive outcome of treatment. A third possibility is that typical anorectic symptoms, attitudes, and ideals are not as strong in Finland as in the United States. A fourth explanation might be differences in wording and understanding related to translation of the items into Finnish.

Examining retrospectively the personality of anorectic patients, and especially comparing them with the control and student groups, made it possible to assess various psychological and psychiatric dimensions of anorexia nervosa.

Depression, uncertainty, a weak ego, and sensitivity are characteristic of young anorectic women.

Clear evidence can be shown of the severity, nature, and permanence of the psychiatric disorder related to anorexia nervosa. For this reason, psychotherapy should play an essential role in its treatment.

However, this design does not enable us to determine whether the differences in symptoms between the anorectic and other groups could have been observed already at the onset of anorexia nervosa. The abundance of psychiatric symptoms may be related to the fact that as anorectic symptoms subside, other psychiatric problems emerge or new symptoms develop. These questions are currently being investigated prospectively in clinical samples.

The results suggest that the questionnaire (EDI) used for measuring anorectic symptoms is reliable in the assessment of anorectic patients. Using this in conjunction with a clinical examination could be helpful in assessing the need for psychotherapy and psychiatric consultation.

It would also be important to assess at an early stage the need for psychotherapy or psychiatric treatment of young women suffering from severe weight loss and manifesting "anorectic behavior," since good prognosis is associated with appropriate and timely treatment (Russell, 1985). This concerns all health center physicians, gynecologists, pediatricians, and specialists in internal medicine.

According to the results, the relationships between the parents and separation or loss in relation to the parents are not as significant for the child's mental health as is the child's relationship to the parent. In the anorectic group, these experiences and the happiness of the father—but not that of the mother (as perceived by the child)—were related to the severity of both general psychiatric and anorectic symptoms.

The evidence of poor relationships with the parents partly characterized by a professional engagement of the mother in the anorectic group seems to contrast with earlier findings of familial overinvolvement, especially between mothers and anorectic girls (Minuchin, Rosman & Baker, 1978). The finding can, however, be true and may reflect cultural features such as the high proportion of professional mothers in Finland. Besides, more neglect and criticism has been reported in families of anorectics with bulimic symptoms (Strober, 1981; Strober & Humprey, 1987). As these results are based on information given by the girls after they have received treatment and obtained some perspective on their family experiences, it might be that they are more free to express a criticism that would not have been possible at a time when they were more involved with the family. This is in line with the suggestion that anorectics deny having problems with their parents (Humprey, 1988).

The results of the study suggest that anorexia nervosa, along with its severe somatic symptoms, is manifested particularly by young women with a deviant personality structure, who adopt "anorectic" attitudes and norms and in stressful situations fail to receive the necessary support and understanding from their parents. New prospective studies using the same methods will probably provide answers to some of the many questions that still remain.

References

Almqvist, F. (1985). Anorexia nervosa. Barn och ungdomspsykiatriska synpunkter. *Helsingfors Läkartidning, 3*, 30–36.

Almqvist, F. (1986). Sex differences in adolescent psychopathology. *Acta Psychiatrica Scandinavica, 73*, 295–306.

Almqvist, F. (1987). Erfarenheter av familjeterapi vid anorexia nervosa. *Nord Kongr Familjeterapi 1987*. FAMÖS, Linköping.

Brodman, K., Erdman, A., & Wolff, H. (1949). *Cornell Medical Health Questionnaire*. New York: Cornell University Medical College.

Bryant, K., & Bates, B. (1985). Anorexia nervosa. Aetiological theories and treatment methods. *Journal of Adolescent, 8*, 93–103.

Garner, D., Olmsted, M., & Polivy, J. (1983). Development and validation of a multidimensional Eating Disorder Inventory for anorexia nervosa and bulimia. *International Journal of Eating Disorders, 2*, 15–33.

Humprey, L. (1988). Relationships with subtypes of anorectic, bulimic and normal families. *Journal of the American Academy of Child and Adolescent Psychiatry, 27*, 544–551.

Miller, D., & Carlton, B. (1985). The etiology and treatment of anorexia nervosa. In S. Feinstein

(Ed.), *Adolescent psychiatry. Developmental and clinical approach* (pp. 219–232). Chicago: The University of Chicago Press.

Minuchin, S., Rosman, B., & Baker, L. (1978). *Psychosomatic families: Anorexia nervosa in a context.* Cambridge, MA: Harvard University Press.

Russell, G. (1985). Anorexia and bulimia nervosa. In M. Rutter & L. Hersov (Eds.), *Child and adolescent psychiatry* (pp. 625–637). Oxford: Blackwell.

Strober, M. (1981). The significance of bulimia in juvenile anorexia nervosa. *International Journal of Eating Disorders, 1,* 28–43.

Strober, M., & Humprey, L. (1987). Familial contributions to the etiology and course of anorexia nervosa and bulimia. *Journal of Consult. Clin. Psychology, 55,* 659.

Prediction of Long-Term Outcome in Anorectic Patients from Longitudinal Weight Measurements during Inpatient Treatment: A Cross-Validation Study

Helmut Remschmidt, Martin H. Schmidt, Cornelius Gutenbrunner

Several longitudinal weight parameters derived from weight curves during inpatient treatment and other variables were used to predict the long-term outcome of patients with anorexia nervosa according to the outcome criteria defined by Morgan and Russell (1975). The defined parameters were applied to two samples (n=51 and n=21) from two different clinical institutions. The defined parameters had a fairly good predictive power within the respective sample, but not for the other sample in the sense of a real cross-validation. This result can be explained in terms of sample differences, especially concerning outcome. Nevertheless, the further study of the predictive power of weight measurements seems to be worthwhile.

The main clinical feature of patients with anorexia nervosa is the loss of body weight, per definitionem at least 15% below that expected (APA, 1987). All methods of therapy—whatever their theoretical basis might be—include measures to enhance body weight. Thus, it seems plausible to use longitudinal weight data during inpatient treatment as predictors for the long-term outcome of the disorder. There are several arguments that support the view that weight curves during treatment might reflect positive and negative aspects of the treatment process. Therefore, weight curves as objective measures might not be the superficial data they are very often seen to be. Nevertheless, studies on the long-term outcome of anorexia nervosa, based on longitudinal parameters, are relatively rare.

The following study is part of a larger follow-up study in 103 patients with anorexia nervosa at the Department of Child and Adolescent Psychiatry of the Philipps University in Marburg. The data of these patients are compared with another sample of patients from the Department of Child and Adolescent Psychiatry at the Central Institute of Mental Health in Mannheim.

Today, there exist several follow-up studies on patients with anorexia nervosa that use the same standardized prognostic criteria. Morgan and Russell (1975) have defined criteria concerning the course and prognosis of anorexia nervosa that take into account only body weight and return of menstruation. These criteria have been used widely because they are simple and practicable. We, too, have used them in our study.

For clinicians, who as a rule are not able to follow up their patients, there exist several questions concerning prognosis and long-term outcome:

- What is the role of low body weight for a long-term prognosis?
- Which role does age play at the beginning of the disorders? the velocity of weight gain during inpatient treatment? the variability of the weight curve during treatment? artificial nourishment by naso-gastric tube or infusions? treatment that is very close to the symptoms or treatment that is more distant to symptomatology?

Department of Child and Adolescent Psychiatry, Philipps University, Hans-Sachs-Str. 6, D-3550 Marburg, West Germany and Department of Child and Adolescent Psychiatry, Central Institute for Mental Health, Postfach 5970, D-6800 Mannheim, West Germany.

– What is the role of the family, the kind and severity of psychopathology, self-induced vomiting or abuse of laxatives?

There are, of course, many more questions. Within this study, we restrict ourselves to the very simple weight measurements and to some other variables during inpatient treatment and relate them with the outcome criteria defined by Morgan and Russell (1975). We operationalized these criteria as follows:

1) *Good prognosis*. This category is given if the measured actual weight at follow-up is at least 85% of the ideal body weight and was, according to patient's assertion, above 85% during the foregoing 6 months, and menstruation is regular.
2) *Intermediate prognosis*. This category is used if measured body weight at follow-up is at least 85% of the ideal body weight, but was sometimes or often below 85% during the last 6 months before follow-up (according to patient's assertion), or if disturbances of menstruation are present.
3) *Unfavorable prognosis*. This category is given if the measured actual body weight at follow-up is below 85% of the ideal weight or menstruation has not returned (or is less than 4 times per year).
4) Death caused by the anorectic disorder, its sequelae, or suicide.

In a former study of the first 36 patients who had been investigated during the Marburg longitudinal study, we already investigated the predictive value of weight curves during inpatient treatment on long-term outcome (Remschmidt & Müller, 1987). In these 36 patients with anorexia nervosa (age at onset: 14.5 ± 1.9 years), an attempt was made to predict long-term outcome (follow-up interval 7.8 ± 3.77 years) from weight changes during inpatient treatment (duration of treatment: 156 ± 76 days). Several statistical methods appropriate for the use of longitudinal data were applied.

In a methodological paper (Müller & Remschmidt, 1988), we used several linear and nonparametric approaches for the analysis of longitudinal data of these patients. It could be shown that in the classification procedure of the patients according to Morgan and Russell's prognostic categories only the longitudinal parameters discriminated best between the different prognostic groups.

Practical experiences with the latter methods applied to discriminate between prognosis groups for anorexia nervosa from longitudinal weight measurements during clinical admission were reported. It turned out that the prognosis was mainly dependent on the coordinates of the point at which the weight of the patient stabilizes after an initial weight increase.

Within this study, some new longitudinal weight parameters have been defined for the prediction of the long-term course of the anorectic patients. They have been applied to the data of the Marburg sample as well as to the Mannheim sample, in order to have a kind of cross-validation.

Samples

The Marburg Sample (n=51)

The total sample of the Marburg follow-up study of anorectic patients comprised 103 patients (99 female and 4 male patients) who had been treated as inpatients between 1952 and 1982 at the Department of Child and Adolescent Psychiatry of the Philipps University in Marburg. For this study, 58 of these patients were first selected from whom complete weight courses as well as the outcome according to Morgan and Russell were available, forming the sample MR58.

Although these patients satisfy the ICD-9 criteria for anorexia nervosa, not all of them satisfy the DSM-III-R criteria, since some had an initial weight above 85% of their ideal body weight. For most investigations, we therefore used the subsample MR51 of the 51 (48 female, 3 male) patients satisfying the DSM-

Table 1. Age/sex modification of BROCA formula.

% of body size (cm) – 100		Age	
		<20	≥20
sex	f	80	85
	m	85	90

III-R criteria, too. The mean age at first diagnosis of these 51 patients was 13.4 ± 1.7, the interval until follow-up investigation was 7.6 ± 3.8, and the mean age at follow-up was 22.1 ± 3.5. The mean age at admission was 14.6 ± 1.8 years.

For selection of the sample we used the age-/sex-dependent modification of the BROCA formula given in Table 1. However, for reasons of compatibility to Remschmidt and Müller (1987), for the weight curves and derived longitudinal parameters, we used BROCA–20% = 0.8 × (body size [cm] – 100) for all patients, independent of age and sex.

The Mannheim Sample (n=21)

According to the same criteria as for the Marburg samples MR58 and MR51, the Mannheim samples MA25 and MA21 were formed, including 25 resp. 21 patients. In the subsample MA21, the mean age at first diagnosis was 13.2 ± 1.4 years, the interval until follow-up investigation was 5.4 ± 1.4 years, the mean age at follow-up was 20.4 ± 1.9 years. The mean age at admission was 15.0 ± 1.8 years.

Methodology

The methodology of this study can be subdivided into three parts:

1) First, it was important to define plausible parameters from the longitudinal weight curves that could be operationalized and that could be connected with long-term prognosis (outcome).

2) The second goal was to develop algorithms in order to estimate the curve parameters defined under 1) using the weight measurement data. The term "estimation" is used here in a statistical sense, referring to the fact that the real continuous longitudinal weight curves are unknown. The bases of the longitudinal data are weight measurements at different points in time (e.g., once a week, with some irregularities) and with the possibility of errors. Errors in measurement include also probable influences through manipulations of the patients (e.g., by water drinking before weight measurements).

3) Discriminant analyses.

Typical methodological problems concerning points 1) and 2) emerge in this investigation as in the former ones (Remschmidt & Müller, 1987) concerning the plateau parameters (see below). These parameters are physiologically and psychiatrically very useful parameters, but it is very difficult to define what is described by the term "plateau" in terms of an objective algorithmic definition. Besides that, there are many curves that do not reveal a clear plateau level of the weight curve.

Definition of the Longitudinal Curve Parameters

In this section, the longitudinal curve parameters used in this study are defined without using special mathematical terminology. With the exception of the plateau parameters, we have restricted ourselves to such parameters that can be defined by simple mathematical operations, such as computation of time averages, of maxima and minima, and, for some parameters, computation of the first or second derivative.

If, for example, $g(t)$ denotes the body weight at time t (measured in percent of ideal body weight), t_a the time of first measurement, t_e the time of last measurement, we shall denote by mean (g) the time average of g, that is

$$\text{mean}(g) = \frac{1}{t_e - t_a} \int_{t_a}^{t_e} g(t)\, dt.$$

Further notations are: min(g) for the lowest, max(g) for the largest value of g, |g| for the absolute value of g, g', g" for the first and second derivative of g, respectively.

Plateau Parameters (PLATTIM, PLATWGT)

As already described by Remschmidt and Müller (1987) and Müller and Remschmidt (1988), many weight curves of anorectic patients show a clear plateau in their weight curves, i.e., there exists a point in time at which the velocity of weight gain decreases significantly and no essential further weight gain occurs until discharge of the patient. From such a plateau we obtain two coordinates: the time when this begins (we will denote this time point by PLATTIM) and the corresponding weight at this time (PLATWGT).

As in Remschmidt and Müller (1987), we determined the value of PLATTIM by visual inspection so that this variable has a subjective component.

In cases that did not show a significant plateau, PLATWGT was set to missing value, whereas PLATTIM was set to another special value outside its normal range. This distinction between missing value (time coordinate of plateau unknown) and special value (no plateau occurred) for PLATTIM was necessary to make it possible for the discrimination algorithm CART to put the cases without plateau into a special category (with potentially good or bad prognosis).

Convexity Parameter (CONVPAR)

On the basis of the results of our first paper (Remschmidt & Müller, 1987), the weight curves can be subdivided into three categories:

- Type 1: Rapid and remarkable weight gain at the beginning, then retardation or stagnation of weight gain, continuation of inpatient treatment, though the causes for this treatment continuation might not be explained by body weight. From a mathematical point of view, such curves roughly look like concave curves, which does not mean that the curves are really concave in the strict mathematical sense.
- Type 2: Uniform weight gain from the beginning until the end of the treatment. Uniform weight gain does not mean that there is no variability of the weight curve, but globally the weight gain can be looked upon as a linear function in contrast to a more or less expressed concavity or convexity.
- Type 3: At the beginning of treatment, only a small weight gain, eventually followed by a reduction of weight again, and later a more pronounced weight gain, which can be characterized as a roughly convex course of the weight curve.

As a measure to describe the above mentioned courses of the weight curve we defined the convexity parameter CONVPAR in the following way:

$$\text{CONVPAR} = \text{mean}(g) - \frac{g(t_a) + g(t_e)}{2}.$$

This formula expresses the mean value of weight minus the arithmetic mean of the body weight at the beginning and at the end of the treatment. There is an association of positive values of this parameter in relation to Type 1 of the weight curve and negative values in relation to Type 3 of the weight curves, whereas the values of the parameter around 0 are typical for Type-2 weight curves.

Figure 1 illustrates some artificial examples of convex and concave weight curves with prescribed values of the parameter CONVPAR. The region between the dotted lines of Figure 1 corresponds to values of CONVPAR between 34 and 74 which are associated with a good prognosis in one of the CART decision trees shown below. According to our definition, positive values of CONVPAR correspond to concave functions, whereas convex functions yield negative values. Of course, CONVPAR is zero for linear functions.

It should be stressed again that real weight curves are generally neither concave nor linear nor convex in the strict sense, though this is also not necessary, because CONVPAR is defined for any weight curve.

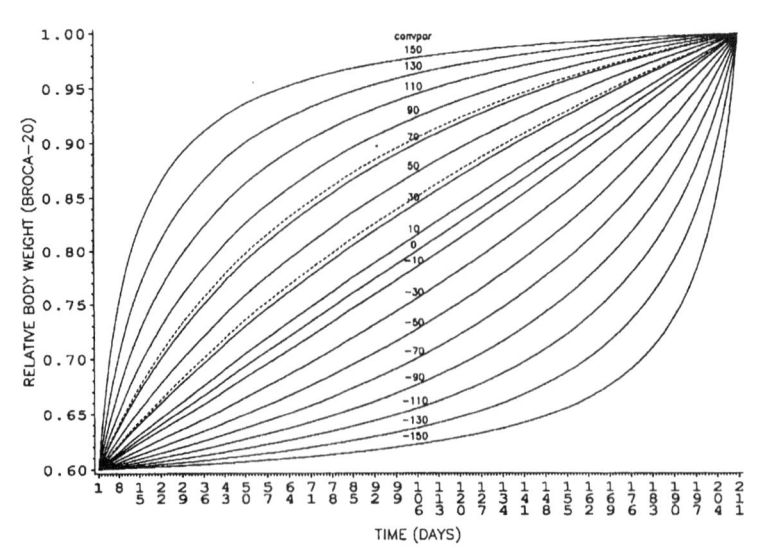

Figure 1. Examples of convex and concave curves with prescribed values of CONVPAR. Region between dashed curves: curves with 34.3 < CONVPAR < 74.1.

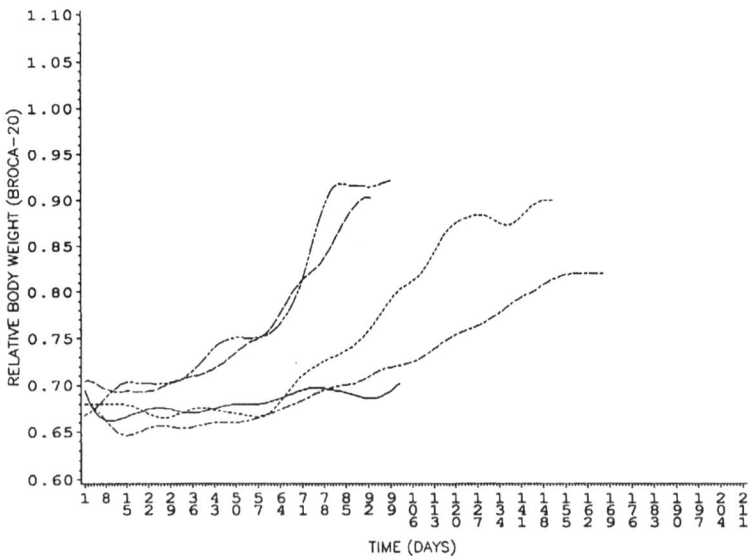

Figure 2. Examples from sample MR51 for weight curves with small values of CONVPAR (–50 to –10).

Figures 2–4 exemplify some real weight curves from the Marburg sample (n=51) with respect to low, intermediate, and high values of the CONVPAR parameter.

To some extent, a high value of the CONVPAR parameter expresses a similar weight curve as an early plateau (low value of PLATTIM) combined with a high stabilized weight (PLATWGT), while continuing inpatient treatment. The convexity parameter has several advantages as compared with the plateau parameters:

- It is defined in a simple and objective way.
- Since it is the difference of two averages, it is easy to compute and has good robustness properties compared to the plateau parameters.

The other longitudinal parameters defined within the following sections of this paper result from a process of differentiation and are thus not as robust as the convexity parameter.

The absolute value of CONVPAR is

Figure 3. Examples from sample MR51 for weight curves with medium values of CONVPAR (40 to 60).

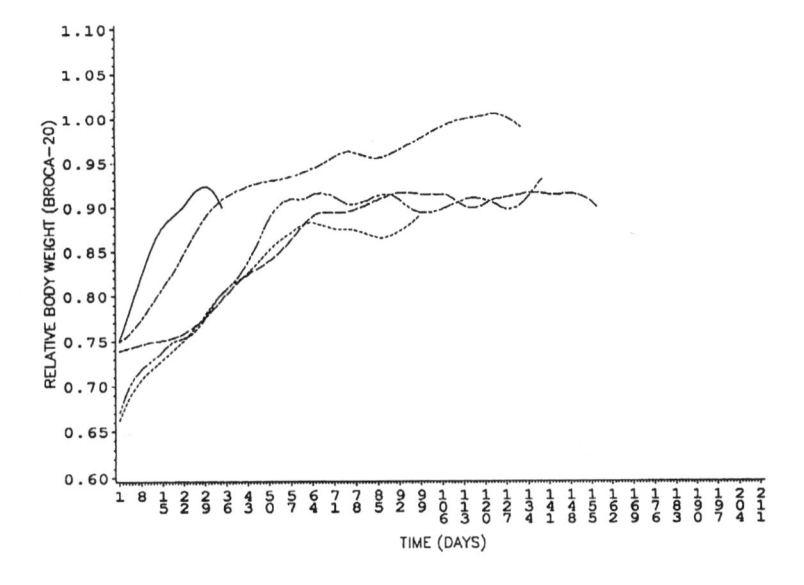

Figure 4. Examples from sample MR51 for weight curves with large values of CONVPAR (80 to 150).

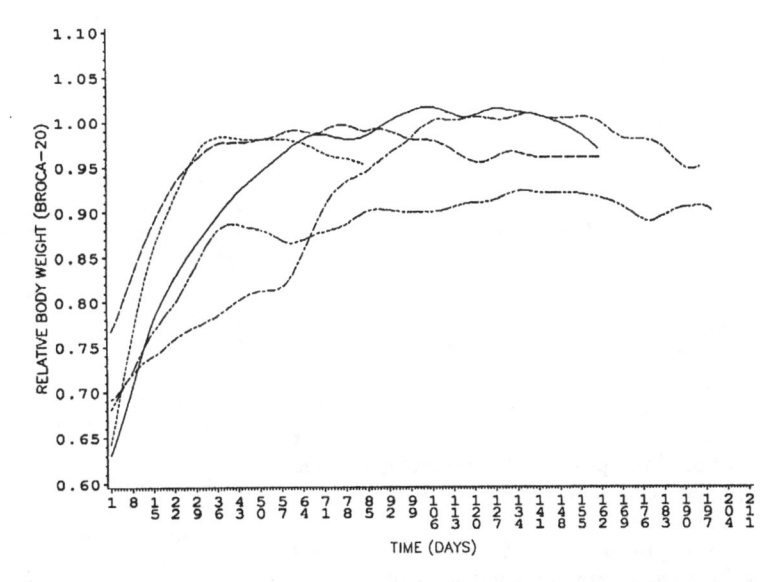

bounded by max(g) − min(g) so that

$$\frac{\text{CONVPAR}}{\max(g)-\min(g)}$$

has values between -1 and +1.

Negative Variation (NEGVAR)

It is an interesting question whether weight losses during inpatient treatment are associated with a poor prognosis at follow-up.

Joining together all the decreasing parts of the curve, we get a continuous decreasing function, the "decreasing part of g." Mathematicians call the difference between its starting value and its final value the negative variation of g. If we divide it by the duration of treatment, we may express the result as an average, mean($|g'| - g'$). This parameter still has the disadvantage that it is influenced by many short decreasing periods (corresponding to short-term variation of weight) in the same way as by long and severe periods of weight decrease. To avoid this, we use a smoothed version $\tilde{g}'$ of the derivative g' of g. Our parameter NEGVAR in its final form thus is the expression

$$\text{NEGVAR} = \text{mean}(|\tilde{g}'| - \tilde{g}').$$

Total Variation (TOTVAR)

Similar to the negative variation, we may define the positive variation by adding together all the increasing segments of g. The sum of positive and negative variation is called total variation. We use the variable

$$\text{TOTVAR} = \text{mean}(|\tilde{g}'|).$$

Maximum Slope (MAXSLOPE)

As done already in Remschmidt and Müller (1987), we use the maximum slope (velocity of weight gain) MAXSLOPE = max(g') as a predictor variable.

Variability (VARIABIL)

In Remschmidt and Müller (1987) a moving-average type estimator was used as a measure of variability (compare also Müller & Remschmidt, 1988). Provided the sequence of weight measurements is dense enough, this statistic is a consistent estimator for the error variance of the process of measurement. This error variance, however, is not a property of the weight curve g.

In the present investigation, we instead used a measure for the variability of g,

$$\text{VARIABIL} = \text{mean}(|g''|).$$

Total Weight Gain (WGTDIFF)

The 8th longitudinal parameter we used was simply the difference between the body weight (in % of ideal body weight) at the end and the beginning of treatment,

$$\text{WGTDIFF} = g(t_e) - g(t_a).$$

Estimation of the Longitudinal Weight Parameters (Curve Parameters)

Kernel Estimation of Weight Curves

Since, according to our knowledge, there are no satisfactory parametric models to describe the time course of body weight during treatment of anorectic patients, we had to use a nonparametric method to estimate the true weight curves from the sequence of weight measurements. The best known methods for nonparametric curve estimation are smoothing splines and kernel estimation. A good reference to nonparametric curve estimation with the emphasis on kernel methods is Müller (1988). In Remschmidt and Müller (1987), we used kernel estimators in a way described, for example, in Gasser et al. (1984). The bandwidth (width of the kernel function) that determines the degree of smoothing and is crucial for the quality of the estimators was determined in Remschmidt and Müller (1987) separately for each individual curve via the RICE criterion (see Müller & Remschmidt, 1988 or Gasser et al., 1984).

This procedure is valid only if the measurement design (i.e., the distribution of the weight measurements over time) is nearly the same for all patients, and if there are no gaps in the sequence of measurements (e.g., 3 weeks without measurement). For our enlarged new sample we had to find a different way.

Problems with kernel estimators generally arise if the density of measurements varies in time within one patient, or if it varies between patients. The problems become still greater if there are "outliers" in the distance (in time) between adjacent weight measurements, that is, if the above-mentioned gaps occur. For example, it may happen that most of these distances are not greater than 7 days, but there are some exceptions where they are 22 days. In such situations, it is natural to think of two solutions: usage of kernel estimators with varying bandwidth or usage of smoothing splines. Kernel estimators with varying bandwidth are, in our opinion, not a good solution for our problem, since the degree of smoothing should not depend on local design conditions but on biomedical facts. Smoothing splines may be a solution, if they are implemented in the right way (not the way supplied with the SAS/Graph interpolation options), but we did not investigate this further. Instead, we propose a modification in the definition of the kernel estimators as proposed by Gasser and Müller (1979) (see also Gasser et al., 1984 or Müller, 1988). Our proposal differs also from the proposal made earlier by Priestley and Chao (1972).

It is not possible to give here a mathematically precise definition, but from a qualitative point of view, the difference between the three proposals may be described in the following way: If the distance in time between adjacent measurements is small (compared to the bandwidth), all three methods yield very similar estimates. If this distance is large, however, the Priestley-Chao estimate is not even defined on the whole time interval, the Gasser-Müller estimate looks roughly like a step function (smoothed a bit), whereas our estimate in this situation resembles a linear interpolated curve with "smoothed vertices." (Expressed in mathematical terms, the Gasser-Müller estimate is the convolution of a step function with the kernel function, whereas our proposal is the convolution of the linear interpolated curve with the same kernel function.)

Because of this modification, we gained the freedom to choose the bandwidth according to biomedical considerations—not according to the largest occurring gap between weight measurements in the whole sample. In our opinion, the bandwidth should be the same for all patients, since otherwise differences in the estimated curves may be attributable to the different estimators.

Using artificial test curves, we decided to choose the Epanechnikov kernel function with a bandwidth of 7 days, which may be described by the following properties: a linear increase of weight over 3 to 4 weeks and a following decrease of the same order are reproduced to 90%, i.e., only 10% are attributed to error variance. If the same increase occurs from one day to the other, with a return to the lower weight at the third day, 90% of this variation is attributed to error variance, and only 10% are transferred to the smoothed curve.

If the duration of the increase is 7 days, 60% are transferred to the curve; if it is 14 days, 80% are transferred (attributing 20% to error variance), and so on.

According to our experience, the bandwidth of 7 days is a good compromise between the demands to preserve essential characteristics of the curve and to eliminate random variation from measurement errors.

On the other hand, the application of the cross-validation algorithm for bandwidth choice (described, for example, in Müller & Ihm, 1985) to individual curves would have led to bandwidths between 2 and 52 days in the Marburg sample, which supports our opinion that this approach cannot be recommended.

For the estimation of the first and second derivatives, we selected the bandwidths 10 resp. 21 days in a similar way, using the IMSE-asymptotic optimal kernels of order 3 and 4, respectively (see Gasser et al., 1984).

The computations were done in two steps, applying a FORTRAN-program of Hans-Georg Müller to the linear interpolated weight curves.

Influence of Gaps in the Measurement Design to the Estimation of Longitudinal Parameters

Gaps in the sequence of weight measurements may not only give rise to problems in curve estimation (discussed in the foregoing section), but may also lead to biased estimates of the longitudinal parameters, even if the best possible curve estimator is used. The convexity parameter is not influenced much by a few gaps, since it is a global curve parameter, computed via integration of the weight curve. On the other hand, it is well known that parameters depending on the first or even second derivative may be severely influenced by gaps or if the density of the measurements is too low.

In order to get an impression of the possible bias and to find a concept of how to deal with gaps, we performed a small simulation study. First, from all patients who had at least one measurement per week without any gap, we selected the five longest curves. The estimated parameters of these curves were taken as "true" reference values. Then, a random sample of 150 curves was generated by introducing random gaps of different length (7, 10, 20 days) and random location into the 5 "parent curves." We compared the resulting estimates with the "true" values from the parent curves, computing empirical bias, variance, and mean squared error.

For these computations, the sample was not only stratified according to the parent curve, but also according to the length of the artificial gaps, in order to get an idea of the "critical" length of a gap.

Two strategies for treating gaps were compared: One was to include into computations (e.g., averaging) only parts of the curve without gap (adjusting then, of course, for the reduced effective curve length), the other strategy was to use the whole curve for computations.

As one must expect, the second strategy introduced some bias especially for the parameter VARIABIL; but to our surprise, this was counterbalanced by a much greater variance for estimates yielded by the first strategy. As a consequence, according to mean squared error, the second strategy was superior. The stratification according to length of the gap suggested discarding all curves with gaps longer than 10 days before computing the sensitive parameters NEGVAR, TOTVAR, MAXSLOPE, and especially VARIABIL, leading, of course, to a rather high rate of missing values for these parameters.

Discriminant Analysis

As in our first paper, we used also in this study the CART classification and regression trees program of Breiman, Friedman, Olsen and Stone (1984) as a nonparametric discriminant analysis. Several weight parameters were used in order to predict the global outcome of Morgan and Russell (1975) at follow-up. For this analysis, the three categories of the global outcome were reduced on two by putting together the categories "intermediate" and "poor" outcome into one category (see Table 2). As Table 2 shows, there are differences between the Marburg and the Mannheim sample. These differences diminish, of course, the chances of a cross-validation between the two samples.

For the analysis of the predictive power of variables during inpatient treatment for the global outcome at follow-up, we included besides 8 variables derived from the weight curves, two additional variables: age at beginning of the disease (AGEDIA), and artificial nourishment (yes or no; ARTNOUR). Other studies have demonstrated that age at the beginning of anorectic disorders is important for the long-term prognosis. The variable "artificial nourishment," on the other hand, is related with the weight curves: On the one hand, artificial nourishment is influenced by the patient's condition at beginning of the treatment, and on the other hand, it influences also the course of weight gain. Finally, these two variables had also been used for the prediction of long-term outcome during our first study.

Nevertheless, the number of ten predictive variables was too high in relation to the number of patients in the different samples (n=58/51/25/21): A reduction was necessary. By using the classification and regression trees, four methods for selection of variables were considered:

1) The CART method implies together with an internal cross-validation already a selection of variables. The decision trees created by

Table 2. Distribution of global outcome in the four samples.

| Sample | | Global outcome (Morgan & Russell) | | | | |
		1	2	3	4	Sum
MR58	n	38	6	12	2	58
	%	65.52	10.34	20.69	3.45	100
MA25	n	9	12	2	2	25
	%	36.0	48.0	8.0	8.0	100
MR51	n	35	4	10	2	51
	%	68.63	7.84	19.61	3.92	100
MA21	n	8	9	2	2	21
	%	38.10	42.86	9.52	9.52	100

inclusion of all ten variables are, however, insufficient, which confirms our experience from previous analyses.

2) Another method is to use the CART program first with all variables and then using a second course of the CART program by selecting those variables that had reached the highest variable importance in the first step. For the concept of variable importance within CART, see Breiman et al. (1984, p. 147).

3) A third method that is simpler and independent of the CART program is a heuristic one, namely, to use a univariate test for the different predictive variables between different groups defined by the outcome variables and to classify the variables according to the p-values. This procedure has little theoretical support since it ignores the multivariate structure of the problem, though it was rather successful in the past, at least to our experience.

4) Finally, another method consists in using an alternative discriminant analysis with automatic selection of variables (e.g., stepwise logistic regression or all possible subsets logistic regression). This procedure, however, seemed not to be suited to our problem, because of a quite large proportion of missing values in those longitudinal variables that depend on derivatives of the weight curve.

For the following analysis, we used the third method for each of the four samples by selecting three variables using the t-test for unequal variances for the interval-scaled variables and Fisher's exact test for the dichotomous variable "artificial nourishment" (ARTNOUR). By using these variables for each of the four samples, a classification and regression tree was calculated.

The predictive power of classification procedures in the case of two classes is usually expressed by the four parameters specificity, sensitivity, negative predictive value, and positive predictive value (see Table 3).

Table 3. Classification matrix.

		Outcome good	medium/poor	
Prediction	good	a	b	a+b
	medium/poor	c	d	c+d
		a+c	b+d	n

Measures of predictive power:
Specificity SPEC (%) = 100a/(a+c)
Sensitivity SENS (%) = 100d/(b+d)
Negative predictive value NPV (%) = 100a/(a+b)
Positive predictive value PPV (%) = 100d/(c+d)

These four parameters have been estimated for each of the CART decision trees in three ways:

- by internal cross-validation (built into the CART procedure) by the leaving-one-out method (in the sequel abbreviated as L-1-out method);
- as proportions of correctly classified cases within the learning sample, which normally leads to too optimistic estimations;
- by calculating the number of correctly classified cases within the other sample (e.g., application of the decision tree from the Marburg sample in the Mannheim sample and vice versa). This procedure is a real cross-validation that allows simultaneous testing of the validity of the results in more general populations.

The last method can be expected to yield the lowest estimates, because structural differences of the samples may play an important role, besides differences by chance.

Results

Four Decision Trees and Their Estimated Predictive Power

As already described above, the three most important variables were selected for each of the four samples MR58, MR51, MA25, and MA21, and a CART decision tree was generated with those three variables as input. The four resulting trees are shown in Figures 5–8.

The most plausible tree which also performed best in the real cross validation is tree MR58 (Figure 5). The input variables for this tree are ARTNOUR (artificial nourishment), AGEDIA (age of first diagnosis), and CONVPAR. The decision nodes are based on the two variables AGEDIA and CONVPAR, whereas the variable ARTNOUR occurs only in surrogate and competitor splits: If age at beginning of the disorder is below 12.5 years, a good prognosis is predicted at follow-up after several years. If the patients are older than 12.5 years, another decision node related to age is important. For those patients whose anorexic disorder started before 15 years of age, the prognosis is good if the convexity parameter (CONVPAR) varies between 34.3 and 74.1, whereas the long-term prognosis is poor for those patients for whom this condition does not apply. On the other hand, for those patients whose disorder started beyond the age of 15 years, the prognosis is good if the convexity parameter of their weight curve is below 74.1, and poor if the convexity parameter is over this value.

The numbers at the branches of the tree in Figure 5 are the numbers of cases in sample MR51 going left and right at the nodes, respectively. The numbers in brackets refer to the full sample MR58.

Table 4 demonstrates the four parameters that characterize the goodness of classification. The table shows the goodness of the classification derived from the decision tree of the total Marburg sample (MR58), for the reduced Marburg sample (MR51), and the reduced Mannheim sample (MA21). The first column shows the estimates of specificity, sensitivity, negative and positive predictive values by using the leaving-one-out method. The second column for the learning sample

Table 4. Estimated predictive power for decision tree MR58.

Parameter	L-1-out	Learning sample	MR51	MA21
SPEC (%)	74	79	77	63
SENS (%)	80	85	87	54
NPV (%)	62	91	93	45
PPV (%)	88	68	64	70

(Sample/Method of estimation MR58)

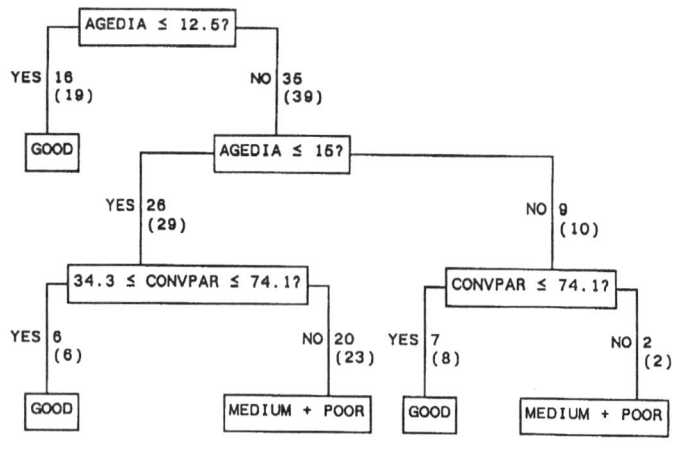

Figure 5. Decision tree MR58, applied to sample MR51 (only cases with initial weight 85% ideal body weight). In parentheses are the number of cases if the tree is applied to the full sample MR58. Variables included age at first diagnosis (AGEDIA), artificial nourishment (ARTNOUR), convexity parameter (CONVPAR).

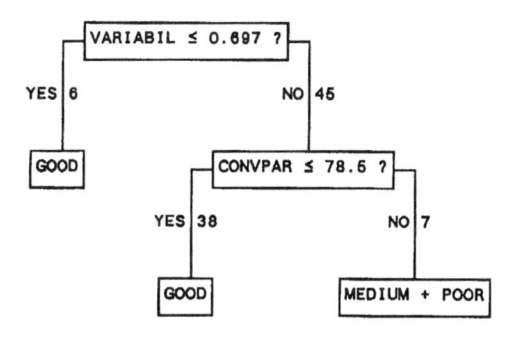

Figure 6. Decision tree MR51, applied to sample MR51. Variables included artificial nourishment (ARTNOUR), convexity parameter (CONVPAR), variability (VARIABIL).

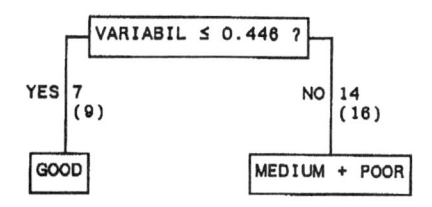

Figure 7. Decision tree MA25, applied to sample MA21 (only cases with initial weight 85% ideal body weight). In parentheses are the number of cases if the tree is applied to the full sample MA25. Variables included convexity parameter (CONVPAR), variability (VARIABIL), weight difference between beginning and end of stationary episode (WGTDIFF).

(total Marburg sample), the last two columns show the same values for the reduced Marburg and Mannheim samples.

Figure 6 demonstrates another decision tree using artificial nourishment, convexity parameter, and variability of the weight curve as predictive variables. The decision tree was derived from the reduced Marburg sample (MR51). It becomes evident that a good prognosis at follow-up can be predicted by values of the variability parameter below 0.697. For those patients whose weight curve is characterized by this condition, the prognosis is good and remains good (n=6). For those whose weight curve has a variability value above a critical value of 0.697 (n=45), the convexity parameter becomes important. If this weight curve parameter is below 78.5, the prognosis at follow-up is favorable (n=38), whereas for those patients for whom this condition does not apply (n=7), the prognosis is poor.

Table 5 exemplifies the goodness of the classification for this classification tree. It becomes evident that the characteristic parameters for the goodness of classification are modest, especially in the reduced Mannheim sample (MA21).

A third decision tree is illustrated in Figure 7, using the input variables convexity parameter, variability parameter, and weight difference. The decision tree was derived in the complete Mannheim sample (MA25), and was administered to the reduced Mannheim sample (MA21). The reduced Mannheim sample includes only patients whose weight at intake was below 85% of the ideal body weight. In brackets are the numbers of patients in the original decision tree derived from the total Mannheim sample (MA25).

It becomes evident that in this smaller sample only the variability of the weight curve has a predictive power for the long-term outcome after 5 years.

Table 6 illustrates for this tree the four parameters characterizing the goodness of classification for the total Mannheim sample (MA25), the reduced Mannheim sample (MA21), and the reduced Marburg sample (MR51). As with tree MR51, the real cross-validation estimates (column 4) are modest.

Finally, the last decision tree is demonstrated in Figure 8, using as input variables

Table 5. Estimated predictive power for decision tree MR51.

Parameter	Sample/Method of estimation MR51			
	L-1-out	Learning sample	MA21	
SPEC (%)	97	97	100	
SENS (%)	38	38	0	
NPV (%)	77	77	38	
PPV (%)	85	85	—	

Table 6. Estimated predictive power for decision tree MR25.

Parameter	Sample/Method of estimation MA25			
	L-1-out	Learning sample	MR21	MA51
SPEC (%)	56	67	63	42
SENS (%)	75	81	84	50
NPV (%)	56	67	71	65
PPV (%)	75	81	79	29

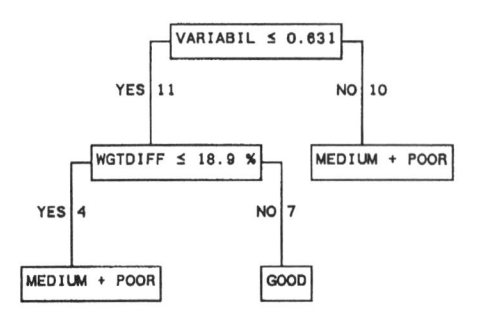

```
                VARIABIL ≤ 0.631
           YES 11          NO 10
    WGTDIFF ≤ 18.9 %          MEDIUM + POOR
  YES 4         NO 7
 MEDIUM + POOR    GOOD
```

Figure 8. Decision tree MA21, applied to sample MA21. Variables included convexity parameter (CONVPAR), variability (VARIABIL), weight difference between beginning and end of stationary episode (WGTDIFF).

the convexity parameter, the variability parameter, and the weight difference. The decision tree was derived from the reduced Mannheim sample (MA21). It becomes evident that two of the three variables were included into the tree: the variability parameter and the weight difference parameter.

Table 7 shows the quantities characterizing the goodness of the classification, in the first column by the leaving-one-out method, in the second column in the learning sample, and in the third column the decision tree is administered to the reduced Marburg sample (MR51). The results are not better than those of the foregoing two trees.

Comparing the four trees, we see that the tree MR58 (developed in the full Marburg sample) attains the best results in two directions: First, in its own (Marburg) samples, it shows the best compromise between high sensitivity and high specificity and secondly, it performs best under real cross-validation (Mannheim sample). Finally, the tree MR58 allows the most straightforward interpretation, as we will see in the next section.

Table 7. Estimated predictive power for decision tree MR21.

Parameter	Sample/Method of estimation		
	MR21 L-1-out	Learning sample	MA51
SPEC (%)	75	88	34
SENS (%)	77	100	66
NPV (%)	67	100	67
PPV (%)	83	93	30

Discussion of the Results

As already mentioned above, the samples of the Marburg and the Mannheim hospitals are different: They differ with respect to the follow-up interval (Marburg: 7.6 ± 3.8, Mannheim: 5.4 ± 1.4), and they differ with respect to the proportion of favorable and unfavorable cases at follow-up. Both differences are correlated with each other, because several studies have shown that long-term prognosis is related with the follow-up interval. But the already mentioned difference remains stable if we reduce the Marburg sample only to those patients with a follow-up interval of at most 6 resp. 4 years. This is demonstrated in Table 8.

With respect to age at onset of the disorder (MR51 = 13.4 ± 1.7; MA21 = 13.2 ± 1.4) and with respect to relative (% ideal body weight) weight at intake (MR51 = 72.8 ± 6.8; MA21 = 72.5 ± 6.9), the samples are comparable. It is not possible here to discuss the possible reasons for the different distributions of outcome at follow-up, but it is clear that they restrict the applicability of the decision trees developed from one sample to the sample from the other clinic. The best results in this direction are achieved by the tree developed from the full Marburg sample (MR58): Applied to the reduced Mannheim sample (MA21) it yields a YOUDEN-index (SPEZ (%) + SENS (%) – 100) of 17%, and a predictive gain (NPV (%) + PPV (%) – 100) of 15%. This is a positive, though modest result. The positive association of observed and predicted outcome, however, is not significant (p=0.39, Fisher's exact test). The other three decision trees do not reach posi-

Table 8. Distribution of global outcome and katamnestic interval in Mannheim and Marburg sample.

Sample	Good outcome	Medium/poor outcome	
MA21	8	13	21
	38.10%	61.90%	100%
MR51	35	16	51
	68.67%	31.37%	100%
MR51, interval ≤6J.	14	9	23
	60.87%	39.13%	100%
MR51 interval ≤4J.	5	2	7
	71.43%	28.57%	100%

Table 9. Estimated Youden-Index.

Decision tree	L-1-out-estimate	Real cross-validation Sample	Estimate
MR58	54	MA21	17
MR51	35	MA21	0
MA25	31	MR51	−8
MA21	52	MR51	0

Table 10. Estimated predictive gain.

Decision tree	L-1-out-estimate	Real cross-validation Sample	Estimate
MR58	50	MA21	15
MR51	62	MA21	—
MA25	31	MR51	−6
MA21	50	MR51	−3

tive values for YOUDEN-index and predictive gain in the sample from the other clinic (Tables 9, 10).

The decision tree MR58 can also be interpreted best with respect to previous results (Remschmidt & Müller, 1987; Müller & Remschmidt, 1988): Besides the assertion that age at onset under 13 years implies a good prognosis, it asserts that a poor outcome can be predicted if the weight curve has one of the following shapes:

- Rapid initial weight gain and long inpatient treatment while the weight curve does not go up any more, eventually also going down.
- Very slow weight gain in the first part (6–7 weeks) of treatment.

A very rapid initial weight gain was seen in patients with severe symptoms of dehydration provoked by laxative or diuretic abuse or vomiting. Increased weight in these patients shortly after admission is the result of normalization of water balance, not a true gain of adipose tissue. In many longitudinal studies, however, laxative abuse or vomiting is connected with poor outcome (Theander, 1985; Lacey, 1983; Mitchell, 1986).

In some patients, a very high initial weight gain may be the consequence of a behavioral treatment program. During the "operant" phase, ward privileges are attached to weight gain, for example, making telephone calls or visits at home. Normally, external confirmation becomes unnecessary and self-observed signs of progressive improvement maintain the course of behavioral change. Patients with "poor outcome" might not become independent of external reinforcements and start to lose weight as soon as the therapist's control measurements stop. This explains why the weight curve does not rise any more or even descends throughout long inpatient treatment.

As we all know from psychotherapy, in anorectic patients weight gain and change of body configuration needs some time to be really accepted and worked through. Those who do not take their time in therapy and try to gain weight as quickly as possible without coming to an understanding of their disorder may not recover completely and are prone to relapse.

On the other hand, initial weight gain should not be too slow. A very slow rise of the weight curve could indicate an intense fear of gaining weight and a severe distortion of body image resulting in refusal of therapeutical interventions. Patients with severe "weight phobia" might be at greater risk for a poor outcome.

A favorable outcome is predicted for the group of patients with an age at onset between 13 and 15 years, if the weight gain is a bit faster (but not too fast) in the first half of treatment, slowing down a bit in the second half, the inpatient treatment being continued not too long after the ideal body weight has been reached.

These young, nonchronically ill patients take their time to respond to therapeutical interventions. They take weight gain as a positive experiment in small steps to test particular beliefs and assumptions connected with eating disorders and continuously learn to alter them while becoming more and more independent of the therapist. This result is in line with our previous analyses (Müller & Remschmidt, 1988).

The diagram in Figure 9 shows, for the tree MR58, the values of the predictor variables "age at onset," "artificial nourishment," and "convexity parameter" as well as for the target variable "outcome at follow-up" in the reduced Marburg sample MR51. The framed areas are the regions where the decision tree predicts intermediate or poor outcome. Thus, a star or cross in the framed areas corresponds to a "false positive," whereas a square or triangle in the nonframed area corresponds

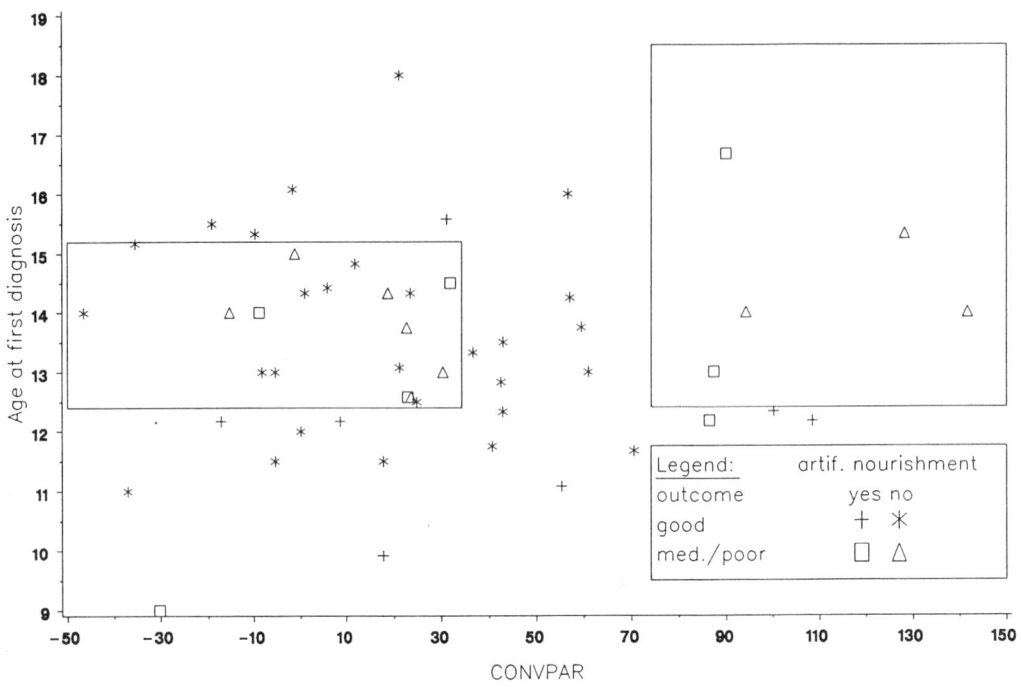

Figure 9. Application of decision tree MR58 to data MR51, represented in the scattergram. Framed areas: regions at which the decision tree predicts medium or poor outcome.

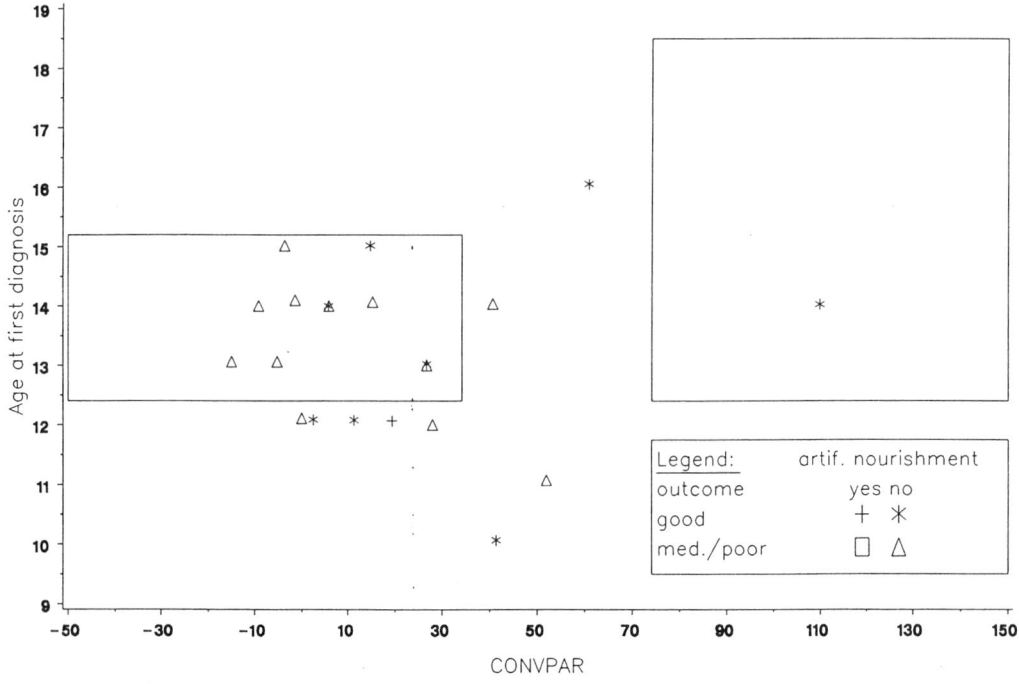

Figure 10. Application of decision tree MR58 to data MA21, represented in the scattergram. Framed areas: regions at which the decision tree predicts medium or poor outcome.

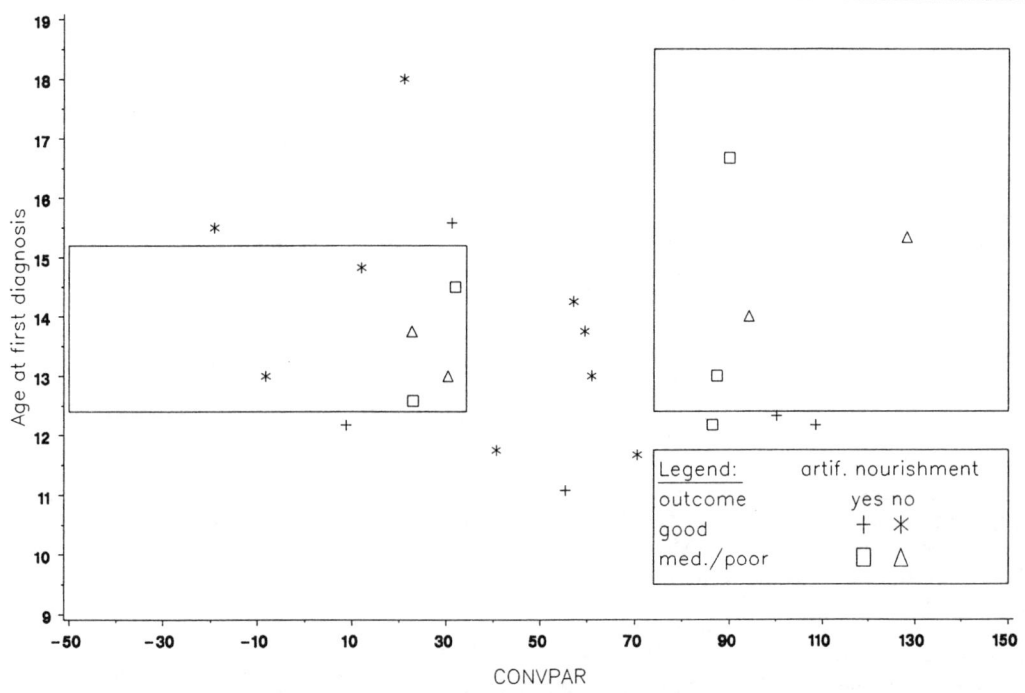

Figure 11. Application of decision tree MR58 to cases of sample MR51 with katamnestic interval not more than 6 years. Framed areas: regions at which the decision tree predicts medium or poor outcome.

to a "false negative," (predicted outcome good, actual outcome intermediate or poor).

Figure 10 shows the same for the reduced Mannheim sample MA21. The structural differences to the Marburg sample are evident: The unfavorable results with high values of the convexity parameter (>75) do not exist. Within the range of CONVPAR between 0 and 70, good and unfavorable cases cannot be separated, whereas for CONVPAR < 0, unfavorable cases dominate. In the Mannheim sample, age at onset has not such a strong predictive power as in the Marburg sample.

Figure 11 shows the structure of the Marburg sample MR51 remains stable if the sample is reduced to cases with a follow-up interval up to 6 years (n=23). This means that the structural differences between the Marburg and Mannheim sample cannot be explained only by the different follow-up interval.

General Discussion and Conclusions

This study assesses the predictive power of different longitudinal parameters derived from the weight curves of anorectic patients during inpatient treatment for the long-term prognosis of anorexia nervosa. Besides eight longitudinal parameters, two other parameters were used, namely, age at onset of the disease and artificial nourishment (forced feeding) during inpatient treatment. As an outcome variable, the three category global outcome score of Morgan and Russell (1975) was used, putting the last two categories (intermediate and poor prognosis) together. All patients fulfilled the criteria of ICD-9 for anorexia nervosa. As a nonparametric discriminant analysis, the classification and regression tree (CART) algorithm developed by Breiman et al. (1984) was applied for the group discrimination. This method has the attractive feature that for each predictor variable, a dichotomous decision (node of the tree) according to the value of the variable leads to the final classification decision in a terminal node and is therefore especially suitable for clinical applications. This algorithm was used with the leaving-one-out cross-validation to assess the correct prediction rate. In our former study (Remschmidt & Müller, 1987; Müller & Remschmidt, 1988), we predicted long-term outcome according to the Morgan and Russell criteria to a high extent. In this former study, the apparent prediction was correct for 96% of the patients with a good or intermediate prognosis and for 89% of those with a poor prognosis. But the built-in cross-validation of the CART program did not deliver such good results. According to the cross-validation, 86% of the good resp. intermediate cases were predicted correctly, but only 44% of those with a poor prognosis (Remschmidt & Müller, 1987). The aim of this study was to have a real cross-validation. For this reason, the method was applied to two samples from two different clinical institutions. The samples were comparable with respect to age at onset of the disorder and initial weight at the beginning of inpatient treatment, but they were different in terms of the outcome categories and follow-up interval. For these reasons, the generalization of the results from one sample to the other may not have been sufficient. Though there is a correlation between good outcome and follow-up interval (Niskanen et al., 1974; Vandereycken & Pierloot, 1983; Fichter, 1985), a reduction of the two samples to approximately the same follow-up interval (up to 6 years) did not change the differences between the samples. Therefore, this variable is not the crucial one.

If the analysis is restricted either on the Marburg or the Mannheim sample, the predictive results are better. For instance, the estimation of the goodness of classification for the total Marburg sample (MR58) reveals for the reduced Marburg sample (MR51) a specificity of 77% and an apparent sensitivity of 87%, which is not bad. The cross-validated estimates in sample MR58 are 74% and 80%, respectively. A similar result was obtained within the Mannheim sample (Table 6). If we look at how adequate the estimation of the reduced sample is by using the measures derived from the total Mannheim sample (MA25), we find a specificity of 63% and a sensitivity of 84%, with cross-validation in sample MA25 yielding 56% and 75%, respectively.

Thus, the conclusion is that the different longitudinal weight parameters do have a fairly good predictive power within a sample, but an insufficient predictive power for another sample, i.e., the generalization is not yet sufficient. As the CART program has an built-in cross-validation, there is also some kind of control of the described process of prediction. Nevertheless, a real cross-validation has not confirmed a high predictive power of the different weight measures as in our first study (Remschmidt & Müller, 1987; Müller & Remschmidt, 1988).

Finally, the question arises whether there might be other variables during or before inpatient treatment of anorexia nervosa that could be able to give a better prediction of long-term follow-up than the weight measures. In another study, we found that premorbid eating disorders are of high predictive power for the long-term outcome (Remschmidt, Wienand & Wewetzer, 1988, 1990).

References

American Psychiatric Association (1987). *Diagnostic and statistical manual of mental disorders* (3rd ed., rev.). Washington, DC: APA.

Breiman, L., Friedman, F., Olsen, A., & Stone, C. J. (1984). *CART: Classification and regression trees.* Belmont, California: Wadsworth.

Fichter, M. M. (1975). *Magersucht und Bulimia.* Berlin-Heidelberg-New York: Springer-Verlag.

Gasser, T., & Müller, H. G. (1979). *Kernel estimation of regression functions.* (Lecture Notes in Mathematics 757). Berlin: Springer-Verlag.

Gasser, Th., Müller, H. G., Köhler, W., Molinari, L., & A. Prader (1984). Nonparametric regression analysis of growth curves. *Annals of Statistics, 11*, 171-185.

Lacey, H. (1983). Bulimia nervosa, binge eating, and psychogenic vomiting: A controlled treatment study on long-term outcome. *British Medical Journal, 286*, 1609-1613.

Mitchell, J. E., Davis, L., Goff, G., & Pyle, R. (1986). A follow-up study of patients with bulimia. *International Journal of Eating Disorders, 5*, 441-450.

Morgan, H. G., & Russell, G. F. M. (1975). Value of family background and clinical features as predictors of long-term outcome in anorexia nervosa: 4-year follow-up study of 41 patients. *Psychological Medicine, 5*, 355-371.

Müller, H. G. (1988). *Nonparametric regression analysis of longitudinal data.* (Lecture Notes in Statistics 46). New York: Springer-Verlag.

Müller, H. G., & Ihm, P. (1985). Kernel estimation techniques for the analysis of clinical curves. *Methods of Information in Medicine, 24*, 218-224.

Müller, H.G., & Remschmidt, H. (1988). Nonparametric methods for the analysis of longitudinal medical data, with an application to the prognosis of anorectic patients from longitudinal weight measurements. In Société Adolphe Quetelet (Ed.), *Proceedings of Invited Papers. XIVth International Biometric Conference at Namur/Belgium,* July 18-22, 1988. Gembloux/Belgium: Société Adolphe Quetelet, pp. 229-240.

Niskanen, P.J., Jääskäläinen, J., & Achte, K. (1974). Anorexia nervosa, treatment, results, and prognosis. *Psychiatrica Fennica, 5*, 257-263.

Priestley, M. B., & Chao, M. T. (1972). Nonparametric function fitting. *Journal of the Royal Statistical Society, B34*, 384-392.

Remschmidt, H., & Müller, H. G. (1987). Stationäre Gewichts-Ausgangsdaten und Langzeitprognose der Anorexia nervosa. *Zeitschrift für Kinder- und Jugendpsychiatrie, 15*, 327-341.

Remschmidt, H., Wienand, F., & Wewetzer, C. (1988). Der Langzeitverlauf der Anorexia nervosa. *Monatsschrift für Kinderheilkunde, 136*, 726-731.

Remschmidt, H., Wienand, F., & Wewetzer, C. (1990). Langzeitprognose bei der Anorexia nervosa. Eine Verlaufsuntersuchung an 103 Patientinnen und Patienten. *Münchner Medizinische Wochenschrift, 132*, 29-32.

Theander, S. (1985). Outcome and prognosis in anorexia nervosa and bulimia: Some results compared with those of a Swedish long-term study. *Journal of Psychiatric Research, 19*, 493-508.

Vandereycken, W., & Pierloot, R. (1983). Long-term outcome research in anorexia nervosa: The problem of patient selection and follow-up duration. *International Journal of Eating Disorders, 2*, 237-242.

Name Index

Abou-Saleh, M.T. 78, 80f
Abraham, S.F. 45, 50, 52
Achenbach, T.M. 130, 135
Achte, K. 135f, 167
Aimard, G. 45, 53
Albala, A.A. 82
Almqvist, F. 137ff, 141, 148
Althoff, P.-H. 77, 81
Altshuler, K.Z. 71, 81
Amir, A.P. 105, 109, 112
Amsterdam, J.D. 23, 29, 75, 81, 84
Andersen, A.E. 66, 82
Ansseau, M. 21f, 26
Apfelbaum, M. 74, 84
Appelt, H. 87ff, 94
Arana, G.W. 78, 81
Ardaens, K. 75, 83
Askevold, F. 62, 66, 104, 112
Asnis, G. 23, 28
Astrup, A. 34, 43
Avgerinos, P.C. 82

Baciewicz, G.J. 25, 29
Backmund, H. 74, 83
Baker, L. 2, 12, 61, 67, 123, 148, 148
Baldessarini, R.J. 78, 81
Banilivy, M.M. 1f, 12
Bannister, R. 43
Bantle, J.P. 25, 28
Barnes, K.T. 25, 27
Barradas, M.A. 35, 44
Bates, B. 137, 148
Baumgartner, A. 78, 81
Bayliss, R. 77, 83
Bean, J.A. 60, 67
Beck-Friis, J. 75, 84
Beckmann, H. 52
Bedig, G. 74, 84
Beeber, A.R. 25, 28
Beil, C. 52
Bell, C. 95, 101
Bemis, K.M. 92f
Benedict, F.G. 14, 26
Bennett, S.M. 26f
Ben Tovim, D.I. 95, 101
Berger, M. 31, 44, 52, 74, 77, 83f, 92f
Bergman, J.G. 12
Bermeyer, H.U. 29
Berry, E.M. 66

Beumont, P.J.V. 45, 52, 75, 81, 92, 94f, 102
Biederman, J. 69ff, 81, 84
Birch, J. 2, 12
Bisdee, J.T. 65f
Bjarke, B. 43
Bjorntorp, P. 26f, 29, 68
Bjorum, N. 23, 28
Bledsoe, T. 14, 29, 84
Blinder, B.J. 83
Blondheim, S.H. 66
Blundell, J.E. 73, 80, 83
Bohr, Y. 2, 12, 93
Bond, P.A. 50, 52
Bonfils, S. 74, 84
Böning, J. 78, 84
Born 90
Borroughs, J. 128, 135
Bossert, S. 92f
Bouchard, C. 64, 66
Bowen, M. 123
Boyar, R. 75, 83
Boyle, P.C. 26f
Bradford, G.E. 26, 28
Brambilla, F. 23, 27, 75, 82
Brandes, J.S. 66
Brandt, H.A. 67
Breiman, L. 133, 158f, 166
Bremer, J. 54, 58
Brinch, M. 128, 136
Brinkmann, W. 31, 44, 70, 84
Brinks, M.J. 105, 109, 112
Brodman, K. 139, 148
Broocks, A. 37, 39, 43f
Brown, G.M. 25, 27f
Brown, L.B. 62, 67, 95, 102
Brown, T.A. 85, 93
Brown, W.A. 27
Brownell, K.D. 26f
Brozek, J. 13, 28, 70, 83f
Bruch, H. 2, 11, 93, 103, 105, 109, 112
Brunswick, D.J. 23, 29, 75, 84
Bryant, K. 137, 148
Bryant-Waugh, R. 1, 12
Buree, B. 95, 101
Burger, A. 14, 28
Burroughs, J. 10f, 60, 68
Button, E.J. 2, 11, 93, 95f, 101, 104, 112
Buvat, J. 75, 77, 82f
Buvat-Herbaut, M. 75, 77, 82f

Cameron, J.L. 19, 27
Campbell, D.T. 119, 122f
Campbell, P.G. 95, 102
Cantwell, D.P. 10f, 128, 135
Carlton, B. 137, 148
Caroff, S.N. 23, 29, 75, 81, 84
Carroll, B.J. 25, 27, 79, 82
Cash, T.T. 85, 93
Casper, A.M. 104, 112
Casper, R.C. 23, 27, 45, 52, 70, 77, 82, 92ff, 101f
Ceaser, M. 74, 82
Celsius 13
Cerfontaine, J.L. 21, 26
Chaitin, B.F. 83
Chaloner, D.A. 65, 67
Channon, S. 70, 82
Chao, M.T. 157, 167
Charney, D.S. 21, 27
Chauplannaz, G. 45, 53
Checkley, S.A. 21, 25, 27
Chetri, M.K. 14, 29, 84
Chiodo, J. 66
Chlond, C. 28
Chopra, I.J. 14, 27
Christie, M.J. 95, 102
Chrousos, G.P. 28, 82
Clarke, M.G. 2, 10f
Cleveland, S.E. 112f
Cobbin, D.M. 45, 52
Cocchi, D. 23, 27, 75, 82
Cohn, D. 23, 28
Collins, J.K. 95f, 102
Consolazio, C.F. 14, 27
Cooke, J.N.C. 14, 27
Cooper, B. 12
Cooper, P.J. 1ff, 10ff, 20, 27
Cooper, Z. 66
Coppen, A. 25, 27
Coppenolle, H. van 103
Coryell, W.H. 25, 29
Coscina, D.V. 95, 102
Costa, D. 25, 28
Cowen, P.J. 65f
Crandall, C.S. 66
Crisp, A.H. 1, 11f, 15, 27, 60, 62, 66f, 78, 81, 95, 101f, 112, 128, 131f, 136
Crisp, A.M. 104, 112
Crombach, L.J. 111f
Cronghan, J. 67
Crowe, R.R. 60, 67

Crowley, G. 16, 28f
Cullberg, J. 2, 12
Cunningham, S. 85, 93, 96, 102

Dally, P. 112
Dandona, P. 35, 44
Darby, P.L. 61, 66
Dare, C. 62, 68
Dashwood, R. 35, 44
Davies, A.O. 34f, 43
Davies, E. 96, 102
Davies, R.K. 23, 27
Davis, C.T. 43
Davis, J.M. 45, 52, 70, 82, 92, 93, 95, 101f
Davis, K.L. 24, 26f
Davis, L. 167
De Ruyter, M. 78, 83
Degroote, T. 115, 123
Dekirmenjian, H. 45, 52
Depreitere, L. 85, 94, 103, 112
DeSilva, W.P. 70, 82
Deuster, P.A. 26, 28
Dibble, E.D. 59, 66, 69, 82
Dickhaut, B. 24, 28
DiMascio, A. 44, 84
Dixon, K.N. 74, 83
Dobbs, R. 1, 12
Docter, R.F. 14, 28
Doerr, P. 15, 27f, 42ff, 77, 84
Dolce, J.J. 85, 92, 94
Douglas, E. 123

Eastwood, M.R. 3, 12
Ebert, M.H. 31, 37, 43, 52, 66, 82
Eckert, E.D. 70, 82, 92f, 95, 97, 101f
Eckert, M. 34, 44
Edelbrock, C. 130, 135
Edminson, P.D. 54, 58
Egbert, M. 82
Eisler, I. 10, 12, 62, 68
Eliahou, H. 66
Ellinwood, E.H. 74, 82
Emrich, H.M. 52
Engstrom-Lindberg, M. 2, 12
Erdman, A. 139, 148
Evered, C. 54, 58
Extein, I. 23, 27f
Eyckman, L. 113

Fahrenberg, J. 130, 135
Fairburn, C.G. 1f, 10ff, 65f
Fairburn, C.P. 20, 27
Fairchild, C. 16, 23, 28f
Farber, J. 23, 28
Faust, J. 26, 28

Feighner, J.P.E. 93, 130, 135
Feinberg, M. 82
Feingold, M. 62, 67
Fereira, A.J. 123
Fichter, M.M. 2, 12f, 15, 28, 31, 34, 42ff, 53, 69f, 75, 82f, 85, 88, 93, 95, 102, 130, 135, 166f
Filser, J.G. 45f, 48, 50ff
Fischer, M. 45, 52
Fisher, S. 104, 112
Fiske, D.W. 119, 122f
Flechtner, H. 85
Fleming, J.E. 23, 27
Fohlin, L. 42f
Forgatch, M.S. 122f
Foss, I. 54f, 57f
Fosson, A. 1, 12
Fourcade, J. 53
Fourlinnie, J.C. 77, 82
Franck, G. 21, 26
Fransella, F. 93, 96, 101, 112
Frazier 132
Freeman, C.P.L. 95, 102
Freeman, R.J. 96, 102
Frenckell, R. v. 21, 26
Freud, S. 69, 82
Freyschuss, U. 43
Friedman, F. 158, 166
Fries, H. 104, 112
Frisch, R.E. 66
Frohman, L.A. 23, 27, 77, 82
Fujii, S. 28, 77, 83
Fukino, O. 23, 28, 77, 83
Fukushima, D.K. 78, 84
Fulton, C.L. 23, 29
Furnham, A. 96, 102

Gallucci, W.T. 26, 28, 82
Gardner, R.M. 95f, 102
Garfinkel, P.E. 1f, 12, 25, 27f, 42f, 61f, 66, 69f, 74, 82, 84f, 87, 89f, 92ff, 102, 104, 112, 131, 135f
Garner, D.M. 1ff, 6, 12, 42f, 61f, 66, 70, 84f, 87, 89f, 92ff, 102, 104, 112f, 131, 135f, 139, 147, 148
Garton, M. 55, 57f
Gasser, Th. 156f, 167
Gattaz, W.F. 45, 52
Geenen, V. 26
Gentler, A. 71, 83
George, G.C.W. 75, 81
Gerlinghoff, M. 31, 44, 70, 84
Gerner, R.H. 25, 27, 78, 80, 82
Gershon, E.S. 59, 60, 66f, 69, 71, 82
Ghandi, M. 14

Giles, D.E. 23, 29
Gillberg, C. 54f, 57f
Giordano, G. 23, 27
Giunings, S. 21, 27
Giusti, M. 23, 27
Glanville, K. 96, 102, 127f, 131, 136
Glassman, M. 26, 28
Gless, K.H. 16, 27
Goebl, G. 34, 44
Goff, G. 167
Gold, M.S. 23, 26f
Gold, P.W. 28, 43, 80, 82
Goldberg, D.P. 3, 12, 104, 113
Goldberg, S.C. 45, 52, 70, 82, 85, 92f, 95f, 101f, 113
Goldstein, G. 123
Goldstein, R.S. 83
Gomez, J. 75, 77, 83
Goodwin, F.K. 53
Goodwin, G.M. 65f
Goodyer, I.M. 2, 12
Gordon, E. 53
Goris, M. 103
Gräf, K.J. 78, 81
Graham, Ph. 1
Greden, J.F. 82
Green, J.K. 10f, 128, 135
Greenwood, M.R.C. 26f
Gross, H.A. 31, 43, 50, 52
Gull, W. 59, 67, 69
Guroff, J.J. 60, 67
Gutenbrunner, C. 130, 134f, 150
Guthrie, L.F. 74, 82
Guze, E. 93
Guze, S.B. 130, 135
Gwirtsman, H.E. 25, 27, 78, 80, 82

Haak, D. 16, 27
Hafstad, K.M. 21, 27
Hageman 132
Haier, R.J. 25, 27
Hall, A. 61f, 66f, 70, 82, 128, 136
Hallstein, E.A. 113
Halmi, K.A. 45, 50, 52, 69f, 78, 82, 84f, 92f, 95f, 101f, 104, 113, 132
Hamilton, D. 70, 81
Hamilton, M. 24, 27, 72, 82
Hamont, J.R. 59, 66
Hamovit, J.R. 69, 82
Hampel, R. 130, 135
Hampton, M.C. 1, 12
Hand, D. 10, 12
Hand, O. 113
Hannum, J.W. 123

Name Index

Harding, G.B. 60, 62, 66f, 128, 131f, 136
Harmatz, J.S. 69f, 81, 84
Harper, A.E. 26f
Harper, G.P. 69, 84
Hartshome, J. 60, 66
Harwood, J. 25, 27
Haskett, R.F. 82
Hawker, F. 70, 82, 136
Haynes, S. 122f
Hayward, A.E. 83
Hefti, F. 41, 44
Heiberg, A. 62, 66
Heiss, W.D. 52
Helbing 70
Hellman, L.D. 75, 78, 83f
Helzer, J. 67
Hendren, R.I. 69, 73, 82
Henninger, G.R. 21, 27
Henschel, A. 13, 28, 70, 83
Herfkens, R.J. 74, 82
Herholz, K. 50, 52
Herman, C.P. 38, 43
Herpertz-Dahlmann, B. 70f, 78f, 82, 69
Hersen, M. 123
Hersov, L. 148
Herzog, D.B. 1, 12, 69, 73, 82, 84, 127f, 136
Heufelder, A. 22, 27, 31f, 34, 43
Higgs, J.F. 2, 4, 12
Hippocrates 13
Hobin, P. 78, 83
Hodgson, D. 26, 28
Hoehl, C. 28
Hoffman, G.W. 74, 82
Hole, K. 58
Holland, A.J. 59, 62f, 66f
Holsboer, F. 77f, 82
Hotta, M. 80, 83
Houben, M.E. 104, 113
Houseworth, S. 84
Howard, E. 23, 27
Howells, K. 65, 67
Howlett, D.R. 50, 52
Hsu, L.K.G. 60, 62, 66f, 85, 93, 102, 127f, 131f, 136
Hudson, J.I. 60, 67, 69, 78, 83
Hudson, M.S. 69, 83
Huenemann, R.L. 1, 12
Humphrey, L.L. 62, 67, 148
Hunter, M. 95, 101
Huon, G.F. 95, 102

Ihm, P. 157, 167
Iker, H.P. 25, 29
Isaacs, A.J. 75, 77, 83
Isager, T. 128, 136

Izumiya, Y. 75, 77, 83

Jääskäläinen, J. 135f, 167
Jackson, D.N. 122f
Jacobs, A.C. 52
Jacobs, C. 60, 68
Jacques, I. 113
Jaeckle, R.S. 80, 83
Jame, W.P.T. 66
James, N.M. 65, 82
James, V.H.T. 14, 27
Jimerson, D.C. 31, 43, 82
Johansen, J.H. 54, 58
Johnson, H.L. 14, 27
Johnson-Sabine, E. 2, 10, 12
Jonas, J.M. 60, 67, 69, 83
Jöreskog, K. 120, 122f
Jupp 95

Kafka, F. 69
Kalliopuska 95
Kalucy, R.S. 95, 102, 104, 112
Kaminer, Y. 62, 67
Kaplan, A.S. 25, 27
Karibe, C. 23, 28, 77, 83
Karoum, F. 84
Kassett, J.A. 60, 67
Kathol, R.G. 80, 83
Katz, J.L. 71, 75, 78, 83f
Kawakita, Y. 75, 77, 83
Kaye, D.W.K. 61, 67
Kaye, W.H. 31, 37, 43, 45f, 52, 66, 69, 82
Kazuba, D.M. 67
Kedward, H.B. 3, 12
Keeser, W. 75, 82, 130, 135
Keesey, R.E. 26f
Keitner, G.I. 25, 27
Keller, M.B. 127, 136
Kelly, J.T. 20, 28
Kemper, J. 92f
Kemper, K. 69f, 81, 84
Kemsley 15
Kendler, K.S. 24, 26f
Kennedy, S.H. 25, 28, 69, 84
Kenrick, J.M.T. 2, 12
Keys, A. 13, 14, 24, 28, 70, 74, 83
Khan, A. 77, 83
Killam, K.F. 44, 84
King, A. 61, 67
King, M.B. 2, 10, 12
Kiriike, N. 75, 77, 83
Kirkegaard, C. 23, 28
Kirkpatrick, S.W. 95, 101
Kirstein, L. 23, 28
Kittl, S. 2, 12, 24, 28, 83
Kittle 69

Kiyohara, K. 23, 28, 77, 83
Kjellman, B.F. 75, 84
Klee, H.R. 16, 27
Kline, M.D. 25, 28
Knibbs, J. 1, 12
Knippenberg 106
Kobayashi, N. 23, 28, 77, 83
Koch, H.J. 93, 95, 102
Koch, S. 52
Kog, E. 62, 67, 114f, 122f
Köhler, W. 167
Kollar, E.J. 14, 28
Koopman, R.F. 95, 102
Kopin, I.J. 31, 37, 43, 46, 52
Koroum 77
Krass, J. 95, 102
Kream, J. 78, 84
Krieg, J.Ch. 31, 44, 52, 74, 83, 92f
Kronfol, Z. 82
Kryzwicki, H.J. 14, 27
Kuhs, H. 78, 83
Kumagai, L.F. 28, 83
Kunze, D. 83
Kupfer, D.J. 25, 28
Kürten, I. 78, 81
Kuznesoff, A.W. 39, 44
Kyle, S.B. 26, 28

Lacey, J. H. 78, 81, 163, 167
Lacour, J.R. 53
LaDu, T.J. 70, 82
Laenen, P. 113
Laessle, R.G. 2, 12, 24, 28, 37f, 42ff, 69f, 73, 83
Lafeber, C. 103, 105, 109, 113
Lake, C.R. 31, 37, 43, 52
Landis, D.H. 21, 27
Landon, J. 14, 27
Landsberg, L. 32, 38, 43
Lasegue, E.C. 59, 67, 69
Lask, B. 1, 12
Latimer, P.R. 66
Lauer, C. 74, 83
Laurent, B. 45, 53
Lauridsen, U.B. 23, 28
Lavau, M. 26, 29
Lavori, P.W. 127, 136
Le Couteur, A. 54, 58
Lefkowitz, R.J. 35, 43
Legros, J.J. 26
Lehmkuhl, G. 85f, 92, 94
Leibowitz, S.F. 42, 43
Leibrich, J. 61, 67
Leichner, P. 71, 83
Leifeld, J. 39, 44
Leigh, D. 61, 67
Lemaire, A. 75, 77, 82f

171

Name Index

Lemmel, W. 65, 67
Leon, G.R. 20, 28
Lepretre, J. 75, 83
Lepretre, P. 77, 82
Leslie, R.D.G. 75, 77, 83
Levi, L. 14, 28
Levin, J. 78, 84
Levitsky, D.A. 26, 28, 65, 67
Levy, A.B. 74, 83
Lichtwald, K. 16, 27
Liebman, R. 123
Lifschitz, F. 1f, 12
Limacher, B. 70, 84
Linnoila, M. 77, 84
Linsell, C.R. 25, 28
Lipton, M.A. 44, 84
Lissner, L. 65, 67
Liu, J. 39, 43
Ljunggren, J.G. 75, 84
Lloyd, G.G. 66, 68
Logue, C.M. 60, 67
Lohr, N. 82
Lonati-Galligani, M. 34, 44
Loosen, P.T. 23, 25, 28, 77, 83
Lopez, J.F. 80, 83
Loriaux, D.L. 28, 75, 82, 84
Luck, P. 35, 42, 44
Luger, A. 26, 28
Lund, R. 15, 28, 42ff
Lyons, K. 62, 67

MacFayden, J. 70, 81
Macintyre, C.C.A. 66, 68
Maeda, Y. 75, 77, 83
Maes, M. 78, 83
Maier, W. 82
Mandell, A.J. 14, 28
Mann, A.H. 1ff, 10, 12
March, V. 59, 68
Martin, D.M. 23, 27
Masberg, J. 85
Mason, J.W. 80, 83
Masurd, A. 80, 83
Matousk, L.O. 14, 27
Maxwell, M.E. 60, 67
Mayer, J.M. 123
Mazzochi, G. 23, 27
McCabe, M. 95, 102
McGrath, P.J. 23, 28
McGuffin 63
Meadows, G.N. 2, 12
Meermann, R. 85, 87f, 93, 103f, 113f
Meister, J. 93, 95, 102
Melamed, E. 41, 44
Melander, A. 14, 28
Meller, W.H. 80, 83
Mellonby, J. 29

Mendels, J. 23, 29, 59, 68
Merrouche, M. 74, 84
Mertin, D. 28
Mester, H. 78, 83
Meyer, J.K. 75, 83
Mickolson, O. 13, 28, 70, 83
Mignone, D. 23, 27
Mikhailidis, D.P. 35, 44
Miles, W.R. 26
Miller, B.C. 119, 122f
Miller, D. 137, 148
Milman, L. 123
Minuchin, S. 2, 12, 61, 67, 114, 123, 148
Mitchell, B.W. 1, 12, 25, 163
Mitchell, J.E. 28, 167
Mohs, R.C. 24, 26f
Moldofsky, H. 85, 92f, 95, 102, 112, 131, 135f
Molinari, L. 167
Molitor, P. 92, 93
Möller, H.J. 82
Monck, E. 1, 12
Moncrieff, C. 95f, 102
Montgomery, L.C. 26, 28
Morgan, H.G. 60, 62, 67, 79, 83, 87, 90, 93, 127f, 130ff, 135f, 150f, 158, 165, 167
Morley, J.E. 73, 80, 83
Morley, S. 85, 93
Morrell, W. 60, 68
Mortara, R. 23, 27
Morton, R. 65, 67
Moses, N. 1f, 12
Mrosovsky, N. 65, 67
Mullen, P.E. 25, 28
Müller, B. 78, 84
Müller, E.A. 23, 27
Müller, E.E. 23, 27, 75, 82
Müller, H.G. 130, 133ff, 151ff, 156f, 163, 166f
Müller, H.-U. 45
Müller, W.E. 45, 50, 52
Munoz, R. 93, 130, 135
Murray, R. 62, 67

Nagata, T. 83
Nagataki, S. 28, 83
Nakagawa, T. 23, 28, 83
Napierski, C. 104, 113
Negri, F. 75, 82
Neill, J. 28
Nelson, R.A. 14, 27
Nerup, J. 23, 28
Neubauer, M. 77, 81
Newball, E.U.M. 2, 12
Newman, M.M. 69, 84
Niebel, G. 85, 93

Nielsen, S. 128, 136
Nieman, L.K. 82
Nishita, J.K. 74, 82
Nishiwaki, S. 75, 77, 83
Niskanen, P.J. 135f, 166f
Nobile, P. 23, 27
Norris, D.L. 95, 102
Norris, P.D 23, 25, 28
Novacenko, H. 23, 28
Nowlin, N.S. 62, 67
Nudel 34
Nunnally, J.C. 106, 113
Nurnberger, J.I. 66, 69, 82
Nussbaum, P. 70, 84
Nylander, I. 1, 12, 65, 67
Nystrup, J. 128, 136

O'Hanlon, J. 66
O'Malley, B.P. 23, 25, 28
Ofers, B. 34, 44
Oleesky, D. 78, 81
Oler, J. 23, 29
Olesen, N.S. 136
Oliveri, M. 122f
Olmsted, M.P. 2, 12, 90, 93, 139, 147f
Olsen, A. 166
Olson, D.H. 122f
Oppenheimer, R. 65, 67
Opstad, P.K. 58
Örbeck, H. 58
Ornsteen, M. 78, 81
Orsulak, P.J. 16, 23, 28f
Owens, M. 69, 84

Pahl, J.J. 31, 44f, 52f, 70, 84
Palmblad, J. 14, 28
Palmer, J.O. 14, 28
Palmer, R.L. 2, 10ff, 23, 25, 28, 65, 67
Papageorgis, D. 95f, 101
Papart, P. 21, 26
Parienti, V. 25, 28
Parker, D. 25, 28
Patten, S.R. 20, 28
Patterson, G.R. 122f
Patton, G.C 2, 12, 66f
Pawlik, G.C 52
Pequignot, J.M. 45, 51ff
Peterson, D.W. 26, 28
Peyrin, L. 45, 50ff
Pfohl, B.M. 25, 29
Philipp, E. 41, 44
Philips, T. 95, 102
Pickar, D. 77, 84
Pierloot, R. 62, 68, 104, 113, 135f, 166f
Pimstone, B.L. 75, 81

Name Index

Piran, N. 69, 78, 84
Pirke, K.M. 2, 12f, 15f, 19, 22, 24, 27f, 30f, 34, 37ff, 41ff, 52f, 65, 67, 69f, 73f, 83f
Platte, P. 38, 44
Ploog, D. 37, 43f, 52
Polivy, J. 38, 43, 139, 147f
Pope, H.G. 60, 67, 69, 83
Post, R.M. 46, 53
Pottash, A.L.C. 23, 27f
Powers, S.K. 26f
Prader, A. 167
Prange, A.J. 23, 25, 28, 77, 83
Presta, E. 26, 29
Priestley, M.B. 157, 167
Prirtera, M.R. 25, 29
Probst, M. 103
Probst, R. 85, 94
Proctor, L. 85, 93
Propping, P. 71, 84
Psaltis, K. 92, 94
Puig-Antich, J. 23, 28
Pungold, J. 136
Pyle, R. 167

Qualls, C.B. 25, 27
Quitkin, F.M. 23, 28

Racadot, A. 75, 83
Raggatt, P.R. 77, 83
Raleigh, M. 37, 43, 52
Rasmussen, K.M. 65, 67
Rastam, M. 54f, 57f
Rauch, I. 87, 92f
Rees, U.M. 94
Register, A. 85, 94
Reichelt, K.L. 54, 58
Reiss, D. 122f
Reitman, E.E. 113
Remschmidt, H. 69f, 72, 79, 82, 84, 93, 127, 130, 133ff, 150ff, 156, 163, 166f, 78
Rich, J. 123
Richman, N. 1
Riedel, W. 34, 44
Riemann, D. 52, 74, 83
Rigaud, D. 74, 84
Rinn, R.C. 95, 101
Rittmaster, R. 82
Rivinus, T.M. 69ff, 81, 84
Robb, J. 26, 28
Robins, E. 93, 130, 135
Robins, L.N. 67
Robinson, D.W. 26, 28
Robinson, P.H. 74, 84
Robinson, S. 28
Rockwell, W.J.K. 74, 82
Roffwarg, H. 75, 83

Rollins, B.C. 119, 122
Rolls, B.J. 26, 28
Rose, J. 61, 66
Rosman, B.L. 2, 12, 61, 67, 123, 148
Rosse, J.L. 113
Rossner, S. 68
Rost, W. 52
Roth, P. 26
Roth, R.H. 37, 44
Rothenberger, A. 45
Routtenberg, A. 39, 44
Rowe, E.A. 26, 28
Roy, A. 77, 84
Roy-Byrne, P. 25, 27
Rush, A. 16, 28f
Russel, C.S. 123, 124
Russell, G.F.M. 1f, 12, 14, 20, 28, 59f, 62, 66ff, 79, 83, 87, 90, 93, 95, 102, 104, 113, 127f, 130ff, 135ff, 148, 150f, 158, 165, 167
Rutter, M. 54, 58, 136, 148
Ryan, R.M. 92, 94
Ryle, J.A. 59, 67

Sacchetti, E. 75, 82
Saelid, G. 54, 58
Salkin, B. 10f, 60, 68, 128, 135
Salmond, C. 70, 82
Salmone, C. 136
Salmons 96
Sambauer, S. 37, 44
Schenck, H. v. 14, 28
Schiele, B.C. 70, 84
Schifferdecker, E. 77, 81
Schildkraut, J.J. 30, 42, 44, 84
Schlesser, M.A. 16, 23, 28f
Schmidt, H. 74, 83
Schmidt, M. 84, 70, 130, 134, 136, 150
Schnabel, E. 92f
Schreiber, J.L. 59, 66, 69, 82
Schulze, C. 92, 94
Schwartz, D.M. 2, 12
Schweiger, J. 65, 67
Schweiger, M. 24, 28, 34, 44
Schweiger, U. 24, 28, 31, 34, 37, 39, 41ff, 70, 83f
Schwingenschlögel, M. 28
Scott, D.W. 62, 67f
Selg, H. 130, 135
Selvini-Palazzoli, M. 61, 67
Sever, P.S. 35, 43f
Severin, B. 136
Shaffer 136
Shafrir, E. 66
Shapiro, L.R. 1, 12

Shaw, M.A. 65f
Shepherd, M. 3, 12
Sherry, D. 65, 67
Shibash, T. 80, 83
Shonz, F.C. 86, 92, 94
Shrager, E.E. 26f
Shur, E. 21, 25, 27
Sian-Ex 87
Sicotte, N. 63, 67
Siero, F. 113
Sigafoos, A. 122f
Silverman, J.A. 42, 44, 59, 68
Simmonds, M. 14, 29
Sir Bayliss, R. 75, 83
Skinner, M.L. 122f
Skude, G. 14, 28
Slade, A.P. 21, 25, 27
Slade, P.D. 2, 12, 92ff, 101f, 104, 113
Slade, P.O. 112
Slater, G.R. 14, 28
Slim, E. 70, 82, 136
Smeraldi, E. 75, 82
Smith, A. 67
Smith, H.M. 26
Smith, S.R. 14, 27, 29, 78, 84
Smoller, J.W. 24, 29
Snyder, P.J. 23, 29, 75, 81, 84
Solyom, L. 95f, 101f
Sörbom, D. 120, 122f
Spana, R.E. 85, 94
Spira, J. 45, 52
Spitzer, R.L. 67
Spyra, B. 34, 37f, 41, 44
Stancer, H.C. 85, 93, 95, 102
Steel, J.M. 66, 68
Steiger, A. 82
Steiner, M. 82
Steinhausen, H.Ch. 88ff, 92, 94ff, 102, 127f, 131, 136
Stellar, E. 26f
Stern, S. 62, 67
Sternbach, H.A. 23, 27
Sternberg, D.E. 21, 27
Stevens, J. 65, 67
Stewart, J.W. 23, 28
Stichler, W. 38, 44
Stone, C.J. 166
Stone, E. 35, 44
Stonehill, E. 1, 12
Storlien, L.H. 26f
Strauss, B. 87ff, 92, 94
Strober, M. 59f, 68, 71, 84, 95, 102, 104, 113, 148
Strupp, B.J. 65, 67
Stunkard, A.J. 24, 29, 43
Sturge 136
Sturzenberger, S. 10f, 128, 132,

173

135
Stutte, H. 93
Suy, E. 78, 83
Sweeney, D.R. 23, 27
Sydenham 13
Szmukler, G.I. 1ff, 10, 12, 62, 68

Takaishi, M. 5, 12
Tamai, H. 23, 28, 77, 83
Tanner, J.M. 5, 12, 14
Targun, S.D. 25, 29
Tarika, J. 82
Tarnopolsky, A. 10, 12, 113
Taylor, H.L. 13, 28, 70, 83
Theander, S. 14, 29, 60, 68, 128, 132, 163, 167
Thijs, P. 104, 113
Thoma, W. 94
Thomae, H. 69, 84
Thomas, C.D. 95, 102
Thomas, D.L. 119, 122f
Thompson, J.K. 85, 92, 94f, 102
Thompson, M.G. 2, 12
Thompson, P. 102
Thoren, C. 43
Timsit-Berthier, M. 21, 26
Titlestad, K. 58
Todd, T.C. 60, 123
Tolstrup, K. 128, 131, 136
Toner, B.B. 70, 84
Touyz, S. 92, 94ff, 102
Treasure, J. 59, 63, 66ff
Trygstad, O. 54, 55, 57f
Tuschl, R.J. 34, 37f, 44

Unden, F. 75, 84
Unvas-Moberg, K. 65, 68

Van Coppenolle, H. 113ff
Van de Loo, K.J.M. 103, 105, 109, 113
Van Knippenberg, A. 113
Van Troos, H. 104f, 113

Van Wouwe 103
Vandereycken, W. 43, 62, 67f, 85, 92, 94, 102ff, 111ff, 122f, 135f, 166f
Vanderlinden, J.L. 102, 111, 113, 115, 123
Vecsei, P. 16, 27
Vertommen, H. 114f, 122f
Viaro, M. 61, 67
Vigersky, A. 75, 84
Vigersky, R.A. 112
Vigne, J.P. de 82
Vinik, A.I. 75, 81
Vulpillat, M. 74, 84

Wadden, T.A. 24, 29
Wagner, J.J. 52
Wakeling, A. 1f, 12, 35, 42, 44
Walkey, F.H. 61, 67
Walks, D.M. 26, 29
Wallet, H. 113
Walsh, B.T. 78, 84
Walsh, N. 66
Warnhoff, M. 27, 31, 39, 41, 43f, 70, 84
Waterman, G.C. 10f
Weeney, D.R. 23, 27
Weiner, H. 69, 71, 75, 83f
Weiner, M.F. 81
Welch, G. 61, 67
Wellbourne, J. 136
Wellhöfer, P.R. 14, 29
Westgren, U. 14, 28
Wetterberg, L. 75, 84
Wewetzer, Ch. 127, 136, 166f
White-Phelan, P. 20, 28
Whitehouse, A. 2, 10, 11, 95, 102
Whitehouse, R.H. 5f, 12
Wienand, F. 127, 136, 166f
Wienhard, K. 52
Willi, J. 70, 84, 132
Williams, J.B.W. 67
Williams, P. 10, 12, 113

Williamson, D.A. 26f
Williamson, D.H. 29
Wilson, I.C. 25, 28, 77, 83
Wingate, B.A. 95, 102
Winnek, H.Z. 24, 28
Winokur, A. 23, 29, 59, 68, 75, 81, 84
Winokur, G. 93, 130, 135
Winter, W. 123
Witchy, J.K. 23, 29
Witkin, H.A. 104, 113
Wittchen, H.-U. 2, 12, 69, 83
Woerner, I. 85, 92, 94
Woerner, W. 85, 92, 94
Wolff, H. 139, 148
Wood, K. 1f, 12, 25, 27
Woodruff, R.A. 130, 135
Woodruff, S.B. 93
Wooley, S.C. 85, 94
Wooley, W. 85, 94
Wurtman, R.J. 24, 29, 41, 44
Wynn, V. 14, 27

Yager, J. 25, 27
Yang, M.U. 26f, 29
Yerevanian, B.I. 25, 29
Yorgelun-Todd, D. 60
Young, E. 82
Young, J.B. 32, 38, 43
Young, R.J. 66, 68
Yurgelun-Todd, D. 67, 69, 83

Zerssen, D. v. 29, 77, 82, 84
Ziegler, M.G. 31, 43, 52
Ziemer, R.R. 113
Zimmerman, J. 25, 29
Ziolko, H.U. 128, 131, 135f
Zitzelsberger, G. 37, 44
Zulley, J. 74, 83
Zumoff, B. 84
Zung, W.W.K. 72, 84
Zutt, J. 69, 84

Subject Index

adenylate cyclase 34
adipositas, premorbid 132
adolescents
    female 1
    male 1
adoption studies 62
adrenergic receptor function 34
adrenoceptors 21f, 34f
    alpha-type 41
affective disorder 1f, 69ff *see also* depression
    familial load 69f
    gonadotropins 75
    peripheric thyroid hormones 78
    TRH-test 59f, 69ff, 77
age, relation to eating disorders 1ff
aggressive impulses 14
alcohol abuse 60, 71, 77
alpha-adrenoceptors *see* adrenoceptors
amenorrhea 4, 14, 19ff, 75, 78ff
    see also menstrual cycle
    primary 138
amino acids 24
amitryptiline 73
anaerobic glycolysis 34
Anorexia Nervosa Inventory for Self-Assessment (ANIS) 130
antidepressants 70, 75, 81
    tricyclic 73
anxiety 11
apathy 24
appetite 74
artificial nourishment (forced feeding) 132, 150f, 159, 165
autism 58
autonomy 5f

behavioral methods 114ff
behavioral treatment program 163
beta-2 receptor, lymphocytes 34f
beta-hydroxy-butyric acid (BHBA) 15f, 73
    plasma levels 23, 32
binging 60
biological
    marker 25
    model 65
blood
    groups 63
    pressure 34, 42
    sugar 79
bodily appearance 3
body
    attractiveness 88

deindividualization 105
denial 103ff, 107f
depersonalization 105
dissatisfaction 95, 107f
estimation 86
estrangement 103ff, 106f
experience 92, 103ff
    age 110
    questionnaire 103ff
    study levels 110
image 85ff, 163
    distortion 2, 85ff, 95ff
        definition 95
        questionnaire 104ff
    disturbances 92
    ideal 85
    influence of age 98
    influence of socioeconomic status 98
    influence of weight 98
    prognosis 95
pattern 129
self-consciousness 107f
shyness 103ff
size estimation 95
width 107
bradycardia 42, 138
Broca formulae 70, 152
bulimic features 87f, 96, 128, 138

caloric
    intake 20
    restriction 19, 37f
carbohydrates 20, 25, 32, 41
Card Sort Procedure (CSP) 123
cardiovascular functions 30f
CART, classification and regression trees program 133, 158
catecholamine metabolism 45ff
Child Behavior Checklist 130
classification tree 160f
clinic populations 2
clonidine test 13ff, 21f, 41
    for depression 21
cohesion 114
compulsive symptoms 128
concentration 24, 74
conduct disorders 60, 77
confiding relationships 4
conflict 114
    avoidance 61
    resolution 2, 61, 114
construction strategies, Goldberg 104

175

contact behavior 132
convexity parameter 153f
Cornell Medical Index 139, 141f
cortex 38
corticotropin-releasing factor (CRF) 42, 80
cortisol
    catabolization 17f
    half-life 18
    nocturnal plasma levels 18
    secretion 17, 35
    suppression 13ff, 18
    secretory episodes 18
course of disease 86
    acute 128
    chronic-persistent 128
    intermitting 128
    simple chronic 128
    type 128
course, long-term 127ff
CRH *see* CRF
criteria 127f
cross-validation study 158
cultural
    passage 61
    pathogenesis 61
cycle *see* menstrual cycle 20

dance students 2
dehydration 138, 163
delta-norepinephrine 31
depression 1, 19, 24, 30ff, 42, 60, 69ff, 128, 143
    see also affective disorder
    role of starvation 69
depressive reactions 71
dexamethasone
    absorption 18
    distribution 18
    metabolization 18
    plasma levels 18
    suppression test (DST) 13ff, 16, 75, 78
        depression 78
        predictive potential 78ff
diagnostic
    criteria 1, *see also* DSM-III criteria and MAS
    interview schedule 63f
    issues 85ff, 95ff, 103ff, 114ff
dietary
    behavior 89
    restriction 18f
diuretic abuse 163
Draw-a-Person Test 96
DSM-III criteria 4, 55, 103, 130, 137f
DSM-III-R criteria 30, 55, 70, 95, 151
DST *see* dexamethasone suppression test

Eating Attitudes Test (EAT) 1f, 87
    subscores 9f
eating

control 1ff
    disorder examination 63f
    Eating Disorder Inventory (EDI) 139, 148
educational achievement 1f
emotional
    overinvolvement 3, 9f
    stress 50
endocrinology 13ff, 15f, 30f, 42f, 69ff, 74ff
energy
    consumption 34
    efficiency 26
    fatigue 72
    loss of 72
enmeshment 61, 114
environment 62
Epanechnikov kernel function 157
epidemiology 2ff, 59f
epinephrine 34
estradiol 20f, 74f
estrone 75f
etiology 2, 59ff, 69ff, 74, 86
    role of the family 59ff
exercise 1
    ergometric 34

factor analysis 121
familial
    factors 2, 59ff, 114f, 135
    load, eating disorders 71f
familiality 62ff
family
    adaptability 114
    characteristics 140f, 144f
    cohesion 114
    discord 3
    Environment Scale (FES) 123
    history information 70
    interaction concepts 114ff
    interactional patterns 114f
        evaluation 121f
    model 114
    observation methods 114f
    overinvolvement 121f
    psychiatric disorders 59f
    relationship 4f, 87, 129, 131, 140, 144
    research 122
        methodological issues 122
    studies 59ff
    therapy 135
famine, definition 13
fasting 13ff, 88
    definition 13
Feighner's criteria 130
follow-up 79f, 127ff, 137ff, 150ff
    interval 130, 132
food
    abstinence 25
    digestion 32

Subject Index

efficiency 26
ingestion 32
Freiburg Personality Inventory (FPI) 130
FSH 19f, 74f

ganglionic blockade 38
gastric emptying 74
genetic vulnerability 59ff, 65
global clinical score 131
gonadotrophic hormones see gonadotropins
gonadotropin-releasing hormone (GnRH) 42
gonadotropins 13ff, 20, 45, 75
growth hormone (HGH) 21f
    basal levels 21f
    depression 21
    menstrual cycle 21f
    response to clonidine 21, 22
        blunted 13ff, 21

Hamilton Depression Scale (HAMD) 72f
health education
healthy subjects and fasting 13ff
heart rate 34
height/weight ratio 5f
HERIT program 63f
heritability 63f, see also genetic vulnerability
history of eating disorders 59f
homovanillic acid (HVA) 24
hormone secretion, basal nocturnal 16f
hormones see endocrinology
human starvation 13ff
hyperactivity 41f, 85, 88, 105, 134, 138
hypercortisolism 45, 77
hypersomnia 72
hypothalamo-pituitary-
    adrenal (HPA) axis 13ff, 17, 42, 78f
    gonadal (HPG) axis 19, 42
    ovarian (HPO) axis 75
    thyroid (HPT) axis 23f, 75f
hypothalamus 30f
hypothermia 42, 138

ICD-9 130
image-distortion techniques 96
immunradiometric techniques 75
individual psychotherapy 135
infertility 65
inpatient treatment 73, 130, 151
insecurity 88
insomnia 72
internalised rules 5f
intestine enzymes 26
IQ 132
irritability 24
isoproterenol 35

KALI computer program 15
kernel estimation 156f

ketone bodies 79

laboratory tests 13ff, 16
lactate 33f
lanugo 138
laxative abuse 88, 129, 138, 151, 163
Leuven Family Questionnaire 115
LH 19f, 74f
    secretory pattern 19f
libido 24, 74
lipoprotein lipase 26
LISREL (analysis of linear structural
    relationships) 120
locus coeruleus 30
long-term
    outcome 150ff
    prognosis 150f
longitudinal
    parameters 151f
    studies 69, 150ff
    weight maeasurements 150ff
low T3-syndrome 77

malnutrition 74
marriage research 122
MDD (Major Depressive Disorder) 71f
    DSM-III criteria 72f
median eminence 39
medication 73
    antidepresive or neuroleptic drugs 135
menarche 9
menstrual cycle 4, 19f, 65, 138
    anovulatory 20
    dysfunction 75
    ovulatory 20
    regular 138
menstruation 4
    painful 138
mental
    retardation 58
    stress 50
metabolic rate 26
methoxy-hydroxy-phenylglycol (MHPG) 37
MHPG 45ff
    chromatogram 47
    depression 45, 50
    fractions 45ff
    glucuronide 45
    sulfate 45ff
Minnesota Experiment 14f, 24
MMPI 130
mononuclear leucocytes 35f
mood 30ff, 42
moodyness 24
MOPEG (4-hydroxy-3-methoxy-phenylglycol
    sulfate) 39f
morbid risk 60
Morgan and Russell

Assessment Scales 63f
  criteria 79f, 87, 90, 127f, 150f, 158
mortality rate 127
mothers' eating problems 7f
motoric activity 24
Multiaxial Classification Scheme (MAS) 130
multitrait-multimethod matrix 119
Munich University Starvation Experiment 15ff
muscular mass 34

naso-gastric tube 135, 150
neuroendocrine regulation 14ff
neuroendocrinological changes 13ff
neuroendocrinology 69f, see also endocrinology
neuroses 131
neurotransmitter 30ff, 65
  metabolism 52
noradrenergic
  activity 42
  depression 42
  neuron 35
  system 30ff
norepinephrine (NE) 30ff, 45ff
  metabolism 45ff
    central 45ff
    pathways 51
    peripheral 45ff
    starvation 45ff
    weight gain 52
  plasma concentrations 31
  turnover
    central 42
    exercise 39f
    peripheral 42
nutritional hypotheses 14ff

obesity 1
obsessionality 2
occupation 131
offspring of eating disorder patients 131
onset of the disorder, age 132f
opiates, endogenous 65
orthostatic test 31f
osteoporosis 20f, 66
outcome 80
  age and onset of disease 160f
  life quality 146
  long-term 150ff
  prediction 150ff
  role of age 150f
over-/underweight 1
overeating 3
overinvolvement 148
overprotectiveness 61, 114, 123

parental
  control 3
  rules 3f

partial syndrome 2ff
pathogenesis 137
peptide complexes, protein-associated 54ff
peptides 54ff
  patterns in anorexia nervosa 54ff
  patterns in schizophrenia 54
  urinary excretion 54ff
perinatal events 62
personality structure 132, 148
pharmacological treatment 73, see also medication
phobia 128
physical exercise 26
  MHPG 50
plateau parameters 152f
platelets, alpha-2 receptor 34f
polysomnographic studies 74
postmortem study 37
pregnancy 95
premorbid
  adipositas 132
  eating disorders 132
preoccupation with food 3ff
preoptic area 38f
prepubertal onset 1
prevalence 2f
progesterone 20f
prognosis 80f, 86, 90, 160f
prognostic factors 128f
projective tests 96
prolactin 15f, 23, 74f
prostaglandin E 34
protein-calorie malnutrition 14
proteins 20, 32, 41
psychiatric
  consultation 148
  disease of parents 129
  symptomatology, premorbid 128, 129
  symptoms 1, 139
psychobiology 13ff, 30ff, 45ff, 54ff
psychodynamics 137
psychological phenomenology 13ff, 137
psychomotor
  agitation 72
  therapy 103
psychopathology 72ff, 151
psychosocial adaption 131
psychosomatic
  families 114f
  patients 114f
psychotherapy 65, 148
purging 1, 18

questionnaires 114f
  weak points 111
radioimmunoassay techniques 25
rapid eye movement (REM) 25
reduced caloric intake 13ff, 23

Subject Index

relationship
   with father 144
   with mother 144
restlessness 105
restrained eaters 37f
restricted food intake 18, see also caloric restriction
rigidity 61, 114

schizophrenia 54, 60
second messenger system 34f
self-
   appraisal 85
   concept 85, 92
   confidence 88
   perception 85ff
   report methods 114ff
   report screening questionnaires 2f
   reported eating disorders 5f
semantic differential 95ff
semistarvation 14, 24
serotonin 24
sex distribution 71
sexuality 129, 132
size-estimation techniques 96
sleep rhythms 74
slenderness 88
slimness 26
   urge for 103ff, 107f, 109
social
   background 144
   class 1f, 132
   competence 85
   reality 109
socioeconomic distribution 71
somatic complaints 128
stabilization of weight 133
starvation 30ff, 41f
   acute 41
   chronic 41
starving conditions 13ff
stress 75, 77, 78f, 80
   emotional 50
structural equation modeling 114ff, 120f
suicidal ideation 72
suicide 127
sympathetic nervous system 22, 30f
   central 30f
   peripheral 30f

symptomatology 72ff, 85, 144, 163
T_3 32, 35, 75f
   plasma levels 23
T_4 75f
therapy 92, 135 see also treatment
   concept 92
thermoregulation 30f, 42
THRESH program 63f
thyrotropin 75f, see also TSH
tiredness 24
treatment, symptom-oriented 150
TRH 75f
   test 13ff, 23f
      depression 23f
tryptophan 24
TSH 13ff, 74f
   response, blunted 77
twin
   model 64
   study 59ff
tyrosine 41
tyrosine hydroxylase 41
   activity 37

vigilance 24
VMA (vanillylmandelic acid) 45ff
vomiting 1, 88, 96, 129, 134, 138, 163
weight
   control 1ff
   curve 150ff
   deficit 72ff
   dynamics 135
   fluctuations 18
   gain, velocity 150f, 156
   measurements 150ff, 156
   parameters 135
   phobia 163
   restoration 13ff
   /height quotient 89
Witkin's body-concept scale 104
worthlessness 72

yohimbine 35, 41
yoyo dieting 26

Zung Self-Depression Rating Scale (SDS) 72f
zygosity (twins) 62